In Search
of Our Roots

In Search
of Our Roots

How 19 Extraordinary
African Americans
Reclaimed Their Past

Henry Louis Gates, Jr.

Skyhorse Publishing

For Angela De Leon

Contents

PREFACE IX

INTRODUCTION: FAMILY MATTERS 1

PREFATORY NOTES ON THE AFRICAN SLAVE TRADE 15

MAYA ANGELOU 23

QUINCY JONES 41

MORGAN FREEMAN 58

TINA TURNER 80

PETER J. GOMES 104

SARA LAWRENCE-LIGHTFOOT 130

TOM JOYNER 153

BENJAMIN CARSON 179

OPRAH WINFREY 200

WHOOPI GOLDBERG 225

MAE JEMISON 242

T. D. JAKES 260

LINDA JOHNSON RICE 287

KATHLEEN HENDERSON 308

JACKIE JOYNER-KERSEE 325

DON CHEADLE 344

CHRIS ROCK 361

BLISS BROYARD 380

CHRIS TUCKER 397

HOW TO TRACE YOUR OWN ROOTS 415

ACKNOWLEDGMENTS 425

INDEX 427

Preface

"The reader must not expect me to say much of my family. Genealogical trees did not flourish among slaves."

—Frederick Douglass, *Life and Times of Frederick Douglass* (1892)

WHILE LIVING in England as a graduate student at Cambridge University, I had my first brush with genealogy envy. It was then that I saw nifty genealogical registries like Debrett's Peerage and Burke's Peerage, which record the family trees of upper-class Englishmen and women in great detail—and at no cost to them! I felt a pang. I was a little jealous of those fortunate enough to be able to trace their ancestry just by flipping through those volumes full of centuries-old names.

I admit that when Alex Haley's miniseries *Roots* aired in 1977, that pang intensified, and I came down with a bad case of what I've called roots envy. From the time I was nine years old, when I first laid eyes on a picture of my great-great-grandmother Jane Gates in a scrapbook, I had been fascinated with genealogy—my own genealogy, not yet the genealogy of others. She looked so odd to me, so "African," especially in contrast to the skin tones of her son and his son, my grandfather, both of whom looked white. As soon as I saw her photograph, I began to grill my parents for whatever names of whatever ancestors they could remember.

But until I saw *Roots*, they were just names jotted in my little notebook. Now, not far off from starting a family of my own, I wanted to know who I was. I wanted to be like Alex Haley and trace my roots back to the slave ship on which Jane Gates's first African ancestors arrived, back to Africa itself to find the ethnic group and village from which they descended. It's funny, but I thought of my African ancestry as singular, as "the" African on my father's family tree, concretized by that photograph in a way I couldn't replicate on my mother's line. That's the other thing: I only thought of my family tree as having two lines: my father's line and my mother's line. It took me years to think of all the branches in between, which I think of as the interstices of the tree, the branches within the shell or the frame. Sounds silly, I know, but that's how I thought of it.

I had no idea how much there was to learn, no idea of the number of surprises that could be found on a person's family tree or in their DNA, especially my own: it turned out that both my maternal and paternal lines traced not to Africa at all, but to Europe! In other words, I was descended from a black man who had fathered a child with a white woman on my mother's mother's line, and from a white man who had fathered a child with a black woman on my father's father's side. As if that information wasn't enough, genetically I was about equal parts European and sub-Saharan African according to my genome, meaning that roughly half of my ancestors, going back about five hundred years, would have been "white," and the other half, more or less, "black."

Remember what I said about those peerages I'd come across in England? Little did I know when I'd stood over them three decades earlier that half of my ancestors looked something like the people whose names appeared on those austere pages.

Astonishing discoveries such as these were to be found within the branches of the family trees of the guests who so graciously agreed to appear in the first iteration of *Finding Your Roots*, the two PBS series *African American Lives* (2006) and *African American Lives 2* (2008). In the decade since they aired, genealogy has become something of a national pastime. DNA science has grown increasingly precise, and the widespread digitalization of vital records around the world has made the obstacles to searching for our roots more surmountable than ever before. The Internet, of course, has kept up with the demand. In the section of this book called "How to Trace Your Roots," I have updated the links to the websites that my team and I found so useful all those years ago, and on which I continue to rely today.

When this book was first published in 2009 as a companion to these series, I was not overstating it when I called the nineteen participants pro-filed in it "extraordinary." To detail the accomplishments and endeavors of each one since then would surely fill another volume. But there are postscripts to the stories of four of our guests that I would be remiss in not sharing.

When I sat down with Ben Carson for our exploration of his roots in 2006, he was a world-renowned surgeon, known for his unimpeach-able skill in the operating room. Following his retirement from medicine in 2013, he traded pediatric neurosurgery for politics, and his became a household name. In 2015, he joined a crowded field of contenders running for the Republican Party's nomination for president. As of this writing, he stands to become part of President Donald Trump's cabinet, as secretary of the US Department of Housing and Urban Development (HUD).

In 2008, I introduced Tom Joyner to his great-uncles Tom and Meeks Griffin, who in 1913, at the height of the Jim Crow era in South Caro-lina, were convicted of perpetrating a murder they did not commit. They were sentenced to death by electrocution. Armed with the knowledge we provided, Tom set out on a quest to clear his ancestors' names. In 2009, almost a century after their execution in 1915, Tom's great-uncles were pardoned for their wrongful conviction by South Carolina Parole and Par-dons Board. It was the first time the state had issued a posthumous pardon for a capital crime.

Finally, since the first publication of this book, two of our guests—two of my dearest friends—passed away, Peter Gomes on February 28, 2011, and Maya Angelou on May 28, 2014. Each of us is irreplaceable, of course, but some departures, some absences, leave gaps in the very fabric of our civilization, as does the passing of Peter and Maya. I am only grate-ful that we were able to give them the gift of their ancestry before they were forced to take leave of us.

Henry Louis Gates, Jr.
February 5, 2017

Introduction:

Family Matters

MY GRANDFATHER died in 1960. I was ten years old. I didn't know my grandfather well, but I was endlessly fascinated by him—or, more correctly, by the way he looked. He looked like a tall white man to me, a white man with straight white hair, slender as a rail, with pencil thin lips, a white man's lips, the sort of lips that you paint onto a cartoon face with a single red line. I loved him, I suppose, insofar as you can "love" a person whom you never got to know. I loved him in the way that you love a grandparent with whom you have not had the opportunity to exchange intimacies, or to create them. I loved him because I was supposed to, formally, by contract, because my daddy did. I don't know what his relationship with his other grandchildren might have been, but "Pop" Gates, born in 1879, was not exactly big on carrying on conversations with his seventh son's second son. He'd pat me on my wooly, basketball-round head and give me a gracious and inviting smile, possibly bemused, I have since suspected many times, at how this nappy-headed milk chocolate–colored boy could have sprung from his light and bright and damned near white youngest son's loins. Standing next to my father at Pop Gates's open casket, just before the funeral director shut it forever, signaling the start of the service, I thought that my grandfather looked as if he had been turned to stone, an alabaster mask unexpectedly covering the blue-veined face of what had so shortly before been a flesh-and-blood human being, even if that flesh had been almost translucently white.

I thought he looked, well, hilarious, a ghostly white papier-mâché mummy, and so I began to laugh. At the same time, it seemed, my father began to laugh as well. My dad has a deliciously wicked sense of humor, and part of getting to know him—of overcoming my older brother's advantage of the firstborn son who had bonded so deeply with our father over sports—was recognizing and responding to his wit. I was ahead of him on this one, I remember thinking. Pop Gates looked just plain ridiculous lying in that purple-velvet-lined casket like an albino mannequin, I thought, and Pop apparently felt the same way. Too much talcum powder, perhaps? As I turned my face upward to share the joke with Daddy, I realized to my horror that not only was my father not laughing, he had begun to cry. Not only was he crying, he was weeping loudly, howling almost, big tears running down his own scarcely black face. I was so startled, so surprised, so taken aback that I had misread the entire situation, that I began to weep almost as loudly as my father. "I appreciated that, boy," he said to me as we headed back to our seat in the front row of family mourners. "Don't be ashamed, don't hold back. Just let it flow." Glancing around at the congregation through a sheet of sheer terror, afraid that I had embarrassed myself, and my father, by my inappropriate laughter, only then did I realize that no one had seen me, all souls in the Kight Funeral Home having been riveted, as I was, on the fact that my father, the funniest man I know, had, apparently for the first time in forty years, when a milk-truck had run over his foot while he'd been sitting on a curb watching the results of a New York Giants baseball game on one of those 1920 state-of-the-art electric scoreboards, actually allowed himself to cry in front of somebody. And not just somebody—in this case in front of the whole town, or at least that segment of the colored people in town who mattered. It took me a long time to stop crying, so certain was I that someone had seen how foolishly I'd acted, and in front of my own grandfather's porcelain dead body.

Following Pop Gates's burial at the Rose Hill Cemetery, where our people were among the very few Negroes allowed, well dead, to disturb the eternal sleep of Cumberland, Maryland's, elite white Episcopal citizenry (the Episcopal churches had been segregated since 1890), my father took us back to the Gates family home on Greene Street, where Gateses had been living for almost a century. My brother and I followed my dad upstairs, to Pop's and Nan's bedroom. I had never been upstairs in my grandparents' home before, I remember thinking as I sheepishly followed my dad's footsteps.

Pop Gates had two hobbies, for the first of which he was quite well known in and around Cumberland: He could grow tulips like nobody's business—"like a Dutchman," people often said. As we followed my father, I couldn't help but notice that the walls of my grandparents' living room were lined with framed sets of red, yellow, and blue ribbons. I wondered, why tulips? Without saying a word, my father opened an old trunk, like something I'd recently seen in a Disney movie about pirates. He pulled out dozens of musty leather books, partially used bank ledgers (Pop was a janitor at the bank), books with green and red lined pages, pages bound together with string when the glue had failed. As he slowly turned the pages, I realized that he was showing me scrapbooks, very ancient and disintegrating scrapbooks. The scrapbooks' pages were covered completely, front and back, and were very stiff from the glue. So Pop Gates had kept scrapbooks; that was his second hobby. The articles that Pop Gates had clipped covered various news stories about World War II, local and national crime, accidents, and human interest items. There were hundreds and hundreds of news clips, mainly, all sorts of random headlines about births and deaths, especially murders and fatal accidents. Weddings and funeral notices. Funeral programs and that most curious genre, those laminated bookmarks noting the passing of the dead, complete with a bit of religious verse, a passage of the Bible, birth and death dates, and sometimes even a photograph of the deceased.

But above all else Pop was into obituaries. He had collected hundreds of obituaries; those scrapbooks were like an archive, decade by decade, of Cumberland's colored dead. And apparently not just colored people either; some dead white people (unless they were just light, like Pop) poked their pale visages out of those pages as well, fighting for air among clips of all those Negroes, probably more Negroes than they had ever been close to in their entire lives. Daddy wasn't saying anything to anybody, just silently turning those pages, page after page after oversize page. It was Pop Gates's cabinet of wonders, his mortuary of the Negro dead, with a couple of white folks thrown in for spice or good measure, I guess. I felt as if those scrapbooks were some sort of two-dimensional time machine, a black cardboard portal onto a world I would never know. Old-school Negroes, long dead. Clean, too: three-piece suits and white starched collars, hair slicked down or pressed. After a while it dawned on me that the white people and the colored people were dressed the same way: the sartorial equality of the recently departed, stemmed from the shared aesthetic of Olan Mills's photography parlor. Who were these Negroes? I found myself beginning to wonder. Were these people Pop's friends?

"Look here, boy," Daddy said, startling me as he broke the silence. There, deep in those yellowing pages of newsprint, was an obituary—the obituary, to my astonishment, of one of my ancestors, our matriarch, an ex-slave named Jane Gates. "An estimable colored woman," the obituary said, and a midwife. Next to the obituary, my grandfather had glued this woman's picture to the page. "That is the color people call 'sepia,'" Daddy said. "That woman was Pop's grandmother. She is your great-great-grandmother. And she is the oldest Gates." I stared at that photograph for what seemed like a very long time, not knowing what I was supposed to say. I would stare at it until I had that face memorized, an image of the oldest colored woman I'd ever seen, etched indelibly into my ten-year-old head. Eventually Daddy shut the album and slowly stood up. By the time we made our way back downstairs, the house was crowded with family I knew and family I'd never seen before and would never see again. Enough food to start a restaurant had miraculously been crowded onto their oak dining table with big clawed feet. I headed for the fried chicken and the potato salad, hungry all of a sudden, but not sure what had taken place upstairs, in the room where my grandfather apparently had archived the lives and times of the Potomac Valley's sepiaed dead.

That same year, in the fifth grade, I developed an obsession with my family tree. I peppered my mother and my father with questions about the names of their ancestors, their birthplaces and birthdays, their occupations, when they had died and where. Ever so dutifully I began to write it all down, in a brown spiral notebook. Sometimes I would grow bored and put the notebook away; then, for no apparent reason, I would be seized with the desire to learn more. Eventually, as glossy magazines began to advertise that they could send you your family's "coat of arms," I grew ever more desirous of possessing the knowledge that would allow me to claim, legitimately, one of these—not for the generic "Gates" family but for my own, complete with a chart of the branches of my family tree, each limb of which neatly filled with the births and deaths of my ancestors, the Gateses on one side, and the Colemans, my mother's family, on the other.

Looking back, it seems obvious to me that my career as a historian began that afternoon in 1960, upstairs in my grandparents' home, on the day that my grandfather died. I can still recall the scene vividly—and the passion that consumed me after seeing Jane Gates's obituary, the sense of wonderment that the picture of an actual slave, one from whom I had descended, instilled in me. I was searching not just for the names of my ancestors but for stories about them, the secrets of the dark past of Negroes in America. Each new name that I was able to find and print in my notebook—almost always recalled by my mom or dad—was an enigma for me, a conundrum of the colored past that had produced, by fits and starts but also, somehow, inevitably, the person I had become and was becoming.

But I can remember, too, that searching for my ancestry was always a fraught process, always a mix of joy, frustration, and outrage, as the reconstruction of their history—individually and collectively—must always be for any African American. I knew I had white ancestors. My father was clearly part white, and his father looked like a not-so-friendly version of Casper's grandfather. My cousin Bud had nicknamed Mary, one of our cousins on the Redman side of our family (my father's mother's side) "Casper," because her skin was so terribly white as to appear invisible. Casper the Friendly Cousin. I wanted to learn the names of both my black and white ancestors. Eventually—but certainly not in 1960—I even allowed myself to dream about learning the name of the tribe we had come from in Africa. But there was always a problem with making progress in this search. If you're black, and have tried to trace your roots, surely you know it well: The problem was slavery; the institution of slavery—more correctly, the people who created it so perversely, designed it to destroy any possibility of maintaining the family ties necessary to tracing one's ancestry, through the deviously brilliant act of obliterating our family names, our surnames. Such a simple, devastating but efficient act of erasure! Given all the ways in which a human being could be belittled or dehumanized, how big a deal could the lack of a surname really be? After all, surnames are a fairly recent phenomenon for many of the world's people; indeed, when I first visited Mongolia in 1992, I was startled to learn that the people there had acquired surnames only with the fall of Communism, following soon on the fall of the Berlin Wall. But denying African slaves the right to own and pass down their true names, at least before the law, reinscribed over and over, decade by decade, a permanent state of fragmented identity that slavery, as an organization, depended upon to maintain control as surely as it depended upon the threat—and practice—of violence and violation. This seemingly simple act of naming—or not-naming—interrupted the continuity of family that last names ensure; surnames signifying, as they do, common bonds of blood and tradition and heritage, as veritable links in a chain, a traceable familial chain of being. For us, for those of us descended from the 455,000 Africans who arrived in this country directly from Africa and indirectly from the Caribbean as slaves—80 percent of whom had arrived here by 1800, 99.7 percent by 1820—it was this "traceability," as it were, that the evil genius of slavery sought to take away from us on *both* sides of the Atlantic, making us fragmented and not whole, isolated, discrete parts, not pieces of fabric stitched together in a grand pattern, like some living, breathing, mocha-colored quilt. That is what slavery attempted to do, and as any of us knows who has attempted to restore the branches on our family tree, slavery was, in all too many cases, devastatingly effective in this attempt. But not entirely.

Slavery—the lives and times of the human beings who were slaves— remains the great abyss in African American genealogical history. In spite of an avalanche of scholarship since the late 1960s, the lives of individual slaves—almost four million by 1860—remain something of a historical void. Why? The "great man" and "great woman" theory of history has ensured the survival of heroes of the race such as Phillis Wheatley and Frederick Douglass, Sojourner Truth and Booker T. Washington, Mary Church Terrell and W. E. B. Du Bois. Social history, reacting against this trend to construct historical narrative around the inevitability of the emergence of supremely gifted agents such as these women and men, reconstituted the narratives of large groups of nameless individuals—especially social subordinates such as women, people of color, laborers, and so on. But neither school of historiography has systematically restored the narratives of these individual, and still largely anonymous, actors on the grand historical stage, who emerged in the 1870 federal census with two names, full-blown, like Athena from the head of Zeus. And who might these people be? Your slave ancestors and mine, the very folks we seek to resurrect when we pursue our own genealogy, when we reconstruct our own family trees. These are the people who made American history, decision by decision, day by day. Properly understood, in an ideal world, the narrative of African American history would consist of stories and themes generalized from the rediscovered experiences of our very own ancestors. Collectively, their experiences would become the rule, and not the exception. But historians have not been able to generalize from these myriad experiences created by our ancestors, because their stories remain to be discovered, buried in dusty archives, seemingly unimportant to anyone but a distant family member.

The overwhelming percentage of our ancestors consisted of anonymous, decent, overly hardworking people whose lives have yet to be chronicled. Until their stories are reconstructed and told, these ancestors of ours will not exist as human beings, as agents, as actors in the great drama that is American history because under slavery our ancestors had no names; or no names that the law was bound to honor. Before the law—if not in their hearts and homes, if not in their relationships with other black and white human beings—black slaves were property, complex pieces of property, property that could think and feel, but property nonetheless. You might view slavery as that alchemical institution that strove mightily to transform human beings into things, and surnames were American slavery's Philosopher's Stone. (Harriet Beecher Stowe subtitled the serialized version of *Uncle Tom's Cabin* "The Man That Was a Thing.") Inevitably, it succeeded in this dehumanizing process, most certainly to some extent in their daily lives and absolutely before the law. And how could it not, given all the mechanisms of the state over which it had control? Vested interests used the forces of ideology, religion, mythology, and social norms to reinforce the dishumanity of the slave, day in and day out. I am convinced that this 250-year process of systematic dehumanization continues to have an impact upon a significant sector of African Americans today, crippling our ability to know ourselves and understand our past, to defer gratification, to believe in the future as an extension of a noble and admirable collective past of which most of us remain painfully unaware. For many African Americans, not knowing our own history—not knowing our individual histories, the narratives of our own ancestors who triumphed, by surviving and propagating against tremendous odds—continues to serve as a profound limitation on what we can achieve, on the history each of us can make. We've internalized generations' worth of doubts and fears about who we are as a people, and therefore as individuals, and about what we can accomplish both individually and collectively. And we continue to pay a terrible price for our uncertainty, for this willed ignorance of our past.

With just a little effort, surprisingly, most African Americans can trace their families back several generations. Indeed, the vast majority of us can trace at least one line of our family back to the 1870 census, which was the first census taken after the Civil War and is thus the first census in which all our ancestors appear as people, as citizens with two names, as opposed to property, with no names. The 1870 census lists all black people for the first time with their full names, birthdays, the names of their parents, their children's names, and their occupations. Coming as it does out of the depths of a seemingly lost black past, this census is like a miracle, a godsend to African American history and genealogy. And because it often lists the names of two generations of people who had been slaves, the 1870 census is the bridge between slavery and freedom, between the early nineteenth century and the twentieth. It is the salient mnemonic device enabling us to remember a nameless, faceless past, enabling us to resurrect the secrets of the darkest narrative in the American past.

But what about our ancestors who didn't make it to 1870? What about the ones who didn't live to see freedom? And what, especially, about the very first generation of Africans in our families, the people born on the Mother Continent, thrown into slave ships against their will and brought here to their doom—will we ever know anything about them? Slavery stole their traditional African ethnic identities, then erased their religions and their names. Of course, the slave ships kept very detailed records, including manifests that listed every piece of "human cargo" on board every ship. But with very few exceptions—some records kept by the Portuguese in Angola, for example—the manifests contain only head counts of the slaves who were brought to America, not their names. And so there is no way to know what happened to those people once they stepped onto and off the boat. They went to an auction where they were sold, or to a master who had already paid for them. They had African names before they came here, but they were often stripped of those—and stripped, too, of their family ties and cultural bonds. Some new arrivals would give their children an African first name such as Cudjoe or Cuffee, or a baptized Christian name, such as Patrick, along with a name denoting place of origin, like "Angola." Inevitably, slowly, all those traces of Africa went away. Fragments survived: expressions from African languages, fragments of song, maybe even an African name such as Cudjoe or Kwame here and there; but the obliteration of a conscious knowledge of the African past in the daily life of the African in America was achieved almost totally, with the genius of military precision, by a brutal process of "Americanization" that characterized the plantation system. Africanisms—traces of Africa—survived, of course, but generally unconsciously, in mediated forms.

And without these remnants of a complex cultural past written down, you have no records, and with no written records you have no trail to trace. The roots of African American family trees extend only so far as the shores of the Atlantic Ocean. No farther. That's what the absence of a paper trail was designed to accomplish. And it succeeded, with devastating effectiveness and, unfortunately, with equally devastating social and psychological consequences.

Nevertheless, against the odds, the descendants of the African slaves in this country have searched and searched, despite knowing how fruitless that search was destined to be, as if helplessly trapped in an endless cycle of false starts and false turns, blind people caught in a labyrinth, black explorers hopelessly embarked on a fool's errand. Even before Alex Haley's *Roots* aired in 1977, many generations of African Americans had longed to learn where their ancestors came from in Africa. What languages did they speak? What was their music like? Their religion? Their culture? What gods did they worship? And, most of all, what were their families' names? From what tribe do I descend? These are questions that generations of us have asked and longed to have answered, frustrated by the belief that the answers are long lost in the depths of the dreaded Middle Passage, among the bones of the 15 percent whose journey to America on board European slave ships ended at the bottom of the sea.

Lost until recently, that is. In the past decade, remarkable developments in DNA testing and the retrieval and digitization of archival records have made it possible for us to begin to trace our families back further through American history and, then, ultimately, across the Atlantic. For the first time since the seventeenth century, we are able, symbolically at least, to reverse the Middle Passage. Our ancestors brought something with them that not even the slave trade could take away: their own distinctive strands of DNA. And because their DNA has been passed down to us, their direct descendants, it can serve as a key to unlocking our African past. With cells collected from the insides of our mouths, geneticists can extract small sections of our DNA. The bases of the acids within them form distinctive sequences known as haplotypes, which can then be compared to DNA samples taken from other people around the world. A match means that we've found someone with whom we share a common ancestor. And back in Africa, scientists have spent several decades gathering such samples from tens of thousands of Africans. So an exact match between an American's DNA and an African's DNA reveals a shared ancestor, and possibly a shared ethnic identity, that has been lost for centuries.

When I first heard this, I was overjoyed. After years of being frustrated by my inability to trace my family back beyond slavery, I now saw a way of doing something about it. My excitement coalesced into an idea—an ambitious idea, I admit, but nothing seemed too big for this subject—and I ended up inviting eight prominent African Americans to allow their family histories to be researched for a documentary film series for PBS. Some were friends of mine, some were strangers who became friends. Together we journeyed back through our family trees, chasing down every scrap of paper we could find, every census record, every family Bible, trying to verify every little story and legend. And when the paper trail would end, as it inevitably did, in the horrid darkness of slavery, we traced our African roots through our DNA. We were successful, in some measure, in every case. And the series had such an enthusiastic response that we were able to film a sequel, with eleven new subjects, employing even newer and more accurate DNA tests.

Thus, I have now spent more than three years conducting genealogical research on some of the world's most compelling African Americans. It has been a magical experience for me—indeed, one of the most intensely enjoyable experiences that I have had as a scholar. I was able to reveal to each of these fascinating people, sometimes in astonishing detail, stories about the ancestors on their family trees, demonstrating how they were shaped, consciously or not, by their family members' experiences—often family members whom they had never even heard of! In so doing I invariably ended up talking with them about a host of related subjects—what it means to grow up black in America, what African Americans think of Africa, how we feel about our slave past. These are the issues that I have devoted my professional life to pursuing, the issues I care about the most. I have spent countless hours contemplating them from a variety of vantage points and through an equally wide variety of media. I have to say that it has been a genuine privilege to be allowed to explore these issues so intimately—family matters, after all, no more and no less—with such an interesting group of people. And as time has passed, I have realized how much the experience changed me—how much the individual stories drawn from each family tree changed the way I perceive African American history as a whole, from the ground up, as it were, from the particular to the general: for example, from Oprah Winfrey's great-great-grandfather Constantine to the broad contours of the Reconstruction period. You won't find Constantine Winfrey's story in any American history book, and that's because it has been hidden on the bare branches of Oprah's family tree. Until now. And that is what genealogy can do, especially for black people: Restoring the stories of the lives of the members of our extended families can directly transform the way that historians reassemble the larger narrative of the history of our people. African American history is still a very young discipline, a discipline still very much in process; restoring the branches of even one black family tree can profoundly change the ways that we understand the larger story of who the African American people really are. By telling and retelling the stories of our own ancestors, history can move from our kitchens or our parlors into the textbooks, ultimately changing the official narrative of American history itself.

This book is about those changes. It is a record, in words and images, of what I learned while tracing nineteen family trees from the present, back through the abyss of slavery, and then across the ocean to Africa. Each chapter looks at one of these family trees in detail, focusing on the stories I found especially compelling and meaningful. This is a book about journeys, not destinations; perhaps the surprising secret of African American genealogy is that every aspect of every family story, no matter how seemingly trivial or insignificant, can be a revelation that reshapes how we understand the entire sweep of the black experience in America. As more African Americans trace their family trees, both African American and American history will have to be rewritten. While learning the name of the tribe from whom your African American ancestors descended back in Africa is astonishingly satisfying and, candidly, something of a miracle— learning the names of your ancestors who were slaves and then freedmen and women, and learning the names of the white people who owned your ancestors, and from whom you are descended, can be just as exciting as well. Judging by the emotional impact upon the individuals interviewed in this book, learning the names of one's kinsmen on this side of the Atlantic carries even more emotional weight than learning about one's more re- mote African ancestry. Frankly, I was initially surprised by this.

Ultimately, this is a book about how the experiences of the individuals in our families allow us to reconfigure our nation's collective past, in a re- lationship of part for whole.

After all, history should be the narrative of the sum of the expe- riences of its actors, our ancestors, not just a few of them. How does the fact that Constantine Winfrey managed to barter twelve hundred pounds of cotton for eighty acres of prime bottom land, in the dread- fully racist state of Mississippi in the dreadful year of 1876, the year that Reconstruction ended—how does this affect our understanding of the historical period of Reconstruction itself? Re-creating the history of the individuals in our families is not only a rewarding activity personally; it also allows us a glimpse into that which has been stolen, hidden, or lost, in the collective history of the African American people. So much of the history of our people has been determined by the racial context in which we found ourselves: first by slavery (1619–1865), of course; then by the Civil War (1861–65), followed by the all-too-few years of Reconstruction (1866–76), Jim Crow (1876–1965), and its antidote, the civil rights movement, which we can date from the founding of the NAACP in 1909 to Dr. King's death in 1968. So very many black people were trapped by these supra-forces—pulled down by the sheer weight of racism like an apple pulled to the ground by the force of gravity. Racism was the ether in which our ancestors lived and breathed and moved. Many of our ancestors didn't have a lot of choice over the major decisions in their lives; rather, their choices were delimited by the larger political contexts in which they found themselves. But all too often we let this obscure the fact that our ancestors lived their lives, too. They had daily struggles— ordinary struggles—and I think that much of our "official" history misses that. We can never forget that there are many large trends in black history, but at the same time we must remember that normal, regular black people went about their business each and every day. They loved and hated, worshipped and sinned, worried and aspired. They were defeated in a shockingly depressing number of ways, yet they triumphed as individuals, as families, as a people. Together they created a culture, one of the world's great cultures; a culture with its own language, its own sacred and profane institutions, its own art and music and literature and dancing, its own ways of walking and thinking, shucking and jiving, dissipating and aspiring, its own ways of struggling to survive, enduring, and transcending.

Here, then, are the stories of my friends' families, which vividly bring that struggle to life. They are stories for which I have been searching, in retrospect—a story, in my own case, which I have been writing without knowing it—since I was ten years old, since the day I attended the funeral of my grandfather, Edward Lawrence Gates Jr., after which my father silently led me up a narrow stairway to a scrapbook, an obituary, and a brown-tinted photograph. (When I was twenty-five, I dragged my father down to the microfilm archives of the *Cumberland Evening Times,* in Maryland, specifically to find that obituary, long lost along with all but one of Pop Gates's scrapbooks, from our family's collective archives.) Searching for my own family's story has led me to the stories of other African Americans. And these are the stories that I was able to reveal in the two PBS series entitled *African American Lives*—the stories of the famous and the obscure, janitors and movie stars, doctors and turpentine collectors. These stories are African American history at its most essential, the building blocks of any people's collective narrative. These tiny fragments of human lives illuminate both our selves and our society, who we are as individuals, who we are as families, who we are as a people and as a country. Collectively, their stories make up a new, richer and fuller narrative of America, of the people who created America and the people whom America created. These stories show how we got through slavery, how we survived, how we overcame odds too stark to calculate, to emerge as a people: the African American people.

I hope you enjoy reading these stories as much as I have enjoyed researching and writing them. And I hope that you will trace the roots and branches of your own family tree and tell the story of your ancestors yourself.

Henry Louis Gates, Jr.
Oak Bluffs, Massachusetts
August 16, 2008

Prefatory Notes on
the African Slave Trade

T HIS BOOK is in large measure about slavery and its aftermath, and the impact of that horrendous institution on generations of African American families and some of their more notable descendants, leading figures in the African American community today. Because the stories of these individuals and their ancestors are rooted in genealogical research, they are necessarily based on historical analysis and a few salient statistics about the origins of our ancestors forced into the slave ships and shipped to the United States between 1619 and the 1800s. Understanding this historical background will, I think, help you more fully to appreciate the stories in this book.

First and foremost, you need to understand who our slave ancestors were—that is, where they originated on the African continent. They were Africans of many different ethnic groups from many different regions, taken captive—often by other Africans—and sold to Europeans. They were then put on ships and transported to the New World. Many did not survive the dreadful journey: Historians estimate that 15 percent of those who boarded the slave ships along the African coast perished in the dreadful Middle Passage. Those who managed to survive endured a lifetime of unimaginable hardship, bound by people who carefully and willfully did all they could do in every possible way to strip away every aspect of their slaves' humanity.

All African Americans whose ancestors were born in the New World before the twentieth century are descended from these slaves, and every African American today—unless she or he is descended from a very recent African immigrant—can trace his or her lineage deep into the slave past. While some of our ancestors were fortunate enough to be freed by the Emancipation Proclamation—about 600,000 according to historian David Blight—before the end of the Civil War (three of the individuals whose family lines are discussed in this book descend from slaves who were freed before 1800), about 87 percent of the 3,953,760 slaves in 1860 were freed from slavery only in 1865. But because of the way the slave system worked, few of us know much, if anything, about any of our ancestors from this period, even if they had been freed. We know even less about our African ancestors, of course. While it's not so likely, some may even have been members of royal families in Africa; many more would have been captured in battle, then sold to Europeans as the booty of war. Others were imprisoned because of debt; some were kidnapped. Regardless, however, of how they were enslaved in Africa, still they spoke their languages and knew their names. But here, on this side of the Atlantic, they soon lost those names.

Slavery poses enormous challenges to any scholar seeking to reconstruct its features. Though the practices of slave owners varied, sometimes significantly, in different eras and in different states and in different times, slavery was, almost everywhere, a systemic effort to rob black human beings of their very humanity itself—that is, of all the aspects of civilization that make a human being "human": names, birth dates, family ties, the freedom to be educated and to worship, and the most basic sense of self-knowledge and continuity of generations within one's direct family lines. With very few exceptions—and there were some, oddly enough—each slave had one name only, a first name, that the law and custom acknowledged. No matter what slaves called themselves within the confines of their own communities, within their sheltered and hidden lives as a veritable subcontinent of the plantation, and no matter what their family and friends knew them by, the American legal system did not generally acknowledge those names. (Slaves would usually be listed by first names in legal documents such as wills, estate papers of the deceased, and some tax records, for example. And, remarkably, in the schedules of the 1850 and 1860 federal censuses, eight counties—including Hampshire County,

then in Virginia, now in West Virginia, where some of my own slave ancestors lived—listed the slaves owned there by a first name and a surname;
but these were the exceptions, only eight counties among all the counties
in all the states in America.) And sometimes, though very rarely, notices of
slave auctions would list slaves to be sold by a first and a last name. (I own
one of these advertisements.) How in the world can you reconstruct a family tree consisting of generations of people who had only one name, when
even that name was not often listed in official, legal documents maintained
by the state?

In my efforts to trace present-day African Americans back to their
family roots in Africa, I frequently consult what I consider to be one of
the most valuable and impressive historical research tools ever created:
the Trans-Atlantic Slave Trade Database. This database is a compilation of
the records kept by shipping companies involved in the slave trade. It offers detailed information on 34,941 transatlantic slave-trading voyages that
occurred between 1514 and 1866. Compiled under the direction of David
Eltis, with the collaboration of Stephen D. Behrendt, Manolo Florentino,
and David Richardson, it is the largest uniform, consolidated database of
its kind in the world. The authors estimate that the assembled data cover
at least two-thirds of the slaving voyages that crossed the Atlantic Ocean
to the New World. Of especial interest to us are the voyages to the United
States, either directly from Africa or via the Caribbean.

According to the database, before the slave trade ended in the United
States, approximately 455,000 Africans were brought here against their
will, 389,000 directly from Africa, and another 66,000 from the Caribbean,
according to Greg O'Malley. Meaning that of the 12.5 million Africans
taken from Africa and shipped across the Atlantic in slavery, only a tiny
portion—less than 4 percent—were brought to this country (the remainder, of course, went to the Caribbean and Latin America). Of the 12.5 million Africans who left Africa, 10.7 million arrived in the Americas between
1501 and 1867. For most black Americans—about 90 percent of those of
us living in the United States today—these 455,000 Africans are the basis
of our ancestral gene pool. They are the core source of what are now more
than 35 million African American citizens.

The vast majority of our African ancestors came to the United States as slaves between 1700 and 1820. Most, in fact, arrived in the final decades of the eighteenth century. David Eltis estimates that in 1700 only 4 percent of the original 455,000 had arrived here. By 1750 the figure is 41 percent; by 1800 it is 80 percent; and by 1820 it is 99.7 percent. This means that virtually all African American families had an ancestor here by 1820, if not much earlier. In fact, more than half of us had ancestors living in the United States by the signing of the Declaration of Independence. The black presence is as old as America itself.

The following map illustrates the African origins of the slaves who arrived in North America:

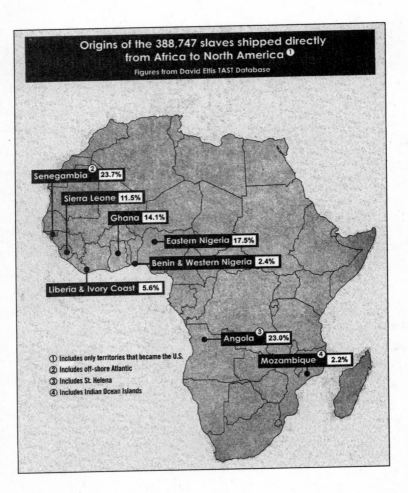

Origins of the 388,747 slaves shipped directly from Africa to North America ①

Figures from David Eltis TAST Database

Senegambia ② 23.7%

Sierra Leone 11.5%

Ghana 14.1%

Eastern Nigeria 17.5%

Benin & Western Nigeria 2.4%

Liberia & Ivory Coast 5.6%

Angola ③ 23.0%

Mozambique ④ 2.2%

① Includes only territories that became the U.S.
② Includes off-shore Atlantic
③ Includes St. Helena
④ Includes Indian Ocean Islands

In other words, if a room were full of black people and we gave each one a DNA test, we would learn that 23.0 percent of us are descended from people who were shipped from Congo or Angola, 17.5 percent of us from eastern Nigeria and the Cameroon Republic, 2.2 percent from Mozambique, 14.1 percent from Ghana, 2.4 percent from Benin and western Nigeria, and 40.8 percent from the countries that range from Senegal and Gambia to Liberia (known as Upper Guinea).

Within these regions there were scores of tribes or ethnic groups who were poured into the slave ships bound for America. Africa was, and remains, one of the most diverse continents, genetically and linguistically, on the face of the earth. Fifteen hundred languages are spoken on the African continent today. But the ancestors of the African American people are surprisingly localized. Linda Heywood and John Thornton have recently estimated that about fifty ethnic groups in Africa primarily made up the body of slaves who became the ancestors of the African American people. These ethnic groups have names today such as Mende, Igbo, Yoruba, and Fon, and these names refer to shared languages and cultural practices. Some of these names would have been used by Africans to describe themselves; others are of more recent vintage. As David Eltis explained to me, "There were some large ethnolinguistic groups such as Mende and Congo, but these were not necessarily part of people's self-identification. Identities would have been developed for much smaller units of people. From Upper Guinea, Mende, Koronko, Susu, Fula, and Mandingo would have been well represented. From the Bight of Biafra (in today's eastern Nigeria), more than half would likely have been Igbo." The slaves who commandeered the slave ship called the *Amistad,* for example, under the leadership of Cinque, identified themselves as members of the Mende people in a Bible they presented to their attorney, former president John Quincy Adams, in 1841. In other words, the names that Africans use to describe themselves today were not necessarily in use during slavery times as a form of self-identification, but many were. What this means is that if we could go back in time and meet our earliest enslaved ancestor, depending on the point in time, he or she may or may not think of him- or herself as

"Mende," say, despite speaking a language that we call "Mende" and living in a "Mende" land. Such ancestors might think of themselves instead as belonging to a specific local group—a group whose name has been long ago lost. For the purposes of this book, and indeed for most work on slavery, we will not attempt to parse the local groups within the larger ethnic identities. If your ancestors shared genetic characteristics with a person who describes him- or herself as Mende today, I will call them Mende here. After all, just because Frederick Douglass thought of himself as "colored" doesn't mean that it would be incorrect to describe him today as an "African American."

Now, of course, once our ancestors came to this country, their ethnic identities were stripped from them, along with their names, religions, and family ties. They ceased to be Mende or Igbo or Kpelle and became Negro slaves, thrown together with people of other ethnicities without any consideration. Over the years the blending of their different ethnicities created the rich mixture—the pan-African identity—that is African American culture today. But it took time. And you can bet that there were some painful intra-African conflicts along the way. After all, what united these many different people of African descent was their color, the continent of their origin, and most especially their condition as the enslaved. There were also, of course, interracial mixtures with whites and with Native Americans—over half the African American people today have at least one European great-grandfather, while that figure for a Native American great-grandparent is much, much less, amounting to only about 5 percent—and all this intermixture contributes to who we are today when we describe ourselves as "African Americans."

I'll have more to say about our "admixture" throughout this book, since this is one of the crucial tests that I administered to each of the individuals who participated in this project. In the broad picture, the geneticist Dr. Mark Shriver has advised me that African American DNA today breaks down something like this:

- 5 percent of African Americans have at least 12.5 percent Native American ancestry (equivalent of one great-grandparent).

- 58 percent of African Americans have at least 12.5 percent European ancestry (equivalent of one great-grandparent).
- 19.6 percent of African Americans have at least 25 percent European ancestry (equivalent of one grandparent).
- 1 percent of African Americans have at least 50 percent European ancestry (equivalent of one parent).

By contrast, Americans of predominantly white or European ancestry have the following mixtures:

- 2.7 percent of European Americans have at least 12.5 percent Native American ancestry (equivalent of one great-grandparent).
- Less than 1 percent of European Americans have at least 12.5 percent West African ancestry (equivalent of one great-grandparent).

These fascinating statistics should, I hope, give us all a better understanding of the genetic and geographical origins of the victims of the African slave trade to America.

Statistics are by their nature very broad and maddeningly vague and anonymous. It will always be so. We will never know even a tiny fraction of the names of our ancestors who were taken from Africa. We will never see their faces, never read their words. They are lost to us forever, because of the devastatingly effective way the slave trade worked in its attempt to erase the past from the present of a slave. Nevertheless, we can now, after all of these centuries, begin to get a sense of who our ancestors were, by analyzing the DNA of their descendants—and by re-creating the lines of the families they started in slavery, the families that against all odds now thrive in such great numbers today. After Nigeria and Brazil, the African Americans living in the United States constitute the third-largest group of black people in the world. Telling the story of their origins and their evolution from the seventeenth century to the present, from slavery to freedom, is precisely what this book attempts to do, through what I hope is a careful history of nineteen extraordinary individuals, individuals whose past—while unique, of course—is also most certainly representative of the world that our ancestors—your ancestors and mine, black and white—created out of the crucible of slavery and the centuries-long battle to become free and equal citizens in the great republic that America is still striving to be.

Maya Angelou

April 4, 1928

MAYA ANGELOU IS ONE of the most resonant voices in the history of American literature. She has written bestselling auto-biographies, books of poetry, and plays that have affected more people than has the work of almost any other black author I can name. In the process she has infused the art form of the autobiography with a densely poetic discourse reminiscent of the old Negro Spirituals. She is also a historian, an educator, and a lecturer who has thrilled audiences with her mesmerizing, resonant, lyrical speaking voice. I have sat in those audiences, spellbound, and I know the power of her voice. So I was de-lighted when she agreed to participate in this project.

As I told Maya at the start of our work, my fascination with family his-tory has been heavily influenced by her writing. Indeed, I cannot overstate the effect that her first book, *I Know Why the Caged Bird Sings,* had on me. I was twenty years old when I read it—and it has been a part of my life ever since. It is a book that I have taught and studied, a book that I love. It was among my mother's favorite books, something we shared. In researching Maya's family's past, I planned to revisit and reexamine some of the characters and settings in the book—to look at scenes and people I thought I knew so well through the lens of genealogy and historical docu-mentation. I was a bit frightened at the prospect. It would be interesting, I thought, as a devoted reader to see how a great artist had molded ex-perience to her own artistic purposes. But as a historian I feared that the power of Maya's work would somehow be diminished by the genealogical or historical experience on which her memories were based. As it turns out, I had nothing at all to fear. Our research only confirmed her memories and has made her work even more rewarding to contemplate. We even found new stories, which I hope that she will one day narrate in her own voice.

Maya Angelou was born on April 4, 1928, in St. Louis, Missouri. Her birth name was Marguerite Johnson, and she was the second child of Bailey Johnson and Vivian Baxter Johnson. I knew from her books that Maya's childhood was deeply traumatic, and I expected that it would be painful for her to talk about. But I wanted to go over the events, exploring them in terms of her family history, and Maya was willing to oblige. She knows how important this history is. Even her famous first name has its origins in her troubled childhood. It was changed from Marguerite to Maya by her older brother, Bailey, when they were very young—and essentially alone.

"Bailey," recalled Maya, "used to call me 'my sister,' because we were buffeted about and I was the only thing that was his. He was so proud of that. Everybody seemed to have lots of other things, but he had just one sister. So he called me 'my sister,' and sometimes he just used to call me 'mine.' And then, when he was about nine, I guess, he read about the Mayan Indians. And he was so taken that he said I was Maya. And I kept the name. I love it so, for many, many reasons. It is history with my brother."

Maya told me that she grew up with little knowledge of her parents. "I was three years old when my parents separated," she said. "And they sent me and my brother—who was five years old—to my father's mother. And over the next ten years, save for one disastrous visit, we never heard from them. We would get a note or a card or a doll about every three years, and we poked the eyes out of the doll and buried it upside down, standing on its head. So I knew almost nothing, really, about them."

The "disastrous visit" that Maya refers to here was an almost unimaginably awful crime. After four years of living in relative happiness with her paternal grandmother, Maya was briefly returned to her mother in St. Louis, where, at age seven, she was raped by her mother's boyfriend. When she confessed to her brother, the family exploded in violence.

Her uncle is reported to have killed the rapist, and young Maya and her brother were sent back to Arkansas to live with her grandmother. It would be years before Maya lived with her mother again—years filled with pain and private torment.

"I was raped at seven and returned to my grandmother," she said with little emotion. "And I didn't talk for six years. Just didn't say a word."

Maya's mother, Vivian Baxter, played a central role in these events, yet Maya and she would eventually reconcile. This is evidence of Vivian's rather remarkable character and of Maya's enormous capacity to forgive and heal. Vivian was born on January 19, 1912, in St. Louis, Missouri. She spent much of her later life in San Francisco—moving there in the late 1930s and becoming active in a wide range of progressive causes. Maya rejoined her mother in 1940 and lived with her through her teenage years, gaining exposure to her mother's views about the world while finding herself drawn into another world—that of dance, literature, and drama. Vivian supported her daughter in all these pursuits—emotionally, if not financially (indeed, Maya worked as a cocktail waitress and a brothel madam in her years as a struggling artist).

Given what I knew of her from Maya's books, I knew that Maya bore Vivian no ill will and in fact admired her mother greatly. But I was still surprised at the rush of feeling that Maya displayed upon seeing a photograph of Vivian that I had brought.

"She is the bravest human being I ever met," said Maya without hesitation. "She was a small woman, and she was a very pretty woman. But she was really tough. She'd fight in bars with her brothers. And they were big boys. And she was also very generous. In Stockton, California, on one edge of town there's a library named for me. And the other edge as you go out, there's a park named for her. She had an organization called Stockton Black Women for Humanity, and they were generous and caring of those in need. All folks in need. She was a terrible parent of young people. But she was generous."

Maya recalls that her mother was also an extremely hard worker, devoted to a great number of causes—from union rights to civil rights to feminism. Over the course of an extraordinarily peripatetic life, she

Maya Angelou's mother, Vivian Baxter, with two family members, around 1980.

worked as a nurse, a real-estate agent, and, almost unbelievably, as a merchant marine. "She was marvelous," said Maya. "A lot of women sailors ship out of San Francisco—white, black, Asian, Hispanic—because of her. They call her 'the mother of the sea.' She was the first. She said, 'I put my foot in that door. They said women can't get in the union. I put my foot in that door up to my ass. Women of every color will get in that union, get aboard a ship, and go to sea.' And they did. She said, 'I'm going to be a seaman.' And she was. I mean, she was all sorts of things. I remember I saw her luggage one time, and there was a huge German Luger. She said, 'If they weren't ready for me, I was ready for them.' She was really all of that. She was marvelous. And I wanted to write a book about her, but she said no. So I write essays, you know, I write around her."

Listening to her talk, it was clear to me that Maya's feelings about Vivian were shaped by her instincts as an autobiographical artist—by the degree to which she is able to appreciate and enjoy her mother almost as a literary creation. It's inspiring to watch. But while Maya is able to celebrate her mother, her feelings about her father remain tortured. I showed her a photograph that we found of him, later in life, when he was working in California as a doorman at the Breakers Hotel, and asked her what, if anything, she could remember about him.

"He spoke some French," she said quietly. "He had been in World War I. He was a proud man, very proud. I didn't like him. I mean, he was likable— but not to me. Because he was quite accustomed to violence. He was a user of violence. He lived in San Diego and had another family in Mexico. He did things that I don't agree with as a person, a human being. And he was phony, too. I never liked him."

Anna Henderson, Maya's paternal grandmother; she essentially raised Maya and sheltered her through years of silence and pain.

Maya's voice was calm as she spoke about her father, but her sentences were unusually clipped, and it was clear that he had caused her a great deal of pain. She seemed palpably relieved when we stepped back and began to talk about his mother, Annie. Annie was Maya's paternal grandmother, and the single most important person in her family throughout her childhood. She essentially raised Maya and saved her from disaster, sheltering her through years of silence and pain, allowing her to grow into the remarkable person she is today. In Maya's books Annie is referred to as Annie Henderson, because Henderson was her second husband's last name. But Annie's maiden name was Taylor, and Maya's eyes lit up at the very mention of her.

"My grandmother was God to me," she said with tremendous awe and gratitude in her voice. "She told me all the time, she said she didn't care what people said about me. People would say, 'You must be an idiot or a moron, 'cause you don't talk.' She said she didn't care. She'd say, 'Mama know when you and the Good Lord get ready, you are going to be a teacher. You'll teach all over this world.' She'd say that often. And I used to sit there and think, This poor ignorant woman, Good Lord. I mean, I would *never* speak. So I can't imagine how she could know that. She went to the fourth grade in school. She taught herself her figures and reading, and she owned a store, but how she could look at me, this little girl, physically and psychologically bruised and say, 'You're going to be a teacher and teach all over the world'—how could she? I'll never know. But each time I go to stand up before five thousand people and they pay to come in to hear a black woman speak, I think about my grandma."

Annie is a fascinating person. She was born in Columbia County, Arkansas, in 1877, the child of freed slaves. During the course of her long life, she would become a leader of the black community in Stamps, Arkansas, owning the only grocery store in that small town. Over six feet tall, powerful and commanding yet immensely kind, Annie left a searing impression upon her granddaughter. "She spoke softly," recalls Maya. "But in church she would shatter the windows. She had this ability. Every Sunday she would sing. The preacher would say, 'And now we will be privileged with a song of Sister Henderson.' And every Sunday my grandmother, for ten years, she sang the same song: 'I am a cold pilgrim of sorrow, I walk in this wide world alone.' I mean, this woman could sing, oh, Lord."

Maya recalls that she rarely left her grandmother's side during the years they lived together. And given this, and the fact that Maya did not speak for many of those years, one might be tempted to think that she would have little memory of the larger world in which she grew up. But in reality Maya was an astute observer of life in the Jim Crow South. She has written about it eloquently in her books many times, describing Stamps, where she spent much of her childhood, as a place in which segregation was so complete that most black children "didn't really know what white looked like."

"I remember never believing that whites were really real," Maya once wrote. And when I asked her how she was affected by segregation, she thought for a long time before answering. "Segregation shaped me, and education liberated me," she said. "And I don't mean formal education.

Or not just formal education. I remember once there were a group of girls who lived on land my grandmother owned. And she owned much of the land behind the town. And they were white. And if they came into the store and my uncle was there, he had to give them anything they wanted, because he was a black man, and although he was crippled, if he didn't do what they wanted, they could simply say he made a pass at them. And that would be the end of it. They could blackmail him. But once they came and my grandmother was there. Uncle Willy had scooted out and gone somewhere next door to save himself. And these girls, one stood up on her hands to show herself. She said, 'Lookit here, Annie.' And she stood up, and she had no drawers on. No panties. So insulting. And I just cried. I wanted my grandmother to show that she was God and zap them. But of course she did no such thing. But I remember when she came to me after the girls were gone, she said, 'Don't cry, sister, don't worry about that, don't worry. It won't always be that way.' And I couldn't imagine the time when things would be different—but it came. Finally, it did come."

This story, to my mind, is a powerfully concise evocation of the pervasive evil that was the Jim Crow era, and the myriad, small ways its forms of insult and humiliation manifested themselves. Its details remind me of so many things I recall hearing from my parents during my own youth, but tiny details most histories of the period ignore. As Maya spoke, I grew increasingly amazed, as she was, that we ever survived those years. But then, moving back another generation on her paternal line, we looked to Annie's parents, Maya's paternal great-grandparents, to see an even worse period in our history.

Annie was the daughter of Mary "Kentucky" Wafford and Emanuel Taylor. Both were born into slavery—Emanuel around 1850 in Louisiana and Mary on August 20, 1853, in Columbia County, Arkansas. We do not know any more about Emanuel, but Mary lived until 1935, and Maya has vivid memories of her from her childhood.

"She was tough," Maya recalled. "She controlled the African American area of Stamps. She was the arbiter of right and wrong. Not talking loud. But tough. She was this tiny woman who had come from Texarkana or Magnolia, wherever she was, with all her daughters, including my grand-

Maya's great-grandmother, Mary Wafford. Born into slavery, Mary was a tiny, tough woman who Maya remembers vividly from her childhood.

mother, twice her size, six feet tall. And she'd walk straight, and she could do anything. She was a former slave. And as soon as slavery was abolished, she renamed herself Kentucky. When asked why—when asked, 'Were you enslaved in Kentucky?'—she said no, that she liked the sound of the name, and she absolutely prohibited anybody from knowing anything more about her background. She said, 'I am Kentucky, and that's all you need to know.' And that's all we ever did know."

Maya clearly enjoys the story of her great-grandmother's name and of the power she wielded in her community. But even though she knew that Mary Wafford spent the first twelve years of her life in slavery, as did many of her relatives, the fact was never discussed in Maya's family. As curious as Maya and her siblings and cousins may have been about their elders, they never asked about their slave pasts. This, as I have found throughout this project, seems to have been the rule in black families. We simply did not talk about slavery. Maya agrees with me wholeheartedly and is as fascinated by the subject as I am.

"We talked about it by not talking about it," Maya said. "Like quilts, right? Younger people don't realize the value of quilts. But during slavery, when people were sold off for any reason, the slave who was sold off would cut off a little piece of his father's shirt or a little piece of her mother's skirt and pin it inside their own shirt. And they would finally make a quilt of those little patches. And a patched quilt had a lot to do with saving one's sanity. You could keep a small piece of your family. To touch it and smell it. And when you had children, you would tell the story. This was your great-grandfather's, this was your grandmother's, this skirt here. But slavery wasn't spoken of. I mean, I had grandfathers and great-grandfathers who were killed, who disappeared, because they spoke back to some white man. And that was never spoken about. We just did not ask, 'What happened to Grandfather So-and-So? What happened to him?' We just did not. Grandmother would not admit to anything. You know? We are fascinated by slavery today. And it's not a minute too soon. We see what has happened. We know that she who does not know where she has come from cannot possibly guide a path to where she has to go. So this generation is avid, eager, champing at the bit to know: 'Tell me more, and let me tell the people more about their history.' It's very important. But it wasn't always so."

This was one of the most moving and poignant insights I gathered throughout this entire project. And for Maya's very reasons, I, too, am always eager to learn more about our ancestors' lives in slavery. The history cannot be lost and forgotten. It is vitally important to the shaping of who the African American people are today, and it has been hidden too long, tucked away in the corners of the historical experiences that our ancestors refused to tell about themselves.

To learn more about Mary, we searched the records of every slave owner with the last name Wafford in Arkansas and the surrounding states. We were extremely fortunate to discover a crucial document that revealed quite a lot about Maya's ancestor. We located the will of a man named William Wafford who lived in Mississippi in the first half of the nineteenth century. This will, dated 1846, deeds William's slaves to his brother, Miles Wafford, and it lists the slaves by name as being Washington, Millie, Dee, Nesendi, and Mary. Since census records tell us that Mary's father was a man named Washington Wafford, born into slavery in Georgia in 1825, it is almost certain that he and his daughter were owned by this William Wafford.

Maya knows that she is very fortunate we found this document. Most of our ancestors from 1825 are invisible to us today, lost in the anonymity of slavery. As Maya took a copy of the will into her hands, I asked her if she often thought about the fact that her ancestors were legally defined as property.

"I think about it all the time," she replied. "I never stop thinking about it. I am maybe consumed by other kinds of activity sometimes, but it doesn't evaporate. Maybe over time it will, but I mean real time—a thousand years. Three hundred and a half years will not noticeably change the positioning of the brain to slavery. So that whites, many of them, will still presume because of my color that they are still better. That their white skin makes them better than I am. But the truth is that many of them are crippled by slavery. And made lesser by it. Many blacks, too, without saying so, find themselves inferior because of their history and don't understand that, 'Wait a minute, that's not true, either.' So it resides with us and will do so for a long time, and we have to be vigilant."

Moving back up Maya's paternal line, we researched her father's father, William Johnson, born in February 1876 in Ouachita County, Arkansas. His father, Maya's great-grandfather, was Simon Johnson, born into slavery in Alabama in about 1825. We were unable to garner much information about him. We could not identify the source of his surname or even precisely identify the date of his death (we believe that it occurred sometime between 1900 and 1910). But our search did uncover a very interesting document: an obituary from 1942 for Simon's wife, Emaline Lankford Johnson, who was Maya's great-grandmother. This obituary reads, in part, "Emaline Johnson, former Negro slave said to be 150 years old, died Friday night at her home six miles southwest of Camden. She was born in what is now Union County, then moved to Camden many years ago. She was married to Simon Johnson in slavery time, who died some time ago. The Negro woman lived through four wars. She could see good and lived in good health until a few months ago."

I find this obituary fascinating, even if it is clearly false as regards to Emaline's age. (According to census records, Emaline was probably about ninety years old when she passed away.) What surprises me about the obituary is the fact that it mentions that Emaline and Simon were married "in slavery." This is unusual because the law didn't recognize slave marriages. In fact, slaves were legally forbidden to marry. Yet this article suggests what we all know: Slaves married anyway. They got around inhumane laws in every way that they could to cement family bonds within their own world, when the white world, the world of the masters, willfully refused to. Maya's great-grandparents, like many of their peers, forged a stable relationship even under the harshest conditions imaginable. And it took a lot of hardheaded willpower and luck for them to sustain that relationship. Maya and I both admired the courage of Emaline and Simon.

Unfortunately, we were not able to trace their ancestors back much further. Emaline Johnson's father was a man named Stephen Lankford. We know nothing more about him than his name. He was Maya's great-great-grandfather, and he is the furthest back we can go along her paternal line. So at this point we began to investigate her mother's family.

Maya's mother's father was Thomas Baxter, born in 1870 in Bainbridge, Georgia, just after the Civil War. Judging from census records, we determined that he came to St. Louis at the turn of the century and was considered to be a "mulatto." In the 1910 census, he is listed as living in St. Louis and working as a Pullman porter.

Maya recalls meeting her grandfather once, during a visit to St. Louis in 1935, just before he died. She had heard stories about his work as a Pullman porter, though she believes that many of them were probably exaggerated. She also heard stories that he was West Indian but again did not know if this was true or if it was simply the way that she identified himself in the racist South to deflect suspicions raised by his fair skin.

"As I heard it," she said, "my grandfather Thomas was from the West Indies. He jumped a ship, a banana boat in Florida, near Tampa, and got a job rolling cigars. He was doing so well that he went back to get his father and brought his father over here. They both worked there in the cigar-rolling thing. And then he married, and he had a child. But then he went away on one of his forays and was told that the owner, the boss of the cigar place, had beaten his father, my great-great-grandfather. So the story goes that he went back and found the white man and took care of that. But then his wife died, leaving him with a newborn called Ira. My Uncle Ira. And he took off walking from Florida with his pistol and his baby and a blanket, and he arrived in North Carolina, and he met up with another woman, quite an older woman. But as I understand it now, that's family lore."

Maya is right. This is family lore. Though the tale is entertaining and quite possibly based on some small amount of truth, we could find no documentation for most of it. The public records show that Maya's grandfather Thomas Baxter was the son of Addison and Jane Baxter, both born slaves in South Carolina sometime in the 1820s. In the years after the Civil War, they are listed in the census as being farm laborers, which means that they were probably sharecroppers. Their son Thomas married Maya's maternal grandmother, Marguerite Savin, in St. Louis sometime around 1909. There are no documents referring to the West Indies, banana boats, cigar factories, or walking trips from Florida to North Carolina. There are, however, documents that tell quite a remarkable story about Thomas's wife, Marguerite.

In *I Know Why the Caged Bird Sings,* Maya describes her grandmother Marguerite as being "a quadroon or octoroon"—and photographs suggest that she was nearly white. When she was a child, this did not confuse Maya. "There were all sorts of light-complected people in the family," she recalls. "Like most African American families, we ranged in color from plum blue to milk white." What did confuse her, as she recalls, was her grandmother's strange accent. Marguerite had what Maya's mother claimed was an Irish accent. The young Maya thought it sounded German. It was, in any event, an accent that she was unaccustomed to hearing in Arkansas—and it frightened her.

Marguerite Baxter was born in May of 1875 in Carlisle, Illinois. Interestingly, Carlisle was a predominantly German-American community. In *I Know Why the Caged Bird Sings,* Maya writes that her grandmother spoke with "a throaty German accent" and that she never lost her taste for the thick, black German bread, called *brot.* Carlisle is undoubtedly where Marguerite developed her German accent and her taste for German food. But what about her own ancestry? Is it possible that Maya's grandmother was German?

Marguerite's death certificate offers some clues. It says that her father's name was "John Savins" and her mother's name was Mary Lee. In the 1870 census, we found a man named John Savin living with his wife—a woman named Margaret—their two daughters, and their black maid: Mary Lee. The census data indicate that at that time John Savin was forty-eight years old. It also indicates that he was a white man, born in Ireland. This suggests that Maya's great-grandfather was an Irishman who lived among German Americans and impregnated his black maid, Mary Lee.

According to the census, Mary Lee was born around 1857 in Maryland. How did she end up working in this white household in Illinois, such a long way from home and from her family? The answer seems to lie in her complex relationship with the Irishman John Savin. Census records show that in 1860 John was living in Washington County, Maryland, and was the owner of one slave: a three-year-old mulatto girl. This was almost certainly Mary Lee, which means that John owned her from the time she was a child, and she worked in his house as a domestic servant after emancipation, moving with John and his family from Maryland to Illinois.

In Illinois, John Savin was to all appearances a prominent and upstanding citizen; he served as justice of the peace and won an election to be the town supervisor. But there was another side to him as well. Looking through local records, we found numerous judgments against him in small claims court for nonpayment of wages and for disputes with neighbors. And in 1875 John Savin was indicted by a grand jury on a criminal charge of suborning perjury. This indictment says, in part, that Savin "did unlawfully and wickedly solicit, instigate, and endeavor to persuade a certain Mary Lee who was pregnant out of wedlock to make a false statement as to who was the child's father." The indictment goes on to say in fact that fifty-three-year-old John Savin was the father and that at the time Mary Lee was seventeen years old.

Soon after the indictment, John Savin made a statement protesting his innocence that was published in the local newspaper in Carlisle. This must have been extremely embarrassing to such an upright citizen. But he had been charged with a felony, and if he'd been found guilty, he would have been sent to jail. So he took his case to the public, such as it was, and said he did not know anything about Mary Lee's pregnancy. And when his case

Indictment of slave owner John Savin, showing that he was accused of impregnating his maid (and former slave) Mary Lee and persuading her to lie about the identity of the child's father.

came to trial, a jury of twelve white men acquitted him.

Given the history of their relationship, both Maya and I are convinced that John Savin was lying. His fellow white townsmen chose to believe his version of the events, but it seems obvious that he was the father of Mary Lee's child. His name was listed on Marguerite's death certificate—seventy years after the fact.

Maya had heard stories in the family for decades about this white great-grandfather but had never been certain as to whether they were true or whether they were like the story of the banana boat that supposedly carried Thomas Baxter up from the West Indies. I assured her that they were most definitely true—and asked her if it bothered her to know that she had white ancestors. "No," she said emphatically and without hesitation. "What's to bother me? You should be pleased at whoever your ancestors are. I mean, you're here."

This is an extremely healthy attitude, I think. Well over half of all African American people have a white ancestor. And while some are bothered

by it, in my experience most, like Maya, are not, which is, I think, an interesting indicator of how willing we are as a people to accept the racial complexity of our family histories, rather than to pretend to some sort of claim
of African purity or embrace embarrassment at how mixed our genetic
makeup actually is. It shows our strength rather than our weakness. I well
remember very painful moments in the late sixties when light-complected
African Americans would sometimes be "called out," or humiliated in public, for having light skin or straight hair. This was the worst time in the
history of community formation of the African American people and it
perpetuated a host of racist myths. One of the surprising aspects of DNA
testing is that it is extremely rare to find an African American who does not
have a significant share of European ancestry.

At this point our ability to trace Maya's family using genealogical
tools had reached its limit. We knew that Mary Lee was born in Maryland around 1857, possibly the daughter of a slave named Ed Lee. But
we could go no further with any kind of certainty. We thus turned to our
DNA testing to see what more we could learn. The first test we ran is
called an admixture test. It analyzes the information in all twenty-three
pairs of a person's chromosomes and provides a general picture of their
genetic constitution and ancestral background. Not surprisingly, Maya's
admixture test indicated that she had 77 percent sub-Saharan African lineage and 23 percent European. Her great-grandfather John Savin obviously played a big role in that result.

We did a second admixture test on Maya, which revealed that among
all of her African ancestors, 45 percent were from Congo Angola and
55 percent were from the large area we call West Africa, encompassing
what are now the countries of Guinea-Bissau, Senegal, Nigeria, Sierra
Leone, Ghana, and others. So she is truly a pan-African person, with roots
spread across an enormous portion of the continent. Knowing that Maya
had lived in Ghana and traveled throughout Africa, I asked her about her
preconceptions of her African heritage. Did she feel kinship, I wondered,
toward any region or tribe?

"Absolutely," she replied. "I went into Aflao once, which is near Keta
at the end of Ghana. The Mende people are there, and I walked into a mar-

ket. There was a woman that looked like my grandmother, Grandmother Henderson. Same size, only physically bigger, and she started speaking to me. She said, 'American,' and they passed all the food they had there to me. And it turned out that Aflao had been raided by slavers who had taken every healthy person out of that town, and some mothers had grabbed their infants by their feet and dashed them against tree trunks rather than see them taken into slavery. But some of the children were left hid and then went over to the next town, and they were kept there until they grew old enough to come back and rebuild their town. And they looked like me. And so there was this woman in the market who figured that I was a part of that group, taken from Aflao to the United States."

I was very intrigued by this horrifying story—and fascinated in that it was close to the story told by Maya's DNA. Not quite accurate, but close. When we analyzed her mitochondrial DNA, tracing her mother's line back to Africa, we did find exact matches with a Mende person—but in Sierra Leone, not Ghana. We also found exact matches with individuals who are members of the Mandinka people in Senegal and with the Balanta and Fula people in Guinea-Bissau, among others.

Both Maya and I of course wanted to know to which of these groups did her first female ancestor belong who was taken into slavery. We knew that Mary Lee, her great-great-grandmother, was born around 1857 in Maryland. So I consulted with professors John Thornton and Linda Heywood, a husband-wife team of historians who teach at Boston University and are among the most widely respected scholars of Africa and the African slave trade. Knowing Mary Lee's birthplace was Maryland gave Thornton and Heywood a departure point for interpreting Maya's DNA. They told me they believed Mary Lee's African ancestors could have been enslaved between 1720 and 1760 as a result of warfare that began in the western part of Futa Jallon in what is now the West African nation of Guinea.

This area, according to Thornton and Heywood, experienced several periods of political instability as the consequence of a jihad led by a Fulani Muslim named Karamoko Alpha, beginning in 1727. The jihad resulted in almost constant conflict in Futa Jallon throughout the rest of the eighteenth century and also expanded to involve ethnic groups in the modern-day countries of Liberia and Sierra Leone. As a result, many local people were taken into slavery, including perhaps Maya's original enslaved ancestress.

According to Thornton and Heywood, most of the leaders of the jihad were Fulbe (although there were also Mandinkas, Susu, and Jalonke people among them), and the Fulbe sold a great many of their war captives to Mandinka and Susu traders, who in turn carried them to the coastal cities in what are now Sierra Leone and Gambia. English slave traders then bought these captives, put them in ships, and transported them to North America. The Trans-Atlantic Slave Trade Database indicates that between 1704 and 1718, 41.8 percent of the slaves arriving in Maryland came from Upper Guinea, the region ranging today from Senegambia to Liberia. Between 1731 and 1745, that region accounted for 33 percent of the Maryland imports. Between 1761 and 1773, the trade increased—as 66 percent of all the slaves imported into Maryland originated in Upper Guinea. Thornton and Heywood believe that Mary Lee's ancestor was most likely imported during one of these periods. This suggests that on her mother's side Maya is in fact descended from a Mende—but from Sierra Leone or Guinea, not Ghana, as the woman in the market thought.

After pondering this information for a long while, Maya began to reflect on its meaning to her—and to our people as a whole. She told me that it is difficult, she thinks, to separate our African roots from our American experience. We are, she said, a truly global people. Her DNA tells her that, and her family history tells her that. And I certainly agree with her.

I then asked her how she viewed her African heritage now that she knew so much more about it. Her answer summed up my own hopes for this project beautifully, in a way that was inimitably Maya's:

"I am an African American," she said. "I have been shown what the African could be. But our heritage is so complex that we have to be simple and we have to consider ourselves global. We have to feel that, 'Wait a minute, human beings are more alike than we are unalike.' And no human being can be more human than another. I mean, Huey Long looked at the people in Louisiana and said, 'I don't see there's any of you doesn't have African blood.' And he was right. We are all in it together. People from Sweden and Denmark and Norway may be more concentrated—for now—but as our flights go longer and our ships go deeper, we will all interchange. So I don't think it's wise to say, 'I'm this and only this because of this.' There is some of me from Ethiopia and some from Eritrea, and some of me is from Athens. And if I go to China, if I go to Uzbekistan, if I go to Capetown, I want to feel absolutely at home. I will not be refused anywhere."

Quincy Jones

March 14, 1933

⩗

NO INDIVIDUAL HAS BEEN more consistently central to African American culture over the past sixty years than Quincy Jones. From the 1950s, when he was a teenager playing the trumpet in some of the country's biggest bands, to the 1980s, when he produced the bestselling album of all time, Michael Jackson's *Thriller,* to today, when he runs a multimedia empire, Quincy has done it all. He is also a close friend of mine, someone I've been privileged to spend a great deal of time with. I have experienced firsthand his musical genius, his passion for black music and history, and I have also seen a very private side of him. I know that for all his glittering success, he is still struggling to come to terms with mysteries that surround his family in the 1930s. Indeed, Quincy was one of my primary inspirations for creating the *African American Lives* film series in the first place.

When, in the middle of the night, I got the idea of creating *African American Lives,* it was Quincy whom I phoned first, the very next day. He had written the musical score for the television series *Roots,* and Alex Haley had become one of his best friends. Moreover, since the airing of *Roots,* Quincy had become a student of genealogy. He knew full well the challenges that Haley faced in trying to trace African American families back through slavery. He knew how many family lines ran dead in that awful period in which our ancestors were purposefully stripped of signal aspects of their identities—names, birth dates, family ties. The idea, I told Quincy, was to do *Roots* for the twenty-first century, using all the most up-to-date research techniques, including DNA analysis. Hopefully, I said, we could build on what Haley and others had done—and even make a few important discoveries. Quincy immediately agreed to be one of my subjects. I will be forever grateful to him for that. Looking up and down his family tree was a most rewarding experience.

Quincy Delight Jones Jr. was born on March 14, 1933, on the South Side of Chicago, the son of Sarah (sometimes spelled Sara) Wells and Quincy Delight Jones Sr. Both his parents were born in the Jim Crow South and were part of the Great Migration of African Americans who fled the omnipresent racism of the region, flooding northern cities across the country in the first half of the twentieth century. In so doing they changed the identity of African American culture as well as the landscape of America as a whole. Sharecroppers became factory workers, abandoning farm life, nature, and the horizon for high-rises and new forms of segregation. They also created a new black culture, one that continues to shape world culture today.

Chicago is a vivid memory for Quincy. He describes it as having been the "biggest black ghetto" in America at the time. "It was a society all to itself," he said, "with totally diversified strata of everything. There were no whites. Just five million black people in the ghetto there. You never saw white people." Chicago's black population of 277,731 in 1940 must have seemed like an all-black universe to seven-year-old Quincy.

Quincy's father was a carpenter, and a very gifted one by all accounts. He had moved north from South Carolina, seeking work, as so many African Americans did in those years. But the work he found was hardly typical. "My father worked for the Jones Boys," recalled Quincy. "They were the biggest black gangsters in history. They started the policy rackets in Chicago. They managed Joe Louis. They were amazing dudes. And my father used to build homes for all these guys."

"My father was capable of any level job," said Quincy, his face lighting up in admiration. "He could do amazing things. And it so happened that he did them for gangsters. It was Prohibition time, the Depression. And in Chicago that was no joke. Really no joke. We saw it all. When I was a kid, my father used to take us to Drexel Wine and Liquor when he had to meet up with the Jones Boys. We were around that kind of thing. We'd go to Drexel and walk up the steps. They had two-way mirrors, you know? Like a mirror they could see through to watch you. And you'd see these guys with stogies in their mouths and tommy guns. My brother and I loved that stuff, just loved it."

Chicago in the 1930s was dominated by mobsters. Organized crime ran everything—in its myriad forms it pervaded every aspect of the city's life. There were crooks in the government and gangs on every block. It

Quincy Jones's father, Quincy Sr., with young Quincy in his arms.

sounds colorful now, but it was an extremely unsafe environment for a young boy, not very different from what so many African Americans are experiencing in today's inner cities.

"In the black neighborhoods," recalled Quincy, "you had the Giles A.C. Gang, you had the Vagabonds, you had the Scorpions. Every street had a gang. It was real tribal. To get to school every day was like a kamikaze trip. They didn't have automatic weapons. They didn't need them. They used to make slingshots out of a clothespin and an inner tube and the tongue of a shoe. And they'd put a steel egg in there. And I'm telling you, you'd think you had got hit by an automatic weapon. They'd kill people, those things. You were grateful just to get to school every day and home alive. You had to fight for everything."

Quincy's grim childhood was made immeasurably worse by the fact that his mother was mentally ill. When he discusses this, his voice imme-

Sarah Wells, Quincy's mother, was mentally ill and had to be institutionalized while Quincy was still a child.

diately changes, the gallows humor vanishes, and a darkness descends. "My mother was taken away to a mental hospital when I was seven years old," he said. "And Daddy was a hardworking man—he was there for us all the time when he *had* the time, but we stayed with foster mothers. Prostitutes, everything. It was an experience. I still, to this day, do not know what the word 'mother' means. It has no emotional meaning to me. I can imagine it. I can see why children need it—and my children have had nice mothers. But 'mother'? The word has no visceral meaning for me. I never experienced it. I don't know what it means."

I can't imagine the pain Quincy must have felt. He told me that the hurt was indescribable—and that it grew worse over time, because he was so young when it happened. His memories continue to haunt him. And he still wonders what went wrong. "She was a brilliant lady," he said in a halting voice. "She just had this kind of active mind. She would write presidents. Presidents would write her back. She got their attention. She was so eloquent.

"I remember them lying her down upstairs," he recalled. "Four guys pushed her down on the bed, and this will never leave me. To see her with them putting the straitjacket on her on the bed. And then they took her away. And the lady next door, she put her hands over my brother's eyes. But I was trying to see."

His mother was suffering from dementia praecox. She was taken to Manteno State Hospital and would live the rest of her long life beset by demons. In and out of institutions, occasionally appearing unannounced in Quincy's life only to disappear again, Sarah Wells never developed any real relationship with her son. It was a different age, when mental illness was poorly understood—and professional medicine, like everything else, was largely unconcerned with the plight of African Americans. Black mental patients received abominable care when we received it at all. I can't imagine the anguish an intelligent, depressed black woman must have faced at that time, or the pain that she must have experienced in the alienation from her children, and indeed the alienation from herself, along with the primitive modes of treatment available for mental illness at the time.

"Something happened," said Quincy. "It could have been the sociological climate then, whatever. She just could not get a grip. And I don't know. They never would tell me. I was so young. But I'm still digging to find out what really happened. Little by little, things come out. Like when my mother died, my cousin George, who I've known since I was five years old—turns out he is my brother, because she got pregnant for the first time on a first date. And her mama said forget it. You know? She said, 'You're gonna have that baby and give it to Aunt Leona.' So that was Cousin George. And so here this dude comes up to me at seventy-two, he tells me he's my brother. I said, 'George, it's too late, man. You've been Cousin George too long.' And that was rough stuff. For him, I mean, repressing that for that long. We used to play together and hang together and everything. It is not unusual, I know. But still. It was rough."

His mother's illness turned Quincy's childhood upside down. When she was institutionalized, Quincy and his brother were sent to South Carolina to live with their grandmother Susannah (sometimes spelled Susanna) Burgess, who was born in 1862. Quincy remembers her well. "She was something," he said. "She was used to hard times. You could tell. She'd come out of slavery, and she just wasn't communicative, you know? And my brother and I were pretty bad. We used to steal money out of her apron. She didn't have that much, but we'd go off and buy candy."

His grandmother lived in dire poverty, but Quincy had already experienced such trauma; the stability his grandmother provided was far more important than her poverty. In fact, at least in memory, the harshness of his new surroundings seems to amuse him almost as much as the mean streets of Chicago did. "She'd talk all kinds of things," he recalled. "How the rats used to come bite her toes at night and all that stuff. And when you're a kid, that's like an adventure. It doesn't freak you out. I think back now, and it was just like a big adventure."

Quincy's rural adventure did not last long, however. Soon after he turned ten years old, he and his brother moved with their father to the other side of the country, to Bremerton, Washington, just across Puget Sound from Seattle, where his father had secured a job in the shipyards. World War II was raging, and the nation needed skilled laborers. Yet, as ever, the African Americans were treated differently. Quincy recalls Bremerton as a small, thoroughly segregated town built around a naval yard. "They put all the black people up on the hill, way out of town," he said. "You had to walk up three miles to this project. And they wouldn't even put phones in the homes. They put in telephone booths, so the black people wouldn't stay after the war."

After growing up surrounded by African Americans in Chicago and South Carolina, ten-year-old Quincy was suddenly part of a very isolated minority. "It was like black people didn't exist," he recalled. "You'd hear George Washington Carver's name maybe once a year, or Booker T. Washington. But it was really like you did not exist." His greatest pleasure, he recalls, was simply to withdraw into his imagination. "I remember lying on the floor and listening to the radio," he said, smiling. "And I'd go crazy. I'd make the Lone Ranger black. And the Shadow. You could make up anything you wanted to, because it was just an audio experience. Without the television you could do anything with your imagination."

It's fascinating to think about what must have been going on in Quincy's young mind in those days. Given what he would go on to create in his later life, I have to believe he crafted some pretty wild episodes of *The Lone Ranger* while lying on that floor. Regardless, however, all the imaginative power in the world couldn't make up for a lost mother. And Quincy was a very troubled youth. By the time he was eleven years old, he was hanging out with a group of boys who spent their days robbing and vandalizing. "We were thugs," he said with hardly a trace of emotion. "We were young, but we were thugs. There's no two ways about it. My daddy would go to work, and we'd go out and tear up everything and hit everything walking."

Quincy seemed headed for disaster, until one night when he and his friends broke in to a recreation center. Instead of raiding this place, like the others, Quincy discovered a piano and started playing it. Suddenly he was hooked on music. "I didn't even realize that I had music in me until then," he recalled. "But that night, you know, we separately went around and broke in to the rooms, and I broke in to one of the supervisors' rooms and opened the door, and I saw a piano over there, and I was getting ready to close the door, and—well, thank God that I listened to God's whispers. I went back in that room and walked over to that piano and just put my fingers on it. I didn't think about it. I just started in on the piano. And everything, every molecule in my body was simmering."

The troubled boy had been transformed. Soon Quincy was going to nightclubs all over Seattle. "I found Basie and Duke Ellington, Louis Armstrong and all of the big bands," he recalled. "Big bands turned my life around. We used to sneak in the back door, because we didn't have any money. I was just a kid, trying to act grown up, with the cigarette, the hat back, you know? Every night I would stand in front of those bands like an absolute addict. Just the idea of four trombones, four trumpets, and five saxophones—a group of black men that were dignified, unified, fun, worldly, and smart and talented. I said, 'This is the family I want to be in!' So I hung around backstage. I talked to every musician who came through. I just hounded them to death, just followed them until they went home."

Quincy's rise from obsessive fan to talented player to master was absolutely meteoric. He began studying trumpet in junior high school and at age twelve started singing in a gospel quartet. By thirteen he was a fixture in the local music scene and friends with the young Ray Charles. "I was corrupted pretty early," he said with a grin. "In nightclubs with Ray, playing strip dances, everything." At eighteen he won a scholarship to the prestigious Schillinger House, now the Berklee College of Music. A year later he dropped out to accept a position in the trumpet section of Lionel Hampton's band, where his reputation as an arranger grew. By the mid-1950s, he was arranging and recording for the biggest artists in the country—and his career has kept on growing ever since. He's been nominated for seventy-nine Grammys, won twenty-seven, produced hundreds of millions of record sales, and been honored all over the world for the past four decades. He has won Sweden's Polar Prize (often called the Nobel Prize of Music) and even has an endowed university professorship named after him at Harvard. And the most charming thing is, he's never lost the fire that he found on that piano as an eleven-year-old boy. If you talk to him about music or anything musical—from the most obscure instrument to the newest fads to a three-hundred-year-old song—even today he lights up with the enthusiasm of a child. His passion simply cannot be contained. It explodes out of him.

I asked Quincy where this passion came from. Surely, I thought, there must have been music in his family somewhere—someone inspiring him, paving the way for his genius. Quincy laughed and shook his head. "My father had not a drop of musical talent," he said. "Not a drop. My mother used to play piano sometimes, but I never was around her much. And anyway, she wanted me to be religious. She said that jazz was the devil's music. She was a Christian Scientist, very serious. And she wanted me to be that way, too."

Looking back on his youth, Quincy sees the beginnings of his art not in the positive influence of any family member but in the absence he felt, in the terrible loss he endured. "That's been one of the most powerful things in my life," he said. "It's something I don't say very publicly. But I remember I used to sit in the closet in Bremerton, and when things would get really rough, I found a way to convert all of it into my music and creativity. It was just like transferring the darkness to the light. As a little kid. I don't know how, but that's what I did. I transferred every feeling I should have given to my mother to the music. I made music my mother. And sometimes now I think that if I'd had a good family, I'd be a pitiful musician. I'll never know. But that's what I think."

It is hard to imagine Quincy as a pitiful musician. And it is easy to see, in retrospect, how he transformed himself by bringing out his own natural talents. His absolute confidence that his genius sprang from pain and loss and a keen sense of loneliness seems convincing, too. And they are a fundamental part of his emotional and artistic makeup. They are who he is, so to speak.

I had hoped that by involving him in this project I might in some small way be able to alleviate some portion of Quincy's pain. I firmly believe that knowing about your ancestors is a grounding experience. It can bring tremendous peace, especially to African Americans, as we have had so much of our past systematically stolen from us. But, of course, the process can also open old wounds. Quincy and I discussed this at length. He told me that he was absolutely eager to learn more about his ancestors, regardless of whether such knowledge brings calm or more pain. "People want to know who they are," he said. "They want to know where they stand on this planet. It's an obsession with me now. When we're young, we're too crazy to care. But I want to know. I want to leave that legacy for my children especially."

He then told me, with a smile, something that is unquestionably true—something that has been the bane of so much African American historical research. "I just want to know exactly what happened, whatever it is," Quincy said. And then he echoed something that Maya Angelou had told me: "Because old-school black families, they don't give anything up." He and I both laughed at that, knowing exactly what it meant. Our parents and their parents kept so many secrets—some for private reasons, some for social reasons. And that can make it very hard to learn what they were up to.

For instance, turning back just one generation down his father's line, we came to Quincy's paternal grandfather, Caesar James Jones. He was born a slave around 1860 in South Carolina, and he died around 1900. Quincy never met him. And much of what he knows about him centers on a secret: Looking at photographs of Caesar, anyone can see that he is obviously part white. Quincy believes that Caesar's father—who would be

Quincy's paternal great-grandfather—was almost certainly a white man. Others in his family may have felt the same, but no one would discuss it openly. "The split in the family is heavy, because his father was white," said Quincy. "There's no two ways about it. But I don't know how it happened or what happened."

We wanted to find Caesar's white father, but with no family oral tradition to lead us, we could not produce any solid evidence, nor could we identify his mother or any siblings. So Caesar's line ends with himself. And we were not able to find out much more regarding his wife, Quincy's grandmother, Susannah Burgess. Census records revealed that her parents, Osborne Burgess and Elizabeth Betsy, were both born slaves on a plantation in South Carolina in the 1830s, but we could go back no further than that.

Fortunately, we were able to learn a lot more about Quincy's maternal line. His mother's father, his maternal grandfather, was Love Adam Wells, born January 17, 1877. Quincy never met Love, but he knew a number of good stories about him. "I heard that he ran a brothel in Mississippi," he said. "And he was running it for some white dudes, and at one point they wanted to put his daughter—my mother—and all of her sisters—my aunts—in that brothel house. So my grandfather, he got a car and drove them to St. Louis, got out, and the guys were on his tail. There's a lot of drama there, which nobody's still explained to me. They don't talk about it."

This is another example of how older generations can be so reticent, so embarrassed, so concerned or bound up in the traditions of their time that they don't realize that for us, what was once shameful is now merely interesting. We aren't worried about embarrassing the dead. We just want to know the story, whatever it was. We want to know the truth.

Quincy was pleased to hear that we'd found several people who were able to corroborate the brothel story about his grandfather—at least in its main details. And he enjoyed poring over some documents we found relating to Love, including his marriage certificate and a page of annotations in the Wells family Bible.

Though Quincy did not know his grandfather, he did know Love's wife, his maternal grandmother, Mary Bell Lanier, who was born August 7, 1879, in Bovina, Mississippi, on what is known as the Gumwood Plantation. Indeed, Quincy remembers Mary Lanier and her home vividly. "I stayed with my grandmother," he recalled. "It was a shotgun shack, you know? Bent, rusty nails over the back door. No lamps and all that. It was ridiculous. But we were there when we were seven years old, so we didn't care. We used to eat the rats. We didn't know the difference. And my grandmother, she was used to that survival thing."

According to Quincy, his grandmother was a loving but stern woman, who retained some beliefs and behaviors that he believes could be vestiges of Africa. "She never called us by our names," he said. "She called us 'Winna.' They say that in South Africa and in the Congo. 'Winna, come here! Winna, do that!' You know? And she was coal black, an incredible lady, just strong as a mountain."

Mary Bell Lanier is also Quincy's link to a very different kind of family—and yet another secret. Her mother—Quincy's maternal great-grandmother—was a woman named Cordelia Dickson. Cordelia was born a slave in May 1857 in Bovina, Mississippi. She was owned by a white man named Judge Pearce Noland, whose property was located near the plantations of an extremely wealthy family, the Laniers. And according to our research, Cordelia had a child—Mary—with a scion of this family, a man named James Balance Lanier. Which means that Quincy's great-grandfather was a white man from an extremely wealthy slave-owning family, a family that descends directly from one of the early kings of England.

The relationship between James Balance Lanier and Quincy's great-grandmother Cordelia Dickson is extremely unusual. I had never encountered anything like it before. Every black person knows that it was common for slave owners to impregnate their female slaves. But that's not what happened in Quincy's family. Cordelia Dickson and James Balance Lanier had a child thirteen years after slavery ended. Cordelia gave the child his father's last name. He was not her master. James Balance Lanier never owned Cordelia Dickson. They were lovers, perhaps. We don't know more. It could have been a violent relationship. It could have

James Balance Lanier, Quincy's great-grandfather.

been a relationship built entirely upon affection. They could have been shacking up. We just don't know. However, Lanier married a white woman shortly after Cordelia conceived her child, Mary, with him, and if the two ever had any contact again, it is not recorded.

"That's heavy," said Quincy. "I can't even imagine in my wildest dreams what times were like that long ago. It's just so unbelievable."

Cordelia Dickson went on to have children with five different men, marrying only once. Interracial sexual relations were not unusual in the South, even after slavery ended. What is unusual is that Cordelia gave Mary Bell the last name of her white father, Lanier. (As we shall see, Morgan Freeman's great-grandparents also were an interracial couple but even more extraordinary, they lived together, and are even buried together.) This act of defiance was uncommon, but Cordelia seems to have been a very uncommon woman. Indeed, she insisted on giving all her children their fathers' names while keeping her own surname, Dickson. Regrettably, we were unable to find out much more about her. According to the available records, her mother was a woman named Minerva, called "Mother Kitty" by the family, and born a slave in 1822 on Judge Noland's plantation. Her father was Henry Dickson, born in 1817 on the same plantation. And that is as far back as we could go on Cordelia's line. Slavery obliterates Quincy's black family at this point.

However, because Cordelia had a child with a white man, our research was not over—not by any means. I then went on to tell Quincy what I knew about James Balance Lanier, most of which involved crime. He owned the Gumwood Plantation, manufactured chewing gum, and was a rich man for a while. But the Civil War ruined his family's fortune, and after parting ways with Cordelia, Lanier seemed to have broken every law he could, from disturbing the peace to carrying concealed firearms to murder. In 1897 he was convicted of killing a black man and sentenced to life in prison. But three years later he was miraculously paroled—not an uncommon outcome for whites who killed blacks in the Jim Crow South. Lanier then went on to become the jail keeper of the town for twenty years and a respectable member of the community.

Going back one generation, we find James's father, Needham Burch Lanier, born November 24, 1815, in Brunswick County, Virginia. This is Quincy's great-great-grandfather, and in his adult life he was one of the biggest slave owners in Mississippi. Moreover, during the Civil War, Needham Burch Lanier served the Confederacy as a valuable spy.

"That's a trip," says Quincy, almost speechless.

Our researchers discovered that Grant's army ransacked the Lanier plantation during the siege of Vicksburg. The destruction there amounted to something more than thirty thousand dollars. That was a lot of money back then, and the family's fortunes would decline significantly after the war. Nonetheless, the Lanier plantations represented the greatest wealth in the area and were at the center of social life during many of the antebellum years. And even though James Balance Lanier was a convicted murderer and his father was a spy, their family has a remarkable pedigree. Indeed, the Lanier family can be traced all the way back to Edward "Longshanks"— also known as Edward I, king of England, born in 1239! So Quincy is one of King Edward I's heirs. As would be expected, such a family includes some incredibly illustrious people on both sides of the Atlantic. On the American side, Quincy's sixth great-grandmother, Elizabeth, was the fourth cousin of George Washington. Tennessee Williams is also a member of this family.

As I told Quincy, there are very few white Americans whose ancestry can be taken back to the thirteenth century. This is extraordinary. But it also illustrates the tragedy of African American history. Quincy can trace his lineage back to the thirteenth century in England—on the white side of his family. But on the black side, it stops much earlier. We hit dead ends for each of his lines in the early 1800s.

Now, this is not unusual. But I was nervous discussing it with Quincy. I was wondering how he felt about his black ancestors as opposed to his white ancestors. Was he hurt to learn that he was descended from these white men—some of whom owned enormous numbers of slaves? Quincy shook his head. "I don't know any of them," he says. "So there's no frame of reference at all. And it's one of the most common things in America, you know, because everybody that's not coal black has got gumbo going in their genes."

This is an excellent way of putting it, I think. And I felt better explaining his DNA results to him at this point—as they confirmed much of what the genealogical research had been telling us. According to his admixture test, Quincy has 5 percent Asian ancestry, 34 percent European ancestry, and 61 percent sub-Saharan African ancestry. We could find no genealogical evidence of an Asian ancestor, but sometimes a low result like 5 percent can be a vestige of some distant Native American heritage—and there have been stories in his family (as there are in almost all black families) of Indian ancestors.

The 34 percent European result is very interesting, however. That number is quite high for an African American. The average African American has 20 percent European genetic ancestry. But only 19.6 percent of the African American people have at least 25 percent European ancestry. Part of Quincy's result can be attributed to his white maternal great-grandfather, James Balance Lanier, but it's likely that he has other white ancestors as well—as suggested by the rumors about his paternal grandfather, Caesar. And looking at Quincy's Y-DNA testing—which traces his ancestry back through all the males on his father's side—we learned that his patrilineal line leads back to Europe, thus corroborating those rumors. So Caesar Jones most likely had a white father, just as Quincy suspected.

Turning to the mitochondrial DNA tests—which trace Quincy's mother through her mother and beyond—we learned that Quincy shares maternal ancestry with the Tikar people, who live today in an area called the Bamenda Grassfields in western Cameroon. It's an area that's famous for its music and art.

Quincy's face lights up when he hears this. "That's amazing," he says. "That's where the bongo's from. I can't believe it, man. I would never have guessed that."

Additional testing of Quincy's mitochondrial DNA revealed partial matches with a member of the Sukuma tribe in Tanzania, the Tonga tribe in Mozambique, and the Fang tribe in Equatorial Guinea (among others). Our consulting historians John Thornton and Linda Heywood both agreed that these results, taken in concert with Quincy's Tikar match, indicate that Quincy's maternal ancestors were almost certainly part of the Bantu migration, one of the greatest migrations in human history. Over two thousand years ago, a small group of Bantu-speaking Africans dispersed from a core area in what we think is southern Cameroon and peopled a huge percentage of the rest of central and southern Africa, bringing a totally new kind of genetic mixture to African populations. This means that Quincy's ancestors had a huge influence on shaping their continent. As they spread out from Cameroon, they changed cultures and languages for thousands of miles—as far south, even, as South Africa.

The test result was also quite significant because, according to the Trans-Atlantic Slave Trade Database, only 2.6 percent of the slaves brought to the United States are from the Cameroon region where Quincy's ancestors lived. Thus, by combining this DNA information with the fact that we know that Quincy's fourth-generation grandmother (Cordelia Dickson's mother, the woman known as "Mama Kitty") lived in Mississippi in the 1830s, Thornton and Heywood were able to reconstruct the crossing story for one of Quincy's matrilineal ancestors, showing how she could have been brought to the United States. It is only a theory, but given what we know, I think it is a good one.

The theory goes like this: We know that people with this DNA profile weren't exported as slaves until quite late in the transatlantic slave trade. So Quincy's ancestor's journey probably took place in the early 1800s, before 1808, when the slave trade was abolished. (Though the illegal importation of slaves continued, by 1820, 99 percent of our African ancestors had arrived in the United States.) Until then his family was minding their own business in Africa—probably in eastern Angola or western Zambia (where they had long since migrated with other Bantu-speaking peoples from their original Cameroon homeland). They were probably members of one of the many ethnic groups that lived in this area—the Chokwe, Lozi, or Bemba—and they were most likely, according to Thornton and Heywood, taken into slavery by warriors of the Lunda Empire. The Lundas, at this time, were fighting almost continuous slave wars with their less powerful neighbors, sending these columns of troops out, building armed camps, raiding the countryside, and then exporting the people that they captured—many of whom were very young children.

Thornton and Heywood believe that after being taken prisoner, Quincy's ancestor and her fellow captives would have been sold to members of the Zombo tribe, who would have transported them in large canoes downriver to the coastal ports of Loango or Cabinda—in what is now the border area between modern-day Angola and the Democratic Republic of the Congo. In the late eighteenth century, the Portuguese had no authority in this area, so the African powers were willing to allow anybody to come and trade, and the English focused their efforts there. The journey would have taken about three months, during which time it was likely that Quincy's ancestress would have been sold through a number of African middlemen. In the port, she would have been traded for about fifty dollars' worth of cloth, salt, or alcohol, and then been loaded on an English ship—a commercial vessel that had been specially adapted for slave transport.

On board the slave ship, Quincy's ancestor and her fellow females would have been kept in separate quarters from the men. The treatment she received would have been slightly less harsh than the treatment received by the men because the crew of the ship would have feared the men and used extreme brutality to suppress any possible revolts. As a woman, Quincy's ancestor was probably spared the worst of this brutality. However, her trip was by no means pleasant. She would have been expected to cook, and of course she would have been vulnerable to rape from anybody on the crew who wanted to rape her. And she would have been kept below deck for long stretches of time, subjected to unbearably humid heat, disease, terrible food, poor water, and no privacy.

After two or three months of this hellish journey, she would have reached either the United States or the Caribbean. And from the Caribbean she would have been shipped to South Carolina or Virginia, and then, perhaps in later generations, her ancestors would have moved on to plantations in the Deep South. That is what we think is the path that Mama Kitty's mama took from western Africa to the plantation in western Mississippi.

"Jesus Christ," said Quincy, after a long silence. "What a saga. That's some tough stuff."

Before we parted, I asked Quincy to tell me if he felt the time we'd spent together had been worth it. Much of what he'd learned concerned his white ancestors, not his black ones. Though we'd shed light on some of his family's mysteries, it was also now clear, I felt, that many of the mysteries were not going to be resolved anytime soon. In some ways we were ending where we began—confronted by the difficulty of doing African American genealogy. But in one significant way, we had moved forward: Quincy could now perceive both his European and his African ancestry in very specific terms, naming a region and a people as his place of origin, his roots, on both his European and his African sides. To him that was more than enough. And it was deeply satisfying to hear him say it. "It's like a closure," he said, beaming. "That's what it feels like to me now. It's a great feeling. It just makes the soul smile, because it's no longer a question mark. Because there's this wandering, you're constantly searching. All your life. You know? We're all searching for ourselves. You want to find out where you came from. And now I know."

Morgan Freeman

June 1, 1937

MORGAN FREEMAN IS SO WARM and personable that I
fear it is easy to overlook all he has accomplished on the stage
and in film, and the deep intelligence that is the foundation
of those accomplishments. Viewed from any broad historical perspective,
his career could not even have been imagined only a couple of decades
ago. Think of it this way: He is a black man who's been paid millions of
dollars to portray God and the president of the United States (long before
we could imagine Colin Powell or Barack Obama actually occupying that
office) in movies that have been shown in every city and town in America.
White people are going to see a black God? A black president? And loving
it? If you had told me when I was a college student that this was going to
happen, I'd have laughed in your face.

To Morgan, however, his accomplishments are an outgrowth of his
strict attention to his craft. He doesn't consider himself to be a *black* actor.
He is simply honing a talent, working at something he loves. He has famously and frequently declared that he never plays a black character, he
only plays a role. To tell you the truth, that distinction had not occurred to
me before. But in exploring his roots, it became clear to me that Morgan
also privately cherishes the many ways in which he is deeply representative of the African American experience.

Morgan Freeman was born on June 1, 1937, in Memphis, Tennessee.
His childhood was chaotic, to say the least. His parents were financially
strapped and fundamentally incompatible. When Morgan was less than

a year old, he was sent to live with his maternal grandmother in Charleston, Mississippi, while his father and mother sought jobs in the North. Following his grandmother's death six years later, Morgan's childhood devolved into a mind-boggling series of moves—from Charleston to Chicago to Indiana to Greenwood, Mississippi. "I went wherever Mama was or my grandmother was," he said. "I never really knew a real solid home."

I was thrilled when Morgan agreed to be in the series. I had interviewed him once before, on the steps of the Lincoln Memorial, for a documentary series about race and class in America. He's a tremendously gifted storyteller, with a wide range of knowledge. But above all—and this is something I truly wasn't ready for—Morgan is extremely modest and self-effacing. As we went over the details of his troubled youth, he spoke casually, as if it were all part of the distant past. When we began to focus on the start of his acting career, he treated it just as casually. In hindsight, I think acting was an escape for him. It offered structure, and it appealed, I think, to a great but unfocused ambition that is probably one of the deepest parts of his character. But I'm not sure Morgan sees it that way. To him, at least in the early parts of our conversation, it all seemed like an accident, a twist of chance.

"I knew I wanted to be an actor when I was around twelve," he said. "I was in this school play. And I was given the role of this kid whose older brother had come back from the war. And at that time, there was an awful lot of competition between schools and school districts and things like that, and it was elevating. We had ferocious competition. And I won best actor. I've got that little pin somewhere. So of course you know the schoolkids come around me and say, you know, 'You've got talent.' And the teachers would say that, too."

Like many successful black people of his generation, Morgan credits his teachers in a segregated school system for shaping him. "I had one teacher," he said. "Her name was Leola Gregory Williams, and from when I was about the age of fourteen to graduation she would say, 'Morgan, there are no limits.' And growing up in Mississippi, you know, being black, you got a lot of the feeling that you are definitely not going to go very far in this world. But I had a sense of myself that I got from my teachers that there's nothing that can stop you. These were all black teachers, of course.

And the feeling was, you can do anything you want to do. You can go as far in this world as you want to go. That was a big blessing."

Even with this positive message, Morgan's opportunities were still limited by the circumstances of race that bound social relations in the community in which he found himself. To a young black man coming out of high school in Mississippi in the late 1950s, at the height of segregation, the world must have seemed a very forbidding place to pursue wild dreams of acting, of all things. Though Morgan was offered a drama scholarship to attend Jackson State University, he chose a much more conventional path and enrolled in the military. It would be several years before he found the confidence and opportunity to pursue his true calling.

"I went in to be a pilot," he says, laughing. "And they give you a battery of tests at the end of basic training to decide how they're going to exploit you, you know? What are you gonna be? What is your aptitude? And mine was for radio. They made me a radar mechanic. I am not mechanically inclined at all. I wasn't bad at it, but I never got the theory of how the thing worked. Magnetron pulse widths? You sit and tell me about that and I'm nodding off. If the thing broke, I could make it run. Using, you know, spit and paper clips. Very often I would fix something, and then someone who knew what he was doing would come in and fix it right. I'd just make it run—tie a rope around this and hold that thing until it'll keep going. I could do stuff like that. But not the schematics and following and knowing how. That's not me."

As he began this story, Morgan spoke with a mischievous grin on his face and a slightly mocking tone to his voice—as if he thought the brash wannabe-pilot of his youth was a joke. But as the story progressed, his tone became more serious. After his training, Morgan was posted to a small radar-station site in Southern California, just east of San Diego. And soon, faced with his responsibilities, he had a life-changing moment. He realized he had no desire to fight.

"I was in San Bernardino at Norton Air Force Base," he said. "And I had gone down to a flight line and sat in the cockpit of a fighter plane. And I was like, 'Hold on, boy, you don't want this. You need a camera here—that's what you really want.' It was one of those epiphanies, you know?

Morgan Freeman in his days as an Air Force radar mechanic.

The epiphany was that the romance with the whole lifestyle was not the lifestyle itself—it was what I got from movies. Playing a role. So I was like, 'Get out of here.' I walked away from it. The idea of becoming a warrior totally evaporated."

After his discharge, Morgan took a bus to Los Angeles and embraced his vague dreams of becoming an actor. "I had a hundred and seventy-five dollars," he recalled. "And when that money ran out, I started walking the streets looking for a job, any kind of job. This sergeant I knew, his wife worked for the board of education. And she managed to get me working as a transcript clerk in Los Angeles City College. That segued into my being able to take acting classes. Still, I had no clue as to how I was going to assault the movies."

For years Morgan struggled to make his dream come true—taking clerical jobs, post-office jobs, fashion-industry jobs, enrolling in acting classes at Los Angeles City College (and flunking them), studying dance and diction, moving between coasts to pursue parts in obscure regional-theater productions, and living, as he said, on nickels and "week-old doughnuts." In the end this dizzying path led to a level of success that is attributable largely, I believe, to an iron will that Morgan hides behind his easy manner and to his belief, nurtured in him since childhood, that he could succeed at anything. Indeed, the more we spoke about his career, the more reflective he became—and the more often he steered the conversation back to his family and to the earliest flowerings of his dreams. After a while he told me that he thought his confidence had first been implanted in him by his mother, Mayme Edna Revere, who had cared for him through the bulk of his childhood, well before he met Leola Gregory Williams in the classroom. It was appropriate, then, that we began our exploration of his family tree by looking at her story.

Morgan's mother, Mayme, was born on March 18, 1912, in Itta Bena, Mississippi. She lived eighty-eight full years, dying in the winter of 2000, and Morgan smiles wistfully at the mention of her name. "Mama was a rolling stone," he says, with real warmth. "Her parents were businesspeople. Her mother was a master seamstress, and her father was a tailor. They owned a tailoring establishment when she was a child. They were doing very well for a black family at that time. But there was a fire. They were burned out, and her daddy went blind 'cause he was running into this fire and trying to get his clients' clothes out. Mama was about seven when this happened. He wound up going to the Lighthouse for the Blind. They taught him how to make brooms. He was walking up and down the street trying to sell brooms. This was a very, very proud man, and it just made him crazy. My mama went on his rounds with him. She was his guide. His hand was on her shoulder, walking up and down the street, until she was ten years old and he died. And so that left the two of them, she and her mother. She was an only child. And very rebellious."

Morgan was one of his mother's five children—four boys and one girl. All four boys had different fathers. "She couldn't stay put, you know," Morgan said sympathetically. "She did support my acting, though. From the time I was a little kid, she would say, 'I'm going to take you to Hollywood.' She fed me the dream. She was very artistic-minded. She didn't want any of us involved in anything like sports. And I was never actually so inclined. I was always kind of fey and was going for the artistic sort of life. My older brother was a jazz musician. He asked for a horn, and Mama went and bought him a horn, and he just grabbed that thing and that was him."

To learn more about his mother, we started by examining the local census records in the Mississippi counties near where she was born. She could not be located in the 1920 census, but the 1930 census shows her living in Clay County, Mississippi, with her mother, Lenora Greenlee Revere. At that time Mayme was eighteen years old, and according to the census she and her mother were both teachers at the Mary Holmes Missionary School in Clay County.

Morgan with his mother, Mayme Edna, sometime in the 1970s.

Morgan had never heard that his mother once worked as a teacher, and he wasn't sure whether he believed it. For much of her life, she worked as a cleaning lady, and Morgan remembers how hard she struggled to make ends meet. "She could have been teaching there," he said. "But if she did, you know, I don't remember. I know they were there. My mother was at the school when she was seventeen or so. But whether she was teaching or studying—I have no idea."

Census records can certainly be inaccurate, so it is possible that Mayme was a student and not a teacher at Mary Holmes in 1930. However, we found a newspaper article from the *Mississippi Sun* citing Mayme as one of several teachers at a school in nearby Tallahatchie County six years later, so clearly she got into teaching somehow. And our research

The Mary Holmes Missionary School in Clay County, Mississippi. Research suggests that Morgan's mother taught at this school for black women in the 1930s.

suggests that the Mary Holmes School was a likely place for her to start. Established by the Presbyterian Church (as we will see, the Presbyterian Church was responsible for the education of the ancestors of Tom Joyner as well), it was the only institution in the entire state of Mississippi devoted exclusively to educating black women. It offered courses in literature, music, business, and home economics, and, significantly, it also trained young women to become teachers. Now, at the time, teaching was one of a limited number of careers available to women, white or black, and while it could be a tough and unstable way to make a living, teaching was a prestigious position within the black community. For many black women, it was their best chance to achieve some sort of economic independence. And Mayme seems to have pursued this career, unbeknownst to her son—at least for a while.

Morgan may not have known about his mother's teaching career, but he was well aware of how forbidding the educational system was for African Americans at that time—as he had suffered under it himself. Indeed, in Tallahatchie County in 1936, there was only enough funding for black children to attend school for four months out of the year, thus ensuring a workforce that was undereducated and underpaid. This was a blatant form of state-sponsored racism that continued well into the 1960s. "The Mississippi legislature," Morgan said, "and Mississippi congressmen worked hard to keep the education of blacks at a minimum because of fear of losing the workforce."

Morgan is absolutely correct about this. While claiming that a longer school year would disrupt planting and harvesting of the crops, white legislators throughout the Jim Crow South strove to guarantee themselves a cheap supply of black labor forever, replacing out-and-out slaves with a group of people whose status hovered somewhere nearer enslavement than to economic and political equality. Morgan's rebellious mother, by becoming a teacher, struggled to fight this pernicious system. And even though she abandoned that career, she placed an extremely high value on education for all her children. "Growing up," said Morgan, "it was as if without education you were nothing. My mother's assertions about education were constant, ongoing. It was in my blood." It was the ultimate way to rebel against a racist system.

The warmth that Morgan displayed as we talked about his mother evaporated quickly when I raised the subject of his father. The two hardly knew each other, and there was no love between them. Yet we were to uncover some intriguing stories about his father's family.

Morgan's father was Morgan Porterfield Freeman, born in Charleston, Mississippi, a small town in Tallahatchie County, on July 7, 1915. His parents were Hubert Freeman and Evie Anderson. Evie was born around 1895 in Charleston, Mississippi. We know almost nothing about Hubert beyond the fact that he was born in North Carolina sometime around 1875 and died in Mississippi in 1942. He and Evie had three boys together: Morgan, Jesse, and Willie Freeman. Our researchers could not find a marriage license between Evie and Hubert, and there is a possibility that they never wed. In fact, the 1920 census lists Evie as being married to a man named Alonzo Cutlip and indicates that she was living with him and her three boys in Leflore County, Mississippi.

Morgan was surprised to learn that his grandmother Evie had had such a complex romantic life, but he was more interested to hear about his uncles, Willie and Jesse Freeman. Morgan remembered them from his childhood but says their fates are an enduring mystery to the family—as both were lost in World War II. "They served in the Pacific, and there is no record of death from the War Department for either one," he says. "I asked Colin Powell to help me find out. But we never found anything."

We were also unable to solve the mystery. But we did find something that I thought might interest Morgan. We learned that on Jesse Freeman's enlistment form he listed his occupation as "actor." Hearing this, Morgan began to laugh. "Yeah," he said knowingly. "My Uncle Jesse was a very good-looking guy. A guy with teeth, you know? He and Uncle Willie hung out in Charleston. They were guys-around-town. Uncle Jesse talked about acting. But, you know, he was a real pool shooter, a whiskey-drinking pool shooter. And I don't know what kind of work he really did. I always thought Uncle Jesse was some sort of a hustler, 'cause he dressed well, had a car, didn't have anything like a grunt job."

Researching Uncle Jesse's life, we found nothing to contradict Morgan. It seems to have been a life of risk, adventure, and hardship, lived on the edges of Charleston's society. By 1930 Morgan's grandmother Evie had divorced Alonzo Cutlip and was a single mother working as a cook. The census of that year indicates that her three teenage sons were working as well. Morgan's father was just sixteen years old, and he's listed as being a road laborer. This certainly must have been difficult work, and after a little more than a decade of it, Morgan's father and his uncles would all be in the military, where Willie and Jesse would lose their lives and disappear. Morgan's father was the lone survivor.

I ask Morgan what he can tell me about his father, and he shrugs. "I didn't know him, really," he said. "First time I remember seeing him, I was six years old. He had on an army uniform. Either he was on leave or he had been discharged. Apparently he wasn't cut out for the military, just didn't have the cojones for it. But all three of Mama Evie's sons were now in uniform. So they offered to let him go. That was their policy then.

I remember him coming to Charleston for a visit around Thanksgiving. And I didn't like him. He was a mean man. It wasn't a month later that my grandmother died. I think she had pneumonia, something like that. Nobody told me. She was only in her mid-fifties, and I was eight."

After his grandmother's death, Morgan moved to Chicago, where both his parents were living. Morgan's father remarried and got work as a barber. Morgan lived with him briefly, for about six months. "Living with him was one of the low points in my life," said Morgan flatly. "And I mean really low points. But that was it—that was the situation. I never liked him, and I never really knew him."

Morgan moved in with his mother when life with his father became untenable. He would remain with her for the rest of his childhood, moving from house to house and state to state before finally settling back in Mississippi for high school. He never lived with his father again—and indeed rarely saw him again. "Looking back," he said sadly, "there were just a lot of bad moments. The worst I can remember was having to go and ask my father for money. I was, like, eight or nine at the time. My mother wouldn't send me to get money from him unless circumstances were just absolutely dire. But we didn't have a phone, and she couldn't go to him. So she thought maybe he would acquiesce if it was his son, and this kid walking in would embarrass the hell out of him, you know? 'Mama said you got to give me some money.' So I went. That was rough."

His father gave young Morgan five dollars and a haircut and sent him on his way. Morgan seems understandably angry and deeply pained by the very memory of his experiences with this man. I'm not sure that he wanted to hear much more about him. Fortunately, there was little to say. His father died in 1961 and left no records of note behind.

There was a good deal more to say about his family, though. Morgan has often wondered about the origins of his surname: Freeman. He believes, correctly, that it derives from the word "freedmen"—which was the word applied to newly liberated slaves. At the end of the Civil War, many of our ancestors took this surname or some variant of it, and it is one of the most common of all black names. Adopting the name Freeman was a significant act, a symbolic breaking of all former ties with slavery—and a means of differentiating oneself from the many former slaves who took the names of their former masters. It is an inspiring name, a name signifying a new beginning, a tabula rasa, connoting a life that commenced in 1865 with the ending of slavery. But it also makes tracking ancestors before 1865 very difficult because it is such a common name. Indeed, we could go back no further than Morgan's paternal grandfather, Hubert Freeman, who was born in North Carolina in 1875.

We had much more luck tracing his grandmother Evie's line. Her father was a man named Albert Anderson, about whom we could learn little. He was born between 1855 and 1870 somewhere in Mississippi and died sometime in the 1940s. Evie's mother, however, was a woman named Lucinda Cain Anderson (aka "Cindy"), born into slavery in Carroll County, Mississippi, in 1853. Searching for documents about her, we found something highly unusual. In the 1930s and 1940s, the federal government sponsored a program through the Federal Writers' Project of the Works Progress Administration (WPA) that sent people throughout the South to interview former slaves. The resulting slave narratives, as they are called—thousands of them—are among the most important historical documents about the antebellum period, oral testimony collected in the Great Depression and transcribed in the vernacular that these former slaves actually spoke. In them, the former slaves testified about their recollections of their own enslavement, near the end of their lives. They are a treasure trove to historians. And among the people interviewed was Cindy Anderson, of Charleston, Mississippi—Morgan's great-grandmother!

In her interview Cindy described her life in bondage, vividly detailing the destruction of black families that was one of the cruelest aspects of the slave system: "My master was Mr. Hub Cain what lived close to Vaiden in Carroll County. Old Mr. Cain bought my father and mother in North Carolina when they was little chillun but after I was born they sold my father to a man named Wright. Colonel Wright. It was nine years after the reb time before I ever seed my father again"—"after the reb time," of course, meaning the defeat of the Confederacy in 1865.

I have never met anybody who had an ancestor who was actually recorded in these slave narratives, so it was an extraordinary thing for me to listen as Morgan read his ancestor's actual words aloud. Morgan had heard family lore about Cindy and was thrilled to see it confirmed. Moreover, Cindy's testimony allowed us to trace her family back even further, because later in the interview she mentions that her father's name was Milton Wright and her mother's name was Sylvia Cain. In addition, Cindy tells us that her parents were brought from North Carolina to Mississippi by their slave owner, Patrick Hub Cain. This means that Morgan's ancestors were part of the enormous forced migration of slaves from the Upper South into Mississippi and Alabama—the migration that populated the Cotton Kingdom and removed the Native Americans in the dreadful Trail of Tears. Almost 1 million slaves were moved from the Upper South to the Lower South along with Morgan's ancestors (among them were also the ancestors of Tom Joyner, T. D. Jakes, Don Cheadle, and Linda Johnson Rice, who will be discussed later in this book).

We looked for information on the slave owner named Hub Cain, and we discovered that in 1860 he owned five slaves. Though the idea of a white man owning just five slaves does not jibe with the popular Hollywood notion of the Old South filled with enormous plantations à la *Gone with the Wind,* such large plantations were actually quite rare in Mississippi and indeed throughout much of the South. In fact, in the years leading up to the Civil War, Mississippi's economy was dominated by small farmers like Cain who owned a handful of slaves and often struggled to stay out of debt. These struggles frequently forced them to sell their slaves, as Cindy describes in her slave narrative.

The final passages of Cindy's narrative are especially fascinating to me. They conclude with these thoughts: "I don't remember nothing else. I didn't try to recollect what took place. I remember more about what happened when the slaves were freed than anything else. Old Master Cain was mad about it. He come stomping around cussing and told us to get out. We didn't have nowheres to get to. But we had to go. We didn't have nothing in the world but some homespun dresses Miss Betsy Ann done made us. We went on a man's place by the name of Mr. Causey and we moved in a little chicken coop of a shed that didn't have no flo' but just a dirt flo'. We had a mighty bad time. I don't see why they didn't let us alone cause us niggers didn't know nothing about being free. I don't remember nothing about it. I didn't try to recollect what took place them days. I never thought I'd be asked no such questions as this no how."

Morgan was as moved by this passage as I was. "I have read a lot of different kinds of narratives about that time," he said quietly. "And you can look at it from two sides. Some of those slave owners were—can we say?—benevolent. They gathered their people together and said, 'Well, you're free.' Others, you know, didn't take that approach. There was a lot of anger sometimes. But either way, imagine you're a slave—what are you going to do? Where are you going? This is why bunches of them walked off and turned around and walked right back. Because the very first thing you realize by the time you get to the edge of the plantation is, 'Where the heck are we going with no money?' And if the whole area is going to be full of people wandering around, there are not going to be any jobs. You know? You're going to have to go back and do what you did. So the idea of freedom was, I think, much easier to endure than the reality."

It is very difficult to imagine making the transition from slavery to freedom in such a hostile world. I have discussed this issue with many of my students and colleagues and with virtually all the people I studied for this project, and it still intrigues and fascinates me, this moment of transition between slavery, a form of social death, as William Wells Brown called it, and the life of a freedman, a semi-free American, as it would develop. Freedom, as Morgan and his ancestor point out, was not a simple proposition. It was complex, frightening, and forbidding. In many ways it was also rigged, as southern whites did virtually everything they could to limit its impact upon the former slaves. It is no surprise, if you think about it, that people like Cindy Anderson found the transition difficult. African Americans were not prepared for it and were not given an adequate chance to make it work—and I believe we still suffer from that today, even though, obviously, some of our ancestors handled the transition surprisingly well.

Unfortunately, we were not able to learn more about how Cindy Anderson handled the transition herself. We know that she died in 1942 in Charleston, Mississippi, just a few years after being interviewed by the WPA. Her brief obituary indicates that she was survived by her daughter Evie, three grandchildren, and four great-grandchildren. But we could learn little more about her—and nothing at all about her parents, Milton Wright and Sylvia Cain, beyond the fact that they were both born into slavery sometime around 1835. Thus the paper trail for Morgan's paternal line ends with them.

It is nonetheless a most fascinating paper trail. Morgan is the only person involved in this project who can reach out and touch a remnant of his family's history in slavery, who can actually recite the words of his enslaved ancestors out loud. He is remarkably fortunate to have this testimony from an actual relative who experienced slavery and talked about it.

"This is the biggest surprise I can imagine," he said.

Turning back to Morgan's mother's ancestry, we came upon another very interesting story from the slave era. His maternal grandmother, Lenora Greenlee, was born on June 16, 1886, in Ethel, Mississippi. Her parents were Elizabeth Carr and Samuel Greenlee, both born slaves in 1850s Mississippi. Examining the records related to these people, we immediately noticed something unusual. Every record that we found regarding Lenora Greenlee lists her as being a mulatto. Where did this mixed-race heritage come from? We were unable to learn anything about Lenora's father, Samuel Greenlee (though a family rumor claimed that he was of Choctaw Indian descent, we could not substantiate it). We were, however, able to identify Elizabeth Carr's parents—Lenora's maternal grandparents—as being Celia (or Celie) Johnson and a man named Alfred Carr. And with them the mystery grew, eventually to resolve itself in the most surprising manner.

There was a large age discrepancy between this couple: Celia was born in 1830, Alfred in 1799, but they were nonetheless very much a couple. In the 1870 census, we found Celia and Alfred living with their eight children. The data also indicate that both were mulatto, but if one looks closely at the original documents, it appears that the census taker or somebody else has written "mulatto" and crossed it out and written "white" for Celia Johnson and "white" for some of the children. Now, this is very, very strange. So we then checked the census for the family ten years later in 1880 and found Celia Johnson listed as being a mulatto while Alfred Carr is listed as being white. What was going on with this family? Why was Alfred white in 1880 and Celia in 1870? To try to answer this question, we looked at census data from before the Civil War, knowing that if either Alfred or Celia was in fact white, then one or both would be listed by name as such, because white people were all listed in the census, whereas enslaved blacks and mulattoes were not. (Free Negroes were listed as well.)

The 1860 census for Attala County does not list anyone named Celia Johnson. It does, however, list Alfred Carr as a sixty-year-old white man, born in North Carolina and working on the farm of a twenty-year-old landowner named Andrew Johnson. This, I believe, is an accurate record. There is no reason to doubt it. And it means that Morgan's great-great-grandfather, Alfred Carr, was a white man who worked as a farmhand in antebellum Mississippi. We then looked into the family history of Andrew Johnson, the man who owned the plantation where Alfred worked, and we found an estate appraisal for his family from 1858. Estate appraisals are very important to genealogists, especially those researching African American families. Whenever a slave owner died, his or her estate was inventoried and appraised. Because slaves were so valuable, these appraisals list each of the deceased's slaves by name and dollar value and, sometimes, by age. Finding an estate appraisal that lists a slave ancestor of a family you are researching is every genealogist's fantasy. And in spite of the fact that we found several of these for the people in this book, this is highly unusual. But in Morgan's case, we got lucky. The Johnson appraisal lists a thirty-five-year-old female named "Celie," valued at $1,000. This, undoubtedly, was Morgan's great-great-grandmother, who later spelled her name "Celia." Alongside her on the list are slaves named Betty, age two, valued at $250; Martin, age eighteen, valued at $1,200; Jim, age eleven, valued at $800; Alex, age nine, valued at $600; Frank, age seven, valued at $500; Erastus, age five, valued at $400; and one mare mule, valued at $150. Some of these young slaves were most likely Celia and Alfred's children. Betty, for example, was, most probably, their daughter Elizabeth Carr, who is Morgan's great-grandmother.

Morgan looked at the documents I had shown him for quite a while. In them he could plainly see his ancestors listed as property alongside a mule—and see also that his great-great-grandfather was a white man who worked with them. This, he and I both knew, was a very complicated situation. Alfred Carr was free; the census indicates he even had some money—a personal estate of two thousand dollars. Celia Johnson was a slave. Their children, therefore, were also slaves, since the children of slaves and interracial unions followed the condition of the mother. (According to Paul Heinegg, an expert on blacks in the colonial period, one of my own ancestors, John Redman, born in the middle of the eighteenth century, was born free because he was descended from a white woman, Jane Redman, who in the late seventeenth century bore a child fathered by a black slave.) In effect not only was Alfred Carr working on Andrew Johnson's farm, but by being involved with Celia he was also producing more slaves for his employer. How did Morgan feel about this?

His response was typical of his character—calm and wise. "We all come from somewhere," he said. "I know from being a lifelong Mississippian that we were slaves. That is my history. I don't really have a problem with it at all. But it's hard to imagine how Alfred could tolerate seeing his own children as slaves. You have to wonder why he didn't buy his family freedom. He had two thousand dollars."

Alfred Carr's behavior is a mystery, we both agreed, especially from a modern perspective. And this illustrates, I think, the vast chasm between our world today and that of the antebellum South, so polluted by slavery. Alfred Carr was not, history tells us, an anomaly. There was a great deal of mixing between whites and blacks during slavery—so much so, in fact, that, as we have seen, geneticists estimate that 58 percent of the African American people have at least 12.5 percent European ancestry, and 25 percent of all African American males can trace their Y-DNA—their father's father's father's line—not to Africa at all but to Europe, largely as a result of the sexual exploitation of black women by white men during slavery.

We don't know what the nature of the relationship was between Alfred and Celie under slavery, but we did learn quite a lot about their relationship under freedom; unlike many, or even most such relationships, theirs persisted from Celie's emancipation to the grave. And in many ways

Alfred's behavior was admirable and extraordinarily unusual. He settled in a predominantly black area with his mixed-race family. (In a sense this white man crossed over into the black community, which would explain why the family confused the census takers for decades.) He sometimes passed as a mulatto, perhaps because it was illegal for him to be with his family unless he did so. His children may have lived in slavery, but Alfred was not the simple coward we might have imagined him to be. He risked a great deal. He basically gave up his life as a white man to be with Celia and their children.

"I bet you any amount of money he was in love with her," said Morgan. "How many kids? What, they had eight children? He could have left. He loved her."

I agree with Morgan wholeheartedly. Alfred and Celia were most likely a very strong, loving couple. And they fascinate me. Researching their story further, we discovered that in 1869, four years after slavery ended, Alfred purchased property with James, his eldest son by Celia. Then, a year later, in 1870, another land deed indicates that Alfred sold the same piece of land to James and to three of his brothers. Although a selling price of fifteen hundred dollars is recorded, there is no way of knowing if money actually changed hands. My strong suspicion is that none did. These people were all family. And it would be very surprising if four very young men who had been slaves had the sum of fifteen hundred dollars just five years after emancipation. So I think this land deal may have been a way for Alfred Carr to appease his conscience. At the very least, it was a seemingly bold and generous way for him to provide for Celia and their children. Of course, when James Carr and his brothers were born, a free white man couldn't marry a slave, so they were illegitimate by definition, and according to Mississippi law, illegitimate children could not inherit property from their father. To get around this, Alfred seems to have come up with this roundabout transfer of property. He managed to find a clever way to provide for his and Celie's children.

Some of this is supposition, of course. We'll never know the truth with any certainty, but this land did stay in the Carr family for generations. And it is, in some ways, an inspiring story—one that is certainly very distinctively American, in all its complexity. It's rare for a white man to have honorably faced the challenge of keeping his mixed-race family together following slavery.

I asked Morgan if he considered Alfred Carr to be part of his family. He nodded vigorously, without hesitation. "Sure. Of course," he said. "There's no getting around that. And he didn't want to get around it neither. Good for him."

One might think that identifying a white ancestor automatically allows us to trace a family back for generations. After all, many white Americans have been able to leave an unbroken paper trail in America since their ancestors first arrived here—be that in 1700 or in 1900. Some also, of course, left paper trails back in the countries that they departed to come here. Some of the people I interviewed for this project had white ancestors whose lineages extended all the way back to medieval times; Quincy Jones, as we've seen, is actually descended from an English king who lived in the thirteenth century!

But even for white people, that's not always the case, as it was in our quest to find more about Morgan's ancestors. In the 1880 census, Alfred Carr stated that his parents were born in France—but we could find no other sign of him in the public record before 1842. We looked in Louisiana, which had a dense French population at that time; in Mississippi, where Alfred Carr worked; and in North Carolina, where he claimed he was born. But we found nothing. He may very well have invented his name and his heritage, since Carr is not a common French surname. It might be an assumed name, an anglicized name. He may have come from anywhere. He was certainly an unusual person.

There is a rather touching coda to this story. As part of our research, we went to the land that Alfred bought and sold to his sons 140 years ago. And there, we found a set of graves. Whatever the nature of their relationship may have been during slavery times, whether or not it started as a relationship between equals of the heart, Morgan's great-great-grandparents decided they would be united in death, just as they were in life. Morgan's family had searched for the grave of Celie and Alfred for years; on the Friday before I interviewed Morgan at his home in Mississippi (a magnif-

The graves of Alfred Carr and Celia Johnson, Morgan's great-great-grandparents, a white man and a former slave. Alfred and Celia were buried next to each other.

icent house built on land owned by his ancestors), one of our researchers actually found their graves and photographed them. They are buried side by side on the old family land, surrounded by the graves of their children. And—romantically, I think—Celia Johnson lies beside Alfred with a headstone that bears the name Celia Carr. There is no evidence they were ever married, but she took his name in common law, and in death.

When I showed Morgan the photograph, his shock was genuine, his pleasure profoundly moving. In fact, his reaction moved me to tears. "That's great," he said. "Buried in the woods together. I've got to go find that grave. That's really great."

The grave is also the end of Morgan's family tree. We could go back no further using genealogical records. His paper trail runs out with Alfred Carr and Celia Johnson. But I think he was very happy with what we'd learned. And as pleased as he was with his genealogical results, he seemed delighted to be turning to the DNA testing, eager to go deeper into his family's past, the anonymous, nameless past of our tribal heritage in Africa.

Morgan's admixture tests revealed that he is 83 percent sub-Saharan African and 17 percent European. He has no Native American ancestry, which refutes the family story that his great-grandfather Samuel Greenlee was part Choctaw. "I'm going to have to tell the Choctaw nation in Oklahoma now that I misrepresented myself," he said, smiling. "I'm not Choctaw at all. But that's okay. That's clarification. It's all good."

I then showed Morgan the results of a second admixture test that we had conducted on the African section of his ancestry. The results suggest that a little over one-quarter of his ancestors came from the area that stretches from present-day Senegal to Liberia—the area called Upper Guinea in the days of slavery—and three-quarters came from the area known as Congo Angola.

To further refine these results, we began to discuss Morgan's mitochondrial and Y-DNA testing. His mitochondrial DNA, which runs back to Celia Johnson and beyond, yielded two exact matches with tribes found in modern-day Niger: the Tuareg and the Songhai. Our historical consultants, John Thornton and Linda Heywood, told me that this suggests that Morgan's first enslaved female ancestor was probably from the area near the Niger River in what is now Mali, perhaps in the vicinity of Timbuktu. In the 1730s this region was the site of wars between factions of the Moroccan army, whose invasion had led to the collapse of the Songhai Empire in 1591, and the local tribes of neighboring areas, including the Fulbe and the Tuareg.

Thornton and Heywood believe that Morgan's original African ancestor was captured in one of the wars and exported to the greater Senegambian area. They tried to decide whether she was a Tuareg or a Songhai but ultimately determined that it would be difficult if not impossible to separate the two—as the shifting alliances that marked the wars resulted in many members from both tribes being taken captive and sold into slavery. However, regardless of what tribe she came from, the fate of Morgan's ancestor is rather clear. She was most likely captured in war and then carried down the Niger River to British and French trading posts where European slave ships waited for their human cargo. The Trans-Atlantic Slave Trade Database tells us that from the 1730s to the 1790s about 12 percent of the slaves entering South Carolina came from ports in what is now Senegal or Gambia. Morgan's original maternal African ancestor was likely among these people.

On his father's side, Y-DNA testing indicated that Morgan's genetic signature provided exact matches with ten Nigerian men who are Igbo. Not only is this a very strong match, but it also makes sense historically. We know that during the late seventeenth and early eighteenth centuries many Igbo people were enslaved by their fellow Africans through kidnapping, wars, and as payment for debts. These captives were frequently sold to English slave traders who plied the waters off the southern coast of present-day Nigeria. Indeed, between 1698 and 1774, captives from eastern Nigeria made up the single largest group of slaves arriving in the Chesapeake region. But they didn't remain in the Chesapeake region. During the eighteenth century, many enslaved Igbo were moved south to North Carolina—which is exactly where we know that Morgan's grandfather Hubert Freeman was born many years later. So, taking the genetic evidence and the genealogical evidence together, Thornton and Heywood were virtually certain that Morgan's first enslaved male ancestor on his father's side was an Igbo who most likely came to the region of the Bight of Biafra, which includes people from what is now eastern Nigeria and the lower portions of modern-day Niger. This news was fascinating to Morgan. He's never been to that part of Africa, but he told me that he intends to go as soon as he can.

As we said good-bye, Morgan lingered for a moment, looking down at the scrapbook containing the research results we had shared. I wondered what he thought about it all. He told me, as many of my guests have, that he found the stories about his family to be deeply moving. They had cleared up some mysteries, he said, but more than that, they had given him a connection to a past that had always been an abstraction for him. He knew he came from slaves—we all know that—but now he had names and faces and even words to put to that knowledge, to bring it to life. And he allowed himself, I think, much to my satisfaction, one brief moment of what seemed like pride—underscored, as it was, by his wit.

"That's very interesting," said Morgan, taking it all in. "I am gonna gloat over this a bit. You know? You can't translate this into gold or silver. But there is a sense of self in the knowledge of where it all might have begun. And I can gloat on that. I can put my hand on that now."

Tina Turner

November 26, 1939

A FTER ALMOST FIFTY YEARS in the music business, Tina Turner is a living legend. Her story, her voice, her face—even her legs—are icons all over the world, and with good reason. Yet to me Tina is more than an icon. She is an artist with a personal style that is inimitably expressive and deeply tied to certain moments in my life. I remember listening to her as a teenager, as a young man, then as a father and husband—and each time she was uniquely suited to the circumstance in which I found myself. She has kept me thinking and tapping my foot and singing along as best I could for as long as I can recall. I wanted to involve her in this project in part just to understand why she speaks to me so directly.

Tina has lived in Europe for the better part of the last two decades, so we met at her home in Nice, in the south of France, near the former homes of James Baldwin and Josephine Baker. Walking me through a series of exquisitely tasteful, very classically decorated rooms, she told me that she has felt more comfortable in Europe than in any place in America since she left her native Haywood County, Tennessee, more than fifty years ago. She fell in love with Europe, she says, when she first toured it in the early 1960s with her onetime husband Ike Turner and insists that she can't imagine going back. Still, Tina is indelibly Amer-ican—and African American at that. Her beliefs and behaviors, both large and small, all stem, I am convinced, from her upbringing in the southern countryside. She was born in rural Nutbush, Tennessee, on November 26, 1939, to a long line of sharecroppers. To begin to understand her—if such a thing is even possible—one must understand how strongly she was shaped by her rural roots in the Jim Crow South, how she transformed herself but never fully abandoned the past.

Tina's birth name was Anna Mae Bullock. Her parents were Zelma Priscilla Currie and Floyd Richard Bullock. Both were born in Haywood County—Zelma on November 18, 1918, and Floyd on July 31, 1912. They were sharecroppers like most of both their families before them. They lived on the land of a white man named Poindexter, surrounded by their parents and siblings. Floyd essentially ran Poindexter's farm.

"Father worked in the fields," recalled Tina. "We all did, but he was just a bit higher than a lot of others around us. Daddy rented the farm and had people working for him. He had horses and pigs and cows and the whole bit. We didn't own the place, but I never remembered suffering from wanting to eat. We ate good."

Despite their relative level of comfort, Floyd and Zelma's marriage was deeply troubled. "My mother was, I think, a typical Scorpio," said Tina. "She was high-tempered, sensitive. Not easy to get along with. You know? I think Ma was spoiled because she was an only child on both sides of the family. She probably should have had a really good spanking, but her father loved her because she was his girl. So she was quite naughty. And she wasn't happy with my father. She always said that she took him away from another girl and she regretted it. So they fought all the time. It was actually physical. And that kind of vein went through her life."

Zelma and Floyd separated when Tina was twelve. At that point, Tina and her siblings moved in with their grandparents, while Zelma moved to St. Louis, where Tina would see very little of her for several years. Floyd moved north to Detroit, and Tina and he had almost no contact until she was a good bit older—and well along on her rise to fame. "He became a dapper man," she says with a hint of bemusement, "very fashion-conscious and all that. Always wore a hat. He remarried up north. And he found out through the grapevine that I was singing, and he'd come and see me,

Tina Turner's paternal grandmother, Roxanna, and her son, Gil Bullock. The Bullocks were sharecroppers for generations in Haywood County, Tennessee.

wearing a suit, wanting to get up onstage and tell everybody he was my father."

With their parents gone, Tina and her siblings were raised by their grandparents—shuffling between her mother's and her father's parents as each saw fit. Her grandparents were thus crucial shaping figures in her life, and hearing Tina's memories of them afforded me a surprisingly vivid glimpse into her childhood. Her stories conjured up a vivid picture of life in the Jim Crow South— and of Tina as a young girl.

Tina's paternal grandparents were Alex Bullock Jr. and Roxanna Whitelaw. Both were natives of Haywood County. Alex was born there on November 23, 1882; his wife was born six years later, in March of 1888. They had fourteen children together—thirteen sons and one daughter. Yet Tina recalls that they lived almost totally separate lives and had wildly differing personalities.

Her grandfather, Alex, she says, was a hard-living sharecropper whose values clashed sharply with those of his religious-minded wife. "The only photograph we had of Papa was after death, in the casket," she said, shaking her head. "He would drink every weekend. She was a church woman, and he was an every-weekend drunk. Just into really being drunk, and he'd come home and flare out and be really crazy. He had this thing he would say—instead of cursing he would always say 'convenal.' I don't know today what 'convenal' is. Didn't know then, either. But when he was 'convenal,' you knew you better get out of the way. He worked all week, and then weekends were his."

When she talked about Alex, Tina's tone of voice shifted from disdain to amusement and back again. And she seemed physically to reenact her grandfather's wild ways as she flashed her warm smile and extended her arms across the room. By contrast, when she spoke of her grandmother Roxanna, Tina withdrew slightly and her voice became more reserved. The warmth was still there, but it was measured, tinged with respect and genuine affection. You could tell that her grandmother had run her house with a firm hand—and that Tina had loved her.

"Grandma was a fine woman, full-on church: the hat, the hair, the apron," said Tina. "Papa stayed away from her, because he knew she was a church woman. That was the relationship. She was a seamstress, she couldn't work the fields, so she did the cooking and the washing and the ironing and cleaned. When I lived with her, it was starch on the dress, the bow on the back. You know? And I was a tomboy. I wanted to get on with the animals and pull out my hair and tear the sashes away from the dress, and she always gave me a spanking because she wanted me to sit in the chair and stay neat and clean. She was like that. She was very strict. Very, very strict. Every day in church, on her knees every night praying, and in the morning, too. Praying and praying. Just a full-on Baptist. And I can relate to the praying, because I kind of picked it up in life and it got me through. But she was the real thing."

On the other side of her family, Tina's maternal grandparents were Josephus Cecil Currie, born in Madison County, Tennessee, in August 1883, and Georgianna Flagg, who was born in February 1887 in Haywood County, Tennessee. Their story is shrouded in tragedy.

"Papa Joe," said Tina, using the family nickname for her grandfather Josephus. "He was a jockey, always wore boots and those English-style pinstripe trousers. But Papa was not around, not much. He was a drinker. He didn't work the fields. He was a jockey for the plantation owner, and it ended up that Papa was hit by a car. He was drunk and coming home, and he was hit, and my grandmother found him on the road."

Josephus Currie (at right), Tina's maternal grandfather, shortly before his death in a hit-and-run car accident.

This obviously must have been very difficult for Tina's grandmother Georgianna, but Tina does not recall how Georgianna responded to her loss. Instead, like so many memories from childhood, Tina's recollections of her grandmother center on the things that a child notices—hair texture, clothes, tone of voice, demeanor, and skin color.

"She was an Indian—and she was different," Tina said of Georgianna. "When she would punish us, she would hit us on the forehead with a spoon, and that was very, very different. When I was with my father's mother, she was totally let's just say as normal as I was. But Mama Georgie was totally different. She didn't dress normally. She dressed in men's shoes, must have been Papa's shoes. And she wore a skirt down to her ankles, and then she wore a dress over that. She had a gap in her teeth, and she dipped snuff. And she drank tea, and she would just walk around humming—she always hummed. She would sit in a rocking chair, hmmm. This is how I remember her. I loved her at a distance, 'cause I didn't understand her."

According to family lore passed down over several generations, Josephus was three-quarters Navajo and his wife, Georgianna, was a "Cherokee squaw" and one-quarter black. African American genealogical research is always difficult, but adding the potential of biracial and triracial pedigrees to the mix presents an even greater challenge. There are so many possibilities to consider. Native Americans intermingled with runaway slaves and with their own black slaves in some areas, though the frequency of such interactions is much, much lower than most of us imagine. And since the blend of African and Native American ancestry in the area of Tennessee where Tina's ancestors lived has never been defined clearly in local and state records, it is virtually impossible to know to what degree any individual actually had Native American ancestry given the available written historical documents.

Understandably, Tina believes the family lore. She is convinced that her maternal grandparents were in fact of Native American ancestry. "They were Indian people," she said matter-of-factly. "My grandmama had red skin, very Indian-like. Really Indian nose, small eyes." Beyond these few remembered physical details, however, Tina had no memories that could connect her grandparents to any Native American group. This meant that testing out the family lore would have to wait for our DNA research.

Regardless of their ancestry, life with both sets of her grandparents, as Tina recalls it, was a life filled with work. Tina's grandparents were not wealthy by any stretch, but neither were they impoverished, and they labored incessantly to maintain their status. "We were average," said Tina. "Not poor nor rich. We bought clothes by seasons. Winter clothes in winter, and in the summer we got summer clothes. I knew the difference, because with some of the people who lived in our area, there was always the smell of urine or uncleanliness. But we were clean."

From her earliest days, Tina worked in the fields with her family, picking whatever was in season—strawberries, watermelons, cotton. "I hated the cotton fields," she said. "There were those hairy worms crawling around. There were the spiders. Terribly afraid of falling on those. So I was always screaming and picking the cotton. And so I couldn't quite get as much in my sack as everybody else. Everyone was picking and pushing it down, and when they went up to weigh it on the scale, their sacks were really full, and I wanted that. I wanted to be as good as everyone else. But I never really got there. I hated it. My hands and cuticles got all ripped up—cotton just tears your hands up. And the sun, the sun was so hot."

Although Tina's family was clearly entrapped within the sharecropping system—working land owned by a white family for wages charged against costs of seed and rent and tools—she feels that segregation and racism were not as pernicious in Tennessee as they were in the deeper South. "I realize now we didn't have it as bad as Mississippi and Alabama and Georgia," she said. "White people in Tennessee were really quite nice. The white people on the plantation that we lived on would invite us down to watch television when a western was coming on. All of our houses were in the back of the plantation owner's. And these people were very nice. They really were almost family."

Nonetheless, Tina experienced segregation in all its forms: sitting in colored-only sections of restaurants, riding in the backs of buses, attending all-black schools, and living a daily life surrounded by signs that said No Colored Allowed.

"We went to town on Saturdays," she recalled. "We called it the hole, because it was downhill. And this is where all the black people were. White people used to sit on top of the buildings watching us, 'cause we were having the fun and the music, the fish. I think we always knew how to have a good time. But there was a lot of crime down there, too, a lot of fighting and stabbing and things. And if we went to the cinema there, well, then we were upstairs, because if the white people were upstairs, they would throw things down on us. So they put black people upstairs, 'cause we knew we'd better not throw things down on the whites. We always knew how it was."

Tina says that she always believed she was destined for a better life than the one Jim Crow Tennessee had to offer, even if as a child she was not sure how that life could be obtained. "At school," she recalled, "I wasn't that smart, but I was liked by everybody—the principal, the teachers, all the kids. I was having a hard time sometimes living with my relatives and so forth, and that probably showed somehow, but everybody liked me a lot as well. I had charisma. I'd walk into a room and I had it.

And I knew I wanted to go somewhere, 'cause I didn't like the cotton fields. I knew that there was something else. I would go to the cinema, and that told me there was something else. So I would dream, you know? I would get the sunglasses and take down my braids and take a cover from the bed and lay it out, and then I'd put on my mother's bra and just be Hollywood. Oh, did I get a whupping! But I was always very dramatic. And I always looked into the yonder, just had a dream, I fantasized a lot about living a different life and being a star."

Tina Turner at fifteen, around the time she left the cotton fields to live with her mother in St. Louis.

I cannot imagine how many young black girls in the 1950s had these dreams; there must have been millions. Tina is one of the tiny minority who lived them. Though as a child she wanted to be an actress, she soon learned that her gift for singing was something special. "I sang in church from the earliest age that you can," she recalled. "I just got up there when I was little, just a little girl leading the choir, always led most of the church songs." No one could have imagined where that gift would lead her.

When Tina was fifteen years old, her maternal grandmother, Georgianna, died and Tina's mother returned to Tennessee for the funeral. She invited her daughter to come live with her family in St. Louis, and Tina jumped at the chance—eager to forsake the cotton fields for the exciting city. The transition, however, was difficult. "I was living with my mother," Tina recalled. "She had rules that I wasn't used to. I was a Cinderella in

Tina as a young woman, having transformed herself into a fixture of St. Louis's R&B scene.

Tennessee. Now I had to get home from school, clean up, do the cooking, the whole bit. And then I was at a new school, communicating with different children, intellectually different. And I was really intimidated. The school was so big, and the northern kids were all different, and it was really quite stressful. But again I won everybody over—the teachers, all the students. I was very liked."

Almost immediately after arriving in St. Louis, Tina began to take her singing much more seriously. She was talented, she soon discovered, and lucky. The city was a music mecca and had been for generations. When Tina arrived, it was just becoming one of the centerpieces of America's burgeoning R&B scene, filled with nightclubs and recording studios on the cutting edge of the nation's tastes. At just sixteen years old, Tina became a regular on the scene. "My sister and I started going to the clubs," she recalled. "Sneaking going, 'cause my mother didn't know. I got involved in it all. It was like I knew I could sing, but I didn't realize that I could *sing.*"

The pivotal moment in Tina's life—for good and bad—occurred in one of these nightclubs when she was called up onstage to sing with Ike Turner's Kings of Rhythm. Ike was a deeply troubled but immensely talented musician with a wealth of ambition and a small following. If Tina did not yet recognize her own skills as a singer, Ike did. He saw in her a ticket to fame and quickly incorporated her into his act, changing her name from Anna Mae Bullock, her birth name, to Tina Turner (supposedly after the TV show *Sheena: Queen of the Jungle*) and relying on her as both a lyricist and a singer. Their first hit together was a song called "A Fool in Love." It was the first time Tina had ever heard her voice on the radio—and the experience thrilled her. (It thrilled me, too; I vividly remember that song: I was ten years old, and it made me want to get a girlfriend, though I wasn't sure exactly what that meant.) Within two years Ike and Tina were married in Mexico. She was barely twenty, but the life that she knew— essentially the life of a rural girl—was gone forever, replaced by something far more complicated, a bit of a fairy tale and a bit of a nightmare, inextricably intertwined.

The story of Ike and Tina has been told and retold countless times. It is a tragic story of abuse, and no matter how many times I hear it, I'm always amazed that Tina survived at all, much less survived to triumph as she did. In our conversation Tina spoke of it bluntly, not shying away from the worst details.

"I spent seven years trying to make the marriage work," she said. "I had brought Ike's children in. We had moved to California. I was really a wife, even though I knew it wasn't quite right, because I knew that Ike's reputation was not what you call that of a married man. But, I had my own house finally. So I was happy. And then it started to fade, because Ike started to do drugs. That was the beginning of the downslide."

Tina stayed with Ike for eight more years, struggling constantly to deal with his drug-fueled rages and need for total control. "I had no say," she recalled, "just none. Whenever he found out that I was doing something, if he didn't like it, he changed it. But when I started to think about leaving, it was like a blank wall. It was, 'Where can you go?' My mother was basically taken over by Ike. He was taking care of the whole family. My sister was just right across the road. I had no place to run. And so that was living for me for years, and it was getting progressively worse, because the fighting was getting worse and the love was totally gone. Everything was totally gone. He did everything against me to push me away."

According to Tina, the physical abuse she suffered was far worse than anything shown in the film of her life, *What's Love Got to Do with It?*— and far more frequent as well.

"The movie couldn't ever have shown it," she said. "There were so many times when he was just in a bad mood when he would take it out on me. And he was like that with everybody—with whoever the secretary was, or sometimes a new musician if he wasn't thinking the same way everyone else was thinking. It was awful. If you didn't have a key to the recording studio, you couldn't get out. And they were fighting in there sometimes. Poor guys didn't even know what was happening. I mean, there were these musicians that Ike was attacking because he didn't think that was what the drumbeat should be. It was a madness kind of a thing. You never knew what was going to happen. I had nightmares of this demon. It was like a black figure, and I remember starting to actually fight it back. Because I didn't like the brutality. I mean, why hit me? For what? Why? And that was going on for a good seven, eight years. Full of the hate building up. A few times I went and got the gun when he was asleep, and I held it there. I was so close. My manager says, 'You better be glad you didn't, 'cause you'd be in prison today.'"

Tina says that she tried to leave Ike multiple times before finally succeeding—after a truly hellish experience. "We were going to Dallas, Texas," she recalled. "And Ike had this pattern of sleeping, staying up five days in the studio, and then we would actually roll him out, into a chair that we had arranged, and take him to bed, and he would sleep straight through. When he would wake up, everything was hurting—the nose, everything. And so we got in the car, and he was in a bad mood. Well, this time the fight started, and I fought back. He hit, and I hit back. And then he was shocked. He was like, 'This MF never hit me.' And he liked to hit, he liked it. But he didn't use his hands. He hit with things like a shoe, and every now and then he would hit me and I would catch it. And this time I really fought back, and I meant it. I was so angry. I fought and I fought, and then he pulled off my hairpiece and he was hitting me on my head. And I knew that there was no going onstage with that, because this whole side of my face had been beaten with a shoe all the way from the airport. And I didn't cry. I was just angry. I just knew that I was leaving. As soon as he went and laid down, I went and massaged him, and then I put a little bandanna on, picked up my hand luggage, and I went out the back way. I didn't know the hotel, and I was afraid. I ran. Fearfully. And 'cause

I was afraid I was going to run into his people and they would say, 'I saw her.' And then I ran out the back side, the kitchen side of the hotel, and I ran down to cross the freeway, and I misjudged the speed of traffic. Big trucks were coming. So I started to run across the freeway. I could have been hit, because a few times I did misjudge the speed of those trucks. But I ran right straight across the street to the Ramada hotel, and I ran in, and I had no glasses at that time, and I just said, 'Excuse me. My name is Tina Turner, and I had a fight with my husband, and I wonder if you would give me a room. I promise you I'll pay you back.' I had a Mobil card, a gas card, and I had thirty-six cents in my wallet, and I said to him, 'This is all I have, but if you would just give me a room tonight, I promise I will pay you.' "

That was the beginning of her new life. She struggled at first without Ike but was ultimately able to build up a singing and acting career that far exceeded anything she had ever achieved with him. Looking back on the story now, she does not downplay Ike's importance in her development, but she can put Ike's influence upon her career in some perspective. She had great talent, she knows, before she met him. And that talent has flourished even more profoundly since she kicked that sadistic force out of her life. She is at peace with what happened, as brutally dreadful as it may have been. And sensing that peace, I realized it was time to return to our investigation of her ancestors—starting with her great-grandparents, whose children had such a strong influence on Tina's youth. Tina knew little about them but was more than happy to learn.

"I still miss my grandmother's house," she said. "I used to get emotional. Because I think that was really home. That is where my happiest days were. And I would have to say that my grandmother's house, obviously in my subconscious mind, still means a lot to me, because I go back there and dream, still have dreams."

We first looked at the line of Georgianna Flagg, Tina's maternal grandmother—whom Tina recalls as the strange woman who wore men's clothes, disciplined children with a spoon, and was of Native American descent. The stories that we were able to uncover about Georgianna's family gave Tina a totally new perspective. Her father, Tina's great-grandfather, was George Flagg, born into slavery in May 1858 in North Carolina. Searching for information about his family, we found a land deed filed January 26, 1889, which indicates that Benjamin B. Flagg, George Flagg's older brother, sold one acre of land that he owned in Haywood County, Tennessee, for twenty-five dollars in cash to a group of men identified as the trustees of the Flagg Grove School House. Now, at that time the going rate for land in Tennessee was approximately seventy-five or eighty dollars an acre. This means that Benjamin Flagg sold his land below market value so that his community could have a school. He made it possible to create what later became the Flagg Grove Elementary School—and according to this deed, his brother William was one of its first trustees.

Tina, who attended this school as a child, was astonished. She had never known that her family helped found it. I tried to express to her how impressed I was by her ancestors. Most black people in rural Tennessee and throughout the South at this time were desperately trying to acquire land, but Tina's family cared so much about our people and about education that they were willing to give their land away to build a school for the black community. (Ancestors of Oprah Winfrey, Tom Joyner, and Chris Tucker would make similar gestures of subsidizing the purchase of land for black schools.) Ten years after the failure of Reconstruction, when public funds were being siphoned off from black districts, Tina's ancestors were fighting back by giving back, and prospering through the acquisition of land.

"It sounds like my people were pretty advanced," said Tina, still stunned at the news. She then told me that she has vivid memories of attending the Flagg school. "Me and my sister had to walk a good hour, it seemed like, to that school," she recalled. "I remember it was just so picturesque. It was a nice school. Just one room and an outhouse, but it wasn't poor. You can't call it high-end, but it was proper desks and a blackboard. I mean, we felt like studying there. And the playground was really big."

I wanted to know how the Flagg family got their land in the first place, but we were unable to uncover sufficient documents to do anything more than guess. However, by returning to Tina's maternal line, we found an ancestor with another very interesting story about land ownership—a story that would lead us back generations in Tina's family.

Tina's maternal great-grandfather was a man named Logan Currie Jr. He was the father of Josephus Cecil Currie (aka "Papa Joe," the jockey who died tragically) and the grandfather of Tina's mother, Zelma. Logan was born in 1842, in either North Carolina or Tennessee—the records are contradictory—and spent the first twenty-three years of his life as a slave. I have never interviewed anyone whose family talked about slavery. Tina's was no exception. She had heard virtually no discussion of her ancestors' slave experiences. Her grandparents did not openly discuss their own parents' lives in slavery. "They wanted to push it behind them," says Tina, echoing the thoughts of many whom I have questioned on the subject.

To find out more about Logan, we tried to identify the source of his surname. We searched the records of every slave owner with the last name Currie in or around Haywood, Tennessee, and we found a slave schedule in the 1860 federal census for a white man named Jesse Currie who lived in nearby Madison County. Slave schedules are very important documents for researchers of African American genealogy. While the United States did not list slaves by name in any official records prior to the Civil War, beginning with the 1850 census, the federal government mandated that slave owners create these schedules in which their property—our ancestors—were recorded by age and gender. The schedules do not contain names, but they offer opportunities to learn about our forebears. Jesse Currie's schedule from 1860 lists a twenty-year-old black male, a thirty-four-year-old black female, and a forty-four-year-old black male. These, I believe, are Tina's great-grandfather Logan and his parents, Betty and Logan Currie Sr. The ages on the schedule correspond exactly with what we know, from later census data, to have been their ages at that time.

This would mean that Jesse Currie owned Tina's ancestors and that they were in the area of Haywood County when the Civil War began. When the war ended five years later, Tina's great-grandfather Logan and his parents became free men and women along with all the other slaves. They were at liberty to go wherever they chose. But, like so many of their fellow ex-slaves, they did not go far. To the contrary, they stayed exactly where they were and struck a deal with the man who had just finished owning them. Our search uncovered a labor contract between Logan and his former master, Jesse Currie, dated January 6, 1866. It was drawn up under the auspices of the Freedmen's Bureau, the government agency that was created after the Civil War to help former slaves. The contract lays out the terms by which Logan, along with his mother, father, and siblings, would barter their labor with Jesse Currie.

"They must have been comfortable with him," said Tina. This raises an interesting issue, I think. I have often wondered what life was like for the newly freed slaves. They called Emancipation Day the "Day of Jubilee," but the word "jubilee" hardly does it justice—at least in my mind. Imagine being the property of a man your whole life, then being tapped on the shoulder one morning and told, "My brother, you're free." How would that have felt? Tina responded in a most realistic manner.

"Well," she told me, "depending on the spirit of the person, they could have been afraid, you know? 'I don't know where to go. I don't know what else to do. I can't imagine another life, other than being here.' "

Tina's insights here are, I think, profound. In fact, I imagine that this reaction to freedom was not as uncommon as we would assume today. And indeed, the historical record indicates that many slaves, like Tina's ancestors, stayed where they were after they won their freedom. Of course, most of these people stayed because they had to for economic reasons. But freedom is frightening—it's a terrifying concept. And it is interesting to me how sensitive Tina is to this. You'd think a world-renowned rock star would be telling me how great freedom was, how unequivocally it should be embraced. But that's not Tina's mind-set. She's seen a tremendous amount in this world, and she knows that freedom has a psychic cost. Speaking from the well of pain that was her relationship with Ike, she described in highly sympathetic terms what a terrified slave might have felt upon becoming free. "When you walk away from a life that you hated every minute of," she says, "you would rather die before you would go back. But still, you may not have anywhere to go. You are not anywhere. You may be dealing with another form of brutality—and maybe not. But it's scary. And

I think that might have been how it was." Tina made the connection herself between the courage to leave one's master and the courage to leave an abusive spouse.

For Tina's enslaved ancestors, life after Jubilee Day must have been frightening enough and economically uncertain enough that they saw fit—wisely, as it turns out—to enter into a bargain with their former owners. Under the terms of their contract, Jesse Currie and Logan Currie's family essentially went into business together. Jesse promised to furnish Tina's ancestors with land and the farming tools, horses, and mules necessary to grow and harvest a set amount of grain and cotton. In return, Logan was to give Jesse three-quarters of the cotton he raised and half his other crops. Beyond that, Logan and his family could use the land and materials as they wished, to grow food and possibly cash crops for themselves. Agreements like this were struck all over the former Confederacy in the wake of the Civil War. They made a certain amount of economic sense. The region had been devastated, and money was in very short supply for everybody. Both the planters and the former slaves needed capital. Such agreements allowed the two sides to barter their resources in a cash-poor economy.

Unfortunately, these arrangements devolved over a relatively short period of time into the highly exploitative system known as sharecropping. It may have started out as a reasonable idea, but sharecropping quickly became the new slavery—a system of unrepayable debt that fixed blacks well below whites on the economic ladder for decades to come.

Of course, I am speaking only in generalities here. As a historian, I know how the vast majority of sharecroppers fared. Tina knows it, too. She was the child of sharecroppers and worked the land herself until she was in her teens. She knows as well as I do that the fate of the average sharecropper was grim. Bankruptcy, economic ruin, and decades of impoverishment were the primary legacies of the system. And yet Tina's ancestors avoided that fate. Her family was better off, if only slightly, than many of their neighbors. And they were successful enough to have essentially donated land for a local school. The main reason for this, I believe, was Logan Currie.

We found two more contracts that Logan signed after he became a sharecropper. The first, dated December 20, 1866, laid out the terms for Logan's farm for the year 1867, his second year of emancipation. Interestingly, this agreement was made between Logan and a white landowner named W. M. Dunaway. Jesse Currie, Logan's prior master, is not mentioned. It appears that the former slave, after one year, grew tired of the former master, and struck out on his own. Maybe Jesse Currie did something; maybe Logan simply needed a year to sort out his feelings, to get used to his independence. We can't tell from the record. All we know is that after one year Logan had the wherewithal to break away from Jesse.

Perhaps significantly, Logan's new contract with the farmer Dunaway is more favorable to him than the contract he signed with Jesse Currie. In the Dunaway contract, Logan still agreed to give the landlord three-quarters of the cotton he raised and half the crops, but he also was to receive the sum of two hundred dollars for his work. His contract with Jesse Currie was just a straight barter. No cash changed hands. But within a year after slavery, Logan was earning cash. And this was crucial to his family's enduring stability—and to the schoolhouse that they were able essentially to donate to their community. The fact that Logan was an entrepreneur, skilled enough as a farmer and a businessman to strike a better deal for himself one year out of slavery, would have ramifications in his family for generations.

In 1880, according to the U.S. census, Logan Currie was still living in Madison County, Tennessee. But he was no longer a sharecropper. He was a tenant farmer—meaning that he was renting land and farming it, paying his bills with his own cash rather than bartering away his labor under the exploitative system. The census also indicates that Logan was married, had at least nine children, and was poor by almost any standard. Yet unlike many blacks in the region, he was earning cash money and had graduated from sharecropping to tenant farming. And that's a very significant thing for his family's security. Moreover, Logan had become a pillar of his community. The records of Madison County indicate that he became a minister and officially married more than fifty black couples between 1870 and 1888.

Marriage, of course, was of enormous significance (legally and sym-bolically) to the recently freed slaves, who made up about 90 percent of the black community in these years immediately following the end of the Civil War. Having been forbidden under slavery to wed, many couples had formed secret wedding pacts, sometimes at great risk. In the years after the Civil War, the formalizing of these pacts and the marriages of new couples became an urgent and fundamental aspect of establishing the foundations of the free black community. Tina is very familiar with this part of our his-tory but was quite surprised and thrilled that her great-grandfather played a role in it. "This is great information," she said, beaming.

Returning to her family tree, we sought to trace Logan Currie back in time. The 1880 census lists his father, Logan Currie Sr., as a widower, which means that his mother, Betty Currie, had died. We could not iden-tify Logan Sr.'s parents, but in 1880 he was living with three of his daugh-ters and his mother-in-law, Lucy Kimbro, a seventy-five-year-old widow who had been born in North Carolina. This means that Lucy Kimbro was Betty Currie's mother and Tina's great-great-great-grandmother.

Searching for the man who may have owned Lucy Kimbro, we iden-tified a white farmer named William Kimbrough who lived in Haywood County in the years before the Civil War. An 1860 slave schedule indicates that William owned forty-nine slaves at that time. Among them is a sixty-year-old woman—which would have been roughly the age of Lucy Kim-bro. Given the age and the similarity of the surnames, our genealogists felt very confident that this was Tina's ancestor.

We then looked at William Kimbrough's 1850 slave schedule to see if we could find a slave matching Lucy's description there, but at that time William Kimbrough owned only nine slaves. Wondering how Kimbrough managed to acquire forty new slaves in ten years, we searched all the records we could find pertaining to his family and found the will of his father-in-law, a man named Nathaniel Macklin, who died between 1850 and 1852. In it, Macklin deeds a great quantity of slaves to his daughter Lucy and her husband, William Kimbrough. This means that Tina's an-cestor was probably once the property of Nathaniel Macklin and may well have been named after Nathaniel's daughter Lucy. Nathaniel's 1850 slave schedule gives further credence to this theory, as it lists a forty-five-year-old female slave—which would have been roughly Lucy Kimbro's age at that time.

Further research revealed that Nathaniel Macklin was born into a wealthy landowning family in Bushwick County, Virginia, in 1771. In the 1840s he moved to Haywood County, Tennessee, and purchased a three-hundred-acre farm. According to the 1880 census, Lucy was born in North Carolina in 1805. If this is correct—and there is no reason to believe otherwise—this means either that Nathaniel Macklin purchased Tina's great-great-great-grandmother en route from Virginia to Tennessee or, more likely, he bought Lucy from a slave trader after he had arrived in Tennessee. Either way, Lucy was taken from her family and her community in North Carolina to be part of one of the largest forced migrations in the history of the United States. As we've seen through Morgan Freeman's family history, between the years 1790 and 1860, the year before the Civil War broke out, over 1 million slaves were forced to move into the Deep South from the Upper South to create the Cotton Kingdom.

Tina was stunned by this story. She struggled to imagine what it was like for her ancestor to be pulled apart from her family in North Carolina and forced to march west to the wilderness of Tennessee. Americans, she told me quietly, don't really understand how much of our country's unprecedented wealth was created on the backs of African slaves. "I don't think it's recognized," she said. "I don't think that the white race wanted it recognized, but we need to bring it forward so everyone can see that it was not just like they were being told. We're the foundation of the money, basically. That's what it comes down to. And we weren't stupid. Doesn't mean because they were slaves they were stupid. You can see that once they were released, they kept going with what they were doing and they grew to where we are."

Tina is absolutely right in this—and her family history proves it. They were exceptionally clever about negotiating the new system.

Lucy Kimbro, born in 1805, is the earliest relative we could trace down Tina's maternal line. On her paternal side, we were able to go as far as her great-great-grandfather Tom Bullock, who was born in North Carolina in the early nineteenth century. But despite our best efforts, we could go back no further. At this point we had exhausted all available records. Every line of Tina's family tree had run to a dead end, to a paperless abyss. There were still, of course, many mysteries on that tree—not the least of which being the rumors, passed from generation to generation, that her mother's family was of Native American descent. But this mystery, as I explained to Tina, could be solved to some extent by DNA testing.

The results were surprising to both Tina and me. Her admixture test clearly indicates that the family legend is just that: a legend. She is 66 percent sub-Saharan African, 33 percent European, and 1 percent Native American. Her family has always believed that it had Native Americans in its recent past. There are innumerable biographies of Tina that claim she has significant Indian heritage. According to her admixture test, however, they are wrong. If both of Tina's maternal grandparents had been three-quarters Native American, the admixture test would have indicated a 37 percent result, not a 1 percent result.

One percent Native American ancestry means that Tina has one great-great-great-great-grandparent who was a Native American. This person probably lived around 1770, maybe earlier. That is simply not a significant amount of Native American ancestry, despite the family legend. Of course, many African Americans think that they have a large percentage of Native American ancestry, but in reality only 5 percent do. This makes sense historically, because there were only three periods in American history when there was significant intermixing between Native Americans and African Americans.

The first period occurred early in the colonial era—in the late seventeenth and early eighteenth centuries—when Native Americans were enslaved just like African Americans, and some mixing occurred in Virginia and South Carolina. The number of Indian slaves was small, but not insignificant, especially in certain colonies. In fact, before 1715 one out of three slaves in South Carolina was a Native American. And I think that this may well have been the era in which Tina's Native American ancestor joined her family, as some of her second- and third-grade great-grandparents were born in Virginia and the Carolinas. This period did not last long, however, as Indian slavery was phased out in favor of the almost exclusively African American slave system we all know about.

The second period of concentrated interaction between blacks and Native Americans was in the mid-1700s, when a number of runaway slaves began seeking refuge with the Indian nations of the South called the Five Civilized Tribes: the Choctaws and the Chickasaws in Mississippi, the Creeks and the Cherokee in Alabama and Georgia, and the Seminoles in Florida.

Opportunities for mixing between Native Americans and African Americans then continued throughout the eighteenth century, because some prosperous members of the five tribes began owning slaves themselves. This is the third period during which blacks and Native Americans had protracted, intimate contact. Some started their own plantations and purchased their own slaves in the southern slave markets. This lifestyle, of course, was interrupted when the federal government forced all the Indians out of Mississippi and Alabama. As we shall see with Don Cheadle, however, proximity did not necessarily lead to admixture, even when the Indians took their slaves with them on the Trail of Tears. And I think it is unlikely that Tina's family became involved with any Native Americans during this period, because these events did not involve the regions in which Tina's ancestors lived.

"All the time I've been thinking I was Indian," said Tina. "And I was dying to find out what tribe it was, and now you tell me that it's no tribe. I guess that's understandable because of the slaves and the whites—I know there was a lot of abuse there."

Tina's intuition here is right. The rumors about Native American ancestry in her family are undoubtedly due to the intermingling of whites and African Americans, not Indians and African Americans. The variations in hair, skin color, and physiognomy that so many black families have attributed to Indian ancestors are almost always in fact the result of a white ancestor. That our people have been historically reluctant to acknowledge this—frequently creating instead a family story about Native American forebears—is, I think, quite understandable given the history between whites and blacks in this country. But the facts speak for themselves. Far more of us have white ancestors than Indian ancestors, and Tina is a perfect example of this. Her European result is 33 percent. This means that Tina is one-third "white." We don't know how, but it's there in her genetic heritage.

"So that's why I love Europe," she joked. "See? Don't blame me. Ike always said I wanted to be white." She sighed. "He'll think he was right all along. But when will the PBS series air?" she asked, suddenly brightening. When I told her February of 2008 (this was August 2007), she exclaimed to my surprise, "Not to worry, then! Ike will be dead." Ike Turner died in January 2008.

Turning to our mitochondrial DNA testing, we moved from our discussion of white and Native American ancestors to the question of Tina's African ancestry, which is after all the great majority of her family tree. We could not find an exact match for her mitochondrial DNA, but we found close matches among many groups, including the Tuareg tribe in modern-day Niger, the Bamileke in Cameroon, and the Turkana tribe from Kenya, among others.

The historians John Thornton and Linda Heywood thought the fact that Tina has several matches for tribes with an eastern Bantu origin, including the Bamileke and Turkana peoples, means that her ancestor probably lived in Central Africa on the fringes of the powerful Lunda Empire, situated in the area that is now Angola. Twenty-three percent of the African slaves in the United States came from this region. During the mid-eighteenth century, the Lunda people conducted a series of wars, the major purpose of which was to capture slaves to sell to the European markets. Tina's female ancestor could well have been captured in one of these wars. Once in the hands of the Lunda, she would have been sold to members of the Zombo people, who were merchants from what is now the Congo. She would then have been carried to the coast and sold to an English slave trader who would have shipped her across the Atlantic to Charleston, South Carolina, and the slave markets there.

To try to identify the African ancestry of Tina's paternal line, we tested the DNA of her half brother, Floyd Richard Bullock. Floyd shares Y-DNA with Tina's father, and their DNA tests yielded almost exact matches with members of the Mbenzele tribe, most of whom live in the Central African Republic, and with the Hausa people, who originally came to Cameroon from northern Nigeria.

Tina recalls that as a child she once met some distant relatives of her father's at a family gathering who were "like Pygmies," she said. "They were very bowlegged and short and very, very dark-skinned, and they didn't speak fluent English to us. So we were all excited, and we never really forgot that small group of people who we didn't understand where they came from. They were never around us ever again."

This is a very interesting memory—as it may have some basis in Tina's African DNA. The Mbenzele people are Pygmies. So it is possible that Tina met some distant relatives of her father's who retained a greater amount of this aspect of their African heritage. She certainly seemed to think so. More likely they were simply short people who spoke an American dialect that was unfamiliar to Tina as a child—the way a Cajun accent might have been. But who knows? That is one of the fascinating things about this project to me. There is so much about the complex African American past that is yet to be uncovered.

Tina did not really care one way or the other. She was happy just knowing that her parents' lines originated at these various places in West and Central Africa. In the final analysis, though, Tina truly comes from all over—from Europe and Africa, from rural Haywood County and from the person she made of herself after she moved to St. Louis from Nutbush, Tennessee, and much later, to Nice, France. Her ancestry in many ways mirrors her personality. She is a very cosmopolitan woman. I ended our meeting by asking her what she thought of this—what her heritage had taught her about herself. Her answer was absolutely, quintessentially Tina Turner.

"I don't think there is a name for me," she said with a smile. "I don't know if there ever will be one. I mean, if somebody told me when I was a girl that I was a third white, I'd never have believed it. But knowing that, and knowing I came from a line of people who were interested in education and being better—that feels good. And I think that runs really strong in me. I always wanted to be better. Even with the life that I was living before I went on my own, I had not achieved that, but I think that was my desire. And I said, reaching into the yonder, 'This is not what I want for myself.' And I did something about it. And today I live as well as I possibly can. I like to dress for dinner, you know? I want to make up for all the years that weren't so great. I want everything nice around me. I deserve it. I paid my dues. It's nothing to be ashamed of. I'm not trying to be anything. I'm being what I am."

Peter J. Gomes

May 22, 1942

THE REVEREND PETER JOHN GOMES is a national treasure—a wise and worldly Harvard scholar, a Baptist minister who has traveled the globe offering care to the powerless and the powerful alike. He is also one of my closest friends, a man I turn to for counsel and just for the pleasure of his company. I love the special combination of the timbre of his voice and the quality of his supple mind. He sounds like a black Pilgrim, if you can imagine such a thing. And he is a unique combination of a deep, free African American ancestry that traces to Virginia, and a childhood spent in Plymouth, Massachusetts, where he still maintains a home at the edge of the sea.

I asked Peter to participate in this project for two reasons: First, I love talking to Peter. He is an incredibly busy man, and the opportunity to sit down with him at length is too rare to let pass. Second, I have heard Peter's family story in bits and pieces over the years, and it has always riveted me. I wanted the chance to study it in detail. These two reasons may not seem significant, but I was not disappointed on either account. As it turns out, we discovered, much to his astonishment, that Peter—along with Sara Lawrence-Lightfoot and I—can trace his ancestry to Negroes freed in Virginia in the eighteenth century. Peter has one of the oldest black family lineages of anyone I investigated.

Peter was born on May 22, 1942, in Plymouth, Massachusetts. His mother, Orissa Josephine White, was born on March 16, 1901, in a prominent African American family in Boston, Massachusetts. His father, Peter

Lobo Gomes, was a cranberry farmer, born on September 17, 1908, on the island of Brava, which is part of Cape Verde, a small country on the west coast of Africa. His parents were, needless to say, very different people. Peter is their only child, and he speaks warmly of them both, relishing many stories about them, including, perhaps most of all, stories of their cultural conflicts. To understand them—and thus to understand the unique environment that shaped Peter—one must appreciate the profound differences in their backgrounds.

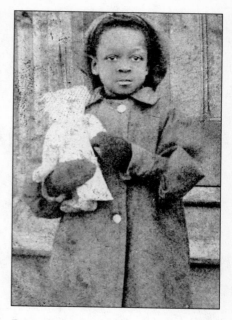

Peter Gomes's mother, Orissa White, was born to a prominent African American family in Boston.

Peter himself starts any discussion of his parents with the story of their courtship. "My mother was a professional old maid," he said with a gleam in his eye. "She wasn't going to marry, wasn't any colored man good enough for her. And her mother said, 'You are getting neither younger nor prettier, my dear. The first good man that comes along, you had better do the right thing.' And my father came along—and my father was fascinated by my mother. They really were from very opposite worlds. She encountered him coming down to Plymouth, driving some friends home from a cranberry bog. He was walking along the road, returning from work. She was lost. So she stopped to ask directions."

According to Peter, his father always described this meeting as "love at first sight." Peter's mother might have used other words, but in the end Peter's father prevailed. "He pursued her," said Peter, smiling broadly. "He used flowers and fruit and candy. He would come up on the train to Boston, walk over to Cambridge where she lived. She didn't have the time for him. But he was smooth. Very smooth. He discovered the way to get to her was through her mother—my grandmother—and her nieces, who

Young Peter with his father, who was an immigrant from Cape Verde, off the coast of Africa.

adored him. And that's how he did it. He was a good-looking man. And they said, 'Orissa, you're not going to do any better than this. You better get on with it.' All the colored men she met, she regarded as shiftless, irresponsible—people who were only there 'cause she had money. Well, my father wasn't interested in that. For some strange reason, he was interested in her."

When they met, Peter's father was an immigrant, less than a decade removed from Cape Verde. Massachusetts was a destination for many Cape Verdeans, in part because its economy was centered on fishing and agriculture—two occupations in which Cape Verdean migrants excelled in their new environment. Upon arriving, Peter's father had discovered that he had a natural aptitude for the cultivation of cranberries, one of the mainstays of the region at that time and still a significant crop for Massachusetts today. He learned the trade very quickly and was soon entrusted with the management of a large cranberry business, supervising a veritable colony of migrant workers.

"My father was a very good organizer," said Peter, "and a very good manager of people. He was also kind of a genius at the horticulture of cranberries. There were lots of Portuguese men in my father's generation who were in the cranberry business around Plymouth. Nearly every other bog either was owned by somebody from Cape Verde or had workers from Cape Verde. It was for Cape Verdeans what cotton was to the colored folks in the South: the crop for people who worked the land. And my father was very, very good at it."

According to family lore, Peter's father came to America because *his* father, Manuel Lobo Gomes, summoned him after immigrating himself. "There are a variety of tales," said Peter. "One of which is that my grandfather kind of wandered over. The Cape Verde Islands were a coaling station for these Yankee ships, and Grandfather apparently knew the harbor very well and was well known as a pilot. Apparently he got on one of these Yankee boats and decided he liked it, and he stayed. Left his family in the old country but sent them back money and goods and whatnot. And then he sent for his youngest son, who was my father. So my father left his brothers and sisters and his mother. And he always wanted to go back. He never did. I remember the only time I ever saw my father cry was when a letter reached him with news that his mother had died. Oh, Father was deeply upset. Deeply, deeply upset."

Peter never knew his grandfather Manuel and wonders how he could have been so hard as to leave his family behind forever. But he suspects that his grandfather must have had a good reason—as his reputation within the family is that of a gentle, hardworking, and very decent man. "My mother," said Peter, "always spoke very fondly of him, and that was unusual, because my mother was not very fond of Cape Verdeans. She didn't speak warmly of them hardly at all. But she liked her father-in-law—adored him, really. She thought he was a wonderful man, and he was very kind to her, and the circumstances that led both of them to this country remain wonderful mysteries as far as I am concerned."

Peter's mother, Orissa, in contrast to his father, came from a long line of distinguished African Americans, running back to eighteenth-century Virginia. Her family thought of themselves as a kind of black aristocracy, with good reason. They owned property in Cambridge, bought cars, and generally lived in a manner that was thought to be much more typical of white families at that time than black, by which I mean that it was thoroughly middle class—indeed, upper middle class. And this caused tensions within her community when she married a man from Cape Verde.

Peter's father also endured tensions within his community due to his choice of spouse. He had grown up in a very ethnically diverse place: Centuries of intermixing between Portuguese colonists and the native Africans who lived in Cape Verde produced an extremely eclectic population, and Cape Verdeans wear this genetic diversity on their very faces, in their skin tones, and in their hair textures. Classifying people by the color of their skin was far more difficult—more subtle, really—in Cape Verde than in 1930s Massachusetts.

"My father," said Peter, "was always described as having married a colored woman, and I think there was resentment there with the other Cape Verdeans who tended to identify themselves as white. When somebody like Father crossed the line as far as they were concerned, that just confirmed in their minds the worst. They would rather be at the lowest end of the white scale than counted as colored people, which made sense in the 1920s and the 1930s. If you had a choice, that's what you did. So there are people darker than I who were Cape Verdeans who trained themselves to be white, and if there was ever an issue about where they fell on the racial register, they always chose the white side of it."

Peter's father, however, was different. He was fairly light-skinned, yet he identified himself as black—or colored, as they said at the time. According to Peter, his grandfather did, too, and this was very confusing to him. "As a child," he said, "I couldn't understand why there were people darker than I who said they were white, because to be colored, as we were in those days, to quote a distinguished book, was an honorable thing, a very honorable thing. And the minority establishment community was African American. That was the community with which my mother naturally identified here in Plymouth. Father was somewhat marginalized in a strange sort of way. But my father always identified with colored people. And by marrying my mother, he was subject to tremendous criticism from his own people for doing that."

Peter believes that his father embraced his black heritage and turned away from his Cape Verdean background in order to please his wife. "He was so into assimilation," said Peter. "I think it was to please my mother.

He didn't spend a great deal of time talking to me, his only son, about the old country and Portuguese culture. He wasn't embarrassed by it, but it wasn't his subject."

These feelings were undoubtedly influenced by the fact that Peter's mother, Orissa, thought of the Cape Verdeans as being decidedly lower-class than the African Americans in general and the black middle class more particularly. Indeed, she referred to her husband's countrymen dismissively as being "his people"—considered them foreigners and treated them largely with condescension (the one exception being her father-in-law, Manuel Gomes).

As a result of these attitudes, according to Peter, many black people in Plymouth thought of the Gomeses' union with disdain as being an interracial marriage, but one with a most curious twist. "To the Cape Verdeans, Mama was always 'Mrs. Gomes, colored lady,' " he said. "And Father was supposed to be white if he had been consistent with the rest of the Cape Verde community. Because they all thought they were white. And so it was very interesting. On the other hand," Peter continued, "My mother was accepted in the upper reaches of the black community because of her style, but also because of her people. She had come from Virginia. Her father was a preacher, she was a princess, and she acted that way, and they understood that. But my father used to say to her—with a sense of irony—'Before I married you, these people who are inviting us to dinner wouldn't give me the time of day, these black Americans.' And that was absolutely true. It was my mother who introduced my father into a social circle that he was excluded from before, and, ironically, he didn't introduce her to any social circles, because by marrying her he essentially left his society."

Peter firmly believes that his independent character and strong moral compass were forged in his childhood observations of his parents. "I inherited all of this, because here I was, the child of this colored woman and this singular man. And so I had a kind of peculiar status, which was a great advantage to me. I was special—or different. Everybody knew it. I wasn't just the colored boy, and I certainly wasn't the Cape Verdean kid. I was all of that and then some, which was a peculiar position to hold."

As an example of this, Peter told me a very interesting story. "I remember," he said, "that in sixth grade in the Mount Pleasant school, we put on a Thanksgiving play. I was Governor Bradford, and the daughter of the chief banker in Plymouth was my wife. She was white as the driven snow. This was in 1955."

This, I think, is truly unusual. No black boy would have ever stood up on a school stage and played at being married to a white girl in Piedmont, West Virginia, where I was growing up at the time. It never would have happened in thousands of towns across the South, not to mention all the big cities in the North. Yet it happened to Peter when he was a boy, and it still warms him to recall it. "I was so proud of myself," he said, "not because this was something interracial. Race never entered into it. It was just that—well, Governor Bradford. That's a big part, and I was given it. And I was very good at it. My father said—and I heard him say it to my mother, he didn't say it to me—he said, 'He thinks he's a Pilgrim.' And I never knew there was anything incongruous about that."

Malcolm X said famously that our people didn't land on Plymouth Rock. Plymouth Rock landed on our people. At Harvard we joke that when the Pilgrims landed on Plymouth Rock, Peter Gomes was waiting to welcome them. And Peter views the world of the Pilgrims with great respect, even reverence. "You see, I grew up with the story," he said. "I knew the story better than anybody else, and I was rewarded for my knowledge. I got a job in the Plymouth library; then I got a job in the museum. I was at the front desk—the voice of the Pilgrim Society. If you wanted to know whether your ancestor was a Pilgrim, I was the guy you talked to. I didn't see anything incongruous about *that*. In Plymouth you grew up on one side of the issue or the other. Either you found the Pilgrims interesting or you despised them. I found them interesting, and I felt I needed to study more, and I did so."

To further complicate the picture, Peter tells me that when he was growing up, he strongly identified with his mother's side of the family—much more so than with his father's side. "My mother had the stronger influence, and she intended that it be so, and it was. My father was very reticent about his family, didn't talk much about the old country. He was very keen on assimilation, which I think was due to the fact that he had married this woman who had very little patience for this Old World stuff. And people marvel, for example, that my father didn't teach me Portuguese, which I should have learned. I now regret that I didn't, but it was just not a done thing, and he wasn't going to do that."

Peter says that he never considered himself to be any race other than black. "I remember in school we still had to designate race, and I always put down 'colored' and then eventually 'Negro.' There was no question in my mind—or in either of my parents' minds—that we were anything other than Negro. I learned all about heroes of the race: Booker T. Washington, Frederick Douglass. And we went to the colored church, the African Methodist Episcopal church and then to the Baptist church. And all I knew about the Cape Verdean culture were these neighbors and other people who weren't quite like us and with whom it was not easy to communicate, because they had a different worldview. I was colored, and they weren't—though they looked just like me. They all were nappy-headed and they were sometimes darker, but they were white. But I never understood that, and that level of discourse was not encouraged in our house."

There was, however, a significant culture clash in the Gomes household, as tastes and preferences in everything from food to language to music differed between his parents. "My mother tried in her early days to cook what she thought Father would like," recalled Peter. "She tried to learn his people's dishes. There is a big rice-and-beans thing, and it has to be done just the right way—it's what we might call a risotto today. And she tried to make this stuff, and it was awful, and I think my father said, 'Let's don't go there.' You know? He just told her to give that up and do what she did best."

I find these stories of intra-black cultural clashes quite instructive and fascinating. The relationship they describe and the racial attitudes they evoke might seem like relics of a bygone era, yet I think they are still occurring today to an unprecedented degree, given the great migration of Africans to the United States since 1990 and the massive influx of black Latin Americans and Caribbeans. In fact, more Africans have come to this country willingly since 1990 than came to this country in the entire slave trade. African American culture is a result of a complex cultural fusion among those fifty African ethnic identities and the Euro-American culture of the master, starting deep in the painful history of slavery. Slavery was many things, but it was first and last a clash and fusion of cultures.

Of course, in 1930s Massachusetts the deepest racial tensions were between blacks and whites, not between blacks and African immigrants. Peter remembers the racism of America during his youth vividly and says that it was a frequent topic of discussion between his parents.

"I was always listening in on adult conversations that were none of my business," he said. "And they were very race-conscious. They were very much aware that the respectable black middle-class people from their point of view were often badly treated. There was a policeman who should have been made chief of police but wasn't. There was a fireman who suffered various indignities. There was a man in the post office. There were all of these situations. They never said to me, 'Now, you watch out when somebody calls you nigger.' They never said that. But I was greatly aware that there were problems. And their way of preparing me for dealing with the real world was to tell me that I was better than everybody else, you know? 'You go out there and you let them know you are the best at this and you are the best at that and you have nothing to apologize for.' That was their attitude for their son. So I did that, and I personally encountered very little that I can recite as racist treatment."

Growing up in Plymouth, Peter found that his cultural life was largely circumscribed by the town's small black community. He was well aware of the difference between whites and blacks—and well aware that he was a member of a decided minority. Yet he says he did not feel "second best" and loves the memories that he has of Plymouth's extremely tight, intergenerational black community. It was here, he says, that he was introduced to the church and to the religious calling to which he has devoted his life. I was fascinated, as we explored these memories, by the degree to which Peter's experience, so remarkably different from my own and from that of most African Americans in this book, still shared many points of contact with the traditional African American experience, especially as it relates to the church's seminal impact on black culture. For example, in talking about Plymouth's black community, I was surprised to learn that Plymouth would fill up with black servants in the summer, attending to their wealthy white employers at their summer homes—and these servants, coming from many different parts of the country, would all gather in Peter's church, filling the young boy's mind with new ideas and influences.

"Plymouth was extraordinary in summer," said Peter. "Because in those days there were still white people who were well-to-do enough to summer in Plymouth for a month or two, and they'd bring what we used to refer to as their help—their chauffeur, their cook, their maid, their nanny, their so-and-so. And they'd set up house in Duxbury or Kingston, and they'd all come to our little church. In wintertime maybe there were a dozen people there. In the summertime it was forty or fifty black folks. They sang songs we'd never heard of before. They loved to show off with their little country cousins. And that's where we heard the latest gospel songs from Chicago and New York and Philadelphia. It was a whole different world. It looked like what I thought Harlem must have looked like. And Sunday night the white people would sit on their porches listening to the singing coming out of Bethel Church. It was a wonderful world."

In later decades similar church gatherings would be filled with talk of civil rights—of marches and boycotts—as well as of music, food, and family. And, in fact, in Peter's youth such things were undoubtedly beginning to be discussed, perhaps out of earshot of curious young boys.

I asked Peter why he thought the church has been so important to the African American community. We take it for granted that it was important to our ancestors under slavery and in the post–Civil War South, but as his story illustrates, even in what I had long considered to be lily-white Plymouth the church was tremendously significant. Why? Peter didn't hesitate to answer. "It was important because it was *ours*," he said. "It was one of the few things that was uniquely and irretrievably ours. Couldn't be taken away. We owned it. And it had an institutional life and identity. It was important to us, and we were important to it. I think that's what the secret of the church is. And I don't think it had anything to do with theology. That was quite secondary. It was ours. Nobody could take it from us, and we

Jacob White, Peter's grandfather, was born a slave and decided to become a preacher after a near-death experience.

could shape how it was going to work."

The black church has certainly been a palpable presence in Peter's mother's family for quite some time. Moving back a generation on Peter's maternal line, we looked at his mother's father. He was Jacob Merritt Pedford White, born a slave in Virginia in December of 1863. Peter never knew Jacob. He died in 1914, long before Peter was born. But Peter remembers that his mother adored her father and was very proud that her son chose to follow his path. "She always talked with great affection about Papa the preacher," said Peter.

Jacob's journey to religion was unusual, far different from that of his grandson. "He was a high flier," said Peter. "He dressed well, he spoke well. He had a big conversion, sort of like the apostle Paul. And apparently, before his conversion, my grandfather lived a wild and crazy life—what they once called a 'sportin' life.' He was charming, facile, very good with words, very romantic. And two things happened to him. First, he met my grandmother, Candace, who sort of tamed him down. And second, he had a religious conversion. He nearly died and was speechless, couldn't see, was in some kind of a state for several days. People prayed over him and whatnot. And the first thing he did when he recovered from this is, he went to see the minister of the Tremont Temple Baptist Church in Boston. And that led him to the Christian faith."

Peter grew up hearing wild, dramatic stories about his grandfather's conversion, in a home peppered with his photographs—in all of which Jacob looks truly magnetic. His wife, Peter's grandmother, had a strong personality as well. She was Candace Annabelle Williams, born in June 1869, also in Virginia. She died when Peter was five, so it is not surprising that he has no specific memories of her. Nevertheless, he vividly recalls that she was treated with reverence by her entire family. "She had her own mythic presence," said Peter, "a very large presence. She was apparently very handsome, very stylish, and very distinguished. And, I am told, had strong views on everything. She was the spine that was in my mother."

Since Peter's grandfather Jacob died early, at the age of fifty-one, Candace had to raise her nine children and manage her household alone. It was an awesome responsibility, but she embraced it fully. "She was the preacher's widow," said Peter, "and so she knew her part, and she did all these sorts of things. She had wisdom. She was the one that said to Mother, you know, 'You better look to yourself, dear, because you are not getting any younger and no prettier.' She knew how the world went."

Our research revealed that Candace and Jacob White met in Virginia and married in 1893. They moved north to Massachusetts a few years later, joining relations in the Boston area. They were southern blacks arriving at the very beginning of what would become the Great Migration, and they entered a world of middle-class life that was virtually unknown to most African Americans from the post–Civil War South, to which they adapted quickly. "They had relatives up here," recalled Peter, "in Providence, Rhode Island, and all around Boston. Very respectable, upper-class Negro relatives. They were not strangers."

Once in Boston, Peter's grandfather Jacob worked as a porter and a waiter. These were tough jobs in some ways, but they represented a significant improvement upon the farm labor Jacob had done in Virginia to support his preaching. More important, Jacob was able to advance his ministry, becoming a deacon at the Union Baptist Church in Boston. Many of the members of this church were displaced southerners like him and his wife. Indeed, many had been born in the Tidewater region of Virginia.

Like so many black churches, Union Baptist was more than a religious site—it was also a hub for the community's social, political, educational, and economic activity. Peter recalls attending Union Baptist Church several times with his mother, long after his grandfather's death. "It was incredible," he said. "When she took me in, she was greeted and hailed. I thought it was magnificent. Of course, when you are young, any place looks vast. But I thought it was Westminster Abbey. I had no idea. It is a small little church. But very inspiring. Their motto was 'Built by Black Hands,' because it was. They didn't buy a derelict church. They built that church with their own black hands."

Long after Peter's grandfather's death, the Union Baptist Church would be central to the black community in and around Boston for decades to come, influencing the political and religious life of the city through the civil-rights era and beyond. "The first black man elected to the city council was a Union man," said Peter, smiling. "There was a great sense of pride, and the people who went to Union Baptist Church thought of themselves as pretty upper-crust. They were high-school graduates at the very least."

Peter himself grew up attending the African Methodist Episcopal church in Plymouth, where his mother played the piano and organized the choir. They later switched to the black Baptist church there, and he has been a Baptist ever since. Peter is quite articulate about how his family's history with the church has shaped and informed his religious beliefs. But the process has been more complicated than I would have ever imagined. "My mother," he said, "had an ambiguous relationship with the church. She was devoted to her father, but the fact that he died so young, in his early fifties—she always blamed the church for that. She always felt they had driven him to death, worked him too hard, never paid him enough, and he was so good, he just put himself out, and she felt she had been abandoned. So she always had that little bit there."

On the other side of his family, according to Peter, was his father, who was a lapsed Catholic and for much of Peter's youth was largely unaffected by religion. "If he'd gone anywhere," said Peter, "he should have gone to the Roman Catholic church. And as an immigrant boy he did go, and he was laughed at because he had funny clothes and an accent. So he didn't bother anymore. And his view was that preachers were a bunch of men who didn't work, who didn't do anything, and lived off women. That was his view of the clergy."

When I was going over our research prior to meeting with Peter, it had seemed to me that Peter came from a long line of ministers and that he had quite naturally fallen into the calling. But given his parents' attitudes, I was forced to reevaluate this theory. And I found myself returning to it over and over in our conversation. What, I wanted to know, had led Peter to the ministry? "The church was on my case," he finally told me. "They thought I was a gifted little kid. I could memorize. I had a good voice. I liked church, it's fun. And of course my mother thought I was going to succeed Grandpapa and to fulfill his ambitions and so forth. So everybody *thought* I was going to be a preacher. But it wasn't that easy."

Peter said that he struggled with his feelings about the ministry for a long time, undoubtedly influenced by the conflicted feelings of his parents. Finally, when he was about fifteen years old, he says that he began to feel a true calling inside him. He spoke about it with his father and, unsurprisingly, received little support.

"I remember," he said. "I can almost feel the sun as it was that day. And I said, 'Daddy, I think I've been called.' And my father looked at me and he said, 'I had always hoped my blood would do honest work.' And I knew enough to know what that meant. He wasn't opposed to what I was going to do, but it was clear he had a very jaundiced view of the black clergy in general. If I was going to become one of them, well, he would accept it. But only grudgingly. And it hurt me. Because in a funny sort of way, even though I was closer to my mother, I wanted to please my father. And it was clear to me that the thing I thought I wanted to do most in life was something he didn't approve of. He did not want me to become a cranberry picker. He wanted greater things for me than that. He was very ambitious, and he and my mother, they shared that ambition. But the clergy?"

After a long pause, Peter shrugged and smiled at me, confident now in the decisions that were so torturous for him to make as a young man. "You know," he said, "everything I have done in my life, I think in a very subtle way has been trying to prove to my father—almost forty long years dead—that I do honest work."

Happily, Peter says, there is a coda to the story. In the fall of 1961, the year Peter went off to college, his father joined his mother in the Baptist church and for the last seven years of his life was an active member of the parish. "He became a deacon in that church," said Peter gleefully. "He gave his life to it, and he said to me, 'If I had known it was going to be like this, I'd have done it years ago.' My mother was so thrilled. And the pastor relied on him, because my father had what the old folks used to call 'mother wit.' He had common sense. He was a very good judge of character, which is why he was a good boss. And he was a great help in the church, though he didn't have any heavy-duty theological stuff. It became a wonderful thing."

I was riveted by Peter's stories about his parents and by his honesty about the struggles they all shared. That their dispute over Peter's choice of a career as a preacher had ended happily during his father's lifetime was a source of genuine pleasure to me, as was Peter's father's certain reconciliation with the church. Turning back to his ancestry, I was delighted that I had a story from his family's past that I thought might deepen Peter's appreciation of his religious roots.

We were able to trace the line of Peter's maternal grandfather, the minister Jacob White, back several generations to find a most compelling story, a story quite unusual in African American history. Jacob's parents were Henry White, born in 1828 in Southampton County, Virginia, and Antoinette Bailey, born in 1830 in Surry County, Virginia. (Genealogical records of the time often spelled the county name "Surrey.") Antoinette's parents, Peter's great-great-grandparents, were Isaac Bailey, born in 1795 in Virginia, and Marya Bailey, who was born in Southampton County, Virginia, in about 1800. These two people were born more than sixty years before the outbreak of the Civil War. And while most of us assume that all of our ancestors from this period were slaves, it's not always the case. In 1860, about 4.4 million black people lived in the United States. Of that number, 4 million lived in the South, while the rest lived in the North and in the West. Of the entire 4.4 million, there were about 488,000 free people of color. Two hundred and twenty-five thousand of them lived in free states, which means, incredibly, that about 261,000 free Negroes lived in states in which slavery was legal. And when the war broke out, most did not move. They continued their lives as free Negroes, unmolested in the main by the Confederates and the war. Reading the slave narratives or standard accounts of black history, we tend to assume that all the slaves who could took the Underground Railroad to the North—but they didn't. Scholars estimate that perhaps only 50,000 slaves escaped to freedom while over a quarter of a million free blacks lived stable lives as free Negroes in the South! This fact shocked me when I first learned it, and I think the vast majority of people—including many scholars—are completely unaware of this puzzling part of our history.

Unbeknownst to Peter, Isaac and Marya Bailey were among this small minority of free blacks in the antebellum South. We discovered this when we searched what were known as the "free registers" of Surry County, Virginia. Every antebellum southern state had its own way of keeping its eye on free blacks. In Virginia, if you were a free black, every three years you had to register with your town clerk, who would record your age, your name, and by whom you had been emancipated. The odds of finding one of your relatives in such a register are slim, but in the case of the Baileys they paid off handsomely. The free registers of Surry County, Virginia, include the following entry: "Isaac Bailey a Negro man was born of free parents, is five feet, five and three quarter inches high, has short hair, narrow forehead, large nose, round nostrils, thick lips is stout, and well made. Rather inclined to be bow legged and is about twenty-one years of age. He is registered in the clerk's office of the county court of Surry of the above description and is number 206 pursuant to an act of the general assembly of Virginia entitled to an act more effectually to restrain the practice of Negroes going at large, this 24th day of September 1816."

This means that Peter's great-great-grandfather Isaac Bailey had become a free person of color by 1816. Peter recalled that his mother often said that some of her people were known as "Free Ishies"—a phrase that I had not heard before and which Peter could never decipher. But it obviously referred to the fact that free blacks were issued papers so that they could prove their status legally in case they were challenged by some white man intent upon returning them to slavery. This, of course, is one of the many chilling aspects of black life in America prior to emancipation. Even if you were free, you had to be able to prove it, and even this sort of deed of registration did not always protect you; you were in constant danger of being reenslaved, and you were often being watched. This is why the description on Isaac Bailey's registration is so carefully detailed—officials wanted to make sure his papers could not be transferred, shared, or used to facilitate another slave's escape.

Peter was surprised and excited to learn that Isaac Bailey had been a free black, and he wanted to find out as much as we possibly could about him. A certificate that accompanied his 1816 registration yielded a very important piece of additional information. It read, in part, "The bearer Isaac Bailey was born of free parents, emancipated by Sam Bailey," and it was signed by a man named Joshua Pretlow. This certificate had been generated because freed slaves in Southampton were required always to carry a written statement from a white person vouching for their status. Every county in the South had some kind of law like this—it is not remarkable— but the paperwork that particular law generated turned out to be crucial in our quest to reconstruct Peter Gomes's family tree. Records such as this explain why it is generally far easier to reconstruct the family history of a person descended from free Negroes than from persons who remained enslaved until the end of the Civil War.

Knowing that a man named Sam Bailey had emancipated the parents of Isaac Bailey and that a man named Joshua Pretlow was willing to vouch for that fact, we began to expand our research. We soon uncovered a list of free Negroes and "mollatoes" (as they wrote it there) compiled by officials in Southampton County, Virginia, in 1821. Here Isaac Bailey and his wife, Marya, are listed by name, as living on the property of Robert Pretlow, a wealthy white landlord and almost certainly a relative of the Joshua Pretlow who had signed Isaac's certificate of freedom. Further research revealed that Isaac and Marya lived on this man Pretlow's estate for over twenty-five years and that Sam Bailey's daughter Ann had married a man named Thomas Pretlow—thus establishing a link between the Pretlow and Bailey families.

This raised a compelling question: Why did these two white families—the Pretlows and the Baileys—emancipate and help support Peter's ancestors? The answer lies one generation further back on his family tree, with Isaac's parents, Ben and Rose Bailey, Peter's great-great-great-grandparents.

Ben Bailey was born in Surry County, Virginia, in 1769. His future wife, Rose, was born in the same area two years later. Both were born into slavery, but unlike the overwhelming majority of their fellow African Americans, they were not fated to die in it. We found a deed of emancipation signed in 1782, which indicated that Rose Bailey—like Isaac Bailey—was freed by a white man named Samuel Bailey! It reads, in part, "I, Samuel Bailey, of Surry County in Virginia, being fully persuaded that freedom is the natural right of all mankind and that it is my duty to do unto others as I would desire to be done in a like situation. And having under my care 17 Negroes whom I have heretofore held as slaves, of the following names and ages, Nat aged about 65 years; Harry about 60; Rose about 11; all and every one of which I also hereby emancipate and set free."

Finding a document such as this is a deeply emotional experience. My face flushed as I read it. And it is as rare as rare can be. Remember: It was written in 1782. The American Revolution was not yet over. Samuel Bailey was on the cutting edge of enlightened slaveholders across an entire new country in the making. He was far ahead of George Washington, Thomas Jefferson, and all but the very most forward-thinking whites of his age. Moreover, he seems to have come from a family of like-minded people. While Peter's ancestor Rose was freed by Bailey, her husband, Ben, is not mentioned. This prompted us to search the papers of Samuel Bailey's relatives, leading us to his brother, Dr. Anselm Bailey. Here we learned that Anselm Bailey, as it turns out, emancipated Peter's great-great-great-grandfather Ben Jr. Peter Gomes is descended on his mother's side from *two* lines of free Negroes, starting in 1782.

Why were these white Baileys so uncharacteristically willing to emancipate the black Baileys, their slaves? The answer, appropriately enough for Peter, lies in their religion. The Baileys were among the most prominent Quaker families in southeastern Virginia, as were their kinsmen, the Pretlows. And unlike most of their countrymen, Quakers believed that America should live up to its ideals of liberty and freedom. By 1800 most Quakers in Surry and Southampton counties had freed all their slaves. What's more, the Bailey and Pretlow families were committed abolitionists, and they worked together not only to free slaves but also to help them rebuild their lives as free people of color. Indeed, documents show that the relationship between these black and white families was very deeply intertwined. We discovered that in 1880, almost one hundred years after the white Baileys had emancipated Ben and Rose, their son, Peter's great-great-grandfather Isaac, was living in Southampton county next door to a white man named D. L. Pretlow. He was a relative of the white Baileys—which means that the two families had stayed in intimate contact for over a century.

"This is *extraordinary*," Peter exclaimed. I concurred. We both became tearful. After a poignant interlude, we then began to discuss how these remarkably unusual stories of freedom in slavery helped us to understand the complexity of relationships between blacks and whites in the slave era.

"I remember," Peter reflected, "my mother used to say how her mother—my grandmother—believed that racial relations in the North would always be difficult, because the colored people and the white people didn't know one another, whereas in the South, even though there had been terrible difficulties, they knew one another and they cared for one another. I could never understand what she was talking about. It was all so abstract. But this helps me understand it, because these white and black families lived side by side, and they had a relationship that we certainly would never have seen between free whites and free blacks in an urban setting in the North before the Civil War. That has to be what Grandma meant. It's really quite extraordinary."

Peter said to me that he now understood that his mother's aristocratic leanings were traceable not to the free Negro community in the North, as he had long thought, but to deeper and longer roots in the South. "That feels pretty good," he said, beaming. "I knew there had been an independent streak in us. I didn't know that it existed in the South. I thought it was a result of their having come north. But it's all the more impressive we are talking about Virginia at the end of the eighteenth century—when there was no particular reason to expect relatively cordial relationships, much less benevolent relationships. It's a wonderful discovery."

I have often heard Peter credit his own success to the nurturing he received from his mother and the high sense of self-esteem that her family possessed—their profound belief that they were part of a black aristocracy and were thus entitled to achieving the highest of aspirations. It is interesting to think that this self-esteem may have originated not in Boston in the late nineteenth century but in Virginia a hundred years earlier, amid all the horror of slavery—not, as it were, through descent from the *Mayflower* but rather descent from a different sort of nobility, a nobility southern and black. I wonder how our nation's history would have been different if these early abolitionists—these Quakers motivated by their desire to do right before God, literally and figuratively in fear of God— had succeeded in ending slavery as an institution at the close of the Revolutionary War. We can only contemplate what American history, and American race relations, would have been like under those circumstances.

"The Quakers," said Peter, echoing my thought, "were really well ahead of everybody else in recognizing the moral compromises of the Revolution. We have had two centuries of trouble because the Founding Fathers could not square their conscience with their desire to maintain the benefits of the status quo, the benefits of slavery. Had they cleaned house at the beginning, who knows what would have happened? Who knows how great this nation could have been? How much we would have been spared."

Returning to his family's past, I was able to take Peter back even further along the Bailey line to Ben's father, Peter's great-great-great-great-grandfather, Ben Bailey Sr. Manumission records indicate that he also was freed by Dr. Anselm Bailey in 1782 when he was approximately forty years old, which means that he was born around 1740. For an African American, this is a bit like an English person being able to trace their ancestors to 1066.

We were able to learn how Ben Bailey Sr. fared as a free Negro because we discovered his will, in which he instructed his estate be sold to pay off his debts and the remaining property to be given to his wife, Lucy. When he passed away in 1802, that estate included three sheep, one heifer, three cows, two yearlings, two sows, two barrows, six shoats, one horse, one bed, one linen wheel, and an assortment of furniture. The total value was appraised at sixty-four pounds. This was a sizable amount of money for a farmer at that time. Ben clearly flourished in freedom.

What's more, knowing that Ben Sr. would have been in his thirties during the Revolutionary War, I wondered if he had perhaps served on either side in the conflict. Our researchers located the February 1778 payroll list for the Fifth Virginia Regiment of the Continental army. It indicates that a man named Ben Bailey served in the regiment. The document does not indicate whether this Ben Bailey was white or black—but his age is roughly commensurate with that of Peter's ancestor. So there is certainly a chance that Peter's great-great-great-great-grandfather may have been a black patriot, as was my own fourth great-grandfather, John Redman, and an ancestor of Sara Lawrence-Lightfoot's, as we shall see.

"I am going to look into that some more," said Peter, eagerly examining the ancient pay record. "That makes me feel pretty good. You know? Short of finding a Pilgrim ancestor or a member of the royal family, this is pretty impressive as far as I'm concerned. I am over the moon with this."

Less than 1 percent of the African American people today can trace their ancestry back to the middle of the eighteenth century. But Peter can. Like every African American, he has deep roots, but because of the heritage of freedom within his family lines he has deep roots that he can name, roots that can be documented.

Looking back on our earlier conversation—remembering the sense of specialness that Peter attached to his mother's family—I wondered if even the subconscious knowledge of these deep roots had somehow shaped her. Peter felt that it definitely had.

"My mother sort of knew this," said Peter. "I think—at least on some level. I don't think she knew these details, but she had this instinctive sense that had been passed to her from her mother and her grandmother.

This sense that we come from people. I remember when *Roots* was on the television. I remember Mother saying, 'What was so special about those people? They didn't seem to amount to very much.' She was very dismissive about the whole thing. And I don't have any evidence, but I think she knew, she had this instinctual feeling, that we come from people who are somebody."

At this point our genealogical research into Peter's family had exhausted itself. On his mother's side, we could go back no further than Ben Bailey Sr. and his wife, Lucy—both born into slavery in 1740s Virginia. And on his father's side, we go back only to his grandfather Manuel Lobo, born in Cape Verde around 1890.

Peter's DNA, however, was able to tell us a great deal more. Peter had assumed that he had some European ancestry because of the Portuguese history in Cape Verde, and according to our results his hunch was correct. His admixture tests reveal that he is 31 percent European and 69 percent sub-Saharan African (he has no Native American ancestry). This surprises him somewhat. "I thought that my father's people were the results of matings between the natives of Cape Verde and Africans, so that whatever white there was in the Cape Verde would be diminished by the African. So that thirty-one percent is higher than I would have imagined."

To my mind the figure suggests that Peter has white ancestors not only in Cape Verde but also in Virginia. Peter has heard family rumors that confirm this. "I remember my mother saying Sandy Williams—who was her grandfather—had red hair. And a Negro with red hair? That's why they call him Sandy, you know? And apparently he got into a fight with this man. I don't know if it was a duel or what, but he resented being called white. I've always heard about that."

Alexander "Sandy" Williams was Peter's great-grandfather. He was born in 1853 in Virginia. That's a long time ago and a world away. And yet stories of Sandy's skin and hair color persist, having been passed on from generation to generation. This, I think, is deeply illustrative of our nation's obsession with race, as well as the African American fascination with the complexity of our family's origins and with a certain fluidity of the color line, especially as measured through the Y-DNA of African Amer-

Incredibly, our research allowed us to discover this man, Christiano Gomes—Peter's genetic cousin!

ican males, a quarter of whom descend from a European male ancestor. Peter agrees with me wholeheartedly, even as he attempts to come to terms with the fact that he himself is one-third European.

Moving on, I told Peter that our testing of his Y-DNA had given us some unusually specific information about his father's line. As you will recall, when we conduct these tests, we isolate the DNA in a subject's Y chromosome—DNA that has been passed down directly through the paternal line, just like a family name from father to son to son. We then compare this genetic signature to global databases of signatures taken from people all over the world today. If we can find someone with the same fingerprint, then we've found a person with whom our subject shares a common ancestor—a distant cousin, so to speak. With Peter we found something special: someone with whom he shares an overwhelming amount of genetic information, so much that we wondered if we might be able to learn more about his father's side of the family from this man. So we contacted him, and we learned that he, too, was born, like Peter's father, in Cape Verde—on Fogo, the island next to Brava, where Peter's father was born. Even more remarkable, this man's name is Christiano Gomes. The surname matches, and—unbelievably—he is living today in Massachusetts and working at MIT, just down Massachusetts Avenue from Peter's church in Harvard Yard: genetic cousins, from the same island with the same surname, working unawares down the street from each other in the same town!

We asked Christiano what he knew about the Gomes side of his family. He told us about his relatives in Cape Verde, all of whom are distant cousins of his. They all live on Fogo today. And they are undoubtedly Peter's cousins as well.

Christiano also told us a fascinating story. He says that the male members of the Gomes family used to practice an unusual ritual: When someone in the family died, they would give up shaving for a month. Peter immediately recognized this as a Jewish mourning ritual. But why on earth would people in a predominantly Roman Catholic African country practice a Jewish ritual? Christiano believes that it is because his direct paternal line led back to Portugal, to a Jew who had been forced to convert to Catholicism in the Middle Ages and then fled to Cape Verde to escape the Portuguese Inquisition of the late fifteenth and early sixteenth centuries. Could this be possible?

To investigate this claim, we combed the Portuguese archives for records containing the name Gomes. And we found that these records list a number of people with this surname who were "judged to be Jews." Some confessed, some recanted their faith, and many were sentenced to death at the stake. This suggested that Peter could conceivably have Jewish ancestry on his direct paternal line.

For final confirmation, we returned to his DNA. Our testing of his Y-DNA revealed a remarkable number of matches among people of Ashkenazi and Sephardic Jewish descent. A map showing the geographic distribution of the people who share his Y-DNA markers revealed no matches with people living in Africa today, but rather a dense concentration of matches in the town of Bratislava, which is located in Slovakia and has long been a center of Eastern European Jewish life. After discussing the issue in detail with historians of sixteenth-century Portugal and Spain, I am convinced that Peter is almost undoubtedly descended from a Jewish man on his father's side—most likely a Jewish man who fled to the Cape Verde islands sometime around the year 1529 when the Inquisition turned its attention to Portugal's Jewish population. There this man had children with an African woman, giving rise to Peter's paternal line—and ultimately supplying Harvard University with one of its greatest religious minds, a devout black Baptist who is passionate about his adopted kins-men, the Pilgrims.

"You must be kidding," said Peter, laughing. "I don't know what to make of it. Every family worth belonging to has Jews in it somewhere or other, so I guess that shouldn't surprise me. The logic is inescapable. It makes perfect sense."

We also tested Peter's mitochondrial DNA to try to see where in Africa his first direct ancestor on his mother's line originated. The tests yielded exact matches with the Fulani people, the Tikar people, and the Hausa people, all in the area of what is now Cameroon. To narrow the results, I spoke with John Thornton and Linda Heywood and learned that slaves were not taken out of present-day Cameroon until late in the slavery pe-riod, which means that whichever tribe Peter's ancestor came from prob-ably lived elsewhere and migrated to this region. The only group among Peter's matches that fits this criterion is the Fulani people. They spread from Guinea and Senegal to present-day Cameroon within a time period that makes sense given the history of slavery. Indeed, the Fulani spread across much of west-central Africa, which was the region that supplied Virginia with many of its slaves—further substantiating the possibility that Peter's original enslaved ancestor is of Fulani descent.

"That's quite extraordinary," said Peter. "I've never heard the word 'Fulani' mentioned in any family business of mine. It's shocking in a way, because there's a strange sort of security in not knowing a great deal about yourself. There's a sense that it is all sort of mystical and lost and nobody ever will find it, so you could sort of invent any past you wanted to. Well, I can't do that now. I mean, there is a reality there, and I will have to learn more about the Fulani."

He said this with a broad smile, as if learning about the Fulani would be a great pleasure to him. But I was struck by his choice of words. I had not really considered, when I began this project, the degree to which some of us may prefer to cling to a sense of mystery about our African and European family past rather than learn the names and ethnic identities of our ancestors. Of course, hearing Peter say it, it made much sense to me. There's something thrilling about the unknown. There are infinite possibilities in a mystery. While I have long yearned for the facts of my ancestry, I can easily understand why another person might feel otherwise.

As we said good-bye, I asked Peter about this. Would he have preferred not to know some of what he had learned? He immediately shook his head and took my hand. "Oh, no." he said. "You want to be somebody, not just anybody—to paraphrase Jesse Jackson. And I am somebody. I am a very particular somebody. There is nobody else like me. And that uniqueness gives a sense of authenticity, a sense of place in the world. For me that is very important. I mean, I know who my people are now, where they came from. So my relationship to places has expanded. Europe, Cape Verde, Africa, Slovakia—that's really sort of mind-boggling. Not to mention Virginia and Plymouth. I've always advocated knowing as much as you can about your place and your past. It gives you stability in the world. You're not just an accident. You're not just a mild statistic. I am thrilled."

Sara Lawrence-Lightfoot

August 22, 1944

S ARA LAWRENCE-LIGHTFOOT is a sociologist, an award-winning author, and like Peter Gomes, my colleague at Harvard. She teaches in the School of Education, where she is a superstar. The people who run Harvard have already decided that they will name a chair after her when she retires. This is a great honor, unprecedented in my experience, and one richly earned. She will be the first African American woman in Harvard's history to have an endowed professorship in her name. I'll be telling my grandkids about her one day.

I was eager to involve Sara in this project, because many years ago I read her excellent book *Balm in Gilead.* Part autobiography, part family history, *Balm in Gilead* recounts the history of a most unusual black family. Sara's family's story stayed with me for more than a decade. And now, with all the advances we've made in DNA and genealogical research, I wanted to look at her family myself, just to see what else I could find. Sara and I were both very happy with the results. Our researchers were able to uncover many things she did not know and offer tangible evidence of things she had long believed from her family's oral tradition but had never been able to prove. In the process, my admiration of Sara's heritage only grew. It is, I believe now, an extraordinarily unique family history—both within the confines of the family stories contained in this book and within the whole of African American history. For Sara is descended from one of the oldest and longest lines of free Negroes in the history of the United

States. While hers is one of three family trees that we analyzed with deep roots in the free Negro community, going back to the first half of the eighteenth century, Sara's line of descent from free Negroes is the oldest and longest that I have encountered doing genealogical or historical research.

Sara Lawrence-Lightfoot's parents, Margaret and Charles Lawrence, a few years before her birth.

Sara was born on August 22, 1944, in Nashville, Tennessee. Her parents, Margaret and Charles Lawrence, were both part of black America's very small, very marginalized intellectual elite of that time. Her mother was a doctor and a psychologist who focused on poor children; her father was a sociologist who specialized in race relations, education, and Marxism. Both were very educated, very political people. There were not many African Americans in the 1940s who had careers like theirs, or who shared the philosophical outlook they had. And Sara is very much a product of her remarkable parents.

Sara spent most of her youth north of New York City in a community called Sky View Acres, an idealistic cooperative, almost a commune, that her parents helped to start in the late 1940s. As Sara described it, it was an interracial community with extremely high moral values, made up of people who were peace activists and civil-rights activists long before such things became fashionable. "My father," she recalled, "had been a conscientious objector during the Second World War, and a number of those men who were doing that kind of work decided that they would try to start a community that was intentionally inclusive—that was a different way of living. It was an incredible experiment."

It was also an experiment that succeeded. Sky View began with about forty-four families, and it survives today with roughly the same number. Indeed, Sara's mother still lives there. And considering when it was founded, Sky View was extremely progressive, part of a burgeoning leftist movement that would become mainstream decades later, including several black-white couples, many of them activists and artists.

Nonetheless, Sara was not a sheltered child. Even though she grew up in this idealistic Garden of Eden, she was exposed to a much wider world and to people whose views were very different from those of her parents. Sky View was located in apple country, surrounded by conservative Republican farmers. "When we got on the school bus," Sara recalled, "they would hold their nose and say 'Nigger' or, more often, 'You dirty Communists.' This was at a time when Communism seemed like the biggest threat in the world. And this community was seen as being very leftist, which it was."

I grew up in West Virginia around the same time as Sara was growing up in Sky View. And when I was a child, we were taught that if somebody called you a nigger, you tried your best to kick his butt. Sara's parents raised her with a different moral code, encouraging the kind of nonviolence that would become a hallmark of the civil-rights movement. "My parents," she said, "taught us if they call you nigger, they must be feeling pretty bad about themselves. They must be feeling as if they have to put someone else down in order to feel good. So my parents just said to us every single day, 'You're gorgeous, you're beautiful, you're fine.' And we thought we were fantastic, and we didn't care what anybody else said."

Sara's parents also exposed her to the absolute cutting edge of black America at the time, welcoming some of the most unusual houseguests one could possibly imagine—Paul Robeson, Marian Anderson, Bayard Rustin. I would have loved to be in that house listening to these adults talking art and politics. So many of us would later discover Paul Robeson or James Baldwin or Ralph Ellison through books and films, in the middle sixties. But Sara discovered them in her living room, more than a decade earlier.

Sara's parents had a very unusual vision for America, a vision we might recognize even today as an unrealized yet admirable goal. It stirred my soul just hearing about it. "They really believed in the idea of a more just society," said Sara. "They believed in integration, real integration. I remember my father saying, when people would claim that integration didn't work, he would say we'd never tried it. We'd never really tried to make the effort to create a society where it wasn't just about desegregation—about bodies sitting next to one another—but instead about developing relationships of trust and rapport and communication between various groups of people, and he felt as if that absolutely had never been tried. And he made a great effort of it. When Martin Luther King came along and talked about nonviolence, this was a person who was almost speaking directly to them."

Thus, from her earliest days, Sara was able to witness the burgeoning civil-rights movement up close. "My father's Ph.D. dissertation was on black activism," she recalled. "So there was this sort of mix of very theoretical and very pragmatic political interest in our house. My parents were always going on peace marches and taking us along. My father went on the first bus rides through the South. And they went to the Selma march. All those things were part of our lives, and we expected them to go off and to come back, or we went with them. And financially, you know, they gave away a lot of their money to the causes that they believed in. My mother always said to my father, 'Don't give away all the money. We need to save some of it to send our kids to college.' And they saved enough for that, but not much more."

Sara's family was so unusual, so uncharacteristic of the black experience in the forties and fifties, that I could not have conceived of their existence in my wildest dreams, growing up as I did in a very small town in eastern West Virginia. They seem like characters in a novel or an idealistic film, so unlike the statistics that characterized black life at this time. I have often wondered what my parents' generation thought when they contemplated the future, especially when they were children. Could they have imagined, in the 1930s or '40s, when they were growing up, the lives that their children would lead? Sara's parents are great subjects to whom to pose this question. They were extremely successful and progressive. Yet could even *they* have foreseen what Sara and her siblings have achieved? I am very curious to know whether it was a surprise to them that they would have a son who was a well-known professor of law (Charles Lawrence) and a daughter who is a Harvard professor of education. I mean, was this a realistic set of goals to envision for their children, even before the *Brown v. Board of Education* decision was rendered in 1954? Were they optimistic about the future? Did they believe that integration would actually come?

Sara herself is not sure. "I think that they imagined us in this place," she said. "But I don't really know. My brother and I, we certainly didn't imagine ourselves this way. I think if you'd asked us at a time when we were growing up, young adults, teenagers, we thought we'd never measure up to our folks."

Nonetheless, Sara is delighted by the ways in which she has followed her parents' path. "The fact is, we find ourselves living lives that are very much like their lives, except probably more visible and more mobile, because the world has changed around us. And this feels like a surprise for everyone—a wonderful surprise. But it surely didn't feel inevitable. I think the teaching-healing legacy that moves through this family over many generations was a force there way before my parents came along. And they experienced that, they gave that to their kids. They got it from their parents. In other words, this teaching-healing legacy—this notion of being identified with what one's parents do, watching them work in the world, leave their imprint on it—it goes back generations. It doesn't begin with my parents, although I think my parents lived it nobly."

Sara and I then began to look at this idea in detail. Her parents were each the product of unusual circumstances—both were born in the North in the early twentieth century and then moved to the South, a reverse migration that almost never occurred in black families in that era. Yet it happened on both sides of Sara's family. I think this has to have had a profound impact on Sara's worldview, on her sense of what it means to be black and an educated person, on what it means about the social responsibility of the educated elite to those less fortunate.

Sara's mother, Margaret Cornelia Morgan, was born August 19, 1914, in New York City. She didn't stay there long, because her father was an Episcopal priest who moved his family from parish to parish, making numerous stops before landing finally in Vicksburg, Mississippi, where Margaret spent most of her youth. Sara's father, Charles Radford Lawrence Jr., was born May 2, 1915, in Boston, Massachusetts. Like his future wife, he also spent most of his youth in the Deep South, growing up in Utica, Mississippi, after his parents moved there to be teachers at the Utica Normal and Industrial Institute, which was a school for African Americans. His parents—Sara's paternal grandparents—were Latitia Burnett Harris (born on October 13, 1893, in Charles City County, Virginia), and Charles Radford Lawrence Sr. (born July 15, 1892, in Knoxville, Tennessee). They settled in Boston after they were married so Sara's father was born in Boston. Yet in 1915 the Lawrences moved back to the South, precisely when so many black people were migrating to the North in one of the great mass movements in American history. This is, as I said, highly unusual. The overwhelming majority of blacks who fled Jim Crow never looked back. Regardless of how bad things might be in the North, they were almost invariably better than what they'd come from. Sara's grandparents are among the tiny minority of black people in the North who made the decision to reverse-migrate to the South. And they did so for the best of reasons: to help others.

"As I understand," said Sara, "they were doing what my parents did after them. They went down to be teachers, to help black communities."

Sara did not know her paternal grandparents well. They died when she was very young. But from talking to her father about them, she developed a strong sense of their characters and motivations, and she thinks that she has some understanding of why they returned to the South. "They thought their work was there," she says. "The most important civil-rights work was there, which was education, and the place where they were needed the most was there."

Looking at photographs of Latitia and Charles, the first thing one notices is that their complexions were extraordinarily light. In fact, the librarian who gave us the photographs of them thought they were white people—and couldn't understand why researchers for an African American genealogy project were interested in them. Sara readily acknowledges this; moreover, she believes that her grandparents' coloring affected their level of success at the time, influencing the way they were treated, by both white people and black.

"My grandfather Charles," she said, "when he was up in Boston, he was working as a porter at the train station, and he looked like a white guy carrying folks' bags. And I think that for sure at that time, and still today, color makes a difference in terms of one's mobility. It was very confusing to him." Even so, Charles insisted on being identified as black—which led to repeated denigration and disrespect of the sort that African Americans received all over this nation at that time. Indeed, according to Sara, one of the reasons Charles wanted to return to the South and work in education was that he believed that the jobs open to blacks were generally intolerable, even in the North.

Sara's grandparents, sensitive to the racism of their day, definitely could have passed as white. Many others did. But they chose not to. I asked Sara why. "It had to do with the deepest, most profound feeling of being identified as African Americans in our society," she replied. "They really felt devoted to the people from whom they came. And they had no wish to pass."

So instead of hiding their race, Sara's grandparents went south, to the Utica Normal and Industrial Institute, seeking to help their people and get at the root causes of the racism they abhorred. Still, even for all their good intentions, the move was quite traumatic. "My grandmother was a very dignified woman," said Sara. "She was very charismatic, very well read, and she hung on to her Boston accent on purpose, you know? She didn't relinquish this northern identity at all. Their house was the one house where everyone who passed through Utica came to dine, white people and black people. George Washington Carver was a good friend. He used to come and dine with them. So there was a way in which I think they brought a kind of intelligentsia, a kind of cosmopolitan reality, to that rural

Sara's grandparents (at left) could have passed for white—but chose not to.

place in the South. But something else which was always true of my father and of his parents, as I understand it, was that they were just respectful of anyone whatever a person's station in life, and so that although they had these relatively fancy friends who passed through, they also were very, very good friends with the people who surrounded them in Utica."

The Utica Normal and Industrial Institute occupies a unique place in African American history. It was modeled after Booker T. Washington's famous Tuskegee Institute, and it pursued the same educational philosophy, a philosophy that seems very alien to many of us today. Students at Utica, both male and female, were there to learn a trade. They were taught how to farm, how to operate machines, how to sew, how to be maids. Its vocational orientation reflected a philosophy of accommodation, of gradual progress. It seems somewhat conservative to many of us now, but in the early twentieth century it was one of the few places in the South offering any kind of decent education to blacks.

As an educator, Sara is especially conscious of both the good and bad embodied in places like Utica and Tuskegee. Indeed, we both have studied Booker T. Washington and his ideas in considerable detail. "I understand it in its time," she said. "I mean, I wouldn't understand it today. Utica trained people for positions in a place in society where they would stay—brick masons, carpenters, largely trades. These are not unimportant, but I think it puts a limit on the possibilities for young people. I think there's a reason to try to educate kids—not train kids, but educate kids—in a way so they have as many choices as possible for as long as possible and so the opportunities are left open for them. But in its time it was a pragmatic and useful strategy for a kind of uplift, a kind of dignity, a training."

I believe that had the Washingtonian educational philosophy been adequately funded, and these well-trained skilled laborers allowed to participate in a free market economy, it could have made a profound economic and social difference for African Americans emerging from slavery and sharecropping. Sara agrees. "When I heard the stories my father told of who the students were at Utica Institute, you know, they were poor, poor rural people. They were from very young ages to very old ages. Most of them working in the fields. And they had the opportunity to learn how to read and write and figure. They had the opportunity to learn trades and participate in a meaningful way in society. It seems to me an important part of our history and not to be denigrated through our contemporary lens."

We found a page from the 1929 Utica yearbook that describes Sara's grandfather, helping us to better understand the man and the culture of the institute. It lists him as "Major Charles Radford Lawrence, Treasurer, Commanding Professor of Tailoring, Director of the Department of Music." And it tells his story like this: "Major Lawrence came to us in 1915 to serve us as commanding officer of the boys. Before he had passed one semester on the ground, he had exhibited his talents in the fields of tailoring and music. As soon as vacancies occurred in these departments, Major Lawrence was used to fill them. When treasurer Anderson resigned in 1921 Major Lawrence was unanimously appointed by the trustees as treasurer of the institute. He is known as the man of a thousand jobs."

Sara was deeply moved to see that her grandfather's career was part of the great African American struggle for knowledge and social mobility. And this struggle was so important to her grandparents that they were willing to leave the relatively safe haven of the North and enter the lion's den of the rigidly segregated South. It was a sacrifice that to them seemed well worth the price, a calling, a personal contribution toward freedom for their people.

The sacrifice, however, was real. It is difficult for us to imagine today how deeply those in the white South resented the rising of their former slaves, how much they wanted to keep them poor and ignorant. There are countless stories of school burnings, Klan raids, and lynchings surrounding the efforts by blacks to educate themselves in this era. Sara's grandparents were taking a great risk. And though they survived and prospered, they must have endured many restless nights, many fears, many humiliations. Sara told me a fascinating story that illustrates this. Apparently one of the buildings at Utica was set on fire and burned to the ground. No one knew who did it. In retrospect, one can assume, of course, that it was probably some local whites, maybe Klansmen. But no one came forward, and in the end two young female students from Utica were arrested for arson. The likelihood that they committed the crime was infinitesimally small, but that's what justice could be like in the Jim Crow era. So they were arrested, and at that point Sara's grandfather became involved.

"There was a big, huge, very ugly, very public trial," said Sara. "And there were lawyers for the side of the kids and lawyers for the side of the school, and both sets of lawyers were big-city lawyers who were white. And my grandfather had to testify on behalf of the school, because he was the dean. And he came, and he testified, and he was ridiculed horribly in court. The lawyers kept on saying, 'You're no colored man, you're no Negro—you're a white man who comes down south, coming here to make trouble.' They actually accused him of not being colored at all. And every time they went to court—and this lasted a long time—he was taunted about this. My dad remembers his friends mocking the trial and feeling an enormous kind of humiliation and sadness for his father."

Justice was not done in this case—or in many others like it. Nonetheless, Sara believes that her grandparents never regretted their decision to move south—and never wavered from their purpose. "To them," Sara said, "education was about liberation. Education was about dignity. And I think what they shared together was this view of uplifting the community, and it was through education that you did that—it was the primary vehicle."

Turning to an old photo of the Utica faculty, Sara told me that she believed that her grandmother Latitia was an equal to her grandfather, if not the motivating force in the decision to move south, driven by her own special love of education. "I think particularly my grandmother was about intellectual development," she said. "I mean, I think that she was a real reader, she was a real thinker, she was an orator, and she really believed in and loved the life of the mind. And she passed that on to my father, who passed that on to his kids."

Looking down Sara's paternal line, we sought more evidence of this commitment to education and equality. What we found was generation after generation of free blacks—the longest such line I have ever seen. Their unique collective experience as free people of color in a slave society undoubtedly shaped Sara's parents and their values.

Sara's paternal grandmother, Latitia Burnett Harris, was the daughter of Sandy Mitchell Harris and Sarah Cottman. Both were born free Negroes in Charles City County, Virginia—Sandy around 1842 and Sarah eleven years later. We were able to find a wealth of records pertaining to both these people. Taking Sandy Mitchell Harris first, I explained to Sara that we found his Union army pension application, which states that he served in Company C of the Second U.S. Colored Cavalry in the Civil War. This led us to look for his military service record at the National Archives in Washington, D.C., which in turn revealed that Sandy enrolled in the army on Christmas Eve of 1863 at Fort Monroe, Virginia, which was not far from where he lived in Charles City County. He signed on for a three-year term, one of about two hundred thousand African Americans who fought for the Union.

Company C's descriptive book lists Sandy as having been eighteen years old when he enrolled, five foot ten inches tall, with a "yellow" complexion, black hair, and black eyes. It also confirms his place of birth and lists his occupation as "laborer." Further research revealed that Sandy's regiment fought in the Battle of Newmarket Heights, a pivotal battle in the Civil War that occurred just outside Richmond, Virginia, on September 29, 1864. At that time Richmond was the capital of the Confederacy. The battle would help pave the way for the city's eventual downfall. In it, Union general Benjamin F. Butler led twenty-six thousand troops, including nine colored regiments. The fighting was harsh, lasting for hours, but the Union forces prevailed. We have no idea what kind of involvement Sandy had in the fight, but the documents provide the basis for some guesswork. Sandy began his military career as a private, but his records indicate that he was promoted to corporal on November 1, 1864—not long

Military records of Sandy Harris, Sara's great-grandfather, show that he served in the Union Army and fought in the Battle of Newmarket Heights.

after the battle. This was perhaps indicative of his conduct on the field.

To me, however, the most interesting thing about Sandy's service is not the question of how well he fought at Newmarket Heights but rather the larger question of why he chose to join the army at all. He risked his life to end slavery, yet he and his family were already free. As Sara said, "What a noble, fabulous thing to do. He didn't have to do it. He didn't have to feel so deeply identified with the slaves fighting for their freedom." And she's right. Some Negroes who were free before the Civil War avoided the army, knowing that they already had their freedom and that they faced not only the risk of death in battle but also enslavement or execution if captured by Confederate troops. Yet Sandy Harris took a different view. He chose to fight for the freedom of other blacks. And this sense of service became a leitmotif in Sara's family. People who could have passed didn't pass. People who could have stayed in the North instead headed south to work in impoverished communities. It's a structuring principle of Sara's ancestry. I think some of it may have been inspired by the curious place in which Sandy Mitchell Harris grew up: Charles City County, Virginia.

Sara has written a lot about Charles City County. It was the home of a very unusual community of free people of color long before the Civil War—unusual because there were so few such communities in the South at that time. While the vast majority of African Americans were slaves, Charles City's inhabitants were free. Their lives were circumscribed by laws, customs, and rules but they were nobody's property. While more than half the free Negro population in 1860 in the United States lived in the South, remaining there even during the Civil War, Virginia, a key slaveholding state, had a very large free Negro population, paradoxically, second only to Maryland. In fact, 22 percent of all the free Negroes in the South lived in Virginia in 1860, and two of the three free black families studied in this book can trace their ancestry to free Negroes who lived in Virginia, as did four branches of my own family.

Sara has visited Charles City County and observed that even today many people there physically resemble her father and his parents. "It was a pretty closed community," she said. "But it was an amazing place. Even generations and generations later, there was a sense of belonging and a lot of trust and communication among members of the community."

Since she comes from a long line of free blacks, we were able to trace Sara's ancestry back much further than is usually possible for an African American. We know that free people were listed by first and last name in the census, but slaves had no last names that the law recognized. Since

Sandy Mitchell Harris and his parents were free, we were able to search for them in the 1860 census. And we found Sandy and his siblings living with their father, Mitchell Harris, in Charles City County. Mitchell is Sara's great-great-grandfather. He is listed as being fifty years old, a laborer, and a mulatto with an estate valued at twenty-five dollars. At that time he is not listed as having a wife, just children. So we presumed that his wife was dead and began looking for her in earlier censuses. We found her in the 1850 census. Her name was Martha Harris, and she was sixty-two years old at that time. Her husband, Mitchell, was forty. Her son Sandy was four. If the census is accurate, this means she married a much younger man and was having children with him when she was around fifty-eight. But this is highly unlikely, suggesting an error in the census records or some kind of biblical miracle of childbirth!

We were unable to learn anything more about Martha Harris. But we did find a certificate that was issued to her husband, Mitchell Harris, indicating that he was a free person of color. The document is dated February 21, 1833, and we found it in the minute books of the clerk of Charles City County, Virginia. It reads, in part, "It appears to the satisfaction of the court by the testimony of William B. Blaten that Mitchell Harris, son of Morris Harris, a bright mulatto man, almost white, about 22 years old, the 11 of September last, 5 feet 4 and a half inches high, no visible mark or scar, hair nearly straight, was born free in this county and that the register of the said Mitchell is correctly made."

This is an eyewitness description of Sara's great-great-grandfather. It was also a very important document to him personally, just as it was to Isaac Bailey, Peter Gomes's great-great-grandfather. It proved that he was a free man. He could carry it and show it in case anybody doubted his right to walk the streets on his own—which was a real risk in those days. Free blacks in the South were frequently kidnapped or arrested under various pretenses and sold into slavery. This could happen at any time, so certificates like this were absolutely crucial to a free black person's ability to remain free.

The certificate also led us back another generation in Sara's family, because it names Mitchell's father, Morris Harris. Morris was Sara's great-great-great-grandfather. The earliest instance we could find of any documentation related to him was the 1810 U.S. federal census (which was only the third census ever conducted, the first having been done in 1790). In 1810, Morris Harris is listed as a free Negro and the head of household of five people, all of whom were categorized as being "free persons."

This is exceedingly rare: an African American family listed by name in the 1810 census, free more than fifty years before the Civil War. According to the U.S. census, only 186,446 blacks were free in 1810, about 13.5 percent of all African Americans. Even more remarkably, by moving up Sara's family tree to her paternal great-grandmother Sarah J. Cottman, we were able to travel still more deeply into the past. Sarah J. Cottman was the wife of Sandy Mitchell Harris, the Civil War veteran. Her parents were Tom Cottman and Eliza Brown, and we were able to trace their ancestors way back. Eliza's father was James Brown, born in 1794 in Charles City County, Virginia. He married Sally Stuart, who was born in 1795 and was the daughter of William Stuart. James was the son of Dixon Brown Jr., who was born in 1765 in Charles City County, Virginia, and married to a woman named Lucy.

In the process of identifying these people, we also found a land deed for the Elam Baptist Church in Charles City County. Built in 1810, it is the third-oldest black church in the state of Virginia and was a focal point of the free black community in the county. And records indicate that Sara's great-great-great-great-grandfather Dixon Brown was one of the trustees who created the Elam Meeting House, which later became the church. We found the deed for that property with Brown's name on it. The deed indicates that the land the church was built on was a gift of Abraham Brown, another free black man in Charles City County. We were unable to discern the exact relationship between Dixon Brown, Sara's ancestor, and this man Abraham Brown, but we believe that at the time all the Browns in Charles City County were related. So Sara most probably has some kind of relationship with the man who gave the land for this historic church.

Sara has visited the church and admired its simple, strong, and unpre-

Elam Baptist Church, one of the oldest black churches in the state of Virginia, was founded with help from Sara's ancestors.

tentious exterior. She has long been intrigued by its role in the community—but she never knew that her fourth great-grandfather was one of the founders. "It seems to answer a lot of questions," she said. "It feels as if it is an absolute foundation—an anchor for my own way of being in the world."

We traced Dixon Brown back still another generation to his father, Dixon Brown Sr., born a free black man in 1745 in Charles City County. He was married to a woman named Susannah, who was born somewhere in Virginia in 1750, and she was born free as well. We found Dixon because he filed a claim for providing material to the Continental army during the Revolutionary War. Apparently he gave the army a pair of stillyards, more commonly known as steelyards, which were devices used for measuring and weighing gunpowder. That means that Sara's fifth great-grandfather was a free African American patriot who had the means to offer material support to the Revolutionary War effort. Sara and I were simply blown away by this news, because, as with previous generations of her family, there was a choice involved here. African Americans fought on both sides of the Revolutionary War. The British even offered slaves their freedom, promising that if they escaped and fought on the English side, they would be emancipated at war's end—and many eventually were freed and sent to Canada after England's defeat. But Dixon Brown Sr. was a patriot. For one reason or another, he cast his lot with the vision of freedom offered by his fellow colonists. Little did he know that it would take well more than a century and much hard work by his descendants to fully realize that vision.

Dixon Brown Sr. and his wife, Susannah, were the earliest members of Sara's paternal line that we could identify. They were both born free by the middle of the eighteenth century. We could not identify the names of their parents or ascertain when they became free. (All African Americans are descended from slaves; the only question is when one's slave ancestors became free.) This means that Sara's father's line has an extraordinarily well-documented ancestral history—one of the oldest I've ever seen for an African American family, and the longest line of free Negroes of any person in this book. (Peter Gomes's oldest traceable ancestor was born in 1740 or so but was not freed until 1782.) Her maternal ancestry, however, posed many challenges to our researchers.

Sara's mother, Margaret Cornelia Morgan, was the daughter of Sandy Alonzo Morgan and Mary Elizabeth Smith, both born in 1881 in Richmond, Virginia. Sara met Sandy and Mary Elizabeth when she was a child but remembers little about them. We were able to trace each of their respective families back one generation, into slavery, but then lost the trail. We were hampered by the fact that in the Richmond area it was common practice for slaves to be used as rental property. Slave owners frequently hired out their slaves to other people for a fee, often in different counties. So slaves were constantly moving around, sometimes for months, sometimes for years, and since the records reflecting these movements did not record the slaves by name, it is extremely difficult to tell which slaves were going where. This makes genealogical research nearly impossible.

Thus on the paternal side of Sara's family, we could trace ancestors back before the Revolutionary War, because they were free. But on the maternal side, the legacy of slavery blocked all our efforts.

"I wish I could see them," said Sara. "It saddens me, particularly as we went all the way back on the side of my father. It makes me very sad to recognize that my mother's side of the family shared in the experience of most black folks. That's a silenced period. A terrible, terrible, painful period in our history."

Ultimately Sara's family tree epitomizes the complexity of the African American experience. There was a small percentage of us who were free and a much larger percentage of us who weren't. And these two groups— the tiny numbers of free blacks and the enormous numbers of slaves— existed side by side in the extraordinary place that was Charles City County. Once freedom came, these two groups took similar, overlapping paths, suffering perhaps equally in the Jim Crow years. Yet the heirs of freedom—the rare black people like Sandy Mitchell Harris who could trace his ancestry back to the Revolution—must have possessed a very different philosophical outlook than did the heirs of slavery. Did this outlook drive generations of Sara's family toward such admirable service to their people? We'll never know for sure. But it certainly had to play a significant role. Moreover, I think that the contrasts within Sara's family lines are emblematic of the extraordinary complexity of the African American experience—complexity within the race and complexity in the relationship between black and white America.

Sara and I spent a good while marveling at the accomplishments of her American family before turning our attention to her DNA in the hopes of tracing her roots back to Africa. When we finally did look at those results, we were surprised at what we found. The admixture test revealed that 55 percent of her ancestry was sub-Saharan African, while 45 percent was European. This meant she had no East Asian or Native American ancestry—which was really a shock to both of us. I've known Sara for decades and always presumed that her high cheekbones, her coloring, and her hair were all indicative of some Native American ancestry. Sara's felt that way her whole life.

"I thought there was Native American blood in our family," she said emphatically. "I thought that this mixture came in fact from Charles City. I was always led to believe that this community embraced free black folks and Native Americans and that I just came out of that."

I told her that while the community may have embraced the mixing of blacks and Indians, none of her ancestors did, and she laughed but still seemed truly confused. "Everyone looks at me as Native American," she said. "Even Native American folks look at me and think I'm part Native American. This surprises me a lot."

Perhaps Sara's and my surprise over these results reveals our own unconscious biases. As we have seen throughout this book, almost every African American I've interviewed claims to be descended from a Native American, which is statistically impossible if you think about it, but there are historical reasons for this myth. For many generations African Americans cherished stories of Native American ancestry, undoubtedly at first to assuage the pain of the stigma of "undiluted" blackness. And, as Chris Rock explained to me, it is much easier embracing a putative, mixed black-Indian ancestry than it is confronting the possibility that one's mixed ancestry stemmed from the rape of a black female slave by a white man. Over time, even as that stigma has lifted, the myths of Native American ancestry have nevertheless persisted for the simple reason, I think, that the old family stories have been enshrined as "facts." But there is no question that the claim of Native American ancestry is one of the three biggest myths of African American ancestry, along with "my family was never enslaved," and "my third great-grandmother was an Igbo princess!"

The fact that Sara has an extraordinarily high percentage of European ancestry was not surprising given the family history that we'd uncovered. Many of her ancestors were very light-skinned and could have even passed for white. That they did not is, of course, one of the most stirring aspects of Sara's ancestry.

I asked her if seeing the evidence of her white heritage so clearly displayed in her genetic ancestry was in any way upsetting to her, knowing as we both do that many African Americans are uncomfortable with white ancestry—in part because the union of black and white has historically been intertwined with rape and violence. Sara, however, said that it did not bother her. In fact, she said that "going over this history, it bothers me even less, because I realize these light-skinned folks who were my ancestors were so deeply identified with the oppressed side of their families and with joining in liberating that oppressed side of their family. So it wasn't as if they were running away toward a community that was more comfortable, where they would be safer. They were in fact running toward a community that needed them more, where they were really vulnerable and which required a kind of courageous stance. So I'm thrilled."

I wanted to explore this idea further, so I asked her if having 45 percent European ancestry made her feel less African American than someone who, say, would be 100 percent sub-Saharan African. (I have never tested a person who was 100 percent African.) She replied that it did not matter to her in the least. "I care less about these figures than I do about one's sense of identification with the racial group," she said. "And that identification is psychological, social, relational, emotional, and intellectual, and I think that's sort of more about what do we do with this heritage? Where do we place ourselves? What do we see as our work? What kind of imprint do we want to make on the world. And all of that for me comes from this sort of deep and abiding connection to African Americans."

One of the things that fascinates me about African Americans and their attitudes toward their white ancestry, as I mentioned to Quincy Jones, is that most blacks tend to be far more interested in our African American and African ancestry—and in our percentages of putatively Native American ancestry—than in our European ancestry, in spite of the fact that so many of us have so much of it. Sara believes that this is because most people today, including white people, are eager to affiliate with a minority, with a group that has a history that allows for progress and courage, for resistance and resilience. There is drama and heroism in such ancestry. Perhaps she is right. Perhaps we embrace with pride the triumph of the underdog, the triumph of persisting, of simple survival, and of thriving. Perhaps we embrace the nobility of suffering. I don't know. This project has shown me, however, that regardless of cause, it is clear that today, African Americans privilege their African heritage. As Sara said, "I feel so blessed and thrilled to be African American. I mean, that's my identity, and it always has been, and I understand that there's been a lot of the European part of my origins, but that doesn't make me any less identified as African American."

Unlike most of the people I researched for this project, Sara grew up with a very strong understanding of Africa and an admiration for its diverse culture due to her parents' social consciousness. She was no child of Tarzan movies. She got her information on Africa from the books and dinnertime conversations in her home. "We had big conversations about our African roots," she said. "Now, my parents were very clear that the African American experience was different from the African experience. But we always had lots of African friends coming through our house. We had people who worked in Africa on liberation struggles in the countries there. We didn't think of these people as living in the jungle. We knew African intellectuals and African writers. We knew it was an important place."

Sara has also spent considerable time in Africa—visiting Tanzania, Kenya, and Nigeria as part of her academic work. Nonetheless, for all her exposure, Sara, like most black Americans today, knows next to nothing about her own African ancestry. "My father always said that our ancestors were from West Africa," she told me. "That's what he said, but I don't really know. When I was in Africa, people would always take me for being from North Africa. They would see me as someone from up there—Ethiopia, Morocco. It's because of my mixed look, I guess."

By analyzing Sara's mitochondrial DNA, we found out that her maternal line falls within a large grouping of genetic signatures known as L3d, which is among the oldest of the African genetic lineages. It's believed to have arisen in East Africa about seventy thousand years ago. Sara didn't know what to make of this information. And I couldn't blame her. I mean, seventy thousand years ago in East Africa? That's pretty vague. But by comparing her mitochondrial DNA with samples taken from contemporary African populations, we found significant matches among the Kanuri people of modern-day Nigeria, as well as the Balanta and the Mandinka people, who are found in Senegal, Gambia, and Guinea-Bissau—which means that she is in fact related to the West African people, as her father had predicted. Sara was thrilled to hear this.

We then tried to discern which of these groups might have been the source of her matrilineal ancestor who was taken into slavery. Our research had not revealed much about her mother's family, but we did know that her maternal great-great-grandmother Mary was born in slavery in Virginia in 1831. And according to the historians John Thornton and Linda Heywood, this fact alone makes it very unlikely that she or her mother or her grandmother was Kanuri, because very few Kanuris were brought to the eastern United States. The tiny numbers of Kanuri who came to North America as slaves were sold in the Gulf Coast region in the early nineteenth century, and it is very unlikely that any of them ended up in Virginia. However, according to Thornton and Heywood, the Balanta and the Mandinka people were traded to Virginia in significant numbers during the first half of the eighteenth century. It is therefore highly probable that Sara's ancestor came from among those groups and was brought to North America sometime between 1710 and 1769, which are the years for which we have documentation of the direct trading of slaves between Africa and Virginia. We cannot be certain, of course, but this is quite plausible.

Sara was grateful for her new connection to Africa—even if the connection is not yet fully clear. "If I went back there and visited," she said, "if I looked into their faces, I might see myself. I might see my cousins. So that's identification, and I think I might feel a sense of great connection there."

Nonetheless, like her parents before her, Sara feels that her main obligation in life is to her fellow African Americans. Learning about her African heritage has made her want to visit Africa and to tell her children about their shared ancestry, but it has also made her feel far more focused on the experience of the descendants of the African slaves in the United States. "I think my sense of responsibility and obligation is more circumscribed to this country," she said. "Meaning that I think that most of my work should be about justice for African Americans in this country. It's a very different history. It's a very different experience."

As we parted, I thanked her profusely, still stirred by the stories I'd learned. She was also a bit shell-shocked at the amount of detail we had amassed about the people who'd come before her. "I'm so proud of them," she said. "I feel wonderful to be a part of this line."

I asked her if our experience together had changed her, whether it had made her feel different about herself. She said she wasn't sure. The main thing she felt, she said, was a sense of reassurance. "I have been very fortunate," she said, "to have inherited some of the motivation and the discipline and the comfort that these people expressed in their lives. That feels just good. It reaffirms. And it also helps me understand why my father and my mother were such extraordinary people." This is, I think, one of the greatest feelings one can have—gratitude toward one's ancestors, a sense of fulfillment in knowing that their values have been passed on and appreciated.

Tom Joyner

November 23, 1949

TOM JOYNER is the most influential and dynamic personality in the history of black talk radio. Host of the leading nationally syndicated program *The Tom Joyner Morning Show,* which reaches eight million listeners five days a week, he has won virtually every major award for excellence in media. I listen to him all the time, as much as I possibly can, in my home and in my car, because I find him so inspiring. I love his passion for black people and black history, but I love his intelligence just as much. I think it is fair to say that he is as obsessed with African American history as any scholar, and I think he's done more to bring our history into the lives of everyday people than anyone else in broadcasting, because of his daily Black History features.

I was eager to involve him in this project, and I was very pleased that he was excited to participate. When I called to invite him on board, he told me that he and his father had watched the first PBS series and that if I hadn't asked him to be part of the second series, he was going to kill me! He knows a great deal about his own family, but like any true devotee of learning, he craves more. "I've wondered about this stuff a long, long time," Tom told me before we could even sit down. "Because I see things in myself that I don't see in my father or mother, and I am dying to find out where it all comes from."

Open and warm, Tom sat expectant as I began to share with him the results of our genealogical research on heretofore-unknown branches of his family tree. He was born on November 23, 1949, in Tuskegee, Alabama, and is particularly interested in his family's relation to this town—justifiably so. Tuskegee is a resonant place, a crucial place in black history. Tom, in fact, believes that this town, as much as his family, shaped him into the man he is today—a "classic overachiever," as he calls himself. I once visited his studio and was surprised to see a framed photograph of Booker T. Washington, the founder of Tuskegee Institute, hanging on his wall.

"I have been thinking more and more," he said, "that the reason I've overachieved, is because of where I grew up. Tuskegee is a community of black overachievers. Starting with Booker T. Washington and then the Tuskegee Airmen and then along to Lionel Richie. George Washington Carver was in there, too. It just goes on and on. You know? And those are just the ones you know about. There is a whole community of these people—black role models—who were my neighbors and whose children were my classmates."

Both of Tom's parents came to Tuskegee because of its famous airmen program, created because the U.S. Army Air Corps was forced, by a 1941 court order, to recruit and train black pilots. These were the first African Americans to fly for the U.S. military, and they ultimately served with great honor and distinction in World War II, but the army fought them every step of the way. Indeed, they tried to get rid of the unit right at the start by requiring that anyone who wanted to join needed to have a college education, knowing that this would eliminate the vast majority of African Americans from applying. Only a tiny number of blacks had had access to higher education. The policy, however, backfired. The few who qualified applied in droves, flooding the War Department with applications and ultimately crowding Tuskegee with the best and brightest African Americans in the nation.

"Tuskegee," said Tom, "was unlike any other place on earth when it came to black people. It was just filled up with all kinds of smart folks."

Tom's father learned about the program from the black newspapers that were widely circulated at the time. "The Pullman porters would throw them over the side of a train," said Tom, smiling, "and little boys like my daddy read the papers—the *Pittsburgh Courier,* the *Baltimore Afro-American,* the *New York Amsterdam News.* And that's how he found out about the airmen program. He was a college graduate, he was teaching school. Teaching math, I think it was, and he wanted to be a pilot. And when the airmen program was announced, when they recruited blacks for the program, their requirements were that you had to be a college graduate. Period. You didn't have to be in the military. You could be a civilian, and you could go straight in if you'd gone to college. So he came to Tuskegee."

Tom's mother was also a part of the Tuskegee Airmen program, serving as a secretary to one of the commanders. "Back then," Tom recalled, "if you were an educated woman—a college graduate, a teacher, or a stenographer as she was—well, they would place you on jobs around the country. She was placed in several locations—some black colleges—and she eventually ended up at Moton Field, which is named after Robert Russa Moton, who was Booker T. Washington's successor at Tuskegee. And my mother was a secretary to one of the white commanders there. That's how they met. She carpooled with my dad. And Daddy took advantage of the car pool."

Tom's father was unable to complete the military program, but he remained in the town and settled down with his carpooling partner. As Tom points out, the town at that time must have had the most highly educated black community per capita in the world—and that's where Tom was raised. So perhaps it is not by chance that he ended up a champion of black culture and history.

"Growing up," Tom recalled, "we were rich in pride, rich in awareness of who we were. I mean, this little town was like ninety percent black—and probably eighty percent of the black population were college-educated. So it was the place to be."

Of course, Tuskegee was not free from the pervasive racism of Jim Crow Alabama. Even though its population was overwhelmingly black, all the commerce of the town was controlled by the tiny minority of white citizens. Not surprisingly, as Tom often points out, Tuskegee, with its brilliant black population, was on the very cutting edge of the civil-rights movement. There was a Tuskegee bus boycott before the Montgomery Bus Boycott—in fact, Rosa Parks came from Tuskegee. She was a very well-educated person. It is a total myth that she was some tired cleaning lady. She was very much prepared for the role she played in the civil-rights movement; indeed, it is fair to say that Rosa Parks was typecast for her part, starting with her background at Tuskegee.

Tom has vivid memories of growing up amid the burgeoning civil-rights movement. "When I was a boy," he said, "I was delivering the *Montgomery Advertiser,* and this is when they had two papers. You had the black edition and you had the white edition—even the paper was segregated. I delivered the colored daily paper. And I remember that the news was different, you know? They wouldn't print it in the white *Montgomery Advertiser* when Dr. King wanted to march on Dexter Avenue—you had to get that from the colored edition."

The civil-rights movement in Tuskegee is actually what drove Tom, more or less by chance, into the business that has made him so successful.

"I stumbled into radio," he said, laughing. "I was going to the protest marches. And every weekend there was a march, and parents always took their children to the marches. And so we were marching every Saturday for something—voter registration, desegregating a church. This particular Saturday we were protesting the fact that the radio station—the one radio station in town—didn't play any black music. It played background music for the merchants of Tuskegee. But they wouldn't play black music. They played Enoch Light. We wanted to hear some Aretha, some Wilson Pickett, some Motown. And so we were out there."

As Tom described it, this rally was not large, nor was it significant to the larger civil-rights movement. But it changed his life—even if he didn't know it at the time. Hearing him tell the story was a beautiful thing, as he masterfully mixed small and large details, mingling personal history with vast social changes, just as he does so expertly on his show.

"The rally wasn't that big of a deal to me," he recalled. "Because there was a rally every Saturday. But I was a fat kid. And they had sandwiches— peanut butter sandwiches. You know, peanut butter was invented there in Tuskegee, so peanut butter was everywhere. Thanks to George Washington Carver, of course. And a free peanut butter sandwich on a Saturday was good enough for me. So we're out there protesting. And the owner of the radio station comes out, and he says, 'I see you all out here every Saturday protesting something. I don't need this. So I'll tell you what: I'm going to give you your music once a week on Saturday afternoon. Who wants to do it?' So the hand that didn't have a sandwich in it went up."

This was a transformative moment in Tom's life, perhaps the most important decision he ever made, yet he recalls it as being a simple lark. "It just seemed like fun," he said. "You know? The most fun job in the world is being on the radio. Wasn't it fun listening to it? I thought it must be fun to actually do it, and so I put my hand up. And at that time, what I wanted to do up to that point was, I wanted to be a truck driver. I wanted to be a long-distance truck driver, because at the service station on the highway up the street from where we lived, black truck drivers would come and fill up and tell all the shorties these lies about their adventures on the road and how they had women. I was fascinated at that. I was fascinated by the lies, and so maybe that's how I got into the business. I wanted to lie like them. And I've been in the business ever since. That's the only thing I've ever done, is radio."

Though Tom jokes about it, I think that the town of Tuskegee gave him a vision of the way black people could live, and that vision has shaped his career and indeed his whole life. To put it crudely, I see part of his mission as being the Tuskegee-ization of all America. And every day he fulfills this mission by helping black people to understand that we can achieve—in business, in politics, in science, in the arts, and in ordinary life.

"I don't even look at it as a vision," said Tom, responding to my interpretation of his work. "Because I was never brought up or taught that there was anything that I could not do, so in my mind there are no limits. You know? If I want to go to the moon and do a show from the moon, a live show with an old-school band? If I put my mind to it, I can do it. I really believe and have proven that if you can dream it, you can achieve it. But Tuskegee is important to that. Because Tuskegee was a place that taught me how to do something even if I didn't know how to do it or want to do it. It taught me how to dream and how to get a job done."

To better understand Tom's relationship to this remarkable town, we began to look at the lives of his parents, who took very different paths to meet in their Tuskegee car pool. Tom's father was Hercules L. Joyner, born on February 4, 1918, in Plant City, Florida. His mother, Frances Lincoln Dumas, was born February 12, 1916, in Clifton, Alabama.

Growing up, Tom felt neither rich nor poor. "I felt nurtured, loved, felt some pain 'cause I got my ass whupped a lot, but I was definitely loved. And I know now that my parents were role models of mine. I didn't think of it then. They were hardworking people. Pops got up every day, went to the VA hospital, got paid on Wednesday, saved his money, had a few side hustles. My mama was a secretary on campus. She helped students with their dissertations. She'd type them and edit them. They were limited, you know, by being African American at that time; that limited their life choices. But they did everything they could. I mean, my parents both graduated from black colleges. They did their best. They were the typical American family that worked, saved for their kids to go to school, and they also saved for vacations. The whole town did that."

Tom is keenly aware of how different his opportunities in life and life choices have been from those of his parents.

"When they came along," he said, " 'separate but equal' was the law of the land. *Brown v. Board of Education* hadn't happened yet, either. So I had a lot more opportunities than they did. But they didn't talk about what opportunities they had missed. And I never felt, 'Oh, if I were white, I could have done that, or I can't do that because I'm a Negro.' Never in my whole life. I thought if I studied harder, I could have been more than I am. Yeah, I did all right for a C student, I'm thinking, you know?"

When Tom was growing up, his family, like so many other black families I've researched, did not talk about their past, even though they lived in one of the most illustrious black communities in the nation. They simply didn't talk about the generations that had come before them or the experiences of their parents and grandparents. In fact, Tom said his father began talking more about the past because of Tom's involvement with this project than he'd ever talked before. The timing couldn't have been more perfect: Tom's father died just after we had filmed a special family reunion that Tom convened so that we could share the results of our research with his relatives.

"Pops is eighty-nine years old right now," Tom told me then, laughing, "and he is telling me more stuff than I've ever heard him tell anyone. And I don't know why. I mean, you tell me—you're the historian. Why are our parents like that? Is it that they were ashamed and they didn't want to think about where they came from?"

Sadly, I can't answer Tom's questions any better than he can. I share his concerns, and I believe that shame and circumspection played a role in the reticence of older black generations, but I also think there are other, deeper reasons for what amounts to their collective silence—reasons of safety, reasons of pride, and reasons that are so specific to the culture and experience of those who survived slavery that we can never understand them. But of course that doesn't mean we should give up trying. We may never fully grasp the experiences of our ancestors, but genealogical projects like this one give us the chance to come much closer, especially if you are fortunate enough, and determined enough, as Tom was, to share the results systematically with older relatives—an extraordinary process, actually, almost a complex form of collective family therapy.

Going back one generation on Tom's father's side, we looked at his paternal grandfather, Oscar Albert Joyner, born in St. George, South Carolina, on April 8, 1882. Oscar is one of the most significant figures in Tom's family, a man whose impact was felt for generations. Indeed, though Tom knew him only briefly, he believes that his own character and his drive to achieve flow directly from his grandfather.

Oscar was clearly ambitious, even as a very young man. He began working as a Pullman porter in the early 1900s—which at that time was a very difficult job to get. Oscar never talked about it, though. In fact, the only reason Tom knows anything about Pullman porters is from doing the narration for a television documentary about them. "The producer got in touch with me and wanted me to do some narration on it, and I said, 'Well, my grandfather was a Pullman porter.' But I didn't know what that meant. Turns out being a Pullman porter back then—it was huge."

The Pullman porters were indeed very significant in African American history, and it is fascinating to me how many of the people I've researched have a Pullman porter in their family's past, including Whoopi Goldberg's paternal grandfather, Robert Johnson Sr., and Maya Angelou's maternal grandfather, Thomas Baxter. These men traveled all over the country, earning money and gaining access to ideas and opportunities that had previously been denied rural blacks. Over time, Pullman porters organized into one of the most important unions in American history and helped launch the civil-rights movement. But for Tom's grandfather the opportunities offered by this coveted job were overshadowed by the struggle that actually performing the work entailed. It was a service job, a service job black men performed for middle-class white men and women. The opportunities to be humiliated were, accordingly, enormous.

"I asked my father about his dad," said Tom. "And eventually I came to find out that it was really rough for a black porter back then. You talk about racism and being treated like a slave? Well, if you were a porter, you got a pocketful of tips. Back then that was a lot of money but the things you had to do? The humiliation. The things you had to put up with? 'Nigger, come here, fill up that bourbon. Didn't you hear me? Don't be looking at my woman.' You know? You had to avert your eyes."

Rather than bear the humiliation, Tom's grandfather decided to transform himself. He saved his wages and slowly paid his way through college. Then he decided to become a doctor. This was an extraordinary leap for an African American to take. There were almost no black doctors in the early twentieth century. But Oscar was able to gain admission to Meharry Medical College in Nashville, Tennessee.

Tom believes that his grandfather probably got the inspiration to be a doctor from seeing white doctors on the trains. "I think that's where he got the whole idea from," he said. "'Cause he was a Pullman porter for a long time, and the passengers were doctors, professors, high-society people, and I'm thinking that he saw the way they lived, the way they worked, and that's where he got the desire to be a doctor. I don't know where else he would have gotten that from."

Meharry Medical College was one of the few medical colleges open to African Americans in the early 1900s. When Oscar Joyner graduated in 1908, he became one of only three thousand black physicians in the whole United States. That's less than 2 percent of all doctors in the country. He was in a tiny class of well-educated black men and women. And just as surprising is what Oscar did with his medical degree: Eschewing the wealth accrued by his peers, he sought to treat the poorest of the poor.

"My grandfather went to a migrant town, Plant City, Florida," Tom said. "He could have gone to Chicago or to Durham or to Philadelphia or to Atlanta. There were a lot of choices. But I guess he liked helping people who needed help the most. If *he* didn't help them, who would? And I think I got a lot of my own philanthropy interests from him. You know, people ask me all the time, 'Why do you just help black students in black colleges?' And I say, 'If *I* don't, who will?' And so I think maybe he chose Plant City, that migrant town, for the same reason."

Tom remembers his grandfather Oscar vividly from his childhood. "He was quiet," said Tom. "But he had some great sayings, he had a lot of funny wisdom, like, 'Leave a Negro alone long enough and he will blow his own brains out.' That was one of his. And, 'A hungry monkey will eat red pepper.' He had all kinds of these different sayings and stuff. I laughed at them all the time. I didn't always know what I was laughing about, but I laughed."

Tom also recalls that Oscar had a certain style and flair that seemed out of place in rural Florida, where he practiced. "He would just ride around in his Buick," Tom said. "He was a big shot with a Buick. Plant City is not a big metropolis. It's a migrant town, but that's where he worked. Just serving these black migrant workers. They didn't have any money, so he was paid in strawberries and oranges, whatever they were picking. He could have been a lot richer. But he chose to do otherwise."

Tom feels that his grandfather had a deeply positive influence on his life. However, Oscar's relationship with his own children was strained by his professional choices—a situation that, as many have observed, is not at all unusual or specific to black people. Successful professionals, of course, frequently alienate their children, or are alienated from them. In Tom's family, Oscar's children did not appreciate their father until much later in life.

"Thing is," Tom said, "my grandfather wanted my father to be a doctor, and he pushed for it. But my father didn't want to be like his daddy.

My father, like me, was a mama's boy. And my grandfather was always gone, because there were people sick all the time, you know, so he was gone all the time. His wife's heart was broken by that. And my father, being a mama's boy, didn't like seeing his mother's heart broken. So the last thing he wanted to be was a doctor. In fact, he told me that Doc used to send money back to Meharry College just so that Meharry would accept my daddy when he applied. He said Doc would send a couple hundred dollars back to Meharry, and it ain't like he had a whole lot of money. He had a whole lot of fruit, ain't had a whole lot of cash money. But my daddy didn't want that. He wanted to be a pilot. So he didn't ever apply to Meharry. And I didn't hear stories about how great Doc was when I was a kid. I only found out how amazing his life was much later."

This, I think, is a familiar story, compressed into just a few of its details. I can sympathize with all involved—the hardworking father, the lonely son and wife. It's a tragedy of sorts, but in the end Tom's father came to celebrate Oscar. I wonder if Oscar felt appreciated.

Oscar's wife, Ruth Griffin Joyner, is as interesting to me as the doctor himself. She was born in 1897 in Chester, South Carolina, the daughter of Franklin and Julia Griffin. Like her husband's family, her family had deep roots in South Carolina, and their ancestors were most likely brought there directly as slaves from Africa. Yet Ruth and Oscar did not meet in their home state. They met in Florida, as Oscar was beginning his practice and Ruth was trying to begin a new life. The story of Ruth's journey from South Carolina to Florida has been shrouded in mystery for generations. Tom himself knew nothing about his grandmother's background in South Carolina. "All I know is she left home and she ended up in Florida and she didn't stay in touch with her people," he said. Our research, however, revealed a tragedy at the story's core.

According to public records, Ruth's family owned 130 acres of land in Blackstock, South Carolina, which is just outside Columbia. There had long been rumors in the family that the Griffins suffered a terrible blow just before Ruth moved away. According to the rumors, Ruth's two brothers were lynched. We looked for the death certificates of her brothers—Tom and Meeks Griffin—and found out that the truth was even worse.

On September 29, 1915, Tom and Meeks were executed by the state through legal electrocution, for a crime they almost certainly did not commit. These men were Tom's great-uncles.

We looked into this case and discovered that in 1913, Tom and Meeks Griffin—along with three other men—were charged with killing a Confederate Civil War veteran, a white man named John Lewis. An all-white jury found four of the five defendants guilty, Tom's great-uncles among them, and they sentenced the four to death. The Griffin brothers claimed that they were innocent, and they appealed their case all the way to the South Carolina supreme court. But the conviction was upheld, and Tom and Meeks Griffin were sent to the electric chair.

Further research revealed that Tom's great-uncles were convicted largely on the testimony of one witness, the fifth defendant. He was an African American named John "Monk" Stevenson, and he turned state's evidence. This seemed odd to me—and I'd say that, based on the record, it was exceedingly odd. We found a sworn statement made during the appeals process by a woman named Hattie Budget. Hattie was an African American in jail for disorderly conduct at the same time that the five Lewis defendants were held awaiting trial. In her statement Hattie claimed that Stevenson spoke to her in privacy in the prison kitchen and said, "I changed my mind and put it on these four 'cause some of them

Tom Joyner's great-uncles, Tom and Meeks Griffin, were unjustly put to death by electric chair in 1913.

FIVE NEGROES KILLED IN THE ELECTRIC CHAIR

South Carolina Makes Record for Legal Electrocutions in One Day.

Columbia, S. C. September 29 —With protestations of innocence on their lips, five negroes—Meeks Griffin, Tom Griffin, John Crosby, Nelson Brice and Joe Malloy—were electrocuted at the state penitentiary this morning for

murder. The time consumed in the separate executions amounted to one hour and ten minutes.

Joe Malloy was convicted for the murder of Prentiss Moore and Guy Rogers, two white boys of Marlboro county, on Thanksgiving day, 1911, while the other negroes received sentences for the killing of John Q. Lewis, an aged confederate veteran of Chester county, on the night of April 24, 1913.

Five legal electrocutions in one day is a record for South Carolina.

Schadd Is Acquitted.

Clearwater, Fla., September 29.—William Schadd, of Safety Harbor, Fla., charged with killing O. A. Stemple, father of Guy Stemple, the state's most important witness in the Mendenhall case, was acquitted today. Judge Reaves held that the state had no case against him.

are the richest Negroes in that country and had the money to pay for their lives and I had borrowed a gun from one of them the day before old man Lewis was killed."

Now, this statement could mean that Stevenson was desperate and named Tom and Meeks because he knew they came from a relatively wealthy landowning family and he thought that they had the money to defend themselves. But it could also mean that Stevenson was jealous and resented Tom and Meeks because they had so much money and such high status in the community. It is probably the result of some combination of both. Regardless, Hattie's statement strongly implies that Tom and Meeks had little or nothing to do with Lewis's murder.

We also found another statement made by Mary Gill, an eighteen-year-old girl who was in jail at the same time for defaulting on her bail. Referring to Stevenson, it reads in part, "He said Meeks Griffin, Thomas Griffin, John Crosby, and Nelson Brice did not have anything to do with killing Mr. John Lewis and they knew nothing about it. He, Stevenson, killed old John Lewis."

These two statements, taken together, strongly suggest that Stevenson, the man who turned state's evidence, was the man who committed the murder and that he pinned it on Tom's uncles and these two other men. Yet Stevenson's testimony was accepted, and all four of his codefendants were executed. How in the world did the prosecution win a conviction with such flimsy evidence? It's not as if they chose to believe the word of a white man against a black man—which would have been just as bad, of course, but also understandable given the racial climate of the day. No, they took the word of a clearly untrustworthy black man against that of some of the black community's most outstanding families. Why? I don't know, but the story infuriates me.

My anger was compounded when we discovered that the defense had only two days to prepare for the trial. Two days. There is no way that they could have prepared a defense in so short a time. Essentially, the moment that Tom and Meeks Griffin were accused of the murder, they were powerless to defend themselves. Why did the state do this to Tom's ancestors? Were they simply trying to knock down wealthy blacks? This is certainly one possible explanation.

Tom was deeply disturbed by this story and wanted to know if anything had ever happened to John Stevenson. Unfortunately, we don't know. There is no evidence that he was ever convicted of lying or of his likely role in the murder and the unjust conviction of the Griffin brothers. This underscores a larger point that Tom fully appreciates: This was not an isolated incident. Justice in the Jim Crow South was notoriously racist. Between 1912 and 1920, of the forty-seven people who were put to death in South Carolina, forty-four were black. And as the story of Tom's ancestors shows—and DNA appeals recently have revealed—we have to wonder how many were also innocent and were railroaded by the system, as the Griffin brothers were.

After these events, which amount to little more than a legalized lynching, the entire Griffin family left South Carolina. They'd had to sell their land to pay for the lawyer to defend Tom's great-uncles. So the whole family just split up, with Tom's paternal grandmother, Ruth Griffin, going to Florida.

Though she quickly met and married her husband, Oscar, it must have been quite a shock for Ruth to leave behind so abruptly and forever her home, family, and the comforts she'd known in South Carolina for rural Florida. Yet despite this, and despite the fact that she may have been heartbroken by Oscar's long absences, Ruth seems to have made a great deal of her life in Plant City.

"My grandmother was a schoolteacher," said Tom. "All the kids around there were taught in Plant City by my grandmother, and she also had some side hustles. Like, she was a beautician. She had a beauty salon right there at the house. And she also had a greenhouse, and she did flower arrangements. She was good at whatever she did."

Ruth Griffin Joyner died in 1966. Oscar passed away six years later. We were able to trace both their families back another two generations to slaves born in the early 1800s—a very good result for black ancestors not freed before the Civil War—and there the paper trails ran out.

Turning to Tom's maternal line, we found a wealth of incredible stories. His mother's parents were Isaac Lafayette Dumas, born on November 26, 1882, in Prairie Bluff, Alabama, and Nettie Lavinia Stanback, born on January 2, 1891, in Raleigh, North Carolina.

In the 1930 census, Nettie and Isaac were living in Wilcox County, Alabama. He was a farmer, and she was a teacher at a school run by the Presbyterian Church. This struck me as somewhat unusual, because Nettie had been born in North Carolina during the early days of the Great Migration. The vast majority of migrating African Americans at that time were moving north. Yet Nettie—like Sara Lawrence-Lightfoot's parents—had gone in the exact opposite direction—to Alabama, to the heart of the old Confederacy and the new Jim Crow South. This was a mystery, and by looking at the occupations of Nettie and Isaac's neighbors in the 1930 census, we began to unravel it. We noticed that Tom's grandparents were part of a community of black farmers and teachers centered on a number of mission schools in Wilcox County. All of these schools had been started by the Presbyterian Church. Nettie was living deep in the racist South because she wanted to help her fellow African Americans.

By interviewing Tom and his family, we began to develop a full picture of this impressive woman. Tom's aunt, Janet Keys, who is ninety-two years old and the family's unofficial historian, told us that Nettie's older sister had wanted to be a missionary in Africa but had decided instead that she was needed more in Alabama. So she moved there to be a teacher, and Nettie followed her.

In the late nineteenth and early twentieth century, there was little in the way of public education available for African Americans in Alabama—and indeed throughout the South in general. Most white southerners, of course, wanted to keep it that way. They wanted to keep black workers in the fields breaking their backs for unfair wages, not going to school. The situation was so grotesque that at the start of World War I, for every dollar spent on a white child, two cents were spent on a black child. In many places the only hope for black people who wanted an education was the church. While the state had decided to deny blacks an equal education, a few Christian groups, such as the Presbyterians, felt compelled to help and started opening schools for blacks in the nineteenth century (as we saw in the case of one of Morgan Freeman's ancestors). These schools were oases of opportunity, and Tom's ancestor was drawn to one.

Nettie met her husband, Isaac L. Dumas, at the school where she taught. He was a farmer and what we might call today the property manager of the school. But he was hardly a typical farmer of that era. Isaac had received an agricultural degree from Tuskegee Institute, where he claimed to have been taught by Booker T. Washington. Apparently Isaac would frequently refer to Booker T. Washington as "Mr. Washington" and quote him extensively, saying things like, "Don't be good, be good *at something.*" This was clearly an exceptional family. My appreciation for them deepened when I learned that Isaac's parents—Isaac Dumas and Frances Briggs—had donated ten acres of land to create the school where Nettie taught. According to Tom's Aunt Janet, the elder Isaac Dumas, an illiterate former slave, was frustrated by the fact that white children went to school for eight months each year while African American children went to school for only two or three months. So he sold his land for one dollar to the Presbyterian Church to create a school for the children of freed slaves.

"That is heart—I like it!" said Tom, ecstatic to hear that his great-grandfather had in essence donated his land for a black school.

Our research showed that Isaac Dumas was born a slave in 1851 in Alabama and that his wife, Frances Briggs, was born into slavery in 1855 in Alabama. It also showed that their commitment to education put them at great risk. Many in Alabama did not want black children to be educated. In 1895, for example, arsonists burned a nearby mission school to the ground, and no one was ever charged with the crime. Yet Isaac and Frances remained committed to their vision and prospered. By the end of their lives, Isaac's will tells us that they owned over a hundred acres of land and one of the first cars in the area, something that many white people across the nation coveted but could not afford.

Turning back to Tom's family tree, we uncovered a fascinating story of a completely different nature. Nettie's parents were Zacharia Stanback and Janet Wilson Hall. Zacharia was born a slave in Virginia sometime between 1838 and 1851. His wife, Janet, was born into slavery in North Carolina around 1859. We found photographs of Janet from the late nineteenth century that show her as a regal woman. Tom's Aunt Janet told us that

Nettie Lavinia, Tom's maternal grandmother, headed into the heart of the Jim Crow South to teach at one of Alabama's few black schools.

when she was growing up, it was accepted as absolute incontrovertible fact that Janet's mother was a slave named Jane Hall and her father was Jane's owner, a white man named Ed Hall.

"That's where my light skin comes from," said Tom, laughing.

According to Tom's aunt, Jane Hall and Ed Hall had a relationship like that of Thomas Jefferson and Sally Hemings. In fact, his aunt said that Jane Hall was Ed Hall's "wife," in every way but legally. We wanted to use DNA to investigate this family legend. Unfortunately, Robert Hall, who is the only male in the black Hall family, never fathered a son so it was impossible to obtain a Y-DNA sample that could definitively tie the black male Halls to the white male Halls through a common paternity test. Instead we had to look for documentary evidence that would either support or debunk the family story.

In the 1870 census, we found Tom's great-great-grandmother Jane Hall living with her daughter Janet and her son Robert. Their neighbor is "Edward Hall," a retired lawyer who is white. And by turning back to the 1860 slave schedule of this Edward Hall, we learned that he had owned eighteen slaves. None are listed by name, just by their age and gender. And yet this is enough to tell us a great deal. Back in 1860, Tom's great-great-grandmother Jane Hall would have been thirty-five years old and her daughter Janet would have been less than a year old, while her son Robert would have been two years old. And on Edward Hall's schedule, he owns a thirty-five-year-old black woman, a two-year-old girl, and a nine-and-a-half-month-old boy. The children's races are listed as "M"—which meant "mulatto."

This suggests that these three people are most probably Tom's ancestors. And since this evidence is exactly consistent with Tom's aunt's oral history, the evidence is quite persuasive that Edward Hall, a white slave owner, is in fact Tom's maternal great-great-grand-father. Tom immediately wanted to know about Edward Hall. "Was he a good white man or a bad white man?" he asked. This is the first question I would have asked if these people were my ancestors. It is a very natural question. But it is, of course, a hard one to answer. How are we to assess relationships of slaves and masters when they are as complicated as this?

Janet Hall, Tom Joyner's great-grand-mother. Documents indicate that Janet was the daughter of the slave Jane Hall and her owner, Ed Hall.

Our research revealed that Edward Hall came from a very illustrious family with deep roots in both Europe and America. His father, Tom's great-great-great-grandfather, was a man named John Hall, who was one of the first three supreme court justices in the state of North Carolina. And John's father, also named Edward Hall, was a Scots Irishman who migrated to North America in 1763 and died in Pennsylvania. His line can be traced all the way back to a man named Isaac Hall, who was born in the north of Ireland in 1686. This means that Tom is from the tribes of Northern Ireland as well as Africa, which amused him to no end.

We found a color portrait of John Hall, Tom's third great-grandfather, who was born on May 31, 1767, in Waynesborough, Virginia. He died in 1833 in Warrenton, Virginia, and probably had this portrait painted because of his position on the North Carolina supreme court, serving between 1818 and 1832. He had peculiarly striking blue-gray eyes and a distinctive hairline. When I showed it to Tom, he exclaimed, "Look at his eyes! So this is where my eyes came from—and my strange hairline," apparently resolving a quandary that has confounded his family and no doubt haunted Tom all these years. The likeness is unmistakable, actually. I was frankly as astonished as Tom was.

Unfortunately, researching Edward Hall's family tree did not help us to learn anything more about his character—or about the enslaved mother of his children and, following slavery, his common-law wife, Jane Hall. Based on what we discovered about the length of their relationship, I believe that Jane and Edward Hall—like Morgan Freeman's ancestors, Alfred and Celie Carr—were bound together by love. They had a long-term stable relationship and three children. They did not marry, but such a marriage would have been impossible in North Carolina after 1715, when the state passed a law to prohibit interracial marriages (a law that wouldn't be changed until 1967). Virginia also early on forbade miscegenation, and Georgia followed suit in 1750, while colonial South Carolina only "exacted serious penalties" if children were produced. Accordingly, Edward and Jane did what I suppose was the next-best thing: Edward kept Jane and their children next door. Unlike many white men in similar relationships, he didn't go out and find himself a white wife and start a new family. He remained devoted to her, even after she ceased to be his property. I asked Tom's family, during the family reunion he convened a month after I first interviewed him and a month or so before his father died, what they thought, and even they debated whether this could be a relationship based on love, with the sentimentalists (like Tom and me!) prevailing, I believe.

But beyond this we could find out virtually nothing more about Jane Hall. The 1870 census indicates that she was born in 1824 in North Carolina. Her parents are not listed, and we couldn't make even an educated guess about them from Edward Hall's records. So her line disappears in the tomb of slavery, even though she herself fared much better than many of her peers.

Turning back to the line of Tom's great-grandfather Isaac Dumas, we were able to identify his father, Ralph Dumas, born into slavery in 1815 in Georgia. Ralph was fifty years old at the end of the Civil War. We looked for public documents to tell us how he fared after he was freed. The documents tell a sad story. The 1870 census indicates that Ralph's wife—Tom's great-great-grandmother Caroline Collier, a former slave—died between 1868 and 1870, right after slavery ended. Ralph then remarried—unhappily, it would seem, as an 1884 court document from Wilcox County, Alabama, indicates that he filed for divorce after his wife abandoned him. Her reasons? According to the document, Ralph claims that she left him, saying "she was not going to stay with no poor Negro."

"There ain't nothing changed, really," Tom said, and laughed, looking at the divorce papers. "Life was tough on a broke brother even back then."

Like the vast majority of former slaves, Ralph was not a wealthy man. But his situation apparently was unusually dire. In all our research, we never found anybody too poor for marriage. "Well," said Tom, "money is the number one reason for divorce even today."

We tried to trace Ralph Dumas back into slavery, searching the records in Alabama to find slave owners with the same last name, and we found the will of a white man named Obediah Dumas, recorded in 1834. Once again, incredibly, we were able to find a black person's ancestors by name in the records of the white man who owned him. I can't stress how rare this is, and how lucky every researcher feels when she or he strikes this particular vein of black ancestral gold. In it, Obediah bequeaths fifteen slaves to his "beloved wife," Mary Dumas. And here is where the story becomes complicated. The slaves are listed with first names being Tony; his wife, Clara; and their twelve children, including a boy named Ralph. These are Tom's great-great-grandfather Ralph Dumas and great-great-great-grandparents Tony and Clara Dumas.

Because Tom talks about African American history every day on his radio program, he knows as well as any of us that slavery was an integral part of our past, but seeing this document with the names of his ancestors who were slaves stunned him. After a long pause, he gathered himself and said quietly, "I knew that we were slaves. But put it in front of you like this and it's kind of chilling."

Tom immediately wanted to know if Tony and Clara had come over directly from Africa. As we shall see, Obediah Dumas brought Tony and Clara to Alabama from North Carolina sometime in the 1820s. This means that Tom's ancestors were part of the great forced migration of blacks into what became the Cotton Kingdom between the 1820s and 1860.

Obediah's will is both interesting and unusual, not only because it refers to Tony and Clara by name but also because they are referred to as husband and wife, with Ralph listed as their child. Most slave owners did not honor marital bonds between their slaves. The slaves, of course, had their own marriages, but the law did not recognize these unions, and so white people were not bound to respect them. To the contrary, they often made significant efforts to violate these bonds and to separate husbands and wives, breaking up black families and forbidding black unions. But this man Obediah recognized the marriage of Tony and Clara, even in the legal language of his will.

Tom thinks it is perhaps indicative that Obediah was a "good slave owner as slave owners go." He is probably right. It certainly indicates that Obediah accorded his slaves a small measure of respect as human beings—even if the law of his country did not.

Obediah's will contained another fascinating detail. It declared that at the death or remarriage of his wife, the slaves Tony, Clara, and their children would be emancipated. So old Obediah was somewhat better even than we thought. Not only did he recognize the sanctity of their marriage, but he wanted them to be free, and he left this world comfortable in the knowledge that he had done all that was necessary to ensure Tony and Clara's eventual liberty. Unfortunately, the situation turned out to be more complex than it seemed at first. Obediah Dumas owned forty-one slaves when he died, but the only ones he freed in his will were Tony and Clara and their six children, suggesting a deep personal relationship.

"I wonder why he was so good to them," said Tom. I wondered the same thing myself. And I am not certain, but I have a guess as to the answer. Obediah's will contains what I consider a clue. It says that this family of slaves had served Obediah "faithfully" since his youth in North Carolina. This tells us that he brought them from North Carolina to Alabama—and perhaps it also suggests that Tony and Clara helped Obediah build his business through their toil, and that in recognition of this he tried to free them in his will.

Tragically, Obediah's wife did not share her husband's views. She never remarried, but before she died, she wrote her own will, leaving to her niece three slaves: Tony, Clara, and Ralph. In direct contradiction of her husband's wishes, Mary Dumas denied Tom's ancestors their freedom. This seemed illegal, until we discovered that in 1834, the same year that Obediah Dumas died, Alabama passed a statute prohibiting owners from manumitting slaves in their wills. So when Mary died, Tom's ancestors remained enslaved. She could have attempted to honor her husband's wishes, but she chose to give them to her niece, in violation of her husband's will.

"That was my family," said Tom, shaking his head in shock, imagining how terribly painful this change of course must have been for them.

But the story does not end there. The executors of Obediah's estate claimed that the terms of his will had been violated by his wife. These executors were white men, of course, but they, too, tried to come to the rescue of Tom's family. They went to court to demand that Tony, Clara, and their children should be freed, just as Obediah had ordered. And over the next four months, both sides made their case to a court in Wilcox County, Alabama. But on January 4, 1848, a judge decided against Obediah's executors and declared that Tony and Clara's manumission was indeed null and void and that the property of Mary Dumas could be lawfully given away in any manner that she had decreed.

Though Ralph would live to see freedom at the end of the Civil War, this meant that Tom's great-great-great-grandparents Tony and Clara, who knew they were supposed to be free and lived between Obediah's death and the death of his widow with all that joy and expectation, spent the remainder of their lives enslaved. What elation they must have felt when told about their master's wishes; who can imagine the pain of learning that Mary Dumas had violated the terms of her own husband's will?

"That's messed up," said Tom. "Can you imagine what it must have been like for them dragged back into slavery? They had it by law. They had it. It's heartbreaking. Makes me wonder what would have become of them had they been freed. Like they should have been."

It is terrible to think about these poor people, Tom's ancestors, who had the sweet taste of freedom in their mouths only to have it turn to ashes. For me, even just researching these events is heart-wrenching. It brings slavery to life for me as very little else has ever done.

"I get calls and e-mails all the time," said Tom. "I get them from white listeners who say, 'Why can't you black people just get over that?' Well, there is no apology. There hasn't been an apology. These were my people, they were slaves and we know slavery was terrible. And they were going to make it out. They had it. From being faithful to a slave owner, helping him build his business, and then him having enough heart to recognize them as human beings, recognize their marriage vows, which he didn't have to do. At his death he was going to do the right thing. And then even his buddy tried to do the right thing. How am I supposed to get over that without an apology? I sure would like to have an apology."

I agreed completely with Tom. And I did not know how to console him. But before we left Tony, there was one more interesting story I wanted to tell. In researching Tony's life, we found what's known as a mortality schedule for Wilcox County, Alabama, in 1860. It records Tony's death as a slave at the age of seventy—and it lists his place of birth as Africa. So Tom's great-great-great-grandfather Tony Dumas was born in Africa around 1790. And since the importation of slaves ended officially in this country in 1808, we can surmise that Tony would have been younger than eighteen years old when he was transported across the Atlantic in a slave ship and was sold to the Dumas family in North Carolina. That's a remarkable amount of detail to uncover regarding the life of a man who came to this country over two centuries ago and lived his whole life with no rights or legal last name.

By learning that Tony was born in Africa, we suddenly found ourselves with a unique opportunity to learn even more about him. If we could find one of Tony's direct male ancestors, we could trace his Y-DNA back to his original homeland. Tom did not qualify for this role, because he is related to Tony through his mother's line and thus does not share Y-DNA with him. However, we were able to locate a distant cousin of Tom's who is a direct male descendant of Tony's—a man named Reginald Thredkil, whose family still resides in Wilcox County. Reginald is directly descended from Tony on his father's side, so the DNA in Reginald's Y chromosome is identical to the DNA in Tony's Y chromosome.

We took Reginald's Y-DNA and saw that it was an exact match with the Y-DNA of the Balanta people from what is today the country of Guinea-Bissau. So Tom's maternal great-great-great-grandfather Tony Dumas was most likely born there. As I explained to Tom, this makes sense historically. We know that a very old slave-trading network existed across this part of West Africa. It would have been very easy for Tony to have been caught up in that network. We also know, from David Eltis's Trans-Atlantic Slave Trade Database, that between 1800 and 1808 there were dozens of slave voyages that carried members of the Balanta people across the Atlantic. What's more, the prime age for male slaves at the turn of the nineteenth century was between fifteen and twenty-five, which is roughly how old Tony, born in 1790, would have been.

"How do you think he was captured?" asked Tom, and I told him it was probably through a war between neighboring African tribes. As Tom knows, slavery was a huge business for different African kingdoms. The stories that we were told as kids—stories about white men jumping out of the bushes and grabbing African boys and girls—perhaps occurred occasionally, but slavery was a well-organized business. Slavery was also a highly profitable business, one based on Africans selling other Africans to Europeans. Indeed, some African societies waged war specifically and primarily to capture slaves to sell to Europeans.

Tom was fascinated to learn that he has distant relatives among the Balanta people today. What's more, as I explained to him, this is not his only African link. Using the same Y-DNA tests that allowed us to trace Reginald Thredkil's DNA back along his father's line to Africa, we tested

Tom's Y-DNA to see where his father's father's father's line originated. The results were quite surprising. We found matches among the people now living across Russia, Ireland, Germany, Poland, Austria, France—and most of all in Scandinavia and in the United Kingdom, especially Ireland.

The most likely explanation for this is that Tom's Y-DNA was carried to the British Isles some thousand years ago by the Vikings, who pillaged and plundered Europe for centuries. So not only does Tom have an Irish ancestor in Edward Hall and an African ancestor in Tony Dumas, he most likely has a Viking ancestor as well. "I've looked around my family," said Tom, shocked. "I've never had any idea of that. Vikings? I haven't even ever seen anybody else in my family who had gray eyes."

Turning to our other DNA tests, Tom's admixture test revealed that he was 62 percent sub-Saharan African, 35 percent European, and 3 percent Native American. The high level of European ancestry was not surprising, given what we had learned from our genealogical work. Tom was even more eager to learn what DNA analysis could tell him about his African ancestry.

Tom's mitochondrial DNA revealed matches with people across the continent, including Angola, Cameroon, Ethiopia, Senegal, and Morocco. However, the closest matches came from groups in modern-day Sierra Leone; 11.5 percent of the African American people descend from slaves who come from this region, and Tom has exact matches with people from four of its major ethnic groups—the Limba, the Loko, the Mende, and the Temne. The historians John Thornton and Linda Heywood believe that the evidence is clear: Tom's original African female ancestor was almost certainly from the area that is now Sierra Leone, and most likely Mende.

Furthermore, Thornton and Heywood told me that Tom's mtDNA results dovetail perfectly with the patterns of the slave trade to North America during the eighteenth century and with what we learned about Tom's family from our genealogical research. The oldest direct maternal ancestor that we were able to identify in Tom's family was his great-great-grandmother Jane Hall (who had children with the slave owner Ed Hall). Jane was born in the northern interior of North Carolina in 1824, but her master's family, the Halls, had moved to that area from Virginia in 1792. According to Thornton and Heywood, this means it is likely that Jane Hall's mother and/or grandmother was born in Virginia. The Trans-Atlantic Slave Trade Database tells us that the Africa-to-Virginia slave trade was over by 1775, but a number of Sierra Leone slaves did arrive in Virginia between 1750 and 1775. In fact, during this period five ships came to Virginia from Sierra Leone, the most in any twenty-five-year stretch. Thornton and Heywood think that it is very possible that Jane's grandmother was imported in one of these ships.

Neither Tom nor I have ever been to Sierra Leone. But the country has an intriguing history. It was founded in the late eighteenth century as a British colony and was first populated by African American slaves who had been given their freedom as a reward for fighting with the British in the American Revolution. Over time the British sent many former slaves from their empire back to this colony, much as the Americans would later send freed slaves to Liberia.

"Now I know where to go on my next visit to Africa," said Tom gleefully. "I'll be going over to Sierra Leone. Like a scene from *Roots:* 'Africa! I have found you!' This is all pretty amazing. I might not go to work in the morning. I'm going to be up all night."

I asked him if he'd be going to Ireland anytime soon to check out that side of his ancestry, and he smiled broadly, saying, "Yeah, I got to go. I never really liked St. Patrick's Day. I was always a little nervous. But I've got to go now."

He was as excited as anyone I'd involved in this project, and I told him that I thought his was a remarkably compelling African American story. He quickly cut me off, saying, "It's not an African American story—I have an American story, don't I?"

He's right, of course. His story is profoundly American—and African, Irish and Scandinavian, Mende and Balanta—a great example of how deeply mixed we all are.

In parting, Tom left me with a warm handshake, and then I heard him, as he turned away, calling out to his father, who was sitting in the next room, "Pops, wait till I tell you this." Tom was so moved by his family history that he assembled his family for a reunion about a month after we had our interview, so that Johni Cerny, the genealogist who researched his family tree, and I could share these stories, with Tom's dad at the center of a group of some two dozen family members who ranged in age from a newborn to a person eighty-eight years old. I have never participated in or heard of a family reunion quite like this. We discussed the nature of the relationship between Ed and Jane Hall, the origins of the color of Tom's eyes, the tragedy of Tony and Clara Dumas. It made me realize that all families should share a ritual such as this, a ritual or replenishment based on knowledge of the ancestors on their collective family trees.

Benjamin Carson

September 18, 1951

D R. B EN C ARSON and I graduated in the same class from Yale, the Class of 1973. As the director of pediatric neurosurgery at Johns Hopkins University, Ben gained a reputation as one of the most accomplished surgeons in the world, saving countless children's lives. Most famously, in 1997 he won international acclaim for separating a pair of conjoined twins connected at the brain in a twenty-eight-hour operation.His success is all the more impressive, I think, because he grew up in dire poverty, in a segregated nation that was set up to keep him there. He is truly someone who triumphed against all odds.

Looking at his family, I wanted to learn how this happened. In the process I found myself asking questions that have animated me for decades—questions about my own family and about the generation in which Ben and I grew up. We are unique, I believe, for having come of age in the maelstrom of the final chapter of the civil-rights era, shaped by parents of an earlier generation, people who might have harbored very little hope for their own future or their children's future, who were continually victimized and humiliated by racism but who nonetheless worked incredibly hard, fought for their dignity in innumerable ways great and small, embraced hope rather than despair for their children, and ultimately saw a better world emerge. How did these people—our parents' generation—pass their values on to us? How were they themselves the product of their parents' values and of a world that most of us today cannot even imagine? The answers, in Ben's family, are rather complex,

Ben's mother, Sonya Carson (at left), posing with family members.

sometimes contradictory. They nonetheless make for a fascinating story.

Benjamin Solomon Carson was born on September 18, 1951, in Detroit, Michigan, the second son of Sonya Copeland Carson and Robert Carson. Both his parents came from large families in rural Georgia and were living in rural Tennessee when they met and got married. His mother was only thirteen on the day of her wedding. His father, a Seventh-Day Adventist minister, was twenty-eight. Neither saw any future in the Jim Crow South, so when his father finished his military service, the couple moved north to Detroit. Ben was born shortly afterward.

"There were opportunities in Detroit," said Ben, "which for my parents meant opportunities in factories. My father got a job in the Cadillac plant, and he was able to purchase one of those little GI homes, which was a big deal."

GI homes were tremendously significant, not only to the Carsons but to all Americans in the late 1940s and early '50s. Indeed, these homes were among the most prominent features of the nation in the post–World War II era. Faced with a tremendous housing shortage (almost no new homes had been built during the war) and a massive number of returning veterans, these affordable, sometimes tiny single-family dwellings were built across the country, giving rise to new suburbs and entire city neighborhoods that were quickly filled with lower- and middle-class whites and a smaller but equally fortunate group of blacks. Through this era of property ownership, many working-class Americans entered the middle class. It was an almost unprecedented housing boom—and Ben's family benefited from it.

"We were in southwest Detroit, in an all-black neighborhood filled with these little GI houses," recalled Ben. "They just had maybe a thousand square feet, something like that. But they had individual little yards and many of them had a little garage and some had a little fence. And everybody was very proud of their property. Everybody had hedges, little trimming and shrubs—and they were meticulously taken care of. People were just very, very proud of these things, because in most cases it was the first time they had been home owners."

A decent job in a factory, a home of their own—things seemed to be going very well for Ben's parents in the earliest years of his life. But Ben doesn't remember that time. What he remembers, his face hardening, is the aftermath, as terrible secrets within his family destroyed their prosperity before it really even began.

"My mother," said Ben stoically, "discovered that my father had another family. And I don't think words could possibly describe the suffering that she went through over that. The only thing, really, that I think kept her from completely losing it was that she knew she had to be there for us."

Ben was eight years old when his parents' marriage fell apart. Recalling it, his voice trailed off and then returned, the pain still fresh, still holding on to the questions he'd had as a boy. "I'd be all over my mom with questions," he said, "asking her, you know, 'Why can't I wait till my dad comes home?,' and that kind of thing. And then finally she says, 'He's not comin' home anymore.' I don't even like to think about it."

In the wake of the divorce, Ben's family was devastated, both emotionally and financially. His mother could no longer afford their GI home, so Sonya took her two sons to live with her sister in Boston. Ben vividly recalls the move as a disaster. "Boston was a very different kind of place," he said, "boarded-up windows and doors, sirens, gangs, murders, rats, roaches—the whole nine yards. Everything that would be depicted in the worst of the movies you see on television, that was there. Our heroes were the drug dealers, because they brought candy for the kids. We would look forward to seeing them. Both of my cousins who lived with us were killed. That's the kind of environment it was."

Luckily for Ben, after two years of near-constant chaos in Boston, Sonya took her boys back to Detroit, determined to give them a better life. Detroit was safer then, but it was also a place where she had no family to support her. I asked Ben what kind of hardships his mother faced as a single parent. "Tremendous financial burdens," he replied, without hesitation, "because my father, even though he was ordered by the court to pay alimony, that was not forthcoming. And so she had to work very, very hard. Many times she would leave the house at five or six in the morning, and she wouldn't get home until eleven or twelve at night, going from one job to the next, cleaning people's houses. She was a domestic. And obviously that was extremely difficult for her."

It was also extremely difficult for Ben and his brother, who were now left to themselves for long periods of time. "She would leave instructions for us," he recalled. "We didn't always do them, but for the most part I think we tried actually very hard not to disappoint her, because we knew how hard she was working. We knew that she was doing it for us. I mean, she was absolutely determined that we were going to be successful. And she learned a lot of things being a domestic, because she was observant. She'd say, 'These people I work for, they have a lot of money, but one thing I noticed is that they study, they plan. They don't just sit around looking at TV and drinking whiskey all day.' Sometimes she would even take us out to their homes. And then we would come back into our neighborhood, and you'd see this guy sitting on the corner with a brown bag. And she'd say, 'Which environment would you prefer? You actually have the ability to choose.' That was inspirational."

Despite her memorable words, cleaning houses is grueling work, and Ben's mother's schedule was nearly overwhelming. Her life during those years, Ben believes, was filled with sacrifice and private pain. "My mother was a beautiful woman," he said, "as you can see from her photographs. She had no end of suitors. But she would make it absolutely clear to them that her sons were her priority. She basically sacrificed her own life to make sure that we were successful. And still, a lot of people were always trying to figure out how she was able to make ends meet—saying that she must be sleeping around, she was selling her body, you know? All this kind of stuff. And she would just have to put her blinders on. That's the kind of person she was."

Sonya Carson's challenges as a single mother were compounded by the fact that both Ben and his brother, Curtis, struggled in school during their early years—something that one might find hard to believe given the fact that Ben became a world-renowned surgeon. Ben insists it was true, however, and often tells stories about how poorly he did as a young schoolchild. "I was a worse student than you can possibly imagine," he said, laughing. But Ben also knows that the situation was far more complicated than that. He was growing up in Detroit, one of the most segregated cities in America, in an era when civil rights was still largely a dream and racism dominated the lives of black children. Ben's poor academic performance was primarily a product of this environment.

"I can remember," he said, growing very animated as he expanded on this idea, "as a fifth-grader being at a school where I was the only black kid in the class. The teacher expected me to be at the bottom of the class. And there was no other expectation than that. In fact, there was another class called special ed, and it had all the blacks in it. The only reason I wasn't in special ed was because I was a scrawny little kid and everybody in special ed was big and bulky and liked to fight, so they figured I would probably be killed in there. So they left me in the regular classroom. But I didn't think I was smart, and they didn't think I was smart, and I lived down to the expectations."

I've heard this story before, and it always fascinates me. Why did that change? How did he transform himself? Ben credits Sonya. "My mother," he said with obvious pride, "was a maverick. I thought I was incredibly stupid, and all my classmates and teachers agreed. But my mother did not agree. She would always be saying, 'Benjamin, you're much too smart to be bringing home grades like this.' She would always say that, and she would encourage me. She was very unhappy because she knew what lack of educational opportunity had done for her. She never got past third grade—and she wanted something better for us. So she was always encouraging."

But encouragement was not enough. Ben and his older brother continued to do very poorly in school, until their mother decided to overhaul their lives by limiting their television viewing and requiring that they instead spend their spare time reading books from the Detroit Public Library and writing book reports on them. Soon the boys were giving their mother two or three book reports every week, then sitting by while she pored over them. This new routine had a transformative effect upon both boys. It is all the more remarkable given the fact that Ben's mother couldn't read.

"She was almost totally illiterate," said Ben, "but we didn't know that, because she would make little underlines and check marks and stuff like that on our reports. Now, you know, she couldn't read them. Couldn't even read a word. But she'd say, 'Let's discuss your book report.' And then if we started talking about it, she could discuss it. So she fooled us. She was a smart woman. She just couldn't read."

To my mind, this woman was a genius. Those book reports made a huge difference in Ben's life, as he himself freely acknowledges. "In the beginning I didn't like the idea at all," he said. "Everybody else was out having fun playing. But after a while I discovered that between the covers of those books I could go anywhere, I could do anything. And so my horizons began to change significantly. I began to read about people like Booker T. Washington, how he was born a slave and taught himself to read when it was illegal for slaves to read—read everything in sight and became an adviser to presidents. This stuff stirred my heart. And then I started reading about animals. I really got into science, and pretty soon I was the only one who knew answers in class. It was totally shocking to all my friends. And to the teachers, too. But after a while, you know, they started getting used to me being the one who knew the answers, because I was the one who was reading."

The almost desperate quest for knowledge has been a crucial driving force in the black community since slavery. It has enabled countless African Americans to overcome seemingly insurmountable obstacles, and stories like Ben's never fail to inspire me. Watching him recall his mother, with her check marks and underlines and probing questions about books she could not hope to read, I could see a proud thrill rise up in him. It was these books, and his mother's passion for knowledge, that changed his life. And he's still excited about it almost four decades later.

"I read everything I could get my hands on," he said with a huge smile. "If I was waiting for the bus, I was reading a book. On the bus, reading a book. In the bathroom, reading a book. It didn't matter. My mother would

tell me to stop reading and eat my food. It made just an enormous difference in me and my academic performance."

But as Ben's grades began to improve by leaps and bounds, he found
his teachers—who were all white—divided. While some encouraged him,
others were deeply disturbed by his transformation, as it violated their
profoundly racist stereotypes.

"I remember in the eighth grade," he said. "They would give an award
for the student with the highest academic performance, and it was me.
And one of the white teachers got up and berated all the other students
for letting a black person be number one. She said, 'This colored boy is
getting better grades than you are! You know that's not right!' I mean, she
got up in front of the assembly and bawled all the kids out, said, 'You guys
are not trying! How can this black person be number one?' "

I asked Ben how this made him feel—it would have just about driven
me mad with rage. "It did anger me a little bit," he said, "but more than
that, it just made me feel like showing her. You know? Just showing her
what I could do." He then told me that his mother taught him how to deal
with racism when he was very young, and that her lessons stayed with him.
"My mother," he recalled, "said that if you go into an auditorium full of big-
oted people, *you* don't have a problem, *they* have a problem. And I internalized that. I refused to take on other people's problems, their negativity."

This attitude has served Ben well. His academic success in high school
led him to Yale, where he initially felt like a fish out of water but ultimately
thrived. He went on to the University of Michigan Medical School, and his
career exploded when he decided to focus on neurosurgery. He began his
residency at Johns Hopkins in 1977, at a time when there were only eight
black neurosurgeons in the world. After his residency ended in 1982, he
was recruited to serve as chief resident in neurosurgery at the Sir Charles
Gairdner Hospital in Australia. He stayed there just a year before returning to Johns Hopkins to become the chief of pediatric neurosurgery, an
impressive title for a man just thirty-three years old.

I asked him if he still experiences racism now that he is world-famous.
"If I do," he said, "I ignore it. As a neurosurgeon, what I try to do is improve people's lives. The last thing I think about is race. When I'm sitting
there and I'm looking at my list of patients, I don't think of them as a white

patient or a black patient or a Hispanic or a Chinese patient or whatever. It just isn't a factor for me. But I do realize that it is a factor for some of the patients. That was particularly true early on in my career. People didn't know what I looked like, and they would get sent to this clinic. And they'd say, 'Where's the white man?' You know? I would walk in the room, and they would say, 'When is Dr. Carson coming?' But I just ignored it. Still do. Like I said, it's somebody else's problem."

Over the course of his impressively successful career, Ben has never failed to credit his mother. "My world, my opportunities, have been so different from hers," he said. "My mother would obviously have never had an opportunity to go to Yale University, or to go to medical school, or to become a neurosurgeon. Never. And I think clearly we have these opportunities because people like her were willing to put themselves on the line, because they didn't want another generation to grow up like they did."

Turning to his family tree, we started to explore Ben's ancestry by looking at his mother's line. Sonya has had such a profound impact on his life. Perhaps because of her, he is convinced that it's important to know about ancestors he has never met and never will meet. "Remember," Ben said, laughing, "my mother, she didn't just appear. She had to come from somewhere. That determination, the will not to just be like everybody else, not to just give up? That came from someplace, and that came through my heritage to me. It goes all the way back to Africa someplace, I'd have to think. I suspect that some of my ancestors were people who just didn't accept the status quo." Our research revealed that he was right.

I began by asking Ben if his mother ever talked about her own childhood when he was young. "Not very much," he said. "You know, it was a difficult childhood." It was also a complicated one. Sonya was among the youngest of upward of twenty children; more details of this large family would come to light in our explorations of Sonya's father's ancestry. Many of her siblings were significantly older than she was and had already left home, so to ease the burden on her parents Sonya was sent to live with different siblings on a rotating basis. Such arrangements were not uncommon, but they were hard on children. Sonya was also a sickly child who was often unable to attend school. It was, according to Ben, a miserable childhood to the degree that it was any kind of childhood at all. It ended, of course, when Sonya married at age thirteen. "She was looking for a way out," said Ben, "which was my father, I guess."

Searching for clues about Sonya's ancestry, we spoke to a number of her relatives and pored over the records of Harris County, Georgia, where her family has very deep roots. There are still many Copeland families in the area today, both white and black, though not all of them are related to Ben. There are also at least five roads called Copeland in Harris County.

We learned that Sonya's parents were John Martin Copeland and Ruby Stanley. Both were born in Harris County—John Martin on March 15, 1888, and Ruby sometime in January 1894. Ben has vague memories of his grandmother Ruby. "I remember she used to like snuff and used to spit tobacco juice across the room," he said, grimacing, before adding what so many of us remember about our grandparents: "She was a pretty serious person. If she said something, you did it." But beyond this, Ben could recall little about his grandmother. And unfortunately, our research was not able to uncover much more.

Ruby's parents, Ben's great-grandparents, were Coleman Stanley and Lucy Smith. Coleman was born a slave in 1831 and does not appear in any census record before 1900, so it's hard to determine what he did under slavery or after emancipation before the turn of the century. We tried to locate Coleman's former owner by looking for white families in the area with his surname. But there were no Stanleys in Harris County, Georgia, until after the Civil War, when black people started using the name.

Ben was interested to learn that we were able to locate an 1860 slave schedule; it listed a white man named John D. Stanley who between 1850 and 1860 acted as an agent for an estate that included fifty-one slaves. Agents were essentially brokers. They sold slaves for rich men or, as in this case, for their estates, and they took a cut of the proceeds. Because they were frequently responsible for the distribution of large numbers of slaves, they had a major impact on the African American communities where they worked and sometimes had a great deal of day-to-day contact with slaves. So, I told Ben, it was possible that a slave like his great-grandfather Coleman Stanley might have taken the name of his broker. The broker may have been unusually kind or may have done Coleman some sort of favor. Anything is possible, including, of

Ruby Stanley, Ben's maternal grandmother, around 1950.

course, the possibility that Coleman simply heard and liked the name Stanley and took it for himself after he was freed.

We looked for the papers of this broker John D. Stanley, hoping to find something that might connect him to Coleman and thus maybe lead us back to Coleman's parents and beyond. But we could not find anything. Their connection is tenuous, albeit intriguing. Although John D. Stanley did not live in Harris County, he seems to have had a great deal of business there. And in that pivotal year of 1870, when former slaves appear in the census for the first time, there were a lot of black people there who had adopted the name Stanley—Ben's ancestor among them. Could they all have taken their name from this one slave broker? There's no way to tell with the evidence we have. But it is an interesting possibility, and it suggests how vast, complex, and economically intricate the slave industry was. We often think only of the masters and their slaves, forgetting all the agents, middlemen, and handlers who made the horrible engine turn.

Unfortunately, I had to explain to Ben that we were unable to prove a link between Coleman Stanley and the white slave broker John D. Stanley, which meant that Coleman's paper trail runs out at this point. We have no idea who his father or mother was. So many of the branches of black family trees end with this sort of stunted growth, as it were, stunted by the absence of written records.

We did find Ben's great-grandmother, Coleman's future wife, Lucy Smith, and her parents, Emily and Green Smith, in the 1870 census, where Lucy is listed as being a ten-year-old female farm laborer. But, like her husband's, Lucy's trail goes cold at this point, too. We could find out nothing more about her parents. As with many former slaves, her family name appears out of nowhere in the 1870 census. There were no large slave-owning families named Smith in the region. So that brought an end to our research on the family tree of Sonya's mother, Ruby.

At this point Ben was growing a bit frustrated with all the dead ends in our research. I couldn't blame him, but this is the nature of African American genealogy. We were luckier when we looked at Sonya's father's line. Ben did not know his grandfather, John Martin Copeland, but his mother's cousin Tom Copeland furnished a number of fascinating stories about him. Tom recalled that John migrated to Tennessee from Georgia in the early 1940s. In Georgia, Tom said, the Copelands were sharecroppers who also "dabbled in moonshine," working for "a white man who never paid what he owed." Tom claimed that an argument with this white man led to a killing—and ultimately forced John Copeland and his brothers to flee to Tennessee. For perhaps obvious reasons, we were unable to substantiate this story. We did learn, however, that Ruby worked as a waitress in Tennessee, and that John did a lot of work as a mason. Cousin Tom supported this, noting that John and his sons built the foundations of a large number of homes in the Chattanooga area, including many homes that still stand today.

Ben's mother's cousin Tom also asserted that John and Ruby had twenty-four children together, several of whom died in infancy. In Ben's autobiography, *Gifted Hands* (1990), he wrote that his mother was the twenty-third of twenty-four children. While that number is quite possibly correct, our genealogists were able to confirm in the paper trail only twenty-two of those children, nineteen of whom were born to Sonya's parents. The first three were born to John Copeland and his first wife, Ollie Simpson; their marriage record, dated 1906, still exists in the courthouse of Harris County, Georgia. By the time John and Ollie's third child was born, around 1910, John appears to have entered into a relationship with Ruby. Although no marriage record was found for them, John and Ruby Copeland were identified in the 1910 census as a husband and wife who had been together for two years.

Here John Copeland's first family, including his three recorded children, disappeared from the paper trail, and his second family was about to grow tremendously. The first documented child born to Ben's maternal grandparents was Barney (sometimes listed as Bonnie) Copeland, born in 1911 or 1912; their last—their nineteenth on record—was Adale, born in Tennessee in 1938. Based on the census from 1910, John and Ruby had been living together as husband and wife for three or four years by the time Barney was born, so it is very possible that undocumented children preceded Barney. Whether the number of Copeland children was twenty-two or twenty-four, however, the abiding fact is that Sonya came from an extremely large family, and her place in it had far-reaching consequences. Complicating factors in reporting basic data were legion in the Jim Crow South, from infant mortality to rural living and migrations to rearing by other family members and beyond, and this divergence of the paper trail from family oral history is not at all uncommon in African American genealogy.

Despite the discrepancies in determining the precise number of children in the sprawling Copeland family, we came closer to closure when drilling down into Ben's maternal grandfather's own ancestry. Further research revealed that John Martin Copeland was the son of John H. Copeland and a woman named Indiana Ash, who is sometimes listed as "India Ash" in various records. Looking at the 1870 census, we found a number of pages related to this Ash family, including something that Ben and I found truly remarkable.

In 1870, "India Ash" is listed as being nine years old, living with her father, Thomas Ash, and her mother, Millie. There are also two other households in close proximity to theirs with the name Ash. And even though the relationship between these households is not spelled out in the census, we can reasonably guess that they are family, because of their names and because of where they lived. And according to the census, in one of the Ash households near India's lived a man named James Ash, listed as a one-hundred-year-old black male. And here's the kicker: His birthplace is listed as Africa.

I strongly suspect that this man, James Ash, is Ben's ancestor, and that his claim of being born in Africa is correct. This is so unusual: a hundred-year-old black man, telling the census takers in 1870 Georgia that he was born in 1770 in Africa! Our genealogists told me that they rarely find an ancestor in the 1870 census whose birthplace is listed as Africa. There were a lot of African American slaves who were born in Africa before 1770. For example, by 1776, the year of the signing of the Declaration of Independence, 75 percent of our African-born ancestors had arrived in the United States. But almost all of them were dead by 1870. I have done years of genealogical and biographical research, and I have never found anybody from this era who listed his or her birthplace as Africa, except in the case of Tom Joyner, about whose family history we've just read. Tom also descends from an ancestor listed in the 1870 census as having been born in Africa.

Ben was positively captivated by this revelation and wanted to know what his relationship was to this James Ash. By examining the names and the ages of all the people in these neighboring Ash households in 1870, I told him it seems likely that James Ash could have been the father of Indiana's father, Thomas Ash, and of her Uncle Green, which would make James Ash Ben's great-great-great-grandfather.

Of course, we cannot say this with certainty. And we were unable to find out anything more about James Ash. We tried to find a likely slave owner for him but could not, because no white family by the name of Ash lived in this region at any time between 1790 and 1860. So the family must have kept the name from some earlier association, or maybe they just made it up. All we know about James is that he lived an incredibly long time and that he was born in Africa. And this latter fact, while enthralling, is not much use in tracing his roots. Hunting for an enslaved ancestor who was born in Africa in 1770 presents an almost insurmountable genealogical challenge, greater even than finding slaves in the records of their owners. This is because, with very few exceptions, slave ships didn't keep records of their passengers' names, since the passengers were seen as property, not as human beings. They weren't listed by name, just by gender and age. Hence there's no ship manifest bearing evidence of James Ash's journey to America. Like all slaves, he came over as an anonymous piece of black cargo. So it would be extremely difficult to pinpoint how and when James Ash arrived in this country. One can speculate, but that is all. And Ben, a scientist, is not especially interested in speculation.

The 1870 census did contain one possible clue about the Ash family in the generation that came after James. It indicates that Indiana Ash's Uncle Green was born in Virginia in 1805, while his younger brother, Thomas, Indiana's father, was born in Georgia in 1810. This corresponds historically with a large movement of white settlers and their slaves from Virginia to the Lower South between 1790 and 1830, spurred by the invention of the cotton gin in 1793, which opened up the cotton economy in the South, eventually leading to the removal of the Native American people from Mississippi and Alabama in the Trail of Tears. (Don Cheadle's family history is inextricably intertwined with the Trail of Tears, as we shall see.) Before the invention of this machine, cotton was extremely difficult to harvest and thus very unprofitable to grow. But the cotton gin allowed for the crop to be harvested in huge quantities by unskilled laborers, creating a massive demand for slaves. In fact, many scholars think that slavery was dying before the cotton gin was invented. After its invention, however, slavery expanded dramatically into the Deep South, with an enormous forced migration of African Americans from Maryland and Virginia into plantations in Georgia, Alabama, and Mississippi. Between 1790 and 1801, the amount of cotton exported by the United States went from 889 bales to 92,000 bales. By 1820, that figure was about 500,000 bales. The birthplaces of Green and Thomas Ash indicate that they were part of that migration (their father, James Ash, was probably part of it, too). Unfortunately, despite this information, we were unable to find any evidence connecting the Ash family to any slave-owning families in any of these states. So Indiana Ash's line runs out here.

Ben was now very satisfied with our work. Who wouldn't be happy to know the name of his first African ancestor? But the journey was not over, not by any means. We were able to find out a lot more about Ben's mother's family by turning back to Indiana's husband, Ben's maternal great-grandfather John H. Copeland. Records revealed that he was born in June of 1858 in Harris County, Georgia, and was owned by William Copeland Sr. This man William, it turns out, was the head of a very wealthy family. He and his son, William Copeland Jr., had adjoining properties, and between them they owned fifteen thousand acres and well over a hundred slaves. Their family documents contain a heart-wrenching story about

Ben's ancestors, a story illustrative of how it is possible to discover facts about black slave ancestors even before the 1870 census.

When William Copeland Sr. died in 1859, his estate was divided up among his heirs. The records from that estate division show that his slaves were split up into five numbered lots worth exactly $6,783 apiece. The lot numbers were then written on pieces of paper and shaken up in a hat. William's heirs gathered around and reached into the hat, each heir pulling out one of the numbered lots. That's a savagely cold thing to do, if you think about it. They pulled out a number, and that number represented a group of human beings, African American human beings, Ben's ancestors among them, who were then uprooted and redistributed, not only from their old owner to a new owner but also from old family ties to new ones. And there was no appeal.

The records indicate that the Copeland slaves were almost certainly not divided by family relationships, meaning that the estate did not try to keep mothers and fathers and their children together. To the contrary: They assigned dollar values to each slave and divided them up evenly, as if they were cattle or bales of hay, simply numbers or ciphers on a page. So families were broken apart. I explained to Ben that this was a horrible thing but was common practice. He wanted to know what happened to these ancestors. I explained that the records show that some of the Copeland slaves were deeded to William Copeland Jr. and thus remained in Harris County. But others were dispersed to relatives in Talbot County and Greene County, which are located halfway across the state of Georgia from each other. And Ben's ancestor John H. Copeland—his mother's grandfather—was a part of Lot Number 3, which was inherited by William Sr.'s son Alexander Copeland, who lived in Talbot County. John was only two or three years old at the time.

So Ben's great-grandfather, as a toddler, was forced to leave his home and his mother and family behind to move to another county because of his master's will.

Ben was profoundly saddened by the story. "It's not something you want to think about," he said. "I mean, I just can't imagine how incredibly difficult and painful it had to be. It makes you want to cry to think that that would happen to anybody, much less somebody who was related to you.

And a two- or three-year-old little boy?"

Fortunately, the story has a happy ending. Searching through the 1870 census, we learned that following the Civil War John H. Copeland was able to make his way back to his family in Harris County. The census places him there as a twelve-year-old boy, living with a seventy-four-year-old man named Spencer, a woman named Patience, and a younger female named Dicy. Looking back at William Copeland's estate papers, we could see that Spencer was owned by Copeland prior to that estate division of 1859. Could Spencer be John's father or his grandfather? We're not sure, but if so, that would make Spencer Copeland either Ben's third or fourth great-grandfather.

Regardless of his relationship to Spencer, John Copeland accomplished something most unusual. Any historian of the black experience will tell you that most families dispersed in the way that Ben's was never saw one another again. Black newspapers and magazines published after the Civil War are filled with ads looking for lost relatives, saying simple, plaintive things like, "Have you seen a boy named Green Ash or John Copeland?" The vast majority of those ads went unanswered. Ben's family offers an inspiring exception. His great-grandfather spent years in Talbot County away from his family, but at the end of the Civil War, with emancipation, he made his way back home. So many of our people were unable to accomplish this; it was something of a miracle. Slavery often arbitrarily created families and just as arbitrarily divided or destroyed them. Scholars still puzzle over the relationship between this horrendous aspect of enslavement and the disproportionate out-of-wedlock birthrate—69 percent—that characterizes black childbirth today. But family, for Ben's ancestor, was everything, something he fought to regain after slavery ended, even as a child.

"He was obviously determined," said Ben quietly. "Maybe that's where my mother got it from."

This concluded our genealogical research of Ben's mother's family. On the Ash side, we had been able to trace his oldest ancestor to a birth before the Revolutionary War, an extraordinary accomplishment for a black person who was not freed before the Civil War. On the Copeland side, we

This 1870 census indicates that Ben's great-grandfather, who had been separated from his family by slavery decades before, was able to make his way back to his family—an extremely rare occurrence.

went back well into the early nineteenth century. For African American genealogy, this is a great success. But I wondered how Ben would view it. I asked Ben if he found it frustrating to learn how recently his family tree ran out. If he were English, we might possibly trace his family lines back to the late Middle Ages or the Renaissance. I wanted to know if that bothered him. "No," he said matter-of-factly. "I'm glad to know what I know." But still, he said, he was eager to learn more. And as more records are unearthed and digitized, perhaps we will be able to learn even more about Ben's family's origins.

"Black people in this country," he said, "for the most part don't really get to hear very much about their roots, you know? We're all told you came from someplace, but that it's really not that important. But everybody wants to feel that they know where they came from. Everybody wants to know what their ancestors did, how they contributed. If you don't have that in our society, you are kind of lost. Even if you don't know it."

I couldn't agree more. I asked Ben if when he was a kid he'd ever wanted to know about his roots. Did he ever want to know about his ancestors? Did he even think about it? His answer struck a deep chord with me.

"I thought about it," he said. "When I used to look at some of the Tarzan movies, for instance. They would have the various tribes, and I would wonder if there was some connection with me. I wanted there to be a connection. So I would sometimes imagine myself running through a forest, you know? Free as a bird. I would sometimes fantasize about that. That was very appealing to me. I wondered, too, about my enslaved ancestors. Many times, in fact. I mean, I always wondered what it was like to be enslaved. And I thought about how difficult it must have been and what incredible strength it must have taken to endure that. And the thing that used to really tug at my heartstrings was thinking about families being torn apart."

Clearly, Ben's own experience shaped his feelings about his ancestors, even those he never knew. In the midst of a broken home, he worried about the families of forebears, living centuries before him under even worse conditions. I asked him if he'd been aware of this primal connection.

"Yeah, I think that's what made me think about it," he replied. "I mean, I just think about a mother and her children. Suppose you transport us back and we're slaves. You know how hard my mother worked to try to make a life for us, and then somebody comes along and just takes that away? I can't even imagine the pain."

Turning to Ben's DNA testing, I hoped to offer him some further understanding of who these lost children might have been. But almost immediately I found myself engaged in a very different kind of task. The first admixture test we ran revealed that 20 percent of his ancestry can be traced back to Europe. This means that at least one of his ancestors was fathered by a European, probably one of the slave owners. Even though we don't have a written record to prove that, we have access to a more accurate record, which is the genetic record.

I asked Ben how it felt to know that his genes reflected this painful aspect of slavery. "Some of my best friends are white men," he replied, half joking. "It doesn't surprise me. There was a lot of that going on in those days. I would be more surprised if it didn't turn out that way. It doesn't really bother me that much, because, you know, people are people, and people alive today aren't necessarily responsible for what happened two hundred years ago."

Since most of us in the African American community have a white ancestor, this is certainly a healthy response. But most of us are also much more interested in the African side of our ancestry than in the European side. Very few black people go to the family history library in Salt Lake City and say, "I want to explore my white roots"—Thomas Jefferson's descendants notwithstanding. And I could see Ben became visibly excited as I handed him the results of our two other DNA tests, which allowed us to trace his lines back to Africa. The first of these tests revealed that he shared a common patrilineal ancestor with many of the Makua people from northern Mozambique. "That's fantastic," he said, elated.

I then explained to him that this result is uncommon. Only 2.2 percent of all slaves who came to the United States were taken from this area of East Africa. In fact, the Makua tribe lived on the opposite coast from where most of the slaves who came to America originated! So we did a lot of research trying to determine whether we'd made a mistake or not. What we found out was that his Y-DNA results did make sense historically, because of the machinations of the intra-African slave trade. As the historians John Thornton and Linda Heywood explained to me, although very few slaves came from East Africa to the Americas, the Makua people were one of the two main groups traded from that region. The Makua became a target of interest particularly after 1808, when the United States banned the importation of slaves, which greatly cut down on the slave trade but did not completely eliminate it. Accordingly, the slavers had to use their imagination. So they began deemphasizing trade on Africa's west coast and started trading in East Africa. Thus some slaves were brought to the United States illegally after 1808 from that region.

This gave a clue as to when Ben's ancestors would have been enslaved. In addition, according to Thornton and Heywood, most of the Makua who came to the United States as slaves went to Latin America or other parts of the New World first. This means that it is very likely Ben's paternal ancestors were taken initially to the Caribbean and then to the southern United States as part of the illegal slave trade. And tragically, it is very likely that this ancestor came when he was very young, because the Makua from Mozambique often were shipped as children. Unlike the slaves taken from West Africa, a disproportionate number of those slaves from southeast Africa were very young people.

Ben's matrilineal DNA test results were even more complicated. We found matches with tribes all over the African continent: with the Bamileke in Cameroon; the Bassa, Yoruba, and Edo in Nigeria; the Mende in Sierra Leone; the Turkana in Kenya; and with Bantu-speaking representatives of the Cabinda exclave in west-central Africa (modern-day Angola and the Democratic Republic of Congo). Thornton and Heywood believe that of these varied results, Ben's first enslaved female ancestor probably came from the Cabinda exclave, as many Africans from this area were shipped to South Carolina after 1770 and this comports with Ben's family history (his oldest traceable direct maternal ancestor was his great-great-great-grandmother Emily Smith, born near the South Carolina border in Harris County, Georgia, in 1859). Of course, with so many matches it is impossible to say for certain. And Ben seems very happy just to know that his genes are dispersed so widely across Africa.

"It makes me feel connected," he said. "It makes me feel that something that was missing has been filled in. It's a wonderful feeling. Will it make me a better person? Probably not. Does it make me happy? Yes. It's inexplicable, but it fills in something in your heart. It's almost a religious experience."

As I prepared to leave, I asked Ben to look over the journey we had taken together, to try to decide whether he thought the slave heritage in his family's past had affected him personally. He seemed intrigued by this question, as he had been throughout our whole conversation, but uncertain at first how to answer it. After a long pause, he said, "I don't think that it's affected me in a negative sense. But I do think that maybe some of that determination, some of that drive that is demonstrated by the family, the ability to get back together after years of being separated and being separated by hundreds of miles—perhaps has something to do with some of the determination I have experienced in my own life and that my mother has. I think some of that probably came from my ancestral tree. And my hardheadedness, too, you know? That has to come from somewhere."

With that, he smiled, we said good-bye, and Ben ran off, hurrying to see a patient who most probably would not be surprised at his race. We had both come a very long way from new student orientation at Yale during the first few weeks of September 1969. How times had changed, I thought. If anyone had told either of us how our lives would have unfolded over the ensuing three decades, we probably would have laughed in that person's face. Because of our long friendship, it was enormously satisfying for me to assist Ben in the tracing of the branches on his extraordinary family tree. He has given so many children the gift of an extended life; I wanted to give him this small gift in return.

Oprah Winfrey

January 29, 1954

OPRAH WINFREY is one of the most famous people on earth. I wanted to involve her in this project from the moment I conceived it, because she fascinates me, as she apparently does just about everyone else. I admire her tremendously for what she's accomplished, who she is, and what she represents to African Americans. There's never been anybody in our history quite like her. This fuels my curiosity at its most basic level. I am dying to know how this woman, a descendant of illiterate slaves in Mississippi, dirt-poor scratchers of the soil, became the inimitable "Oprah," a cultural icon wherever human beings watch TV or film.

I'm also, I must admit, quite curious about the possible sources of certain aspects of her character. I think that Oprah somehow is as close to an Everyperson as any human being has ever been—she appeals to white people and black people and just about every other shade of people, males as well as females. She has an uncanny capacity to name the zeitgeist, the spirit of the time, to identify the key issues that most concern us as human beings at any given moment. And I want to know where that capacity comes from—what her family tree might tell us, if anything, about the source of this extraordinarily rare capacity for empathy and communication. Of course, there's no way to know for sure. There never is. There are tens of thousands of biographies of famous people, and none of them explain their subject fully. Yet each can teach us something, bringing us per-

haps just a little closer to
an explanation that makes
sense. And that's what I set
out to do here: get a little
closer to an understanding
of what makes Oprah tick
by looking at her ancestors.
I got a lot more than I bar-
gained for.

Oprah Gail Winfrey
was born January 29, 1954,
in Kosciusko, Mississippi,
a rural town just north of
Jackson. Her parents were
poor, young, and unmar-
ried. Her father, Vernon
Winfrey, was twenty-one
years old when he fathered
Oprah. Her mother, Ver-

*Oprah Winfrey's father, Vernon Winfrey,
opened his own barbershop in Nashville in
the 1950s.*

nita Lee, was just nineteen. Both came from families that had been in
this area in Mississippi since the days of slavery. And like many African
Americans of their day, they both fled the rural South—part of the Great
Migration of blacks looking for better economic opportunities in northern
cities. But their journeys took very different paths.

Vernon Winfrey served in the army, got an honorable discharge, and
moved to Nashville, Tennessee, taking with him the work ethic that he
had learned on his father's farm. By the late 1950s, he was reaping the
benefits of his decision to go north. He ran his own barbershop in Nashville—which he still does and at which he works every day—and his own
house. He met a woman and got married. He was happy, stable, and comfortable.

By contrast, Vernita moved to Milwaukee in 1954 and felt compelled
to leave her infant behind for several years, to be raised by her maternal
grandparents, Hattie Mae and Earlist Lee. Oprah had little understanding

of why her family had been torn apart. She was told that her mother had moved to Milwaukee to have "a better life" there. She grew up confused about basic aspects of her family. But she has vivid, formative memories of those years she spent with her grandmother, Hattie Mae Lee. And it seems that right from the start she knew she would grow up to achieve more than the Jim Crow South was allowing her family to achieve.

"I remember," Oprah said, "standing on the back porch and looking through the screen door, and my grandmother was boiling clothes in a big black pot. And she said, 'Oprah Gail, I want you to pay attention to me now. I want you to watch me, because one day you're gonna have to learn how to do this for yourself.' And I watched and looked like I was paying attention but distinctly recall a feeling that 'No, I'm not. This will not be my life.' She worked for a white family and used to always say to me, 'What you want to do is grow up and get yourself some good white folks. You want to get good white folks, like me.' Because her white folks let her bring clothes home, and many of the things that we had came from her good white folks. And I think her idea of good white folks was just that they give you things and you get to bring food home. But I also think it meant for her that you at least got to keep a piece of your dignity—a piece—and that's the best you could do. And so she'd say, 'I want you to grow up and get some good white folks.' And, you know, I regret that she didn't live to see that I did get some good white folks workin' for me, yeah. She couldn't imagine this life."

Oprah was observing firsthand the rural poverty that drove so many African Americans northward and the forces of racism that permeated every aspect of life in the Jim Crow South. But Kosciusko was also the only place she'd ever called home, and before she was old enough fully to understand its limitations, her mother insisted that she join her in the North. And so the six-year-old Oprah moved to Milwaukee. The difference between life in Mississippi and life in Milwaukee was profound, and the experience was deeply traumatic for her.

Prior to the move, Oprah says she had no relationship with or memory of her mother. "I'd only been raised by my grandmother," she said. "I knew I had a mother, but all those years my primary relationship was with

Young Oprah with her grandmother, Hattie Lee, and family. Hattie Lee raised Oprah until she was six years old.

my grandmother, and all of a sudden just one day I'm packed up and put in a car and told, 'You're gonna go live with your mother now.' It was horrible. But something inside me clicked. I knew that I was going to have to take care of myself—that I didn't have my grandmother anymore."

In Milwaukee, Oprah's mother was collecting welfare, working as a maid to earn a bit of extra money—and starting a new family. "My mother had another child," remembered Oprah. "And she was living in the home of a woman named Ms. Miller. And Ms. Miller was a colored lady, but a very light-skinned colored lady who did not like colored people."

Oprah began to cry at the memory of that household. "I instantly knew that Ms. Miller did not like me because of the color of my skin," she said. "I was too dark, and Ms. Miller would say it. My half sister Pat was five years younger than me, and she was light-skinned, and my mother was staying there because Ms. Miller loved my half sister. And I was put out on the porch to sleep. I wasn't even allowed in the house to sleep, and it was because I was brown-skinned, which didn't compute for me because my mother was brown-skinned, too. But I realized she was okay to Ms. Miller because she had Pat."

I found this story very moving—and deeply illustrative of the horrible ways that African Americans have internalized racism, the ways we've visited pain on each other. It is an unfortunate but vital part of our collective history, an experience that, sadly, is shared by thousands and thousands of people. Our people have long been color-struck. I know because I experienced those feelings myself. I remember, as a kid, being proud that my father was visibly mixed—that his whole side of the Gates family was light. Many of them even looked white; some could—and did—"pass," and they had "good hair," straight hair. And I thought that was wonderful. You didn't want to look like Nat King Cole, even with his beautiful process, his glistening chemically straightened hair. You didn't want to be too "dark."

Oprah recalls sensing this situation the minute she walked into the house where her mother was living. Nevertheless, she was powerless to change things—and her life began to spin out of control. Between the ages of six and fourteen, she moved back and forth between Milwaukee and Nashville, alternating between the homes of her mother and father, growing ever more isolated until disaster struck.

"I was nine years old," she said, her voice trembling. "And I got sent back to Milwaukee for the summer and ended up staying there, because my mother had said that she was going to marry her boyfriend and we were going to be a family. But the summer of my ninth year, things changed immensely for me, because I was raped by the boyfriend of my mother's cousin, who my mother was also living with. He became a constant sexual molester of mine. I thought it was my fault. I thought I was the only person that had ever happened to, that it would not be safe for me to tell. And so I was sexually molested from the time I was ten to the time I was fourteen in that house."

This monster abused Oprah publicly and openly, leaving unimaginable scars. "He practically told everybody," she recalled. "He'd say, 'I'm in love with Oprah. I'm gonna marry her, she's smarter than all of you.' He would say it, and we'd go off to places together. Everybody knew it. And they just chose to look the other way. They were in denial."

Alone, with no one to trust or confide in, Oprah saw her adolescence become a living hell. She wouldn't fully understand the profound trauma of these events for many years. Indeed, there was a time in the black community when the sexual molestation of children was considered to be something alien to the black experience, something that happened only in white families, like suicide, supposedly. "I was about forty when I stopped thinking it was my fault," she says. "I got all my therapy on *The Oprah Winfrey Show*."

School was Oprah's only respite, a place where she could feel safe and in control. Her grandmother, Hattie Lee, had taught her to read at an early age, and this gave her a great advantage. "I'd grown up reading," Oprah recalled, "and when I went to my kindergarten class, on the first day of kindergarten I was so bored. I thought, I'm gonna lose my mind with these kids sitting there with their ABC blocks. So I wrote my kindergarten teacher a letter. I sat down and I wrote, 'Dear Miss New.' And I wrote down all the words that I knew. I said, 'I know words.' I knew 'Mississippi,' 'hippopotamus,' 'Nicodemus.' I wrote down all the big words I knew. And so she said, 'Who did this?' And I got marched off to the principal's office, and I got put in the first grade the next day. And then they skipped me to second because I was such a good reader."

This was an integrated school. Oprah never went to a segregated school. But Miss New was a black teacher. And the fact that Oprah's first teacher in kindergarten was a black teacher deeply impressed her. "If she had been white," Oprah wondered, "would I have had the courage to write that letter? I don't know. I remember going home and saying, 'I have a colored teacher.' And she was colored like me. She was brown-skinned. So I felt like I could connect to her and that she would understand me. And so I got myself out of that kindergarten class."

Hearing Oprah talk about her early schooling, I was particularly struck by the contrast between the reinforcing climate she discovered in her school and the alienation she experienced within her home, especially hearing the horrific stories of her sexual abuse. The very idea of education transformed her—school had clearly given her an enormous amount of gratification and self-assurance. At the same time, school could not protect her from the trauma of daily life in her mother's house.

By the time she was fourteen, Oprah was living on the streets of Milwaukee. "I became a sexually promiscuous teenager," she recalled. "I ran away from home. I was going to be put into a detention center and ended up being sent to my father instead. I was out of control."

Oprah's father, Vernon Winfrey, provided a lifeline. The authority that emanated from him, the order and financial security of his Nashville home, and the role model offered by his new wife combined to give Oprah discipline and stability—and a chance to save herself. All of this would eventually lead to a profound transformation. What's more, Vernon provided a renewed focus on education, reinforcing Oprah's earlier passion for learning, which the abuse had served to obscure.

"On the Winfrey side of my family," Oprah recalled, "education was everything. I remember coming home once, and I had a C and my father said, 'C's are not allowed in this house.' And we were sitting in the kitchen, and he opened the door and said, 'You can stay out there with those people if you're gonna bring a C because you are not a C student! If you were a C student, I would let you get C's, but you're not a C student, so you can't bring 'em in this house.' "

However, before any transformation could occur, Oprah was forced to endure another terrible ordeal. When she moved back to Nashville, her father struggled to instill order and discipline in her life. He didn't know the deep, dark secrets of her abuse. He knew only that she was troubled, and he tried to respond. But her father could not imagine the true depths of her problems, or their origin. "He said to me that there would be no association with boys. He didn't know there had already been an association. Because I was pregnant when I came to my father, and my father didn't know it. So he sat down and said to me that he would rather see a daughter of his dead, floating down the Cumberland River, than to bring shame on the Winfrey name. And I knew I was pregnant. I thought about killing myself."

The stress caused Oprah to go into premature labor. Her legs started to swell, and her father sent her to see a doctor—accompanied by her stepmother, Zelma Winfrey. "We went to the pediatrician," Oprah recalled. "And the pediatrician says, 'Either this is the biggest tumor I've ever seen in my whole life or you're pregnant. Are you pregnant?' My

Oprah in a high-school photograph.

stepmother was there in the room. So I said, 'No.' And so he asked my stepmother to leave the room, and then I broke down and cried, and oh, my God, it was bad."

Oprah then had to go back home and tell her father. She doesn't recall what he did or said, only that he was devastated by the news and that she was overwhelmed with shame, falling further into a deep depression, consumed by thoughts of suicide. The story is harrowing—and its ending was tragic. Oprah went into labor shortly after seeing the doctor and delivered a baby who would die a few months later. With that, her father took full control.

"My father," she recalled, "came in and said to me, 'This is your second chance.' He said, 'We were prepared to take this baby and let you continue your schooling, but God has chosen to take this baby, and so I think God is giving you a second chance. If I were you, I would use it.'"

With this second chance, Oprah transformed her life. Thanks to her father's discipline—and with her stepmother's encouragement—Oprah focused on her studies, won a scholarship to study speech, drama, and English at Tennessee State University, where she excelled, realizing all of her enormous intellectual potential. At the age of nineteen, she began coanchoring the news at Nashville's CBS affiliate. And by 1977 she had moved to Baltimore's ABC affiliate, before taking a new job in Chicago seven years later, which would catapult her to the unimaginable heights she has since attained.

Hearing Oprah tell me the story of her early life enabled me to begin to see how she had been shaped, positively and negatively, by her family. And I wanted to find out more about these various family members, about who had raised them, where and how, under what circumstances. I found ample material on both her father's and her mother's sides. Oprah's maternal grandparents were Earlist Lee, born in 1887 in Hinds County, Mississippi, and Hattie Mae Presley, born around 1900. Oprah lived with them for the first six years of her life. They had a tremendous impact on shaping her childhood, even more than was usual for someone of Oprah's generation. Indeed, Oprah is able to describe her grandparents' daily life in vivid, eloquent detail.

"I slept with my grandmother in a big poster bed in the living room," she said. "We had a hearth, and the living room had the bed in it. There was just one big room with the hearth, the bed. People would come to visit, and there'd be the chairs in front of the bed. We called it the front room. Behind the front room was the kitchen. There was no running water. To the side was another room where my grandfather slept. My job in the morning was to go to the well and bring water, then to take the one cow out to pasture. Then my job was to do whatever my grandmother wanted me to do—get the eggs from the chicken without breaking the eggs. When it was hog-killing time, I was the one picking up all the intestines, and I would flick things off here and there. I had all the worst jobs."

Oprah remembers her grandmother making lye soap and homemade shoes and sewing their clothes. "It was a really big deal to get store-bought clothes or patent-leather shoes," she marveled. "It was a rural life. There was no indoor plumbing, no bathrooms. I bathed only on Saturdays. And it was my job to empty the slop jar in the morning. We had the slop jar under the bed. It was my job to keep the irons clean—because we had those irons for ironing clothes, and so when you used starch, they'd have to be washed off and scraped. It was my job to do that. I was a busy little girl."

Hearing her recount the basic level of her family's existence, the amount of grinding labor it took merely to provide the most fundamental features of daily existence, one can't help but be amazed at how far Oprah has come—she is almost like a character in a fairy tale. Yet her memory is absolutely correct: The rural poverty she describes was typical, indeed pervasive, among black people in the South. Oprah grew up in a community of sharecroppers, people bound to the soil by a system that was intended to replace slavery with its mirror image, a system of peonage to which most blacks were chained economically, as surely as they had been chained in slavery. The vast majority of former slaves became sharecroppers, almost as soon as slavery ended, and very few were able to break out of this system and own their own land.

Oprah's father, Vernon, recognized this and encouraged the education of his children as strongly as he could. Unfortunately, Hattie Lee, Oprah's maternal grandmother, had a different imaginative horizon, a horizon delimited in scope by the confines of the sharecropping system, Jim Crow segregation, and its various complex legacies. No doubt because of this set of experiences, she could not imagine encouraging her granddaughter to dream of getting an education so that she could become a doctor or some other kind of professional. Instead Hattie Mae wanted Oprah to grow up and "work for good white folks." And, given the severe limits of her own options, this was a noble and loving enough goal to which to aspire for her granddaughter.

But curiously, one generation back, Hattie Mae's family had taken a very different approach to the harsh system in which they found themselves. Hattie's mother was Amanda Winters, born around 1874 in Kosciusko, Mississippi. Amanda was the daughter of Pearce and Henrietta Winters, both former slaves in Mississippi. All these people seemed to have prized education. Amanda attended a freedmen's school, and for their time she and her siblings were quite accomplished individuals. Her brother, Jesse Winters, attended Wilberforce University, and her sister, Matilda, was a math teacher. Amanda herself taught public school English to black children in the 1890s and 1900s. She seems to have risen high in the community as well. She married Nelson Alexander Presley in 1893. They had eight children together, including Hattie Mae. What's more, after Nelson died (sometime around 1907), Amanda married Charles Bullocks, also widowed and seemingly well-to-do for a black man of his time.

Digging deeper, we discovered something most unusual about Amanda. When the NAACP was founded in 1909, one of its biggest supporters was a visionary philanthropist named Julius Rosenwald. Rosenwald had made a fortune with Sears, Roebuck and Company, and he was really passionate about what we would have called back then "Negro-white relations." Starting in 1912, he gave millions of dollars to help rural black communities set up elementary schools. Remarkably, in 1929, Oprah's great-grandmother Amanda became a trustee of one of these schools—a very rare feat for a woman of her day, white or black. We do not know exactly why she was appointed, but it is probably a sign of how respected she was in her community. Amanda was clearly a very accomplished, able woman. According to our research, she organized not only the school but also the Methodist church in Kosciusko.

How did Amanda's daughter Hattie Mae end up in such difficult straits just one generation later? The answer is illustrative of the precarious status of all African Americans in the Jim Crow South. Whatever gains they made were inevitably fragile, sometimes even the ownership of land, the crucial variable for the accumulation of wealth in this country.

Records show that Amanda and her second husband, Charles Bullocks, borrowed money from the Federal Land Bank. After Bullocks died, Amanda defaulted on payments, and the bank seized their land. Amanda offered to pay her debts with money from her children, but the bank wanted the land. According to Katherine Esthers, who is Oprah's cousin and the family's unofficial historian, they wanted it because they didn't think it was right that a black man—and now a black woman—had owned so much land. So the bank seized it all, along with all of Amanda's belongings. She then moved to her first husband's property and lived in a shanty for the rest of her life, dying sometime around 1940. Thus she was unable to preserve her briefly held prosperity, much less pass it on to her children, although her first husband's land did remain in the family as a more lasting form of wealth.

This story is tragic, of course, but Oprah was thrilled to learn that at the height of segregation her great-grandmother was working to educate African Americans. "It feels like I've carried it on," she said. "It feels like she would be the kind of person you would've had to have been to be able to stand up in a room. I mean, I feel it myself now when I go into a corporate room and I'm the only black face in that room and I'm the only fe-

Amanda Winters, Oprah's great-grandmother, was a trustee of one of the black schools founded by the NAACP.

male. I often say that 'I go forth alone, and I stand as ten thousand,' which is a line from one of Maya's poems."

I nodded in agreement. Oprah's maternal ancestors clearly shared her willpower and her passion for education and the ownership of property.

Oprah now wanted to learn more about these people from whom she descended, and I did my best to oblige her, even though the chasm of slavery began to make things very difficult. Amanda Winters's parents were the eldest generation on her maternal line that we could find. Their names were Henrietta and Pearce Winters. The 1870 census tells us that Pearce was born a slave around 1849, and the 1880 census tells us that his wife, Henrietta, was born a slave in Mississippi around 1854 (Henrietta's last name is not recorded). This census also tells us that by 1880, Pearce and Henrietta were living in Attala County, Mississippi, with their five children, including Oprah's great-grandmother Amanda. Sadly, we know nothing more about these people.

Oprah was disappointed to hear that we could not with certainty trace Amanda's line any further than this. But by going back a branch along Oprah's maternal line, we were able to learn more about the ancestry of her maternal grandfather, Earlist Lee. Earlist's parents were Harold and Elizabeth Lee. According to the 1870 census, Harold was born a slave around 1855 in Hinds County, Mississippi, whereas Elizabeth was born in freedom, also in Mississippi, sometime around 1875. The same census data revealed that Harold's parents—Oprah's great-great-grandparents—were named Grace and John Lee. They both were born slaves in Mississippi in 1833, which means they spent the first thirty-two years of their lives as a white man's property.

It is very difficult to find any records documenting the lives of our slave ancestors during the years that they were held in bondage. As we have seen, the slave system stripped them by design of the last names that they created for themselves, as part of a larger process of officially and legally denying their humanity. Indeed, names, records, language, family structures—all were intentionally repressed by the slave owners.

In Oprah's case, by searching over the records of slave owners in Mississippi, we were extremely lucky. We found an 1860 slave schedule for someone called S. E. Lee, who owned a female slave, age twenty-six, which is how old Oprah's great-great-grandmother Grace would have been in 1860. S. E. Lee also owned a male slave, age twenty-six, which is how old her great-great-grandfather John would have been in 1860. More-over—and this is very important—he owned a male slave, age five, which is how old Oprah's great-grandfather Harry Lee would've been in 1860! No other slaves in the county match these three ages and relationships of proximity to a white person named Lee. You don't exactly have to be Sherlock Holmes to deduce that these people are most probably Oprah's ancestors, even though they stand nameless in their slave owner's records.

Of course, matching ages and genders of slaves listed in the 1850 or

1860 slave schedules with freedmen and -women listed in the 1870 census is not absolute proof of identity, but it is overwhelmingly likely that these three people are Oprah's ancestors on this side of her family, her direct ancestors who were born into slavery and remained in slavery until the end of the Civil War. We were especially fortunate in that this is the only slave owner named Lee in the state of Mississippi whose slaves' ages matched that of her ancestors. And we looked at every Lee in the entire state.

Oprah was deeply moved when I showed her S. E. Lee's slave schedule. This seemingly simple document, almost 150 years old, listing human beings as objects of property, bore evidence of her ancestors' existence. There were her great-great-grandparents, written down as possessions, their ages and color recorded, but not their names. Oprah began to cry. And she cried, I think, because she was shocked to see two human beings from whom she is directly descended listed merely as nameless objects along with "the chickens and the cows," as she put it.

I asked her whether her family ever talked about slavery when she was growing up. She said no, absolutely not. "When you grow up poor and on welfare," she continued, "you don't have time to think about what came before." This is true, of course, but then I suggested that there might be another reason as well—a reason I've contemplated many times regarding the lives of all black Americans, be they rich, poor, or somewhere in between. For years and years, we were embarrassed about slavery. We were embarrassed about our slave past. That's why I think it's so extraordinary that our generation is embracing our slave heritage so very enthusiastically—slavery, the proverbial skeleton in America's historical closet. Some African Americans were so embarrassed by the fact of slavery that they would claim that their family members never had been slaves, a historical impossibility! Slavery has traditionally been difficult for all Americans to deal with honestly and openly. But this has changed with a new generation of African Americans hungry for all the details of their family's past, even the most painful and humiliating ones. We now realize that ultimately these are tales of survival and triumph.

Oprah agrees. "When I did the movie *Beloved*," she said, "it was not as successful at the box office as any of us would have wanted it to be, and

I was asked by so many press people, 'Why would you want to tell this story?' I wanted to tell the story because I find such pride in the story. My strength comes from their strength. That's one of the reasons I work so hard. And I feel like I have not even the right to be tired, ever, because I know I come from this. I didn't know names and backgrounds, but I know I come from this." Indeed, and so do we all.

At this point we had traced Oprah's maternal lineage as far back as the written record would allow. So we turned to her paternal line—and found another wealth of fascinating stories. Oprah's paternal grandfather, Elmore Winfrey, was born in 1901 in Poplar Creek, Mississippi. Her paternal grandmother was Beatrice Woods, born in 1903 in Carroll County. Oprah knew Elmore and Beatrice. Though she saw them rarely after she left Mississippi, she heard plenty of stories about them from her father, and these stories accord with the records that we were able to find.

In some ways the Winfreys were archetypal citizens of the Jim Crow South, where economic opportunities for African Americans were exceedingly scarce. Like the vast majority of their peers, they were sharecroppers, and their lives were brutally harsh. However, in one crucial way they were different. Most sharecroppers were illiterate, because whites wanted them that way. If black farmers couldn't read or count, then they couldn't manage their own transactions. That made them vulnerable, and they could be taken advantage of. (Indeed, if you look at contracts written in the Jim Crow years between blacks and whites, blacks were often paid less than their fair share.) There were exceptions, though. By all accounts, Elmore and Beatrice Winfrey were two of them. Elmore could read and write and understand math. He was reportedly a good businessman who successfully managed his own farm. We found a land deed revealing that in 1942 Elmore spent $3,425 on a 104-acre piece of land, ten miles southwest of Poplar Creek. This is truly remarkable for a black person who lived at his time, either in the North or in the South, but especially in the South.

Oprah was not at all surprised by this news. "I've heard great stories," she said, "about my grandfather being the businessman that he was." She's also heard all about the vicious racism that surrounded the lives of her grandparents and their neighbors—and how education offered the only way out of this morass. "My father," she said, "often tells this story about my grandfather not wanting his wife and daughters to have to go and work for the white man or work in the white man's kitchen, because he understood, many times, that, you know, Mr. White Man would be abusing those women and that there would be nothing that he could do about it. What he always wanted to do was to be able to be the provider in such a way for his family that he would never have to put the women in the family in that position. He understood that education was the open door to freedom for them. So thanks to him, all my father's siblings were well-educated, and every time I went to their house, that's all anybody ever talked about. 'So-and-So was in school, So-and-So's finishing school and graduating, So-and-So's going to college.' It was where I got that belief system. It came from that part of the family."

Talking to Oprah's father, Vernon, we learned another remarkable thing about his parents. Vernon told us that whenever his father encountered white people, Elmore would tip his hat and say "Yes, sir" and "No, sir." Vernon believes that his father felt compelled to do this, and Vernon had trouble accepting that. He feared that his father, however much he may have loved him, was just another Uncle Tom. But years later Vernon was shocked to learn that Elmore was quite the opposite—and that in fact in 1965 he and Beatrice housed two civil-rights workers in a back bedroom of their home. Vernon couldn't believe what his father had done, how much of his economic stability and security he was willing to risk to further this political cause, to which he had seemingly been oblivious for decades.

According to Vernon, the sheriff came to Elmore—a white sheriff, of course—and said to him, "You're one of the most respected Negras in this area. Now, other black people think that you're sending the message that it's okay to support the civil-rights movement." And Elmore replied, "Well, if you want to know what message I'm sending, go to that civil-rights march on Sunday, because I'll be sitting in the front row, sending my message—it's time for a change!"

Oprah had never heard this story before I told it to her. And it surprised her, the same way it astonished her father when he first heard it. It was as if her grandfather, a mild-mannered man, conservative in his habits, had become a fiery black militant, seemingly overnight.

We could not confirm Vernon's account of his father's conversation with the sheriff, but we were able to track down the two civil-rights workers whom Elmore housed—Luther Mallett, an African American from Kosciusko, and Matthew Rinaldi, a white college student from Long Island. Both testify to the role Elmore played in the movement in Mississippi. Indeed, they said that both Elmore and Beatrice were strong supporters of the civil-rights movement and that they had placed themselves in great danger by housing them. They recall that the couple was subjected to violent threats and that there was a cross burning on the lawn of the Winfrey home. They also told us that after a freedom house in nearby McCool, Mississippi, had been burned down by local whites, Elmore used his carpentry skills to help rebuild it, making the dangerous trip between Kosciusko and McCool even as armed Klansmen were traveling the same roads.

Oprah was pleased to hear these stories. They ultimately reduced her to tears of pride. And going back another generation on her paternal line, we found even more remarkable ancestors. Elmore's parents were Sanford Winfrey, born in 1872 in Poplar Creek, and Ella Staples, born in 1874 in Choctaw County, Mississippi. Ella's family can be traced forward to the Staple Singers, who are Oprah's distant cousins. Her husband, Sanford, was a farmer and may have been a teacher as well. Many towns in rural Mississippi had a one-room schoolhouse for black children. Vernon claimed that Sanford was the head teacher and that he taught all subjects through all ages. Friends and neighbors even called him "the professor."

We couldn't find a record of Sanford's being paid to teach, so we cannot confirm Vernon's claim. But Vernon was able to evoke a sense of the importance that education played in his family's life. He says that his father, Elmore, often spoke of how Vernon's grandfather Sanford insisted that his children learn to read and write—and that Elmore had two sisters who became schoolteachers.

Going back one more generation on Oprah's paternal line, we come to Sanford Winfrey's parents, Oprah's great-great-grandparents, Constantine and Violet Winfrey. And here Oprah's deep roots grow even more fascinating to me. In fact, the story of Constantine Winfrey is one of the

Oprah's grandfather, Elmore Winfrey, rebuilding a freedom house in McCool,
Mississippi, with civil-rights workers Luther Mallett and Alan Moonves.

most remarkable stories about a former slave that I have ever encountered.

Constantine Winfrey was born in October 1836 in Georgia and was
married to a woman named Violet, who was born in North Carolina in
1839. She didn't have a last name, or if she did, it was never recorded. It
seems that Violet was acquired in North Carolina, where she is listed as
having been born, and then shipped somehow to Mississippi, no doubt
because of the cotton boom. Constantine and Violet were married around
1859. They had eight children together.

Oprah knew that the Winfrey name came from this man, Constantine—she had heard of him in her family's lore, and she knew him to be
the highest branch on the family tree—but she'd never heard anything

more about him. And she had no idea where his last name came from. I think we found out. Constantine Winfrey probably took his name because he was a slave owned by a man named Absalom F. Winfrey. There is no concrete proof that Constantine was owned by Absalom or that he took his name, but in the 1870 census Constantine is listed as living three houses down from Absalom, and Absalom, like Constantine, also moved to Mississippi from Georgia. Furthermore, an 1850 slave schedule indicates that Absalom had seven slaves, the profile of one of whom fits Constantine exactly.

As for who Constantine was, the 1870 census indicates that at that time he and his wife were living with their five children and that both Constantine and Violet were illiterate. This is of course to be expected, since almost no slaves could read. But I learned something remarkable about Constantine, something that would prove to be consistent among later generations of Winfreys, including Oprah. Ten years later, in the 1880 census, Constantine and Violet are listed again, but now Constantine can read. And he can write.

Oprah and I were dumbfounded. At thirty-five, as a newly freed slave, he couldn't read and he couldn't write. At forty-five, just ten years later, he could do both. In ten years he had mastered literacy as an ex-slave. And that's while he was still having to work as a farmer every day, pick cotton, earn a living, raise and take care of a growing family. What's more, Oprah's great-great-grandfather not only embraced education himself—he emphasized education to his children and to the rest of the colored section of his hometown. We located a report from the Montgomery County School Board dated 1906 indicating that Constantine Winfrey moved an entire schoolhouse to his property so that the black children in his town could get an education.

Why did people on both sides of Oprah's family care so deeply about literacy and education? We don't have a simple answer. Even Oprah didn't know. But she was affected strongly by the revelation. "I can't even begin to explain what that is," she said, "but I think it's deep that that is where I've come from. I mean, I've always sort of understood on the periphery how important education is, and also inside myself, but I didn't know that

that was the root of where I came from."

Indeed, as we have seen, through several of her ancestral lines, Oprah is at the tail end of a long chain of people who loved education. While I cannot prove this scientifically, I happen to believe that this is why she is who she is. Or rather, it is deeply reflective of who she is. But there's another side to the story of her roots, another element that has defined her family since Constantine. And that element is the ownership of land, a factor as crucial to the shaping of her family as education was.

I wanted to discover how Constantine supported himself after slavery. Where did he get this land that he used to feed his family for generations, the land to which he moved this schoolhouse? How did an illiterate slave in 1870 eventually come to own acres and acres of prime farmland within just a couple of decades? As it turns out, Constantine had purchased the land in two different parcels. And the story of those purchases, contained in the land deeds and mortgage agreements, is not only remarkable, it is the only story of its kind that many other historians of this period and I have ever encountered.

Constantine bought the first parcel in 1876 from a white man by the name of John R. Watson. It was obtained through a highly unusual means of payment. According to the deed, Constantine agreed to give Watson eight bales of "lint," or cleaned cotton, in exchange for eighty acres of land. But there was a catch: Constantine didn't have any cotton. To get his land, he had to grow it and pick it first. The deed stipulates that Watson give Constantine usage rights on the eighty acres with the understanding that in two years Constantine would produce his eight bales. Each bale of lint cotton had to weigh four hundred pounds. So that's thirty-two hundred pounds of cotton. To get this much clean cotton, Constantine probably had to grow and harvest about four times as much, because of the debris and detritus contained in harvested cotton. In other words, Constantine had to grow and pick and clean more than six tons of cotton, and do so in two years!

Now, remember: John Watson is a white man, and this is 1876, the year Reconstruction ended and the Old South really started rising again. Needless to say, this was a very bad time for blacks. Moreover, throughout the 1870s the entire country was in terrible economic shape. There was essentially a depression that lasted the whole decade. So white people were poor, and black people were poorer. And these are the circumstances under which Constantine signs this agreement, promising that he would harvest this monster load of cotton in just two years. In addition, the agreement stated that if he could not deliver the eight bales of cotton in the allotted time period, he would be forced to vacate the land and lose all the cotton he had picked. In effect, Constantine Winfrey signed a two-year mortgage, with full payment due at the end of the agreed-upon time. It was all or nothing by the end of those two years. To me this sounds like an absolutely impossible set of tasks to fulfill.

But somehow Constantine pulled it off. And we know that because we found two deeds, both dated 1881, indicating that Constantine Winfrey had satisfied his obligation and owned his land free and clear. What's more, we also found a third deed, from 1882, indicating that Constantine had purchased a second plot of land, another eighty acres adjacent to the Watson plot. He paid $250 for this plot, which was a lot of money in 1882, and which indicates that he must have been doing very well developing his first eighty acres.

So Constantine managed to be a thrifty, productive farmer at a time when the status and power of black people were falling apart in the South. Constantine Winfrey somehow, through sheer grit and energy and determination, managed to thrive. Not only was his land deed unusual, it was possibly unique. I could find no other instance in which a black man used cotton as the payment of a mortgage in the former slaveholding South.

Oprah rightly sees this land as the heroic monument it surely is, for this was the very first property that any member of her family ever owned. It was this farm that sustained and supported her family for generations. Just as important, it was this farm that played a crucial role in furthering the progress of Poplar Creek's black community, by becoming the literal foundation for their education. This is fascinating to a historian like myself, because it's a patent reminder that the black community never consisted of one economic or social class. It had parts, or economic subdivisions. Even in the earliest years following slavery, the black community had a very distinct class structure, a structure that was sometimes based on color, sometimes based on education, sometimes based on property ownership. Among the slaves freed following the Civil War, this was really the start of the black middle class. And of all these factors contributing to class status, property ownership was most important, because it had the potential of being the longest-lasting.

Stories such as those of Constantine Winfrey are all too rare in our textbooks. If we encountered this story in a film, either Watson would abscond with the eight bales of cotton or the Klan would burn Constantine out shortly after he had constructed his new home! Tragically, we know that such betrayals did occur all too frequently. But such success stories like Constantine's, no matter how rare, reveal how truly complex and variegated was the multilayered set of economic and social relationships between black people and white people in the postbellum southern United States. Stories such as these are no doubt far more common than previously imagined, and they wait to be discovered in the historical records of our individual ancestors, hidden under the lush foliage of the branches of our family trees.

Constantine Winfrey's remarkable story is also where the paper trail of Oprah Gail Winfrey's family tree ends. Constantine and his wife outlived slavery and made their respective marks on history. Prior to them, however, there's no written record of any of Oprah's ancestors, at least none we've yet been able to find. The slave system obliterated any vestige of them. So now it was time to turn to DNA in the hopes of tracing her family all the way back to Africa.

Before we conducted her DNA analysis, I asked Oprah how she'd felt about Africa when she was growing up—was it somewhere to which she wanted to be connected? Or was she embarrassed about the images of Africans she saw on television and in films? Today she is deeply connected to Africa, devoting large amounts of her time and resources to humanitarian causes there, but she freely admits that when growing up she was embarrassed by her African roots, just as many of us in our generation were. "I was ashamed," she responded. "If anybody asked, 'You from Africa?' in school, I didn't want anybody to talk about it. And if it was ever discussed in any classroom I was in, it was always about the Pygmies and the, you know, primitive and barbaric behavior of Africans. And so I remember wanting to get over that period really quickly. The bare-breasted *National Geographic* pictures? I was embarrassed by all of it. I was one of those people who felt, 'I'm not African, I'm American.' They were primitive."

Oprah's honesty was quite refreshing. And I daresay her views were held by most African Americans until very recently. As a preadolescent I recoiled just as Oprah did. But also like Oprah, when I saw positive images of Africa during the Black Power era, and then when I started to study Africa in college and in graduate school, as I began to understand more, I began to feel a deep connection to the place and its people. Today, like most African Americans, Oprah sees Africa as it really is—a vast continent, full of diverse cultures, ancient civilizations, and boundless beauty. After centuries of separation, we're eager to reconnect on many levels—spiritually, economically, and politically.

I asked Oprah what she most hoped DNA would answer about her African ancestry. She told me that she's often been told she was a Zulu—a descendant of that great South African nation who fought so hard and so effectively against the British for so many years. She said, "When I'm in Africa, I always feel that I look Zulu. I feel connected to the Zulu tribe." The Zulus are legendary, and Oprah has talked about her possible Zulu connection more than once on her television program. She said to me that it would be a great shock if it turned out she was not a Zulu. I hoped, for her sake, that the test results would verify her instincts.

But Oprah's DNA told a different story. Our analysis of her mitochondrial DNA, which bears evidence of her maternal line's lineage, revealed that Oprah shares genetic traits with people in three parts of Africa: the Kpelle people in Liberia, the Bamileke people in Cameroon, and a Bantu-speaking tribe in Zambia. We also found identical matches to her among the Gullah people in South Carolina.

These results meant she could not be descended from a Zulu. Indeed, as it turns out, none of the Africans brought to America as slaves had Zulu heritage. The Zulu homeland in southern Africa was simply too far away from the main centers of the trade for any Zulu person to have been captured and sold into the transatlantic slave trade.

Oprah needed a moment to process this information. She still feels that

spiritually she is a Zulu—which is a very healthy way to think about our putative African or European ancestry. And despite not being of Zulu descent,
Oprah has a very rich African genetic heritage nonetheless: Zambia, Cameroon, Liberia—her genes are spread all over the continent. Indeed, as I explained to her, Oprah's DNA shows up in so many different places because of
the history of Africa. She is herself living proof of how, over centuries, even
millennia, tribes migrated great distances, and people were taken away as captives in wars, or sold into slavery, or married into other tribes.

Discussing her results with the historians John Thornton and Linda
Heywood, I tried to find out where Oprah's first enslaved ancestor might
have come from. The Bantu in Zambia, according to Thornton and Heywood, were generally not victims of the transatlantic slave trade. They
were simply too isolated, and so, for the most part, were Oprah's Bamileke
ancestors, who lived in the interior of modern Cameroon. This means that
Oprah's other exact match—her DNA hit among the Kpelle people in
Liberia—most likely points toward the origin of her first enslaved matrilineal ancestor.

Indeed, this result, combined with her DNA match among the Gullah people in South Carolina, squares nicely with the history of the slave
trade, according to Thornton and Heywood.

The Gullah were a very unusual group of enslaved Africans. During
the eighteenth century, they were brought to islands off South Carolina
and Georgia from an African region that encompassed modern-day Senegal, Liberia, and Angola. Prized for their skills in harvesting rice, these
people were able to remain on these isolated islands for generations,
largely sheltered from direct contact with whites, who preferred to live
away from the pestilential coast—and thus they were able to develop their
own unique language and culture, which have been handed down from
generation to generation along with their own distinctive DNA signatures.

According to Thornton and Heywood, the fact that Oprah's DNA has
been found among the Gullah people suggests that her first matrilineal
ancestor came to the United States through South Carolina and that that
woman's owner later moved down the Mississippi, leading eventually to
the birth of Oprah's oldest known female ancestor, Henrietta Winters,

born in Mississippi around 1850. From South Carolina we can trace a path back across the Atlantic to the region of Africa now called Liberia. We don't know who owned Oprah's first enslaved matrilineal ancestor in America, nor do we know her name. But taking the genetic evidence and this historical evidence together, both Thornton and Heywood agreed that it is highly likely that Oprah was descended from the Kpelle people in Liberia and that her ancestor most likely either was captured in a battle or became a slave as the result of a marital dispute, as was custom in this region. Thus I felt very confident telling Oprah that she shares ancestry with the three hundred thousand Kpelle people who still live in the rain forests of central Liberia.

Oprah was stunned by the news. "That's me," she said wistfully, looking at the charts of her DNA that I had handed her. "I'm Kpelle. I feel empowered by this." And no doubt the Kpelle will welcome Oprah as a long-lost sister, just as warmly as the Zulu have done.

Oprah's admixture results were just as surprising. As we have seen throughout this book, many African Americans claim a considerable degree of Native American ancestry, but most have little or none. Oprah defies this trend; her admixture results are 8 percent Native American and 3 percent Asian. Since these two results can code for each other, we can conclude that Oprah has 11 percent Native American ancestry, placing her among the 5 percent of African Americans who have a significant amount of this genetic heritage. And this is probably the result of the proximity of blacks and Indians in her ancestors' home in Mississippi in the early nineteenth century, before the Trail of Tears in the 1830s.

This concluded our research. When it had begun, Oprah had lived for the past two decades as one of the most famous people on earth, but also as someone who was unable to name her great-great-grandmother, much less assert the identity of her maternal ancestor's original African tribe. By the time we said good-bye, all that had changed. She shared an exact genetic match with an African human being who identifies herself as a Kpelle today. She was the heir of Constantine, a remarkable entrepreneur; of Amanda, a devoted educator; of Elmore and Beatrice, who risked all they had for civil rights. Taken together, the recovery of these ancestors—even the bare-bones stories that we've been able to piece together—help to explain why it would perhaps not surprise some of these ancestors that their

Whoopi Goldberg

November 13, 1955

IT IS IMPOSSIBLE to talk with Whoopi Goldberg for long without being intrigued at her sense of timing, at her capacity to improvise, and by how keen an observer of human nature she is. She seems to take her material from the world unfolding around her, minute by minute—even, or especially, in conversation. Whoopi heard that we were doing this project and sent word that she would like to be involved. From the outset she was passionately interested in the process of finding one's ancestors, saying that she'd love to have her family tree researched because she had no idea who might be on it. "I just want to know who's there," she told me with a sly smile. I was happy to oblige her. The stories we uncovered, however, were not at all what I'd expected. I thought I would perhaps find some hints as to the source or inspiration for her humor. Instead I found myself confronting a fierce, independent line of people who had little room in their lives for jokes—and yet some shared a great deal with their brilliant descendant.

Whoopi was born Caryn Elaine Johnson on November 13, 1955, in New York City. She and her older brother, Clyde, were raised by their mother, Emma Harris, in a housing project in the Chelsea neighborhood of Manhattan. Whoopi's father, Robert James Johnson Jr., abandoned the family when she was very young, and Emma was forced to support her children as a single mother, working a variety of jobs—including teaching and nursing—to make ends meet. While Emma worked, the kids more or less took care of themselves, sometimes not seeing their mother for days at a time or, if Emma was working a night shift, seeing her only in the early morning as she was coming home from work and they were getting ready to go to school.

Though she had many traumas as a youth, struggling with drug addiction and an absent father, Whoopi eventually triumphed, transforming herself into the multitalented, Oscar-winning actress and comedienne we all admire. The transformation must have required great effort and determination. Yet in person Whoopi is almost coy about it, choosing to deflect praise with jokes. Her brother, Clyde, says that Whoopi's eventual success took everyone by surprise. As a child, he says, she was friendly but somehow different. "In retrospect," he added, "she was probably ahead of her time." He has no explanation for where this came from. And he doesn't see any ancestral influence in Whoopi's success. There is no one, he told me, in his family who had any talent as an entertainer.

When Whoopi talks about her upbringing, she focuses not so much on the hardships she endured or the way in which her family shaped her but rather upon the community in which she grew up—a community that continues to inspire her today.

In the late 1950s and for decades beyond, Manhattan's Chelsea was an exciting, wildly diverse neighborhood. "Chelsea was the neighborhood of eclectic people," said Whoopi, smiling broadly. "It was all kinds of economic backgrounds, all kinds of jobs—actors, performers, boxers, nurses, doctors. And there was just every conceivable group of people—white, black, Asian, Puerto Rican, Greek, Turkish, Albanian. I mean, you name it, it was in Chelsea. We all spoke a little bit of Spanish, a little bit of Greek, a little bit of whatever. Whoever was near you, you spoke a little bit of what they spoke. You had to be able to say, 'Could I use the bathroom? Can So-and-So come out to play? Good evening, good morning, good night.' You know? And because not everybody's parents spoke English, you had to find a way. That was the neighborhood."

Whoopi was born the year after *Brown v. Board of Education,* at a time when many blacks were feeling intense discrimination. Her neighborhood seems to have been insulated from the racial politics of the times, however, and she remembers feeling little if any racism, in the streets or in school. "In New York City, you could never be undereducated back then," she said. "You could go anywhere and get any kind of education you needed in public grammar schools and Catholic schools, which is what I went to. And in New York, as far as your color, in the wintertime you don't know who is who. 'Cause everybody has got hats and coats and stuff, so you always were intermingling with people. So it was for me the greatest, greatest place I could have been born. Because it gave me an understanding that fundamentally we are all the same."

As many of the family histories that I've researched for this book have illustrated, throughout the first half of the twentieth century, the Great Migration reshaped the African American population, when thousands of black people moved from the South to the North. But the trade-off of moving to the North to escape southern racism could be costly. Many blacks encountered severe economic problems and experienced profound feelings of isolation and displacement in their new northern homes. To Whoopi, however, growing up in Chelsea, these issues were distant. Her family had come up from the South a generation earlier, and even though new southern immigrants were streaming in throughout her childhood, all were easily absorbed into the neighborhood's diversity.

"How would we tell?" she asked me. "I mean, how would we know? There were just new kids in the neighborhood sometimes. And maybe in hindsight you could say, 'Well, that person was really country.' But there were so many different kinds of people there. And when you're a kid, none of that is important. The white kids, the black kids, the Spanish kids—we were all about how many bottles can we collect 'cause we want some candy. That's what we were into. 'Gee, it's so hot, Mr. Softee is coming.' Or 'Let's get the big wrench to open the fire hydrant so everybody can have the mobile pool.' That's what I knew growing up. I've faced more racism as an adult in this enlightened time than I ever did as a kid. It was a shock to me. I was like, 'Huh? Where did you grow up?' 'Cause, you know, in New York it was just, you were there. It wasn't a discussion about color or any of those things. We all ate the same thing, we all went to the same movies, we all hung in the same places, and it wasn't till I got outside of New York City that I discovered, 'Oh, uh, okay, this is a little bit different here.' "

As a result of her environment, young Whoopi watched the civil-rights movement unfold from a distance, uncertain as to its significance, living in blessed isolation from America's racial woes. "It wasn't until I was older," she recalled, "I mean really into my teens, you know, when I began to realize what was going on. And then for me it was more like, 'How can people be so dumb? What's the big deal with the bus? Why can't you ride the bus?' Because it wasn't something that was in my sphere. In New York you didn't have to deal with buses and sitting at counters. In New York you went where you wanted. So I saw it all on the television and in magazines. I saw Dr. King and the hoses and the dogs. We all saw it. But, you know, it wasn't until I was older that I could sort of figure out what was going on, because it just made no sense to me."

I asked Whoopi how this experience affected her identity as an African American. She shook her head and smiled, bemused. "I don't consider myself an African American," she said. "I never have. I consider myself an American, because all I've known is this country, and so anytime someone hyphenated it, it always made me think that I wasn't entitled to everything I would be entitled to as an American. And regardless of how far back the times of arrival go, I still sort of figure I predate most of the folks that I meet. So I'm an American."

I asked her how her black identity figures into that, and she replied simply, "I never separated them. I am black. It's just what I am. It's like I am female, I am black. And I am American. That's my identity. And it's straight out of New York City. The person who I am was formulated specifically because of what I learned as a kid and the way I had relation-ships with people and the fact that the relationships were not ever based in race but were based in what we are doing. 'Cause, you know, if Tommy Tinsley's mom caught me doing something, she'd beat my behind just as bad as if Ms. Gale found me doing something. The Irish ladies beat your behind, the black lady beat your behind, Mrs. Rodriguez would beat your behind—it didn't matter, you know."

I admire Whoopi's brazen independence, her stubbornly counterintu-itive sense of cosmopolitan identity in an era of ethnic fragmentation. So many Americans of all ethnicities today are angrily territorial about their identities—determined politically and emotionally to erect barriers and police the boundaries. Whoopi, by contrast, is ethnically mercurial and inclusive. She delights in defying cultural stereotypes. "Folks who have not grown up around black folks think we have this mythology connected to us," she said. "They all think we all talk this same way and do this and that and you know what I'm talking about. But it's a mythology. My human education is vastly different from someone who was raised somewhere else. So I don't have some of the same ideas. And that's why I go about my life the way that I do. So people shouldn't come at me like they don't understand my culture, you know? I don't know what that means—'my culture'? I'm here, this is my culture."

Unlike most of my other subjects, Whoopi was not especially eager to talk about her parents' lives. Perhaps she wanted to protect their privacy, which, of course, is understandable. Or perhaps, like many of us, Whoopi sees herself essentially as her own creation—a product of her own brilliant imagination, sui generis, her own branch on her extended family tree. I wanted to see where this sense of independence and individuality came from. Was it just Whoopi's invention, as her brother believes? Was it somehow the culture of her neighborhood in New York City, as she seems to feel? Or were there some antecedents in her family's past, unknown to her perhaps, shaping her identity, as if through mother's milk?

We began by researching her father, Robert Johnson Jr., who was born in 1930 in New York City's Harlem at the end of the Harlem Renaissance. His father—Whoopi's paternal grandfather—was Robert Johnson Sr., born in Georgia around 1898. Photographs show him to be a very light-complexioned black man—bearing, as Whoopi points out, an uncanny resemblance to Edward G. Robinson. Whoopi remembers little about him. "I used to wonder about him on occasion," she said, "but you couldn't ask him anything. He was not a talking gentleman. You did not question him about anything."

When Whoopi was growing up, she recalls visiting her father's parents often in Harlem. But almost all of her recollections of her grandfather revolve around the silence and distance he created. "He was very quiet," she said. "I only saw him occasionally. I always knew he was at my grandma's if the door was closed. And when the door was closed, you didn't make any noise. It was two very distinct worlds, not because it was Harlem and Chelsea but because I think the family connections weren't as tight, you know? So you went to Harlem and you did what you were supposed to do, and then you got home and did what you wanted to."

We were able to learn one rather interesting fact about Robert: He was a Pullman porter, which as we've seen was a very prestigious job for a black man of his era. Being a Pullman porter gave you status within the community. Pullman porters saw the world by rail. They went everywhere. They were sophisticated. Sometimes they had two families, one at each end of their route—which may have helped explain Robert's distant personality. The Pullman porters also played a crucial role in the history of the civil-rights movement. They were the first independent black labor union, organized under the leadership of a brilliant labor leader, the socialist A. Philip Randolph. The Brotherhood of Sleeping Car Porters was a historic, visionary group in African American history, one that would have political influence for generations. So these porters were, as a group, remarkably interesting people, sophisticated and cosmopolitan. But no one in Whoopi's family knew any details about Robert Johnson's career. He simply never talked about it. "As far as I knew," said Whoopi's brother, Clyde, "he was always retired."

Whoopi was not aware that her grandfather had moved to New York from Georgia. And, indeed, in our interviews, nobody in her family knew exactly where in Georgia he came from. Many thought that he came from a town called Pleasantville, but there is no town in Georgia called Pleasantville. So we did a lot of research, and in the 1900 census we found a two-year-old colored child named Robert Johnson living in a town called Faceville in Decatur County, Georgia, just across the border from the Florida panhandle. Perhaps Faceville became Pleasantville after years of repeating. And for this reason and others, we came to believe that Whoopi's paternal grandfather was born sometime in 1897 or 1898 and was living in Faceville by 1900.

Marriage and census records told us that Robert was the son of John Johnson, born in May of 1875 in Faceville, Georgia, and Estella Sherman, born in 1874, also in Georgia. They were Whoopi's great-grandparents. Further research revealed that John Johnson was the son of Alex Johnson and Quilley Williams. Both Alex and Quilley were born slaves in Faceville, Alex in June of 1847 and Quilley in November of 1860. By locating them we had gone back over 125 years in Whoopi's family history. But we lose the thread at this point, because there are so many black people who share the name Johnson. Indeed, when Frederick Douglass—whose birth name was Bailey—escaped from Baltimore, he took a train to New York, riding under the invented name of "Frederick Johnson." But when he got to New York, he said there were so many black people called Johnson there that he wanted another name. So he chose Douglass. And he was right. At that time Johnson was the most common surname among free African Americans in the United States, followed closely by Coleman.

Turning to Whoopi's maternal line, we found a lot more information. Her mother, Emma Harris, was the daughter of Malakiah Harris and Rachel Freedman. Whoopi did not know her grandmother Rachel, who died in 1951, four years before she was born, but she has very happy memories of Malakiah—or Malachi, as everyone called him. "I'd know that face anywhere," she said, looking at a photograph of her grandfather. "During the war he went to France, and all the French girls called him Malachi. He came back and said, 'They called me Malachi!' So he became Malachi. He was a big, tall, beautiful man. I have his smile. It's his smile that you see on me. And I remember Easter Sunday with him. I remember he gave my brother a Brownie camera for Easter, and there were always wonderful and mysterious things going on with him. He'd go places, and then he'd be gone for a while, and he'd come back. He was an adventurer."

Malakiah also led us back to a remarkable story in Whoopi's family's past. According to his death certificate, Malakiah Harris was born in Palatka, Florida, in 1911, and his parents were James Harris and Clander Washington. This is corroborated by the 1910 census, which places the Harris family in Palatka at that time. We could trace the Harris family back no further. However, the 1900 census indicates that ten years earlier Clander Washington was living with her parents—Whoopi's great-great-grandparents—William Washington and Elsa Tucker in Alachua

Whoopi Goldberg has fond memories of her charismatic grandfather, Malachi Harris.

County, Florida. That census also indicates that William Washington was born a slave in Virginia in 1837, and his wife, Elsa, was born a slave in 1845 in Florida. By 1900, Whoopi's great-great-grandmother Elsa had given birth to sixteen children, of whom fourteen were still living. Clander, who is the baby, was born in 1891.

"Sixteen kids?" said Whoopi, laughing. "I barely got through one."

Trying to learn more about these people, we uncovered what I consider to be one of the most remarkable stories from the Reconstruction era. In the years after the Civil War, Alachua County, Florida, was extremely poor, rural and underdeveloped; indeed, the entire state of Florida was essentially a frontier. Its hostile climate kept its population tiny relative to the rest of the settled United States. William and Elsa Washington found themselves there, after slavery, trying to start a new life for themselves under freedom. Given their skills, like the overwhelming number of former slaves, they had little choice but to farm. Obtaining land to farm was everyone's ideal. However, while you might think that uninhabited rural Florida would have been an easy place for the Washingtons to acquire land, it did not prove to be so. You need money to buy land. And most African Americans came out of slavery with nothing. Of course, near the end of the Civil War, General Sherman famously promised freed slaves forty acres of tillable land in his Special Field Order #15, on January 16, 1865—that is the origin of the phrase "forty acres and a mule." But few slaves got their land, let alone a mule.

Fortunately, Reconstruction offered people like the Washingtons another opportunity through what was known as the Southern Homestead Act, a piece of legislation passed by Congress in 1866 that set aside roughly 46 million acres of land—primarily in Florida, Arkansas, Mississippi, Alabama, and Louisiana—for the former slaves and, initially, whites loyal to the Union to claim. In order to take possession of a parcel of this land, the first step was to select a lot and then pay a five-dollar filing fee, which wasn't as easy as it sounds. The program was not well administered. If you

James Harris, Malachi's father and Whoopi's great-grandfather.

wanted land, you had to travel about looking to find a parcel that was available, inspect it, then locate an office to file your claim, which many times proved to be an administrative nightmare.

William and Elsa, however, managed to beat the odds. In November of 1873, the register of entries for the land office in Gainesville, Florida, set down a claim for them, totaling 104 acres. But filing a claim was just the beginning. Now the really hard part began. According to the Homestead Act, in order to own the land you claimed, you had to "prove" your claim by building a home of some kind on it—and then you had to live there and make a wide variety of what were called "improvements" on the land, meaning you had to enclose it, plow it, pay taxes on it, and plant and harvest a salable crop.

William and Elsa Washington had never done anything quite like this before. They had worked land their whole lives, of course, first as slaves

William and Elsa Washington's Homestead Claim in Gainesville, Florida. They would be among the tiny minority of blacks able to keep their land after Reconstruction.

and then as sharecroppers, but this was very different. They had to build and run a farm! Up to this point, they'd been the raw labor that made a farm profitable; now they were taking on the added and incredibly burdensome role of management. They had to make all the decisions about what crops to grow, where to buy seeds, when to plant and harvest, where and how to sell, how to manage the money and buy the equipment. To make matters even more difficult, they had only five years to prove their claim. It must have been terrifying. And this wasn't the only obstacle they faced.

Reconstruction effectively ended in 1876, three years after the Washingtons filed their claim and two years before the deadline they were rushing to meet. And with the end of Reconstruction came the rise of the old white South, as former Confederates and their children took power throughout every state in the region. For Whoopi's ancestors, trying to prove their homestead claim in Florida, what had been a tough prospect

became an even more difficult challenge. Many homesteaders faced arson or other
violence from the angry
whites who resented any di-
minishment of their power.
Some faced lynchings by the
rising Ku Klux Klan. And the
overwhelming majority faced
a pernicious, ubiquitous form
of economic exploitation.
Fighting to keep their land,
most black homesteaders
were forced to take on massive debts, borrowing money
from whites at exorbitant
rates, mortgaging everything
they had, from their crops to
their livestock to their tools.
Of the three thousand Af-
rican Americans who filed

*Whoopi's great-grandmother, Clander
Washington, daughter of William and Elsa.*

homestead claims in Florida, only one in ten was able to withstand these
pressures.

But Whoopi's ancestors were among that group. We found a mortgage
for William and Elsa Washington indicating that they borrowed heavily on
40 of their 104 total acres. But we also found an affidavit, dated 1878, that
proves they eventually became the legal owners of their land. What they
did is an extraordinary accomplishment in African American history. They
were slaves who became property owners in the Old South. They joined a
tiny minority.

Whoopi was elated by this story, crying "We did it!" as I showed her
the deed that proved just how resourceful her ancestors had been. And I
was just as excited as she was. I know it can be difficult for people today
to fully appreciate how important this was. There is nothing surprising

about an African American owning land today. A large number do—and have done so for generations. But in the 1870s, land ownership was rare. Even by 1920 only 25 percent of the African American people owned land. Land ownership was a critical battleground. Land was a primary source of wealth in the nation at that time, and nobody knew this better than former slaves. They had worked the land. Their parents, their grandparents had worked the land. They had seen the land make their owners rich. They knew that if you could own property, you could be independent, meaning you could provide for and protect your family. You had a chance to achieve a measure of economic independence as a black person. Theoretically at least, you could play a small part in the American dream, you could enjoy a certain status and a certain self-sufficiency. The historian John Morton Blum once wrote that the promise of America was land. And that's why William and Elsa's story about property acquisition is a story about freedom—a thrilling story of which we should all be proud.

"I'm going to go to Florida and find that land," said Whoopi, beaming.

I wanted to ask her if she thought differently of her family now, if she thought something had been passed on, not through genes but through sensibility, from generation to generation. I am not sure what I think myself. How could these distant ancestors contribute to the fantastic success she enjoys today? So I posed the question: Did she think William and Elsa had had some influence on her, however small?

"I don't know," she replied. "I have to think about that. But I do know that there is a new little fire building inside me. It's like your head goes up another foot and a half, you know, because they were extraordinary people. They did extraordinary things. I mean, I just think it's wonderful to know that they got their land. So now I will stop saying to people that all I want is my forty acres and a mule, because we actually got it. We got it. Double that, actually."

Trying to learn more about William and Elsa, we found a land deed dating from 1898 that shows William receiving eighty acres of land from a person named Daniel Tucker and his wife, Dinah—at the cost of one dollar. This is significant because it is how family members typically gave each other land back then. They "sold" it for a dollar. And by looking at the 1880 census, we learned that at that time William and Elsa Washington lived in Newmansville Precinct in Alachua County just two houses away from the Tuckers. And remember: Elsa Washington's maiden name was Tucker. So since they lived two houses away and sold land to each other for one dollar, I have to believe that they were related. In fact, given the level of generosity—eighty acres is a lot of land—I believe that the Tuckers could well have been Elsa Washington's parents, which would make them Whoopi's great-great-great-grandparents, another generation of landowners in Whoopi's family line.

Daniel Tucker was born a slave in South Carolina in 1825. His wife, Dinah, was born a slave in Georgia in 1828. We have no idea how or when they ended up in Florida. But, digging deeper, we found that the land the Tuckers gave to William Washington had been purchased by Dinah Tucker in 1871, just six years after all the slaves were freed by the northern victory in the Civil War. Now, how did she get the money to buy all that land so soon after slavery? We don't know. It would be fascinating to find out. Did a white man or woman who used to own it and who particularly liked her give her the money? Did she have a child with a white man? I think this possibility is very likely. Whoopi agrees. There is no way to know, but I'd say there's a good chance something like that happened, some tie of intimacy trumping race.

We were unable to resolve this mystery or add anything else to our knowledge of the Tuckers. In fact, we were not even able to connect them definitively to Elsa Tucker Washington. They may have been her parents; they may also have been neighbors who, coincidentally sharing a name, wanted to sell her some land at an exceedingly low price. But circumstantial evidence suggests that a family tie, and a deep one, was obtained between them.

After William and Elsa, this line of Whoopi's family, like all her other lines, disappears from the written records into the mists of slavery. We could not definitively identify their parents. The paper trail ran out. This understandably saddened Whoopi. "It's like whole stories are gone," she said. "Whole lives are gone. Whole histories are gone. And there is not emotional compensation for that. You know when you sit with folks and they say, 'Well, my family goes back to County Cork or Sicily or wherever.' I'll say, 'I don't know. I think in Florida, maybe?' "

DNA, of course, offers us new tools to explore our heritage and to help us understand our origins. Her admixture test revealed that she was 92 percent sub-Saharan African, 8 percent European, with no East Asian or Native American ancestry, which means that one of her great-great-grandparents or great-great-great-grandparents was probably European—which was, of course, very common due to the treatment of female slaves by their owners. (And perhaps Dinah Tucker and the white man who sold her the land somehow play into this.) However, her percentage of European ancestry is very low for an African American. Most of us have about 20 percent European ancestry. Whoopi is overwhelmingly of African descent.

"I always thought I was a mutt," said Whoopi. "I'll stop saying that now."

We next analyzed her mitochondrial DNA, which tells us about her matrilineal line all the way back as far as it's possible to go. The tests revealed that she shared genetic signatures with people who today identify themselves as Mende in Sierra Leone and with the Kru people in contemporary Liberia. We also found matches with members of the Papel and Baiote tribes from the modern-day Republic of Guinea-Bissau.

These results were somewhat difficult to interpret, because we know so little about Whoopi's maternal heritage. The earliest direct maternal ancestor we were able to locate was her great-grandmother Emmaline Morris, who died in New York in 1953. We don't know anything more about Emmaline. We don't know her birth date, much less her birthplace, much less her mother's name or birthplace. One of our professional researchers described her work on this family line as "an insurmountable task."

Nonetheless, John Thornton and Linda Heywood were able to offer an interpretation of Whoopi's DNA based on their immense knowledge of the African slave trade. They maintain that all of Whoopi's matches could be valid sources of her original enslaved African female ancestor. The Papel and Baiote tribes lived very close to one another in the region that is now Guinea-Bissau, and both were taken into slavery in large numbers. According to Thornton and Heywood, many Papel and Baiote people ended up as slaves in Virginia, South Carolina, and even New York, which was a significant destination for slaves from this region in the 1740s and '50s. Though it is unlikely that Whoopi's direct maternal line remained in New York undocumented from the mid–eighteenth century until the mid-twentieth, it is not impossible. Moreover, since other members of Whoopi's maternal line moved to New York after spending generations in Florida and before that Georgia and South Carolina, it is not inconceivable that Whoopi's direct maternal ancestor followed that path, too—in which case she may well have been a Papel or Baiote sold in South Carolina or Virginia.

In addition, Thornton and Heywood concluded that Whoopi's Kru and Mende results from the bordering nations of Sierra Leone and Liberia make sense, because during the years that the slave trade thrived in the seventeenth and eighteenth centuries, one out of every ten slaves who came to the United States came from this area of Africa. And many of these slaves ended up in plantations in South Carolina and Georgia.

I then told Whoopi that I thought she might be interested to know that many of the slaves from this region were what we might call "hardheaded" slaves or "independent-minded" slaves, meaning they fought and resisted the slave trade. Most famously, Cinque, who led the revolt on the *Amistad* in 1839, was a Mende man from Sierra Leone. Under Cinque's guidance a group of slaves seized control of that ship off the coast of Cuba, killed many of the crew, and tried to force one of the white sailors to steer them toward Africa. It didn't work. They ended up being captured by the United States Navy and stood trial before the Supreme Court. They were defended by John Quincy Adams, in one of the most important cases in our history. And they were freed. It's a very famous story, cherished by African Americans. But the ending isn't as well known as the beginning. And I love the ending—which is that after their trial, after they were freed, they had the choice of staying in the United States or going back home. This was no choice at all to them. They went home, went back to Africa. They were smart and determined people, who refused to recognize the reality of their enslavement and refused to believe that they had lost control over their own lives. Incredibly, they prevailed. And Whoopi is a distant cousin of these people.

"People should stop messing with me," said Whoopi in a kind of half growl. "They should stop messing, 'cause this can come about again!"

When I finished laughing at this, she told me, deadly serious, "That's quite wonderful, though. Really. I think it's pretty amazing. I love the idea that the *Amistad* is in my blood. I love that. I love that there's a cousin or an uncle or whatever who is fifty times removed but, you know, is my blood. I like that. I like that my family, we had skills. We weren't just any-old-body. We knew stuff. We did this."

She seemed extremely happy to learn that she came from such an impressive heritage, on both sides of the Atlantic. I asked her if her parents ever talked about Africa, and she replied, inimitably, shaking her head, "No, they were New Yorkers, you know." I then asked her if she'd ever wondered what part of Africa her ancestors were from. "Not as a kid," she replied. "Because when I was a kid, it was just Africa, the Dark Continent. The animals, Tarzan. But since then, I've grown up, I guess. And this has always become something I hoped I would come to learn about in my lifetime, where I would have some opportunity to find out just who went into this family. And then I can go and see the land and I can go and sniff the air, you know? You want to walk in the places where people who had something to do with your existence walked."

This is in fact one of the most important reasons to do genealogy, especially if you are African American. This sort of knowledge can ground you; I deeply believe this. Knowledge of your ancestry can provide a certain sense of calm about the past, where before there were only questions—hundreds of years of unanswered and seemingly unanswerable questions.

I wanted to know what Whoopi thought of the journey we'd taken. She had known so little about her family when we began. And our journey—like all journeys into the African American past—was incomplete. Despite that, had it been a trip worth taking? Was this information important to her? Had she learned anything about herself? Her answer was very inspiring. "The battles I have today," she said, "they come from people labeling me and trying to whittle away what is mine, you know? My individuality and my place in the nation. This is my country. I always knew somewhere in my gut that we had arrived early on. So I've always said to people, 'You might have come above on the *Mayflower,* but I was below on the *Mayflower.* We came at the same time.' So this is great, because it sort of cements that and makes it even bigger in me. I now know that this is mine. This country, this is mine."

Mae Jemison

October 17, 1956

⁜

D R. MAE JEMISON was the first black female astronaut, an historic accomplishment that has made her a hero to countless people, myself included. She has also been a tireless advocate for children around the globe, founding a number of nonprofits, including one that provides health care for impoverished children in West Africa. Hers is an exceptional story—yet her family's story contains many haunting, painfully familiar reminders of the slave roots we all share. Indeed, I was able to find only some of her ancestors, because their master made gifts of them to his children. Nonetheless, I felt that our dialogue was among the most positive and inspiring that I had with anyone in the course of filming *African American Lives*. This was, I think, a testament to Mae's powerful sense of herself and of her family's influence upon her.

Mae was born on October 17, 1956, in Decatur, Alabama, a small town in the northern part of the state. Her parents, Charlie and Dorothy Green Jemison, like many of their fellow African Americans, could not find good job opportunities in Alabama at that time and so decided to move north. In 1960, Dorothy took Mae and her older siblings, Charles and Ada, to Chicago, leaving her husband behind temporarily. Mae remembers the experience vividly, from a child's perspective.

"My mother went up to Chicago, and then my father closed everything down in Alabama and came up, I guess three or four months later," she recalled. "It was so funny, because I remember we were all expecting my father to come up for so long. We were living with my Aunt Mary, who was my mother's sister in Chicago, in Woodlawn. And we were staying in the basement, and we looked outside and said, 'He's here, he's here! My dad is here!' "

The reunion proved to be a very happy one. At the time Mae's father was a roofer and a journeyman carpenter. Her mother had two years of college but had been doing odd jobs in Alabama. "She used to clean houses sometimes. And she used to sew clothes," recalled Mae. "I remember that's how I learned how to sew. I

Mae Jemison in an official NASA photo.

learned how to do a lot of things from her." The move north gave both of the Jemisons new opportunities. Mae's mother's life especially was dramatically transformed.

"Once we got to Chicago, my dad put my mother through school," said Mae. "She finished up at Chicago Teachers College, did her last two years and then came out and started teaching. Before then she had worked at Spiegel's doing warehouse, so she used to have a hard time getting a job, because everybody said she was overqualified for any of the jobs they had. And my dad, he used to always have two or three jobs. He drove a taxi, worked as the maintenance man for United Charities of Chicago. Then he eventually became a maintenance supervisor. And he always did contracting work, too, remodeling homes. He was one of these people who always had a bunch of jobs."

Clearly, Mae's parents were impressively industrious. They also, like many other African Americans of their generation, knew that hard work was not enough—a black person needed education to rise in the white world—and they treasured education, encouraging Mae from her earliest days to pursue her passions in school. "My mother was a teacher," said Mae, "so she was always very excited about learning. I remember that when I was growing up, I loved space exploration. I mean, even as a little girl—oh, God, I loved space exploration. I followed the Mercury, the Apollo, the Gemini programs. I knew song, line, and verse of everything and always assumed I was going to space. And my parents were my role models. They're how I learned to deal with success or failure. I learned from my mother how to stay up all night and finish a project. She was that way with everything, even with sewing clothes: 'You got to do that until it is completed.' I learned from my dad and his buddies—they loved my assertiveness as a little girl. So when I'd run into guys later on who had a problem with me, it didn't matter, because my dad was the manliest man I knew. And he thought I was fine, so that was that."

Talking to Mae about her parents, I have to confess that I felt a great rush of pride that we came from the same kind of background. Her parents were remarkably enterprising, I thought, and had much in common with my own parents. They worked tirelessly to inspire their children, teaching them to love and treasure education and hard work. They were part of a truly great generation, a generation that we still do not fully appreciate and from whose principles—sadly, I think—too many of our people are straying. Mae agrees. And as we began to talk more about her parents, my appreciation of them only deepened. I was fascinated to learn that Mae's parents were unusually engaged with their heritage and their African roots. This was not the case in my home, or in most African American homes. And I think that this foundation in her black heritage profoundly shaped who Mae Jemison is today; long before "Black is beautiful" became a catchphrase on the streets, Charlie and Dorothy Jemison were proclaim-

Mae as a little girl with her father, Charlie Jemison. Mae's parents placed a premium on education—Charlie worked two or three jobs at a time to put his wife through school.

ing it in their living room.

"When I was a little girl growing up," Mae said, "we always paid attention to Africa. I remember when Miriam Makeba first came over to the United States back in like the early sixties, my mother took us to get our hair cut off, and we were wearing short Afros. And my mother used to talk about how you were beautiful because you were African, how in South Africa women were beautiful without their hair. And I remember also hearing about Olatunji and his 'Drums of Passion'—all those little kinds of things were really important to me."

Chicago in 1960 was still a segregated city. The Woodlawn neighborhood in which Mae grew up was all black, as was her school. Race was a palpable presence in her life. Yet perhaps because of her parents' attitudes and the examples they set, it did not overwhelm her or limit her aspirations. Rather, it seems to have empowered her.

"I knew that there were race issues when I was growing up," she recalled. "When I was in elementary school, I couldn't help notice them. I mean, we're in the middle of the 1960s! But my parents were very aware of everything that was going on. And race never impinged upon me in terms of how I saw myself as a child or how I saw myself as a person in this world. I always assumed I could do whatever I wanted to do, because I had the talent and the skills and all that, the energy to do it. My mother especially was always very aware of things that were going on. My mother knew about the Nation of Islam—she had gone to Nation of Islam meetings. Now, she did not agree with how they wanted to treat women, and she was not about to join the Nation of Islam. But we knew about it. We knew there were choices. We knew about black liberation. That was part of us."

Mae attended all-black elementary schools, where her parents' values were widely accepted. No one complained about her short African-style hair or clothes. In fact, she happily remembers having a sixth-grade teacher who was as excited about her heritage as she was. During the time normally devoted to history, the class departed from the standard European and American history curriculum and actually studied Africa. "I learned about the African countries becoming free," said Mae, smiling. "And I remember this report that I made in sixth grade. It was sort of one of those extra-credit reports, busybody little girl that I was. I drew this picture on the cover with an African in a business suit and another one in tribal garments. Because the whole idea is, there was this world between which people were transitioning very rapidly to sort of Western ideas and lifestyles as well as maintaining their traditional culture. So for me Africa was just always a part of my life. I was always interested. Civil rights, too. That was always part of our consciousness, too. I remember when Martin Luther King came to Chicago and marched in Cicero. I remember Stokely Carmichael, H. Rap Brown, LeRoi Jones. I was aware of all those things that were going on. My mother got the *Liberator* magazine, the *Chicago Defender, Muhammad Speaks*—all of that was a part of growing up, part of the background of things."

Mae believes that this environment gave her levels of self-assurance and pride in her roots that fueled her desire to excel. "I was always very excited about being called African and African American. It made me very confident. I didn't have to worry. I mean I remember being just six years old; my brother and sister were older than me. They always talked about what they knew about how black people, how we invented the traffic light and shoe-lasting machine and all those kinds of things."

When Mae ultimately went to an integrated high school, she expected to do not just as well as the white children but better. And she did. She graduated high school at the age of sixteen and went straight to Stanford, where she majored in chemical engineering and African American studies. (I have to confess that I love the fact that the world's first black female astronaut was an African American studies major!) She confronted sexism and racism within the engineering department, she says, but had the confidence to fight back and succeed. She went to Cornell Medical School, spent summers traveling providing health care in Kenya, Cuba, and Thailand, and she became fascinated with medicine in developing countries. Before joining NASA and becoming the first black woman in space, she even found time to serve as a medical officer for the Peace Corps in West Africa. She's had an engaged and fulfilling life—and still credits it all to her parents and the values they instilled in her.

"I don't know that I can trace it back and say what made my parents so special," she said proudly, "but the stories they told about growing up sort of just blended into everything I knew. They became who I am."

I was fascinated by Mae's parents and hoped to find more about what made them so special. Unfortunately, in the case of her mother, who died in 1993, we were able to journey only a short way into her family's past.

Mae's mother was Dorothy Mae Green, born in Florence, Alabama, on October 27, 1928. Dorothy's mother was named Alberta Inman, born in 1903 in Decatur, Alabama. Alberta had five children and put two of them, including Dorothy, up for adoption when they were very young. Dorothy ended up taking the last name of the elderly couple who adopted her—John and Ada Green.

Though Dorothy seems to have been extremely close to her adoptive parents (she named her first daughter Ada, after her adoptive mother), she knew her birth mother and her biological siblings. And the story of Dorothy's birth mother is very unusual. All five of Alberta Inman's children had the same father. He was Mae's maternal grandfather, and he

Mae around the time of her high-school gradua-tion. Thanks to her parents' influence, Mae graduated high school at the age of sixteen and went on to earn degrees from both Stanford and Cornell.

was a very complex man who wore many masks, using a number of different aliases. According to Mae's family, he called himself Lucius Blount. We spent countless hours searching every possible record for a man by that name or some variation, but we came up empty-handed. And in the end I wonder whether "Lucius Blount" or Alberta herself ever revealed his true identity. This, of course, makes genealogical work nearly impossible. Still, I wanted to learn as much as I could about this situation.

"He was an older man," said Mae, acknowledging that her grandfather was essentially a mystery to her. "And he lived elsewhere, possibly in the North. He came to town from time to time."

Speaking with Mae's older sister, Ada, we learned more. Ada had heard that Lucius was a married man, very good-looking—tall, well educated, and articulate. He was also, according to Ada, very light-skinned and might have been half white.

Ada believes that Lucius met her grandmother, Alberta, when she was a teenager and that Lucius had some business with her father, Jones Inman, a farmer who lived in Decatur. After that, Ada says, Lucius started coming to Alabama every summer from somewhere in the North. She believes that Lucius impregnated Alberta on almost every visit.

Alberta ended up having five children with Lucius, all very close in age. Mae and Ada's mother, Dorothy, was the last. At first, all the children lived with Alberta and her father. At some point, however, according to Ada, Lucius said that he would take Alberta away to the North with him and get rid of his wife. But he wanted to be able to start life over with Alberta "unencumbered." So he promised to arrange adoptive homes for all of Alberta's children. Dorothy and her brother Major were both placed

with elderly, childless couples in nearby Florence, so they grew up knowing each other and were always very close. Moreover, the families that
they were placed with were very kind and supportive; both of them went
to college and flourished.

According to Ada, the other children ran away from their adoptive
homes so often that they were returned to their mother. In the meanwhile
Lucius had vanished, never to return. So three of Dorothy's older siblings
ended up staying with their mother and being raised by her. They kept in
contact with their two adopted siblings and remained close throughout
their lives, but the family had been forever damaged. In later years, according to Ada, the children would tease their mother and quiz her, asking, "How could you give up your kids?" Ada recalls that her grandmother
was ashamed—and didn't like to talk about it. She also recalls that her
children had a lot of enmity and anger toward her.

Mae agrees with her sister. "One of the things that used to really
bother my mother," said Mae, "is that she felt that Gram was not forthcoming about anything, and it really, really upset her."

These feelings are easy to understand. It is very hard for an outsider
to comprehend the desperate choices that Alberta seems to have made,
even given the fact that she was so young. It seems to us today that she
exposed her children to unnecessary pain and hardship. It is a sad story,
both for Alberta and her children. Unfortunately, we could not flesh it out
any further. The only official document we could find regarding Alberta
or any other member of Dorothy's biological family was the 1930 census.
It revealed that Alberta's parents were Jones Inman, born around 1872 in
Decatur, Alabama, and Mollie Ray, born in the same town in 1874. We
tried to find out more about Jones and Mollie, but we lost track of them
around 1910. They seem to have just disappeared from the records. Mae's
sister, Ada, believes that her great-grandfather Jones Inman was half Indian, but this is based only on rumor. And beyond that rumor, I could find
out nothing more about him. Mae's maternal line had run out very early—
thanks in part to the mysterious Mr. Blount.

Fortunately, turning to her father's side, we were able to learn a great
deal. Mae's father, Charlie Jemison, was born in Talladega, Alabama, on

December 31, 1925. His parents were Edward Primus Jemison and Susie Anna Dickerson, both also born in Talladega County, Alabama—Edward in 1902 and Susie in 1906.

Mae knew some of these people in her childhood and had heard stories growing up about most of them. "We knew all about my grandmother, my great-grandmother," she said. "I met a bunch of them, and there was always this idea that there was American Indian in my father's side, which was fairly pronounced even in him. I never knew exactly where it was or how it came about, mainly because I probably didn't pay enough attention to it. But I remember my grandfather, my father's father. He was a teacher of traditional medicine, and I always found him a very fascinating man."

Tracing Mae's grandfather Edward's lines back, we were able to find ample documentation taking us into the slave era—and a rumor that may substantiate Mae's Native American stories. Edward's father, Mae's great-grandfather, was Lewis Jemison, born in 1866 in Mumford, Alabama, which is part of Talladega County. He was the son of Annie and Adam Jemison, both born slaves in Talladega County in the early 1840s. Family members claim that Annie was a full-blooded Cherokee and that her son Lewis refused to call himself black, Indian, or white. "I'm a man and will be treated like one," he liked to say. Sounds like a man ahead of his time, and a stubborn one at that.

Looking for a white slave owner who might have owned Lewis's parents, Adam and Annie, we found a man named Shadrack Jemison, who was a wealthy white farmer in Talladega County. He owned a great deal of property, even after the Civil War. Finding a slave ancestor by name before they were freed is the brass ring of black ancestry. Although, as we have seen again and again, the slaves had no names that the law was bound to respect, sometimes, for legal reasons, an owner had to indicate the specific identity of a certain slave. And poring over Jemison family records, we found a deed indicating that on January 1, 1852, Robert Jemison Sr.—who was Shadrack's father—gave his children large shares of property, including land and some slaves. The deed lists the first names and ages of the slaves whom he gave to each of his children, including a boy named Adam.

Mae could hardly read the handwriting, but there in the deed, she

Sunnyside Plantation in Talladega, Alabama. Mae's great-great-grandfather Adam lived on this plantation under slave owner Shadrack Jemison.

located her great-great-grandfather Adam, listed as being eight years old and worth four hundred dollars! I couldn't believe our luck. Unfortunately, we could not find Adam's wife, Annie, but we did find several artifacts that helped us further imagine Adam's life. First, we found photographs and records concerning a plantation estate in Talladega called the Jemison House. Mae remembers that her parents used to tell her about this house when she was growing up. Looking at the photographs, I can only say that it is a most memorable house—elegant, grand, and imposing. It was built by Shadrack Mims Jemison in 1848, and it is the plantation where Mae's great-great-grandfather Adam was probably living between 1852, when he was given to Shadrack, and the time he was freed after the Civil War.

The house is still standing today, and it bears elegant witness to the economics of enslavement. In fact, it has quite a history. We found an entry about it in a book published in 1957 called *Fascinating Talladega County*. It reads, "In the slave quarters behind the house it is said that the master used to punish refractory slaves by putting them in very heavy irons. This they resented intensely and ever since it was first done the manacled slaves were returned to their quarters and rattled their chains so strongly that they are plainly heard in the big house."

Perhaps that was one of Mae's ancestors rattling those chains! Regardless, this simple passage, based on an experience shared by many slaves, humbled her. "It is incredibly sobering," she said quietly. "If you think about the resilience that those people had to have. You know, when folks talk about perseverance and strength of character, strength of mind, to be able to go through all of that and still have some semblance of family . . ."

But this wasn't the end of our research into Adam's story. As we saw in the case of Morgan Freeman's ancestry, in the Library of Congress there is a collection of first-person slave narratives recorded in the 1930s as part of the Federal Writers' Project, which was part of the Works Progress Administration. Along with that of Morgan's great-grandmother, Cindy Anderson, we found an account by a man called Perry Sid Jemison who was owned by the Jemison family and was about the same age as Mae's great-great-grandfather Adam. So their experiences were likely very similar. They probably even knew each other.

Though Perry's narrative does not mention Adam by name, it describes in general terms how the Jemison family was "scattered about" after the Civil War, and it gives some fascinating insights into what life was like for a young boy on the plantation. It reads, in part:

"I'm Perry Sid Jemison. My mother's name was Jane Perry. My father's name was Sid Jemison. The whole family lived together on the Kahoba river Alabama. . . . There was no food allowance for children that could not work and my grandmother fed us out of her and my mother's allowance. I remember my grandmother giving us pot liquor, bread and red syrup. The first work I done to get my food was to carry the water to the field to the hands that was working. The next work after that was when I was large enough to plow. Then I done everything else that come to the hand on the farm and never earned money in the slave days. . . . Abraham Lincoln fixed it so that slaves could be free. He struck off the handcuffs and the ankle cuffs from the slaves. But how could I be free if I had to go back to my master and beg for bread, clothes and shelter? It was up to everybody to work for freedom.

Mae was pleased to imagine that this man might have known her ancestor, that they may have played and worked together. It gave me gooseflesh. It also got us talking about the hardships that Perry and Adam and all other slaves must have endured even upon being granted their freedom. "Imagine that," said Mae. " 'How could I be free if I had to go back to my master and beg for bread?' " And she's right. In so many ways, as we have seen, the sharecropping system that followed the Civil War sought to substitute a new form of slavery for the old form.

Turning back to her father's mother's family, we focused on Mae's paternal grandmother, Susie Anna Dickerson, born on July 21, 1906, in Talladega, Alabama. Her parents were Charlie Dickerson and Fannie Bradford. Both were born in Talladega County, Alabama—Charlie in 1878 and Fannie two years later.

Mae's sister, Ada, had a very interesting story to tell about her great-grandfather Charlie. According to Ada, Charlie Dickerson was very good friends with a white man named John McKenzie, who came from a wealthy family and owned a lot of property. They were such good friends, in fact, that Charlie stood in for John so that he could get a marriage license to marry a black woman. This was necessary because intermarriage was illegal at the time. What's more, according to Ada, John McKenzie and his black bride began living with Charlie Dickerson and his family in some kind of "communal situation" when McKenzie's family disowned him after he married this black woman. The two friends—white and black—then made a living distilling liquor, and when John McKenzie was arrested for it, Charlie Dickerson went to jail for him, since the two friends knew that a black man would not be allowed to hold on to his white friend's property at that time. Ada claims that McKenzie even gave Dickerson some land when he got out of jail.

Ada heard this story from two white women, who told it to her in the presence of her grandmother Susie Anna Dickerson. Though we could not substantiate it, as many of the pertinent records from this area of Alabama have been lost, Ada believed it to be true—and I see no reason to dismiss her account. Such situations were much more common than we think. As we have seen in the case of ancestors of Maya Angelou, Quincy Jones,

Morgan Freeman, and Tom Joyner, there were many close friendships and sexual relationships (good and bad) between blacks and whites in the post–Civil War segregated South, even though they were illegal.

In trying to verify this story, we became very frustrated. Not only were many local records missing, but we could not find any federal records regarding Charlie Dickerson or his family. As a last resort, we turned to a tool that genealogists often use called Soundex code. It allows one to search for names in a computer database by how they sound rather than how they're spelled. And in the case of Charlie Dickerson's family, it proved extremely useful. We found the Dickerson name recorded in public documents in a wide variety of ways—as Dickinson, Dickerson, Dickason, Dickasons, and on and on. This greatly expanded the range of our search. And in the census records, we found a "Charlie Dickinson," whom we believe to be the same person as "Charlie Dickerson," living with his parents, Wiley Dickinson and Letitia Cunningham, in Talladega County in 1880. Wiley was a former slave born in 1852, and Letitia was a former slave born in 1855. These two people, I am virtually certain, were Mae's great-great-grandparents.

Census records indicate that Wiley Dickinson's father was a slave named Henry Dickerson, born around 1801 in Wayne County, North Carolina. Unfortunately, we know nothing more about him, and we could not identify a possible slave owner for him, so we could not trace the Dickerson line back any further than this. But in the 1870 census, we found Wiley's wife, Letitia Cunningham, living in Talladega County, not yet married, with her seven brothers and sisters and with her mother, Chaney Cunningham. This is Mae's great-great-great-grandmother. She was born in 1835. And searching for white Cunninghams who could possibly have owned her, we found that the largest plantation in the entire area was owned by someone named William J. Cunningham. Incredibly, once again we found some interesting records in which slaves were listed by name—including a will that was written by William's father, Joseph T. Cunningham, dated August 13, 1846. It includes detailed instructions for the distribution of his property and a detailed inventory. There are six pages listing slaves by their first name. Among them, Mae's great-great-

great-grandmother Chaney Cunningham is listed as being worth $125. At the time, she would have been ten years old.

Chaney is included in this will as part of a lot of slaves valued at $2,900. Other slaves in the lot included a man named Bob and a woman named Edy, both listed as being born in 1800. And judging from the rest of the will, it would seem that Joseph Cunningham kept most of his slave families together, which was unusual. It also means that Chaney's parents were probably Bob and Edy. If true, they would be Mae's great-great-great-great-grandparents—and they would represent the end point of one of the longest lines in the ancestry of African American *slaves* that I have ever seen documented.

Mae was thrilled to see her family tree drawn out in such detail down the Jemison line—a joy tempered only by the sadness she felt at not being able to share the information with her father, who died in 2004. "He would have loved this," she said. "It would have really given him a kick." I understood. Sharing my family tree with my father has been one of the great pleasures of my life. I can only imagine the pride that Charlie Jemison would have felt in seeing his long line of ancestors.

At this point we began looking at Mae's DNA tests. Her admixture results were a surprise to us both. They revealed that she had 84 percent sub-Saharan African ancestry, 13 percent East Asian, and 3 percent Native American ancestry. We know where the Native American probably comes from, based on her family stories about it. But nothing in our genealogical research suggested any Asian heritage, which is unusual for an African American. But as I stared at Mae's facial features, her Asian heritage became readily apparent to me.

"I wonder if that's Lucius Blount," said Mae. "Or maybe there were Chinese in Mississippi in the late 1800s doing work projects and stuff like that. Maybe that's the reason." This is possible. Chinese laborers were brought into the Deep South to fill a labor shortage after the Civil War. Mae's mother's family could have become intertwined with them. But I think her DNA is more likely the result of the fact that there was migration across the Bering Strait that intermingled Asians and the Native Americans centuries ago. And, as we saw with Oprah Winfrey, Native American and Asian can code for each other, meaning that Mae could be 16 percent Native American, the most of any person we tested. In the end it is a mystery—though one that Mae is very happy with. "I've been told I look Asian," she said, "and I love that."

She is also very proud of her Native American roots. "One of the things that we don't talk about enough," she said, "is that when slaves would manage to run away, many times they were accepted by Native Americans. Indians would just help them out. It was a very interesting sort of dynamic, and I think if this dynamic ever became well known, that would make the country much stronger. We need to emphasize this part of history." I couldn't agree more strongly, when it can be documented through DNA analysis.

Before turning to Mae's DNA test results regarding her African roots, we spoke again about her parents and their relationship to Africa. "When I was a little girl," said Mae, "I couldn't wait to get to Africa. When I got my own room, I wanted to do it like the Kalahari Desert. And I wanted to put my bed on the floor. My parents, they were the ones who made me aware of things. We listened to the music, African music, my father and mother were very proud of it. I remember when I was growing up, and I wanted to give my parents a special trip. So I got them this brochure to choose a trip, and it had these European tours in it, 'cause I thought it would be easier. They came back, and they said 'Well, Mae, we want to go to Egypt.' So they went to Egypt, and my mother and father said it was the most wonderful thing that they had done, because the people there, they look just like us. We were there before anyone. And they were really excited about being there."

Unlike many of the people interviewed, Mae knows Africa very well, both academically and from working and traveling there. She speaks Swahili and has spent extensive amounts of time in Kenya, Tanzania, and all of West Africa since first going there in the early 1980s. Yet I was delighted to see that she still had her childlike enthusiasm for learning about it. She wanted to know her African roots, she said, just because it would give her so much pleasure. She had no preconceptions, no favorite ethnic group or region. She just loved Africa—and I have to say that I see that love as flowing straight out her parents.

Our initial testing of Mae's mitochondrial DNA indicated that her matrilineal ancestors were among Bantu-speaking East African Kikuyu people. This posed a frustrating question. There were virtually no Kikuyu taken as slaves from East Africa to the New World, so how would Mae's first maternal ancestor get here? Bantu-speaking people who were part of the eastern stream of the Bantu migration passed through central Kenya on their way to central and southern Africa. So people enslaved by the Lunda in eastern Angola and the Democratic Republic of Congo are likely to have genetic markers similar to people in areas such as Kenya. Fortunately, a second round of testing revealed matches with the Koto and Mafa people of Cameroon, the Hausa of Nigeria, the Mende of Sierra Leone, the Akan of Ghana, and the Mandinka of Senegal. These results were diffuse and by no means definitive, but they were much more accessible to interpretation against what we knew about the history of the slave trade.

John Thornton and Linda Heywood explained that several of these matches were unlikely to have been the source of Mae's original enslaved maternal ancestor. The Akan and the Mafa, for example, were people from the forest and coastal regions of West Africa and were far less likely to be victims of slavery than the other groups. Indeed, the Akan sold slaves to the Europeans. The Hausa, Mende, and Mandinka groups were very likely matches, however. What's more, these groups were all associated with the Fulbe (or Fulani) tribe, who were spread from Senegal to northern Cameroon and who frequently intermarried with them, fought wars with them, and kidnapped and sold them into slavery. (Fulbe raiders were notorious slave takers.) And since ethnic membership in these tribes passed through the male line, Fulbe women who married into these other ethnicities may have not been identified as Fulbe. Thus, according to Thornton and Heywood, it is possible that Mae's original enslaved maternal ancestor might be related to the Fulbe. Indeed, they concluded that a Fulbe connection was the most likely explanation for the diffuse distribution of Mae's genetic markers.

They argued that it is also possible that Mae's original maternal ancestor was from the Koto tribe. The Koto were a decentralized society in coastal southwestern Cameroon, and if Mae's first maternal ancestor was from this tribe, she was probably exported through Old Calabar sometime around 1700—most likely after being kidnapped or taken prisoner in a small-scale war. A number of Koto people came to the Chesapeake area in this manner, especially after 1660, and some of them were among the first settlers in the Piedmont region; thus their descendants might have been brought to the Deep South by the internal migration to the frontiers after 1800. In addition, a group of Koto came to South Carolina in the 1720s and '30s and might have been among the pioneers of British and American settlements in the Deep South following the Revolution.

Looking back to Mae's family tree, I saw that the oldest female relative we trace down her matrilineal line was her great-grandmother, Molly Ray Inman, who was born in Decatur, Alabama, in 1874. Her parents, though we could not identify them, were almost certainly slaves. We know that Alabama was settled between 1810 and 1840 by people from Virginia, the Carolinas, and Georgia. Now, many settlers would have brought slaves with them, and, once there, many would have purchased more slaves— not recent arrivals from Africa, because the slave trade was abolished in 1808, but rather they would have purchased them from existing owners, most likely back in Virginia or the Carolinas. All of this is consistent with Mae's second round of mitochondrial DNA testing. It does not allow us to narrow down her results beyond the Koto, Hausa, Mende, Mandinka, or Fulbe (although, again, Thornton and Heywood think the Fulbe match is most likely correct). Nonetheless, these results do give a general picture of Mae's maternal heritage in Africa.

Mae's testing produced the least conclusive results of any of the people in this project. However, I think Mae was the best prepared of all the subjects to handle them. As we said good-bye, she seemed completely happy, comfortable in her knowledge of who she is and what she has accomplished. "I am just proud to be African. Proud to be an African American. It would have been fun to know more, but it's great just to know that. I tell people, 'What difference does it make if you have a position and you mind your table manners and you act just like everybody else? What difference does it make? You have to bring what's unique to you.'

And part of what's unique to me is all our history. What we share. I have never been ashamed of African history or African American history. I'm amazed by how much we accomplished—how much actually happened. We ended up having black doctors, black teachers, lawyers, dentists, everybody. We've had communities who took care of themselves and were self-sufficient when they had very little to begin with, were given nothing and were in fact denied and had stuff taken away from them constantly. To me it's a tribute to fortitude."

T. D. Jakes

June 9, 1957

BISHOP T. D. JAKES is one of the most passionate and charismatic preachers of the Gospel that I have ever had the pleasure of hearing testify to the glory of God. And believe me, since I was a little boy, I have been listening to my share of preachers, starting with Miss Sarah Russell, our very own Sister Holy Ghost, who used to terrify me every Sunday morning because she seemed to be on a first-name basis with the Lord, all the way to great preachers such as Charles Adams and Wyatt T. Walker today. Perhaps it was an easy matter for Miss Sarah to make a young boy quake, but even in my adulthood I have heard sermons that made me wonder, sermons that frightened me, sermons that made me cry. Not only is T.D. Jakes a stirring preacher, but he also seems to possess a genuine compassion for the foibles of us human beings, destined first and last to be nothing more or less than sinners. Will we seek forgiveness for our inevitable sinful ways? T.D. asks us, in a curiously nonjudgmental way. That is the source of his appeal, at least to me: the generosity of his compassion for human nature. Unlike Miss Sarah Russell, T.D. is the voice of a loving, forgiving God, a God who speaks the vernacular of human weakness bolstered by the desire to do good. Miss Sarah was Old Testament Jehovah all the way. I think she relished the idea of the unrepentant burning forever in hell, sort of like a luscious pig slowly roasting on a spit over a roaring wood fire. Miss Sarah would have enjoyed throwing some logs down to Satan, in case he was running short. T.D. would throw water on the flames.

I was curious to see where this compassion came from. T.D. is an imposing, powerful man physically, with an iron handshake and a booming voice. Yet there is something keenly sensitive and vulnerable about him. When we first discussed this project, he said he had long been eager to learn about his ancestors—to find out what he had possibly inherited from them emotionally, for better or worse. And as we explored his past, it was easy to see that while he had endured great hardships, he had grown up in a family that nurtured the very values that make him such a compelling preacher, a family

Bishop T.D. Jakes in Kenya.

that loved him for who he was, and not what someone hoped he would be.

T.D.'s mother and father with their kids in the 1950s.

Thomas Dexter Jakes was born on June 9, 1957, in South Charleston, West Virginia. His mother and father, Odith Patton and Ernest Jakes, came to South Charleston from Hattiesburg, Mississippi, where his father worked in construction and his mother had been a teacher. Many of Jakes's relatives still live in the Hattiesburg area today, and he has vivid memories of visiting Mississippi as a child. "The black community there was a lot like the movies," he said. "They had the fish fries on Friday night; all the neighbors came around—with the singing, the booze, the church with the wood floors, the funeral fans, and the good music. I went to a lot of those family gatherings. It was really interesting."

Every black person over a certain age has heard countless negative stories about Mississippi and the Old South. My daddy used to say that he didn't leave nuthin' in "Mississippi, Miss-abama, and all them missies," which we thought was hilariously funny, isolated from the most virulent forms of racism, like T.D., in the hills of West Virginia. I was quite surprised to hear Bishop Jakes recount how, growing up in West Virginia, he learned about the racism that was an inherent part of the Deep South but that he also heard many positive stories about the black community there. "My father loved Mississippi," he told me. "My father is buried in Mississippi. In spite of the adversity and the racial climate, there was still a lot of love there. My father would get up under a shade tree with a glass of iced tea and think he had died and gone to heaven. He'd talk about fishing down there and growing up down there. He loved it, absolutely loved it. His heart never really left Mississippi. So it was not some horrendous place in our memory."

Though his parents were a part of the Great Migration out of the Jim Crow South, Jakes believes that they moved north for economic reasons more than to escape racism. "Life was grand in Mississippi," he said, "but it was also very poor. The economic opportunities were nil. And people who have ambitions and goals often go looking for the promised land. So we went north. A lot of my uncles migrated to Detroit, Michigan, went to work for General Motors. Then they started making money and buying the big, long cars. They'd get a suit, a tie. They were really excited. They'd come driving back down south, you couldn't tell them nothing. You know?

People getting the first taste of money. A lot of my family did that. Some in Detroit, some in California. We went to West Virginia."

According to Jakes, his parents first traveled to South Charleston because his father was sent there to do construction work and his mother liked the area. "My mother liked the mountains," Jakes recalled. As a fellow West Virginian, I can attest to his mother's taste. There is something compellingly peaceful about a mountain range rimming a river, and Charleston, the state capital, is on the Kanawha River, in a beautiful river valley, surrounded by gently rolling hills—a most idyllic valley, too, befouled only by the stench of the Union Carbide plant located there. Still, those mountains have had a salient effect on all of us who grew up in them. I have often thought that being a "mountaineer"—that's the state's nickname for its citizens—was as important in shaping the peculiarities of my personality as was being black; more so, in some ways, like stubbornness, and hardheaded resoluteness and individualism. T.D., a mountain of a man, shares some of the state's cultural characteristics, no doubt about it.

Jakes was born soon after Ernest and Odith arrived in South Charleston. While T.D.'s parents struggled at first, Ernest was eventually able to launch his own janitorial business, and the family put down its roots. I asked him about his experiences growing up in West Virginia. Not surprisingly, given his age and the fact that Charleston was a segregated city, he told me that he lived in an all-black neighborhood, one that changed abruptly into an all-white neighborhood just across the street. "It was the Berlin Wall," he said, laughing. "Black on one side, white on the other. But our side was a great experience, a real neighborhood, with a deeply rooted sense of community. If you did anything wrong, everybody told on you. Everybody would tell your mother. The whole village raised the children."

My experience as a child was similar, though it came seven years earlier. West Virginia, while certainly better than Mississippi, was no paradise for African Americans, but we made do. The advantage that black people had in West Virginia—and all black people from marginal communities understand this—is that there were so very few of us, compared to the numbers of white people. Blacks comprised about 3 percent of the state when T.D. and I were growing up. Absence—rather, scarcity—breeds a certain degree of tolerance. Critical mass, on the other hand, exacerbates tensions that are understated or only implied. We both benefited from the relative freedom of race relations in West Virginia. The fact that T.D.'s parents could start such a lucrative business, a business based on white clientele, is a sign of that tolerance, that level of latitude even to create a business at all. Still, economic prosperity for blacks breeds anti-black racism; it did then, and it does now.

Of course, the world of Bishop Jakes's youth was rapidly changing. He was growing up as the civil-rights movement was recasting America. He did not attend an all-black school, as his older brother did. And like many blacks of his generation, Bishop Jakes did not experience racism as intensely as his parents and grandparents did. Indeed, he says that the most painful memories of racism centered on the treatment of his father by the white men he worked for—that is, the white men who engaged the services of his company—while running his janitorial business. "I remember," said Jakes, "my father worked for a grocery store, and the way that man there talked to my father made me very angry as a boy. He treated him in a very condescending, disrespectful way. And he wasn't the only one. I had to suppress so much rage about the way my father was handled and treated during those times. I was a little boy, but I just deeply resented the things that he had to go through."

Jakes also vividly recalls the residential segregation of America in his youth, a form of segregation that was both racial and economic and that motivated his passion to succeed. "My mother," he said, "used to take us for rides on Sunday to nice neighborhoods, and they were always white neighborhoods. Anybody black there was dressed like a maid. And my fantasy was to live in a house that my father would have bragged about cleaning."

I can completely identify with the bishop's feelings here. My brother and I still treasure the memory of the day we bought our parents the house that my mother used to clean when she was a little girl. I remember my mother crying and telling us stories about how badly they treated her there—how they mistreated her and accused her of stealing, planting money in sofas to make her look like a thief when she was only twelve years old. When we bought the house, she loved it, and my mother and I cried together that night. It wasn't until T.D. told me this story that I realized how generational my own fantasies, and his, might be, how even our most personal ambitions could be shared by others our own age and could have been fueled by social forces larger than our own personal experiences, experiences shared by a larger group than we could ever understand.

Bishop Jakes smiled as I told him this story about my mother and nodded in sympathy. "It's a major thing," he said, "because it was inconceivable to our parents that things could turn around and get better. And they are better today. We've got a lot of work to do, but it is better than it was for us, and for our parents." In so many ways, the civil-rights movement functioned as a Berlin Wall for racism, separating the past from the future, a delimited life from a life expansive with possibilities—at least for some of us.

Growing up, Jakes saw firsthand how hard African Americans had to work to rise, given the opportunities that they were offered. His father's janitorial company was run with a harsh efficiency. Ernest Jakes and his family did an enormous amount of the labor. Though he owned several trucks, had contracts with a number of big stores in South Charleston, and employed more than forty people, Ernest would do a lot of the cleaning himself, taking his children along as assistants. Because the white owners didn't trust Negroes not to steal, one client would lock them in overnight, to ensure security.

"I remember that when I was a little boy," said Bishop Jakes, "my father would take us into Heck's Department Store at night and they'd lock us in the store. We'd clean the floors until the morning, when they'd come and unlock the door. Once you went in, you were locked in. So I was scared, you know. And bored. After about an hour or so, I was whining and wanting to go see Mama. But Daddy had us working. My job was to get steel wool and clean out the corners of the floors that they were stripping and waxing. And if I fell asleep, Daddy would be nudging me to get back to work again. When the sun rose, a worker would come to the store and unlock the door. Had there been an emergency in the middle of the night,

Lord knows what would have happened."

Whenever Jakes speaks about his father and mother, he always refers to their tenacity, to their tireless work ethic, which he believes he inherited. "My parents were industrious," he said. "They had values. My father started a business with a mop and a bucket. And I can remember my folks arguing in April, tax time, how they were gonna file the taxes. I grew up listening to them talk about business. Sometimes I didn't appreciate it at the time, but in retrospect I realize that they left a mark upon me. I learned you had to work hard and that nobody was gonna give you anything on a silver platter. It affects me to this day. I told my children when they left cookies at the bottom of the fireplace, I said, 'There will be no fat men climbing down chimneys to give you anything for free.' I told them give *me* those cookies, 'cause everything you got, somebody had to work to get it. And those were the kinds of values that my parents taught me, and I'm glad that they did."

I found it profoundly moving to hear T.D. talk about his parents in this way—in part because I knew that the story has a terribly tragic ending. Ernest Jakes was a dedicated entrepreneur, but he wrecked his health by working too hard for too long, unwittingly jeopardizing the prosperity he'd built for his family.

Understandably, Bishop Jakes finds his father's illness very difficult to talk about. "They learned that his blood pressure was 280 over 260 and that his kidneys had been damaged," T.D. recalled in a pained, deliberate voice. "And that was right at the moment that they'd bought the house they were trying to get. I mean, we had a patio, and they were talking about a swimming pool, which was unbelievable for a black family to have a swimming pool. We had central air and a dishwasher. So we had arrived at that point. But then he started spiraling down, healthwise. He died when I was about sixteen. And watching him was terrible."

With his father in the throes of rapidly accelerating kidney disease, Jakes was forced to grow up quickly—too quickly. He was soon playing the role of caretaker, bathing Ernest, watching over his dialysis machine, and witnessing his father's great suffering. "There was no room at that point for a child," he said sadly. "You had to be mature. It was real frightening to see him go from two hundred eighty pounds down to a hundred and thirty pounds. He was shaking and trembling all the time. I can still to this day remember him shaking. And sometimes something would malfunction with the kidney machine, and then there would be blood on the floor. I can remember mopping the blood up and trying to help my mother. I remember shaving him and taking care of him and trying to make sure he had everything that he needed. And my mother held on to a job in all of this, because she had to have the insurance to provide for my father. We had no choice: We had to keep going." The Jakes family had to make a way out of no way, just as the Bible says the Lord will do, if you ask Him.

As we might expect, this experience changed T.D. forever. How could it not? How could watching so closely the physical deterioration of your father not prove devastating? Talk about the great divide in one's life, the wall between the optimism of youth and the reality of adulthood. For T.D., adulthood came early, much too early, coterminous with his father's death. His father's illness not only informs the way he sees the course of a life, it forms the underlying structuring principle of Jakes's philosophy for living, his raison d'être, and, by extension, his faith. "My attitude," he said, "is the result of all the things that happened within my family at this time. My tenacity, my maturity. There was no room for bicycles and Big Wheels and things in my childhood. It wasn't about me. It wasn't about football games. It wasn't about piano recitals. It wasn't about anything except dialysis. And though it was painful, I'm glad for it in a way. It taught me to be responsible. It taught me commitment." It taught him the function of the will, of determination, of sacrifice for a larger cause, of necessary selflessness.

His father's death, he believes, also turned him toward God. "My father left a cavity," he said. "And the Bible filled that cavity. And out of the filling of that cavity came the ministry that I possess today. Because I think a lot of your self-esteem and identity comes from your father and how he perceives you. It's vitally important. One of the great challenges that we have today is the lack of fathers. And my father wasn't absentee. He was just very, very ill. But I was only sixteen, right in the middle of adolescence, asking all the questions: Who am I? Why am I? Where am I?

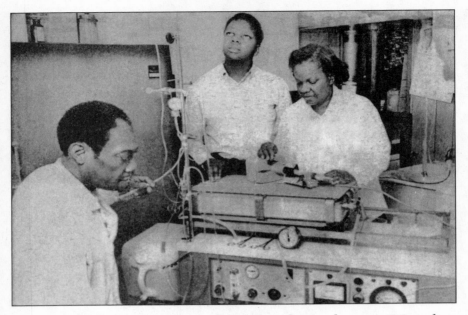

When T.D.'s father, Ernest, was struck by kidney disease, the young T.D. took on the role of his caretaker.

You know? And there was nobody there to fill in those blanks. My father once said to me, 'By the time I figured out what life was all about, it was time to go.' And that struck terror in my heart. That drove me to God for answers."

Though raised in the Baptist Church, Jakes turned to Pentecostalism and was born again in a storefront evangelical church. He was eager to become a preacher but was discouraged by the fact that he was poor and had a slight speech impediment—a lisp, still slightly detectable when he speaks, but oddly appealing, connoting a sensitive side within the thunderous presence that he affects in the spirit at the height of his services. So he enrolled at historically black West Virginia State College, located just outside Charleston, and tried to go to school while holding down a variety of odd jobs. But Jakes's religious fervor did not dissipate, and he soon dropped out of college to travel around the South Charleston area as an itinerant minister, developing his own unique style of preaching. In 1980, still only in his early twenties, Jakes became part-time pastor at the

Temple of Faith Pentecostal Church in Montgomery, West Virginia. His congregation consisted of ten people, but he was on his way. In this same year, he met Serita Ann Jamison, the proverbial coal miner's daughter, who had heard him preach. They soon married and had their first two children, twins, Jamar and Jermaine. To better support his family, Jakes took a job at the nearby, odoriferous Union Carbide chemical plant. He worked afternoons and nights and preached in his spare time until Union Carbide closed its plant in 1982, and Jakes was laid off. He and his family then suffered through a period of great hardship, going without heat, electricity, or water, as T.D. collected bottles to sell and dug ditches to keep his family afloat. This was just twenty-five years ago; never in his wildest dreams could he imagine that in so short a time he would be not only a multimillionaire but on everybody's short list of the world's great preachers.

Despite hustling for dollars 24/7, trying to survive, Jakes never gave up on preaching—and his congregation continued to grow, slowly but undeniably, just enough to attract notice. When he was twenty-six years old, he was able to begin broadcasting a weekly radio program. T.D.'s voice is made for radio, and his radio congregants, spreading word of the power of his sermons by their own word of mouth, soon started making their way to his church. Then he began holding Bible conferences, almost like the old tent revival meetings, explicating the word of God and saving souls, all through a gospel of achievement, of the potential for individual prosperity, spiritual and material. The word spread, while T.D. spread the Word. And the coffers began to bulge.

His colleagues, ever practical even when fighting the temptation of envy, chose him as vice bishop of an assembly of two hundred Pentecostal churches, both because of his charisma and his organizational skills, but also because he could fill the tent. If you can fill the tent, you can fill the collection plate; whereas an isolated preacher fills his or her own coffers, a bishop—the preacher among preachers—has a vested interest in filling yours as well, or rather fills yours by extension. His ministry has continued to expand ever since, through books, television programs, and spiritual conferences. If T.D. has a voice made for radio, it turned out that he has a face and a body made for the camera: In 1996 he moved to Dallas and launched his "megachurch," the Potter's House. Within a year the Potter's House was drawing thirteen thousand people a week. It currently has over thirty thousand members. T. D. Jakes is one of the most successful black religious businessmen in the history of electronic evangelism. Anyone who can publish a book entitled *Woman, Thou Art Loosed* and sell 5 million copies is a force to be reckoned with.

Looking back on his success, Jakes credits the values that his parents were able to instill in him, even despite—more likely because of—the tragic circumstances inflicted on their family's fortunes as a result of his father's illness. "I got into all kinds of devilment," he said. "Just like any other kid does. But the thing that stopped me from staying in the devilment was a sense that I was created to do something. That came from the way my parents raised us, to believe that you had some high purpose. You know? 'Leave your mark on the world, let the world know you was here.' My mama said that. And that left an indelible impression in my heart. I knew I had to make life count. And sometimes I get down on my knees and say, 'God help me to put it in my children what my parents put in me.' And I'm still laboring to make some contribution to this world."

As we turned to his family tree, Jakes told me that he believes we are a deep composite of our parents and our ancestors. I asked him what he meant, and he said he is convinced that the ways in which our forebears resolved issues in their time has an impact on how we live our lives, how we make the choices we make, our family's past guiding us like an invisible hand. Thinking about this idea, which sounded rather mystical to me at first, I have to say that I now find a great deal of truth in it. Researching family history has made me very aware of how patterns of behavior and sometimes whole personalities can echo across generations. Patterns of success and, oddly, patterns of failure—making the wrong choices over and over—often emerge through a person's family history, for reasons that scholars do not fully understand. Common sense and folk wisdom predict this repeating behavior, however, as we all know. But is it true? That is one of the questions this book seeks to answer. And within the bishop's ancestry, as I looked for these echoes, these patterns of repetition, I found many of them—starting with his mother.

Jakes's mother, Odith Thelma Patton, was born March 25, 1926, in Marion, Alabama. Though she was one of fifteen children raised in almost absolute poverty, she was remarkably well educated for a woman of her day—as were most of her siblings. Odith attended high school with Coretta Scott (later Coretta Scott King), graduated at age fifteen, and promptly enrolled at Tuskegee Institute, where she earned a bachelor's degree in home economics. She met her husband, Ernest, after she had finished college and was working as a teacher of children with learning disabilities. She would later serve as the Equal Employment Opportunities Representative for the state of West Virginia.

Education and opportunity were clearly very important to Odith. Her son sees this as a product of her upbringing—and of the challenges her parents faced in the Jim Crow South. "My mother was raised by sharecroppers," said Bishop Jakes. "And for them to have a chance to go to school and to be trained was highly valued. It was a source of pride. They were not the drug generation. They were not the burning-the-bras and to-hell-with-the-war generation. They had a whole different mentality—it was a good mentality, too," the bishop concluded, as we might expect him to do, given his message of up from your bootstraps, so similar to that of another great, conservative West Virginian, Booker T. Washington. And make no mistake about it: The bishop is a social conservative, if liberal on race relations, just as we might expect someone in his position to be. Were it not for the party's silence on the several forms of our society's anti-black racism and its stand against so many forms of affirmative action, many black Christians, I believe, would be Republicans, given that party's embrace of "family values," abstinence, and the repudiation of excess, as well as its condemnation of libertine practices such as premarital or extramarital sexual relations and its glorification of bootstrap capitalism. But race, for most African Americans, still trumps almost everything else, for reasons that some Republicans seem unable to fathom.

In his mother's case, Jakes told me that her stress on deferred gratification and education "comes from the meager way that she grew up," expanding on his theme with great warmth. "My mother would talk about reading books under the bed with a kerosene light late at night, because she shared the bed with a lot of other kids. There might be six or seven of them in the bed together. And my mother said somebody's foot was always in your face. But she would be reading books. And she said that when she read books, she escaped. And she had this strange saying, I remember. She told me to always remember that the world is a classroom and everybody in it is a teacher, and every morning you wake up, don't forget to go to school."

As an educator, I have to say that T.D.'s mother's aphorism is an apt and beautifully succinct sentiment—a marvelously simple yet inspiring charge to her children, one that is deeply reflective of the almost insanely valued commitment that earlier generations of blacks had to the miracle of education, of formal learning, even in slavery. Jakes maintains that this belief in the transformative power of education has stayed with him his whole life. "As I've traveled around the world," he said, "I think, my God! I got to go to the places that my mother only got to read about. It's strange how you pass on visions and goals from one generation to the next." He's right. A belief in the future once inspired even the most vulnerable members of the African American community, deferring gratification so that a new generation could achieve that which one could only imagine, if one dared to.

Of course, the most reliable predictor of a person's economic future is what that person's parents did. But Odith and her siblings achieved so much more than their parents. What was the force behind that? Jakes believes that it was his grandmother, Susie Patton. By today's standards Susie would have been called a preacher, but they didn't allow many women preachers to occupy a pulpit during her time. They called her a "missionary." And by all accounts she was an excellent one. Jakes recalls her being nicknamed "the fire-and-brimstone girl of Morning Star Baptist Church"—I imagine her like Miss Sarah Russell—and he says that her strong principles and strong hand ran the family, like an autocrat's. "My grandmother had a child almost every year," he said. "Every year for fifteen years, and never had a stillborn, never had a set of twins, all natural births, never one born in a hospital. You talk about strong. She was one tough lady."

Unfortunately, our genealogists were unable to learn much about Jakes's maternal grandmother's line. Susie Patton was born Susie Mae Williams in August of 1888 in Marion, Alabama. Records indicate that she was the child of a man named Tye Williams and a woman known only as Sallie, both of whom were slaves in Alabama. And beyond that, nothing more could be found about her family.

We were able to learn a bit more about Susie's husband, the bishop's maternal grandfather. He was Richard David Patton, born in 1874 in Marion, Alabama, which is part of Perry County. A sharecropper, Richard farmed land that had once been the plantation of the Webb family, who were white slave owners in Perry County before the Civil War. This was potentially significant genealogical information, because it was common for the families of former slaves to end up as sharecroppers on the property of their former owners. So we wondered whether the Webb family owned Richard's parents, Leander and Ann Patton, Jakes's great-grandparents. Census data indicates that Leander was a former slave born in Alabama who died before 1900 and that Ann Chatman was a former slave and resident of Perry County who died about 1902. It certainly seemed possible that they had been owned by the Webb family. And if so, there might be records pertaining to them in the family's various estate papers. We decided to find out. We searched all records related to John Henry Webb, who owned and ran the Webb plantation in the years before the Civil War, looking to see if there was any mention of slaves named Leander or Ann. We found one relevant document: a slave schedule from the 1860 census indicating that John Henry Webb owned sixty-eight slaves at that time. But unfortunately, as we know, the slave schedule almost never lists any of the names of slaves, just their age and gender.

The trail seemed to be stone cold at this point. However, interviews with the Jakes family revealed something interesting that allowed us to continue a bit further. Leander Patton, the bishop's great-grandfather, was rumored to have been brought to Alabama as a slave from North Carolina. This is possibly relevant because the slave owner, John Henry Webb, also moved to Alabama from North Carolina. Therefore, it seems quite possible that Leander was owned by Webb in North Carolina and brought

Susie and Richard Patton, T.D.'s maternal grandparents. T.D. recalls that Susie's strong principles and personality ran the family and prompted her children's later success.

with him to Alabama, in this case family lore coinciding with a verifiable fact. But unfortunately, due to lack of records, we can't know for sure. And that's where the paper trail runs out on the maternal side of Jakes's family. Once again, we can see how effectively slavery erased the presence of the slaves as individuals, tracking them carefully as objects of property, of course, but not as people, not as families, not as idiosyncratic, differentiated beings.

Despite these limitations on his mother's side, we were able to learn much more about the paternal side of the bishop's family tree. Going back a generation from his father, Ernest, we found records documenting Ernest's father, Thomas, Bishop Jakes's paternal grandfather and the man for whom he was named. Thomas was born in 1906 in Atmore, Alabama. He appears in many records as "Thomas Jake" with no *s* at the end of his surname. Such discrepancies are normal in African American history, because of the ignorance and lack of education of some census takers and the cavalier manner in which they treated details concerning black people's answers to their questions. (In my own family's records, some of us are referred to as "Gates" and some as "Gate.") The story of Thomas Jake, however, was not normal at all. Indeed, it is one of the most tragic stories I encountered in doing this project—and I have no doubt that it helped to shape Jakes's entire family.

Thomas Jake's death certificate indicates that he died on June 9, 1928, in Lucedale, Mississippi. The cause of death is stated to be "accidental drowning while bathing in swift currents." When I read the death certificate, I noticed that the handwriting was quite distinctive, written in a script that seemed too perfect, too legible, compared to every other word written on that page. That statement read with the clarity of John Hancock's signature by comparison to the other words on the page. I wondered at that; in fact, I wondered what the boldness of the handwriting signified. "Accidental drowning," it had read. How swift did a current have to be to fool a person who swam in those waters virtually every day? Just bad luck?

Thomas was just twenty-two years old at the time; his son, Ernest, Bishop Jakes's father, was only three. I wonder who brought his wife the dreadful news that her husband, overdue for the lunch that she prepared every day and to which he swam from the turpentine factory where he worked, had drowned in the swift currents.

Just as I was about to ask T.D. about the nature of the death and wonder aloud about my worries over the handwriting on the death certificate, he told me that at a family reunion just a month or so before, an older relative had revealed a closely held family secret, a special sort of brutality that some black families, for reasons we cannot always fathom today, kept buried, whispered from generation to generation: "He didn't die in an accidental drowning," the bishop said to me matter-of-factly. "My grandfather would swim back and forth across the lake when he got off work to get back home for dinner. He was working for some company at that time. My grandmother, who was pregnant with my uncle, was waiting for him to come home. But he had had an argument with a white man at work. And they put barbed wire in the lake, so when he dived in the lake, as he did every day, to swim across to get back to his house, he got caught in the barbed wire and he died. My family found him in the barbed wire. They murdered him. On June the ninth. And years later I was born on the day that he was murdered."

As I watched the bishop recount this terrible story, I realized that, as a minister, he probably had been the bearer of dreadful news on many occasions before. "The Lord has His reasons," I could hear him say. "The Lord works in mysterious ways." Not this time. He was angry; this was the Old Testament T.D., throwing logs on the fires of Hades along with Miss Sarah Russell. I couldn't help but wonder how keeping this secret knowledge of the nature of this man's death must have affected his family over the generations; in spite of that horrible murder, his family did not leave the area. They just pretended to believe the overly wrought words written on the death certificate. And when, finally, T.D.'s father moved north to West Virginia, he dutifully took his own children back to the site of the murder for summer vacations, subconsciously bearing witness, I suppose.

This death certificate states that Thomas Jake, T.D.'s paternal grandfather, died of "accidental drowning"—but T.D.'s family remembers differently.

"It's a funny thing," said Jakes, agreeing with me. "The resilience of our people is amazing. We have a strong survival instinct. And that resilience was apparent in my grandmother. She went on with her life. She married again. And he died, and then she married *again.* You know, my grandmother got through three husbands. She outlived all of them. She was tough. I think her faith brought her through. And she sent herself to college when she was fifty, washing white folks' clothes in a pot in her front yard as she sent herself through school. She was tough as nails. I can remember her hitting a cow or something in the head with the back of an ax during killing time, telling my daddy, 'Hold him still!' She was just that way, you know. My grandmother didn't play."

This remarkable woman was Lorena Smiley, born in Montrose, Mississippi, in 1908. She outlived her murdered husband by more than sixty years. And Jakes's face lights up when he talks about her today, remembering her overt toughness overlaying an abiding gentleness. "I loved her," he said. "She was somebody who helped sick people in the community, always carrying food to people's houses in need, feeding the reverend on Sunday. I just loved her to death."

Jakes also recalls his grandmother's work ethic and strong sense of economy, something that he believes has been carried down in his family ever since. "My grandmother had the same furniture when she died that she had when I was a little boy," he said emphatically. "Same exact furniture. And it was funny, because I teach about economic empowerment. My grandmother had about thirty thousand dollars in the bank toward the end of her life, you know? She didn't waste money. My ancestors were always entrepreneurial. They had a respect for finances. And they were self-sustaining. They weren't the types of people to beg or to borrow. You took care of yourself. And I think that's important. We need more of that today. Wish we could put it in the water our people drink," he said, ever mindful of the desperation so many African Americans suffer through every day, in part because of the bad choices they make, in part because they have abandoned hope of progress for the next generation, or generations, their children's children.

Going back another generation, we found that Lorena Smiley's father,

Willie Smiley Jr., had much of that same sense of financial acumen. Born in Mississippi in 1876, he was a deacon in the Methodist Church, a mason, and a lumberman. He owned 180 acres of land and cleared it of timber to support himself. Jakes recalls meeting him as a child and was deeply impressed by his great-grandfather's faith and willingness to work.

I was impressed as well. A hundred eighty acres of land was a tremendous amount of land for a black man to own in those days. As we have seen, the ownership of land was the promise of America, a promise that so few black people could realize before the first half of the twentieth century. Bishop Jakes appreciates this. "It was amazing," he said. "It really was. In fact, after he died, when they sold the land, we were still dispersing his assets among all his heirs and descendants. And I was quite proud of that, because during those times people didn't die with anything—maybe a watch or, you know, a hairbrush or something like that. But he had land."

Willie's father was Willie Smiley Sr., Jakes's great-great-grandfather, born a slave. Jakes has no memories of this man, and we were able to learn only that he was born a slave in Mississippi, without much of a paper trail. So this line of T.D.'s family runs out with the senior Smiley.

However, by returning to the family of the murdered Thomas D. Jake, the bishop's paternal grandfather, we were able to trace the Jakes back a bit further and to uncover several more compelling stories. Thomas's father, Jakes's great-grandfather, was a man named Lemon Jake, born a slave in 1858 in Georgia. In the 1910 census, he is listed as the head of a household, married, and his occupation is set down as "Turpentine Dipper," a trade I'd never heard of before. The phrase was a literal description of what the man did for a living.

This is a small but fascinating detail to me. A turpentine dipper would collect and sell turpentine, getting up early in the morning to hang cups from the trees. Then, later in the day, he would carry a five-gallon jug to each tree, dumping the contents of each of the cups in that jug. When the jug was filled, he would empty it into a larger, fifty-gallon jug. Then he would haul that jug away. That was a tough way to make a living; a backbreaking, labor-intensive job.

Bishop Jakes had never heard of this man before, or his occupation.

But he was intrigued to learn that, like many of the men in his family, Lemon Jake had to perform physically taxing work. T.D. believes, as I do, that he was shaped by this legacy. Moreover, though he did not know Lemon Jake, he had vivid memories of his wife, Nancy Boykens, who was born on September 16, 1874, in Alabama. "I remember her," said the bishop, gazing at her picture. "I went to her funeral. I might have been eight or nine years old. She was the first corpse I ever touched. I'll never forget her. My mother had the idea that when you touched a dead body you'd never be scared of them. So she had me touch Grandma Jakes, and I remember it vividly, to this day. It felt cold and hard, and I spun around on my heels and got out of there pretty quick. I thought, you know, this is not fun." Yet T.D. chose an occupation where he touches the cold, hard facts of death almost every day, in a church with thirty thousand members.

Jakes remembers his great-grandmother when she was living, too. "She was quiet, austere, almost Indian-like," he recalled. "We would go and spend summers with her as part of going to visit my grandmother. She had a woodstove on the back porch. I remember the stove specifically, because they declared that fried chicken couldn't be truly fried if it wasn't fried on the wood. They really believed that. It was great food, great times." I was hoping that he would give me a demonstration, fried-chicken devotee that I am, but he didn't offer to stoke the fire, so I didn't have the pleasure of testing his great-grandmother's theory about the proper way to fry chicken.

To find out more about Nancy, we looked for her death certificate. It shows she died in Waynesboro, Mississippi, on February 23, 1968, and lists her parents as Zenia Jefferson and Sam Boykens. Both were former slaves born in Alabama. Neither were among the fortunate slaves listed in any records, at least that we could find. So the bishop's family line disappears at this point, with the first generation of his ancestors who were born in slavery. Were the next generation of his relatives born in Africa? When had they arrived on these shores? We don't yet know. And so everything that happened in the Jakes family prior to the Civil War is invisible to us.

I asked the bishop how he felt being cut off from his ancestors in this way. "It's a bit disturbing to me," he replied. "The very fact that they were not considered people, that they were considered property, is insulting. I'm glad that things have changed today. But when you think that they were a part of you, it's painful."

Like many African Americans of his generation, Jakes has few recollections of his elders discussing slavery at all. "I think they didn't want us to know how bad it was," he said. "So 'slavery,' that was not a word in our vocabulary." We have seen how all too common this attitude toward slavery was shared by black families. For many of our ancestors, as W. E. B. Du Bois pointed out in 1926, slavery was an embarrassment and a stigma. They simply wanted the horror of it to go away; just as the silence about the murder of his ancestor might attenuate the anguish, perhaps so, too, might silence about slavery exorcise it. Perhaps we could forget it, in a collective act of amnesia. Our ancestors who lived through the Civil War and gained their emancipation wanted to start over as free people, as citizens, as if the past had never happened. And that attitude carried down through ensuing generations. It is a very understandable attitude, but I believe we are still paying the price for refusing to talk about the pain of slavery today. I believe that the African American community—almost 150 years later—is still damaged psychologically and economically by slavery and its aftermath. And I believe we need to understand our history better if we are going to heal that damage. We need to talk about this, even if our grandparents and our parents did not. I have actually met middle-class black people who claimed that their ancestors never experienced the chains of slavery, as if they'd landed with the *Mayflower* at Plymouth Rock and not on a slave ship in Virginia, or Charleston, or New Orleans. As we have seen, all of our ancestors who arrived here before the end of the Civil War came here as slaves. We need to talk our way through slavery and begin to cure its traumas, traumas that have been passed down, generation to generation, lo these many years.

Bishop Jakes shares these feelings with me. Both he and I believe that the legacy of slavery has had a devastating effect on our people collectively, influencing how we feel about ourselves and how we envision our pasts and futures. "There's a great big question mark back there," said

Jakes. "And I think it affects us in obvious and not-so-obvious ways. I believe that each generation passed on not only their power but their pain. It's very difficult to live through so many physical mutilations and rapes and murders and abuse and not pass on in the breast milk a certain tainted wisdom or anger or hostility. I think that our children find it very difficult to process all that. It comes out in their music, it comes out in the drive-by shootings, in the burning of our own communities, and in a certain lost, forlorn feeling that exists in our people." I have experienced that feeling myself, once when I read the latest statistics about the percentage of black teenagers who never graduate from high school and who are, essentially, functionally illiterate. Slavery lives in us today, he seems to be saying, though not by that name. We have internalized its legacy; we just don't know its name, its source, and because of that, we can't exorcise it from the collective life of the race.

Bishop Jakes explained to me that he believes that slavery robbed us not only of knowledge of who our ancestors were but also, in the process, took from us the dignity that comes with knowing that you are a person of inherent worth and value—of knowing that you come from other people who were considered and recognized as a people. There is a curious phrase in the African American tradition: "We come from people." My mother used to say this to my brother and me when we were growing up. I was not sure what she meant, but I knew from the way she cocked her head back when she said it that it meant something very good, something reassuring, in the same way that Peter Gomes's mother proudly pronounced that they were "Free Ishies." And our people come from people, as it were; that is the lesson of African and African American history. This is why I began this project, why I'm determined to put more black individuals—"regular" individuals—into the larger narrative of African American history. Our history belongs to us all, and it should consist of and be shaped by the revelation of the particular details of the actual lives our ancestors led. Because tracing our family stories has been so difficult traditionally, our historians have had to generalize, often from a very limited sample of evidence, of examples. A revolution in family history among African Americans will fundamentally alter the story historians are able to tell about our people's experiences in this country. As the bishop said, "It's very important to fill in the blanks and to better understand who we are and where we fit."

Jakes was very excited at the prospect of learning about his African ancestry. I asked him what he had heard about Africa when he was growing up, and he replied that it was not often discussed in his family—and that what little he heard was generally negative, the stock stereotypes drawn from racist genres such as Tarzan movies. "There was a disconnect," he recalled. "But when I got older, I began to be more curious to see how much was myth and how much was fact about Africa."

I was intrigued—though hardly surprised, given our generation's fascination with Africa—to hear the bishop tell me that he had actually begun the emotional process of trying to recapture his African roots for himself when, in his late thirties, with his ministry growing strong, he started journeying there. In the past ten years, he has gone back repeatedly, almost as a pilgrim. "I didn't really realize what a void was in me until I started traveling in Africa," he said. "I could not sleep the first few nights. Just because of the smell of it, the feeling that it gave me. I can't really describe what it was like for me to get off a plane and have somebody say, 'Welcome home.' And then you try to process: Is that true? Is this home? The food is familiar. Tastes a little like soul food. And so you say, 'Oh, that's where we get that from.' That's why we cook the way we do and that's why we dance the way we do or sing, to hear them sing in the open air and the harmonies that they made. I could not sleep." Anyone who doubts the cultural continuities between Africans and African Americans just has to step off a plane. No serious scholar can question these links, links forged environmentally: after all, what people do not carry with them their culture, their music, their religious beliefs, their ethos, their stomachs?

Jakes has taken many trips to Africa, and unlike most of the people I've interviewed for this project, he had very well-formed ideas about where his ancestors may have come from. Traveling in Nigeria, he has met many people who have told him that he is either Yoruba or Igbo, and he was very eager to find out if either or both are true. Indeed, the desire for this knowledge became almost an obsession with him. "I listen to how much pride they ascribe to who they are culturally," he said, discussing the people he has met in Nigeria, "and I didn't know that I was impoverished culturally until I realized how rich they were. It was their riches that exposed my poverty."

I think that's a beautiful way of putting it. And after hearing this insight, I began to discuss the results of his DNA testing with him. I was quite surprised to learn that his intuitions were absolutely correct. His patrilineal DNA signature, his father's genetic line, places the bishop among the Igbo people of Nigeria. His mitochondrial DNA revealed that his mother's ancestry contains a genetic signature that has been found clustered among the Hausa people living in Cameroon today. The Hausa were originally from Nigeria and were driven into Cameroon during a religious war in the late nineteenth century. This means that he has ancestors of eastern Nigerian descent on both sides of his family, as do about 17.5 percent of all of the African American people today who are descended from slaves.

Jakes smiled broadly when he heard this news. "All of the Nigerians say I act like I'm Nigerian," he told me.

I then explained to Jakes that these are two very noble and accomplished lineages. The Hausa have a reputation as farmers, soldiers, and traders, while the Igbo are famed for their achievements in art, politics, education, and, most of all, for their entrepreneurial or business skills.

What's more, based on conversations that I had with John Thornton and Linda Heywood, I was able to make some educated guesses about how Jakes's African ancestors ended up as slaves in North America. Regarding his patrilineal ancestor, the Igbo, Thornton and Heywood informed me that this tribe's members were enslaved by many different means. Some were kidnapped by African slave traders and some by European slave traders. But a great many Igbo, most curiously, were sold into slavery by members of their own tribe. In essence they used slavery as a form of social cleansing. So adulterers, criminals, and excess children were often sentenced to be slaves—with the blessing of the Igbo priests. The Igbo also used slavery as a way to raise money to satisfy creditors, meaning that some members of the tribe would pawn themselves or their family members to pay off their debts. These practices were highly unusual within

Africa and, obviously, very sad for us to ponder today. Even sadder, a large number of the Igbo slaves who came to the United States were children. Between 1821 and 1839 for example, two-fifths of all Igbo slaves imported into Alabama were children. One of Bishop Jakes's paternal ancestors may well have been among them.

According to Thornton and Heywood, it is also possible that Jakes's first paternal ancestor in America was brought into Virginia or Georgia. We know that many Igbo were sold as slaves in these states in the late eighteenth and early nineteenth centuries. In fact, there is a place near Savannah, Georgia, called "Ebo Landing" ("Ebo" being an antiquated English transliteration of "Igbo"), where, according to legend that is probably based in some measure on fact, a group of Igbo slaves staged a fierce revolt and chose to drown themselves rather than capitulate. The novelist Paule Marshall has written a brilliant short story about this event.

Reconstructing the enslavement of Bishop Jakes's Hausa ancestor on his mother's side is even simpler. This ancestor, according to Thornton and Heywood, probably came from the traditional Hausa homeland in the north of Nigeria, where Islam was dominant and had been from the eleventh century. And she probably came to the United States in the beginning of the 1800s, when the Hausa were attacked by the neighboring Fulani tribe, who sold captured Hausa into slavery. Once enslaved, Jakes's ancestor would have been transported through a network of African slave traders, shipped across the Atlantic, and sold in New Orleans, the primary destination port for slaves at that time. From New Orleans it would have been a short journey to the plantations of Mississippi, where the descendants of this woman still live today.

The bishop is intensely pleased with the results of his tests and very proud to learn that he is in fact a descendant of the people who live in modern-day Nigeria. "I've gone there several times," he said. "And I put on the Nigerian garments, you know, and I've stood in front of the mirror looking at myself, three in the morning, just imagining my ancestors being dragged off in ships. And I've always been fascinated by the food and the culture and the music. And I think their personalities seem somewhat similar to mine. You know, that aggressive, rambunctious Nigerian—I relate to that." I know it is unscholarly to say this, but T.D. "looks like" a Nigerian, even to me.

Thinking back over the journey we had taken together through his family, Bishop Jakes had what I thought was a very stirring set of insights. "My people," he said, "were ambitious. They were trying to get somewhere. And I don't think that they ever totally got where they were trying to go. They died in process, but all of my people died moving. None of them died sleeping. They died in motion. They died working on a goal. And I am still trying to follow that trail they left. Because they gave us hope. There was still a lot of racism out there. And there still is. You knew you might not get what you wanted. But they gave us the freedom to chart our own course."

History is always much closer to the present than we think, lurking in unseen ways, informing how we function, informing our collective condition. This is especially true of race relations in America. I can remember the Jim Crow laws of my youth—the colored bathrooms, the separate water fountains, and all that. The reality is that it wasn't that long ago, even if our children think of this as ancient history. "America likes to think that the civil-rights era and even slavery were a lot further back than they really were," T.D. mused to me. "But it was yesterday. And we're still right up against it. Even slavery was yesterday." Slavery ended about a century and a half ago, not so long ago in the grand scheme of things.

It is hard to come to grips with this fact, to know how to place it in our lives and thoughts. How should we approach and interpret the world, knowing that just a few generations back our ancestors were property, owned by the ancestors of people we deal with on a daily basis today? What is the proper way to understand this? I am not certain. But I am convinced that historians haven't realized sufficiently that our collective history should be told through individual stories like those of Jakes's ancestors, who carved out lives for themselves and their children under some of the harshest conditions conceivable, in creative ways that we can scarcely imagine. Talk about "making a way out of no way," as the black sacred tradition says.

The bishop agrees with me. "I think history gives us stats and figures and names," he said, "but when we put faces with it and we tell the passion of the story, well, then the people become real to us. Particularly with African American history, because we paid such a price to be here. It's not just a gathering of data, but it's a gathering of tears and souls that makes us sing like we do and clap like we do and dance like we do and live like we do. It's because we suffered like we did. Our forms of worship come straight out of our history. They're not just arbitrary. And it's not just emotionalism. It tells a story. Our passion tells a story."

I left Bishop Jakes wondering if these recent revelations—of the murder of his grandfather, say, or his Igbo ancestry, or the long history of entrepreneurs in his family extending back to Reconstruction—would serve to affirm or redirect his dedication to his ministry in ways that he had not conceived before.

Linda Johnson Rice

March 22, 1958

LINDA JOHNSON RICE is one of the most distinguished media executives in America. She's the president and CEO of Johnson Publishing Company, which was built by her father, John H. Johnson, into a publishing empire, the number one African American publishing company in the world, with its flagship *Ebony* and *Jet* magazines. It's quite a portfolio, and Linda is the brilliant heir to its founder. I was somewhat nervous that she wouldn't be able to participate in this project, just because she's so busy. But I was determined to do whatever it took to get her involved—for the simple reason that her family story contains elements not shared even in the broadest sense by any of the other people in this book.

I admired Linda's father enormously. He was one of my heroes. When he died, in 2005, the African American community lost a pillar. John H. Johnson was the first African American to do so many inspiring things—the first publisher to convince major corporations to advertise in a black-owned magazine, the first to make it on the *Forbes* list of the 400 Richest Americans, one of the first to join the board of a major corporation. Simply put, Mr. Johnson—as I called him—was larger than life, an unprecedented success story in the history of our people. Yet even though he has been celebrated by many, I think very few understand how very humble his origins were and how very much he was a product of those roots. His wife, Eunice Johnson, who was a fundamental part of his success, came from a rather different background, but together, John and Eunice were

Linda Johnson Rice at Johnson Publishing with her parents in the 1980s.

one of the great power couples, black or white, of the past century. While John was running his vast company, Eunice was its secretary-treasurer and also served as the director and producer of the Ebony Fashion Fair, the world's largest traveling fashion show. I was eager to explore their stories with Linda and to see how she, growing up, had absorbed the experiences of her parents and how her professional life had been shaped by them.

By her own admission, Linda was unusually intrigued with this project, since she was adopted shortly after her birth by John and Eunice and knows nothing about her biological parents. We were unable to learn anything about them either, though our DNA testing revealed a good deal about her distant ancestry. For this reason our genealogical research was necessarily confined to the lineage of her adoptive parents. This was more than all right with Linda, who rightly feels that her primary identity is as the daughter of John and Eunice Johnson. Family is a social construct, of course. And, at the same time, she knew little about her parents' family histories—both seemed to spend much more energy focused on the present than on the past—so she was eager to learn as much as we could tell her. Fortunately, we uncovered a wealth of compelling detail.

Linda was born on March 22, 1958, in Chicago, Illinois, and adopted when she was three months old by John and Eunice Johnson. At that time John was well on his way to building his publishing empire and Eunice had firmly established herself as a force in the fashion industry. Few couples have been so very successful in their separate realms yet managed to merge these skills under one large rubric. But as we all know, being a good parent is very different from being good in one's profession. The two are often, in fact, in great conflict, and many children of successful people resent their parents' inattention while still loving and admiring them. This isn't the case with Linda.

"All I ever really knew was John and Eunice Johnson as my parents," she said. "And they were just a very loving, strong family. I remember when I found out that I was adopted. I was maybe five, six years old, and my mother told me in a very sort of matter-of-fact way. She said, 'If any kids tease you about being adopted, you should tell them that your parents really wanted you. And they really chose you.' And I've never forgotten that. That has always been deeply instilled in me, and it gave me, I think, a great sense of security."

Linda believes that her own career choice and success flowed naturally out of her parents' support and love for her. They overcame tremendous racial and economic obstacles—they knew how hard it was to make it in American business as an African American. Yet they were able to imbue their daughter with strong feelings of security and confidence. And she has thrived as a result. To understand how this happened, we began to look at her parents' very different backgrounds, starting with her father's.

John Harold Johnson was born on January 19, 1918, in Arkansas City, Arkansas. "His family was dirt poor," said Linda. "I mean, there is no other way to put it. They were dirt poor. They picked cotton. They worked in sawmills. His mother was a housekeeper. And the environment was—filled with racism, you know? There was just a lot of racism there. He never liked Arkansas, never liked the country. He always was a city person. He left his hometown in 1933, and he didn't return for fifty-three years. I think he felt that there was no opportunity for him there and that the racism was so strong there that his memories just weren't good. He just said, 'That's my past. That's what I left behind, a country place that I acknowledge I'm from, but I have moved on.' "

Ironically, John often claimed that the poverty and intolerance his family endured in Arkansas propelled him to his great success, and he frequently cited the fact that not having access to a high-school education was a great "gift" for which he thanked fate. This is highly unusual, of course. Most people thank the presence of an education system for their accomplishments. John credited the absence of it with his success.

"It's because that's what drove him out of Arkansas City," said Linda. "That's what brought him to Chicago. His mother wanted him to get a high-school education. He actually repeated the eighth grade, not because he wasn't bright but because she had to stay another year in Arkansas in order to save up to get to Chicago. So she sent him back to the eighth grade again. There was nothing else. There simply was no high school there for black kids. If there were, he probably would have ended up staying there. He used to tell me he thought he probably would have ended up being a minister in Arkansas City, because that was the best job there."

Hearing this story, it occurred to me that John celebrated the hardship he endured in Arkansas not only because it led to his escape to Chicago but also because it prepared him for what he would encounter there. By transcending the limitations that racism imposed on him in the South, he was undoubtedly better able to navigate the racism of the ultra-white publishing industry that he broke open in the 1940s. And believe me: The racism he must have experienced there in the supposedly liberal world of journalism and advertising is far less understood but was equally as vicious as the anti-black racism that educated black women and men experienced in more traditional professions, such as the law or medicine.

Linda agrees with me. "There were many levels to that," she said. "I mean, even just getting started, as far as getting the magazine printed, finding a printer who would print a colored magazine at that time. He went to several. Nobody wanted him, nobody. They were all like, 'How are you going to pay for it? Who's going to advertise in it? What companies are there that are going to want to reach the colored market? And, more importantly, how are you going to get people to buy it? Colored people ain't got no money.' So he heard all those things in the wonderful, progressive city of Chicago that we love but that was, at that time, very racist."

This is why I think John Johnson is such an inspiring figure. He was a man who dared to dream a dream of journalistic equality. He believed that our people could participate equally in every aspect of American society—economic, social, political. And he put his whole self on the line for that dream. He was a brilliant entrepreneur, a genius as a salesman of his dream.

When he finally found a publisher, he marketed his magazine himself. He encour-

Linda's adoptive father, John Johnson, in an undated photograph from his youth.

aged all his friends to go buy it, and he even went to the newsstands himself and bought out copies so that the distributors would see that there was a demand for it. He knocked on the doors of advertisers and just kept knocking and knocking until they realized that black people wanted this—that black people read and have disposable income and are avid consumers. Banned from purchasing property in downtown Chicago because of his race, Johnson hired a white lawyer to buy a lot in trust, then went ahead and became the first African American to build a major building in the city's downtown area. John proved to white corporate America that black people count—and that black people *can* count—that we cannot be ignored and in fact can be depended upon as a vital purchasing center. Curiously enough, just a few years later, in 1955, the Montgomery Bus Boycott, ostensibly about racial discrimination, proved to be victorious because it so graphically demonstrated the costly effects of segregation, if the black community organized its purchasing power. And the ramifications of

Mr. Johnson's brilliant insight were that major American companies could be shown the value of advertising in black publications. The implications of his accomplishment are all around us today.

"I think he saw a void in the world that needed to be filled," said Linda. "He wanted African Americans to realize how important they were. And how beautiful and intelligent they were. All of the things that you had doubted in yourself, he wanted to be able to say, 'Don't doubt that. We can do it.' And that's because everybody on the outside was telling him, 'You can't.' They were all saying, 'You can't because you're inferior.' And his feeling was, 'You're not. You are absolutely not.' And the odds weren't in his favor.

"Everyone thought he was crazy. And laughed at him. But he believed in himself, and he had a mother who believed in him and who supported him, and I think that carried him through."

"Self-esteem starts at home," Mr. Johnson seemed to be saying to you each month when *Ebony* arrived and as you sat in your easy chair reading his magazines every night, or after hours or on the weekend as you read *Ebony* or *Jet* in beauty parlors or barbershops. He seemed to want to share the process of positive-image creation that his own mother generated in him. That's one of the great lessons I've learned writing this book: It is the rare person who claims to have built him- or herself up from absolutely nothing, with no family support at all. And it was no surprise to me to hear that Linda felt that John's success and vision were a fundamental result of his upbringing. John himself consistently credited his mother the same way.

John's mother was Gertrude Jenkins, born on September 12, 1888, in Chicot County, Arkansas. She was the dominant figure in his youth. His father, Leroy Johnson, died in a sawmill accident in 1926, when his son, John, was just eight years old, leaving Gertrude to care for the family on her own. Though she married a man named James Williams sometime around 1930, she remained focused on John and was extremely devoted to him.

"What happened with my father was his mother," said Linda. "She really saw in him a great deal of potential, and she recognized that that po-

Linda with her paternal grandmother, Gertrude, who mortgaged her furniture as collateral so that John could start his first magazine.

tential could not be fulfilled in Arkansas City. Her son needed an education, and I guess the closest big city where they had relatives was Chicago. So she brought him there, and he went to school, and the support and the guidance and the love that she gave him instilled in him his sense of pride and discipline and determination and the attitude that he couldn't fail."

Linda recalls her grandmother as a powerful, forbidding woman. "She was so strong," said Linda. "I never called her Grandmother. It was always Miss Williams. And she was serious. Brocade suit. Mink stole. Just absolutely, absolutely serious. But I think in her generation a black woman had to be that way. And she was very loving to my father, just not very demonstrative. To a kid she was scary. We went to her house and just sat on the sofa, and you really didn't move around too much. But I know how much she loved her son, and at a young age I recognized right away how much he adored her. He sent her a dozen red roses every Sunday. She came from a tough life—a life where you had to scrap and fight for everything."

Linda is absolutely right. Her grandmother came from nothing. And in her generation either black women were tough or they were crushed.

In his autobiography John said that his mother, Gertrude, had "lived the death of black hope"—a strikingly evocative phrase. And thinking about Linda's grandmother, I cannot help but admire her sheer determination. She gave everything she could to her son, because she believed in him. She moved from the only place she'd ever known—rural Arkansas—to the urban North just so he could go to high school. It must have been terrifying, but she never wavered. And when her son pursued his crazy publishing dream, she backed him all the way. When he needed a loan to start his first magazine, she allowed him to use her furniture as collateral.

"That's right," said Linda, smiling. "That's really believing in your son, when your furniture is all you have. I mean, he mortgaged her furniture for five hundred dollars. That was all she had, and she was willing to put those things out there for him."

Amazed by Gertrude, I hoped to learn more about her background, but our research was unable to uncover much beyond the barest of details. Her mother was a woman named Malinda Lyerson or Larson, born in March of 1870 in Chicot County, Arkansas. Her father was most likely a man named William Jenkins, born into slavery in Arkansas around 1850. Her maternal grandparents were also born into slavery, and the paper trail runs out with them.

Fortunately, we were able to learn more about John's line by looking at the ancestry of his father, Leroy Johnson. Leroy's parents were James Johnson and Leota Crawley. We were not able to learn much more about them than the rough outlines of their lives. Both were born in the mid-1870s in Chicot County, Arkansas, and died sometime around 1930. Our best glimpse of either of them comes from James's draft-registration card, filed on September 12, 1918, as World War I was drawing to a close. It says that James was born December 24, 1874, and lived in Readland, Chicot County, Arkansas, where he worked as a farmer. He is described as having been tall, with a medium build, black hair, and black eyes.

Going back one generation, we were able to identify James's parents—Linda's great-great-grandparents—as being Nelson Johnson, born in Alabama in 1851, and Kesiah Glen, who was born in Arkansas around 1855. They both spent the first years of their lives as slaves. To find out

more about them, we started by looking at records from the years immediately after the end of the Civil War, and we were lucky enough to find
a contract from 1880 in which Nelson and another man borrowed money
from a man named W. W. Ford.

The contract reads, in part, "Nelson Johnson and Isaac Allen desire to
obtain other and further advances of money and to purchase other goods,
wares and merchandise for the purpose of enabling them to carry on the
business of planting and cultivation of a crop of cotton and corn on the
Sunnyside plantation in Chicot County, Arkansas."

This, Linda and I both knew, could be an important clue about her
father's ancestors. As we have seen in the life stories of many of the ancestors of the people in this book, freed slaves often remained on their
former plantations and worked as tenant farmers or sharecroppers. The
contract is dated 1880. Could the plantation called Sunnyside be the plantation where Nelson had been a slave twenty years earlier? We discovered
that the antebellum owner of Sunnyside was a man named Elijah Worthington, and we scoured all the archives we could, looking for his estate
papers. We ultimately found an 1858 Worthington property record. It indicates that on December 14 of that year, Elijah Worthington borrowed
$275,000 from Angelica Van Buren, who was the daughter-in-law of the
former president of the United States, Martin Van Buren. (And the two
were very close—even closer than their relationship suggests. Angelica actually served as first lady when Martin was president of the United States.)

Now, in 1858, the sum of $275,000 was a fortune, just a staggering
amount of money, equivalent to over $5 million today. To prove that
Worthington could repay the debt, this deed contains a detailed list of his
property, including the first names of hundreds of slaves. In this list is the
name of Linda's great-great-grandfather—Nelson—as well as that of his
siblings Matilda and Steven. It also contains the names of Linda's great-
great-grandmother Kesiah, as well as her sister Sylvania and their mother,
Alethia—or "Leafy" as they called her here. All these people were owned
by Elijah Worthington.

"He doesn't look very friendly," said Linda, staring at a photograph
that we found of Worthington. "He doesn't have kind eyes. Doesn't have

kind eyes at all. Looks like a mean old man."

In 1860, Elijah Worthington was the largest slaveholder in the entire state of Arkansas. He owned twelve thousand acres of land and six hundred slaves. Plantations as large as Sunnyside were the pinnacle of the Cotton Kingdom. Slaves labored at narrowly defined, specialized jobs, which provided greater efficiency and productivity and hence greater profit. By 1860, Sunnyside produced seventeen thousand bales of cotton each year, which was an incredible amount.

"This man made a fortune," said Linda, trembling. "A fortune off of African Americans. He used us as he saw fit—for his own benefit and his own gain. That's something that we as a people and the general public needs to know better. We can't forget this. I mean, he had to know better. There is no way you could see a slave every day and be surrounded by African American human beings and not know that this was a big fiction. This is a thinking, breathing human entity so—oh, it's disheartening."

Linda was growing upset—and I couldn't blame her. This part of American history should make all of us sad, black and white: the brutalizing of women and men and the exploitation of their labor. It is our greatest national disgrace. But before moving on, I wanted to talk to Linda a bit more about the kind of life I believe her ancestors lived. There were some surprising details I wanted to share with her. Large plantations such as Sunnyside contained unique slave communities, because the slaves vastly outnumbered the white people who lived there. Generally, this meant that the white people had less contact with them and that black people had greater autonomy. In fact, recent historical research suggests that slaves on large plantations were more likely to have stable families than were slaves on smaller plantations or farms. The irony for her ancestors was that the work was relentless but they could form relatively durable family units. And the reality is that her ancestors did stay together. The bonds formed at Sunnyside endured well beyond slavery.

"I don't see any good in any of this, quite frankly," said Linda without emotion. And again, I concur. As a historian, I find these details fascinating but they pain me deeply as a person. All African Americans, at some point in their lives, allow themselves to wonder what if our ancestors had been allowed to compete on an even economic playing field? Every African American experiences anger, sooner or later, at the huge heritage of brutalization that each of us has had to overcome. I know that I do, and I've been studying African American history for more than three decades.

Looking at Linda's pained face, I asked her if she felt that slavery was still affecting the black community today. "That's a very tough question," she replied. "I think that those who are impoverished and those who have no hope are living the effects of slavery. I think those who work hard and are determined and have discipline and self-esteem and see a better life for themselves don't live that slave way, in that slave mentality. But it's a sad state. It's very complicated. I mean, it can't not have an effect on you. You can't be treated as slaves for centuries and it not have an effect. But I also think that is what made us as a people stronger. And more determined to do better. Like my grandmother. I mean, what made her jump on a train and take her little boy north? There's got to be a better life, there's got to be a better life. So I think it makes us angry and sometimes bitter, but more determined, too."

Before moving on to her mother's family, I had one final note on the Johnsons for Linda. Her great-great-grandfather Nelson Johnson is the oldest member of her father's family whom we could identify, and we wanted to find out what the source of his surname was. Interestingly, Sunnyside's original owner was a man named Abner Johnson, who sold the property to Elijah Worthington in 1840. Nelson was not born until about 1851, and according to the 1870 census he was born in Alabama. So it is highly unlikely he took the name of Abner Johnson, and in the end we're not sure how Nelson got his surname. Johnson is a very common name among African Americans, of course, and it seems entirely likely that Nelson brought his family name with him from Alabama. One thing is for sure: Linda's ancestors did not take the name of their slaveholder, as many slaves did. And they weren't the only ones. Even though Worthington owned 579 slaves in 1860, there were no black Worthingtons in the area in 1870. In other words, none of Worthington's slaves took his surname. What does that tell us about this man? Nothing good, I suspect. Moreover, Worthington, like many slave owners, impregnated some of his female slaves. Yet even Worthington's own mixed-race children adopted their mother's last name and not his.

"They must have hated him," said Linda, looking at Worthington's photograph once more. And I have to agree. He looks brutally tough, and perhaps that's why his slaves eschewed taking his surname.

Turning to Linda's maternal line, we began to trace the lineage of her mother, Eunice Walker. It was remarkably different from that of her father. Eunice was born on February 16, 1916, in Selma, Alabama. Her parents were Nathaniel Walker, born in Alabama in 1886, and Ethel McAlpine, also born in Alabama, but a year later, in 1887. Ethel and Nathaniel were both highly educated. He was a doctor in Selma, and she was a teacher at Selma University, then known as Selma Seminary. Moreover, Ethel was the daughter of a very important figure in the history of the African American church: the Reverend William McAlpine.

"I knew that," said Linda, "But, you know, it's interesting—I hate to say it, but my mother really didn't talk all that much about him. She was very proud of her family, but she didn't spend a lot of time going back in history."

I found this intriguing. I understand when the children of sharecroppers don't want to talk about their ancestry. But Ethel McAlpine was the child of a legendary figure. One might expect that if you had someone like William McAlpine in your family line, you'd be talking about him or her night and day. Nonetheless, I suppose Eunice had so much going on in her life that she had neither the time nor inclination to look back at her remarkable grandfather.

Biographical accounts of William McAlpine tell us that he was born into slavery in Buckingham County, Virginia, in June 1847. They also tell us that he was owned by a doctor in Alabama and served as a nurse to the doctor's children. The doctor's wife, these accounts say, was from the North and she didn't like southern schools so she homeschooled her children, and therefore William learned to read and write alongside them— an incredible opportunity for a slave. In 1864, the year before the Civil War ended, William, then seventeen, underwent a religious conversion and became a fervent Baptist. Thus, when freedom came, he had an education, unlike the vast majority of the slaves, and he also had a calling.

As it turns out, McAlpine was a true visionary. After slavery he went to work as a carpenter but soon became a pastor. He then enrolled in Talladega College and became involved in statewide Baptist organizations. At the 1873 convention of the Colored Baptists of Alabama, he introduced a resolution proposing that a theological school be built to educate young black men. Just seven years after the Civil War, he had a dream to uplift his people through education—and a well-conceived plan to support it. Of course, Linda's great-grandfather faced some serious opposition to his plan. White Baptist leaders assembled and advised against the school— showing that even the church, which by that time had long recognized that black people had souls, did not want them to have the power that education within their own institutions could bring. But William McAlpine was undeterred. In 1878, just five years after he proposed the idea, the Alabama Baptist Normal and Theological School opened its doors with a mission of training and educating black Baptist ministers. That mission expanded considerably over time. The college exists today as Selma University. Since 1878 it has educated thousands of students, doing as much for the black community in Alabama as any institution of its kind.

"That must have taken tremendous courage," said Linda. She's absolutely right. When William proposed building the school, Reconstruction had just ended, and throughout the South many former slaves who'd been waiting to achieve true equality with whites were losing hope. The Klan was rising. Jim Crow was rising. Yet William McAlpine was undaunted by the worsening social and political climate. He worked against all odds to give African Americans a greater voice within the Baptist Church. And he succeeded. Even the white Baptists who had opposed McAlpine had to admit their respect. We found a tribute to him in the records of the Alabama Baptist Convention of 1893, a gathering of the church's white leaders. By this time, in an era in which "separate but equal" would become enshrined in the law, the church had come to embrace William's vision of an all-black seminary at which to educate black ministers. The tribute notes that William McAlpine had become the instructor of the colored ministers at the college and commends him, saying, "He is a man of piety, discretion, energy and education. He has been received by his people with great favor and our brethren who have seen something of his work speak in highest terms of him and his methods. He has organized his brethren into classes and puts the best of books into their hands. We are sure this is the most efficient way to assist the colored people."

This document astonished Linda. Seeing past its condescension, she perceived her ancestors' important accomplishment. "Now I understand why my mother has always been such a strong promoter of education," she said. "It makes total sense. I see why she just was such a driver about supporting young black children and nurturing them. That's where all this comes from. Absolutely, that's where all this comes from."

Thus, along both her father's and mother's lines, we'd found people who had a vision and then created an institution. This is quite noteworthy, and I don't think it's a coincidence. In spite of the socioeconomic differences between her mother's family and her father's family, Eunice and John saw something that they loved about each other, something irresistible—an entrepreneurial spirit, the capacity to dream and to make those dreams concrete. And precedents for this impulse were right there on their family trees.

"A lot of us dream but end up in bars, drinking," said Linda, musing, a bit sadly. "But it's being able to dream and then deciding, 'I'm going to fulfill this dream no matter what.' That's what's important. It's having the determination to fulfill these dreams, and they both did. This is amazing."

Linda and I then turned back to Reverend McAlpine's story. Neither of us was surprised to learn that he did not rest when his school was finished. By the late nineteenth century, African American Baptists across the nation had begun to form their own organizations. They faced stiff resistance from their white peers, who had no interest in sharing religious, social, or economic authority with them. Racism within the church was as bad as it was within the society as a whole. Whites didn't want to worship with blacks, but they wanted to control their churches, and profit from their income. The situation came to a head in 1895, when more than two thousand black clergymen from all over the country came together in Atlanta, Georgia. It was a historic event. Delegates included Adam Daniel Williams, the grandfather of the Reverend Dr. Martin Luther King Jr., and Walter Henderson Brooks, the grandfather of my Harvard colleague Evelyn Brooks Higginbotham. It led to the creation of the entity known as the National Baptist Convention, the first nationwide organization of African American Baptist leaders, a group that would have a fundamental impact on shaping the black community and giving rise to the civil-rights movement in the early twentieth century. William McAlpine was elected as the organization's first president.

Curiously, among the many struggles that black Baptists faced with their white brethren was a struggle over publishing. White Baptist ministers simply refused to publish literature written by black ministers. In response, the National Baptist Convention, under McAlpine, formed its own publishing house, which rapidly became the largest black publishing enterprise in the entire world at that time. So, in a way, Linda's maternal great-grandfather William succeeded in the same spirit as her father did a few generations later in devoting his energy to serving his people by creating separate institutions for African Americans, including publishing houses.

"I never knew that," said Linda, who has been steeped in the family business her entire life. "I never knew it and see how both sides of the family have been so connected with one major, major thread which is publishing. I'm really glad to know that."

The National Baptist Convention was created in 1895, just one year before the Supreme Court decision *Plessy v. Ferguson* made "separate but equal" the law of the land. It has to give us pause to think how a man like McAlpine built upon the rare, if still fairly basic, education that he was allowed as a house slave, an education that gave him a head start and allowed him to transform himself over the ensuing thirty years into an institution builder and an entrepreneur. What if the other slaves had been educated to the degree that William was? Even as the country around him was descending into a new racist madness, he managed to found a seminary, a publishing company, and a national organization that were all so forward-looking, so visionary. And it's instructive to see how his entrepreneurial spirit dovetailed with his vision of social justice. He saw a series of voids in the black community—educational and spiritual voids—and he filled them.

"This is an integral part of my heritage," said Linda. "The church and the school and publishing. It's like braiding hair. It all ties together. It all ties together back into my parents. The way they think and all the things that they stand for."

We wanted to find out more about William McAlpine's experience of slavery. Fortunately, the biographies written about him gave some clues. According to several of them, a Presbyterian minister named Robert McAlpine who lived in Coosa County, Alabama, bought William and his mother from a slave trader around 1850. At the time William was only three years old. The biographies also tell us that the death of the slave-holder Robert McAlpine led to the forced separation of William and his mother—and this trauma shaped his life.

Much of this story matches with the historical record. We found documentation confirming that a slave owner named Robert McAlpine died in Coosa County, Alabama, on March 20, 1855. At this point William would have been about eight years old. The estate records of the deceased slave owner list among his property a boy named Bill, valued at $450, and two women, Emily and Park, each valued at $700. There is no way to know for certain, but it is likely that one of these women was William's mother.

"That's quite something," said Linda quietly, "that you could just slap a dollar value on a human life. And here is a man who is so crucial, you know? In the founding of the National Baptist Convention, and everything. He's reduced to four hundred and fifty dollars."

We found another record, dated October 1855, which details how the heirs of Robert McAlpine purchased items from his estate seven months after his death. It lists farm animals, furniture, and also, of course, slaves. According to the record, one of Robert's sons, a man named Dr. Augustus McAlpine, bought a number of child slaves from his father's estate, including William. Emily, the woman we thought might have been William's mother, was purchased by another McAlpine heir. And Park, the other possible mother of William, had disappeared by this time altogether. Regardless of whether William's mother was Emily or Park, soon after the sale Dr. Augustus McAlpine had moved to Talladega County, taking young William with him, without his mother. William was an orphan; he would never see his mother again.

"I can't imagine," said Linda, "how devastating that must have been. The person you love the most, who nurtured you all your life of eight short years, is torn from you. I'm sure that it was not without a lot of physical and emotional grief and pain. The

Slaveowner William McAlpine's estate records list "Bill, a boy"—referring to Linda's incredibly accomplished ancestor William McAlpine.

loneliness was probably almost unbearable on both sides. To be that callous about a given life is just—it's unforgivable."

We could find out nothing more about William's mother, and neither could we trace William himself back any further. However, consulting the slave narratives that were gathered by the Federal Writers' Project in 1937, we found a very interesting document related to the family. These narratives, which we discussed in earlier chapters on Morgan Freeman and Mae Jemison, were the oral histories of people who were born under slavery and were still alive in the 1930s, and they include an interview with a former slave named Tom McAlpine. Tom indicates that in the years just before the Civil War he was owned by Dr. Augustus McAlpine and lived on the doctor's property five miles outside Talladega. We have no reason to believe that this man Tom was a blood relative of William McAlpine, but it is almost certain that as boys the two lived and worked on the same plantation. They probably knew each other quite well.

In his interview Tom describes the life he and William would have shared: "The doctor just had a small plantation about a hundred acres I suppose. And he didn't have but twelve slaves 'cause there weren't no need for no mo'. He was busy in town a-doctoring folks. He didn't have any time to do any real farming."

Tom also described the limited access to education that he had as a slave, saying, "I ain't never had no schooling 'cepting what I could get out of de little white folks' books myself. We niggers used to tote their books to school for 'em and on the way I would look in de book and get a little learning."

This, of course, suggests a crucial difference between Tom and William. William was much more fortunate than his fellow slaves on the same plantation, because William was in the house, gaining exposure to education alongside his master's children. Tom was in the field, with no such opportunities. And this little glimpse reminds us of how rare William's opportunities were. It is difficult to imagine how much harder Linda's ancestor's life would have been if he had not acquired an education.

"It would have been horrific," said Linda. "Education was their only way out. That was their *only* way."

This concluded our ability to trace Linda's parents' families using the available historical record. We had taken both her mother's and her father's lines back into slavery—and found that they both ended in Alabama in the early decades of the nineteenth century. We were now ready to turn to our DNA research. With Linda, I think this aspect of the project held a unique appeal. Being adopted, her genealogy does not map against her DNA. She knew some details of the history of her parents' families. She knew absolutely nothing of what her DNA might tell her—and she was very excited to learn these links to her natural parents.

"I hope that they were a proud people," she said. "I hope that no matter what their circumstances were, they persevered. Because that is very important to me: No matter what your circumstances are, you persevere."

According to Linda's admixture test, she is 60 percent sub-Saharan African and 40 percent European, which is an extraordinary amount of European ancestry for an African American. This result is higher than for almost any of the other people involved in this project, slightly lower than Sara Lawrence-Lightfoot's and mine, and just a bit higher than Quincy Jones's. The average for African Americans is approximately 20 percent European ancestry.

"That's interesting," said Linda, slightly taken aback. "That's very cosmopolitan—that's for sure. And, well, this is ancestry that has to be respected and understood. But the bottom line is, I am an African American black woman. In no uncertain terms. Fundamentally, what you see is who I am. Because, you know, being an African American, it's cultural as much as it's genetic. I'm a black woman. And culturally I have grown up in the African American community."

Having an admixture of 50 percent myself, I could sympathize with Linda's initial amusement at this statistic, and I thoroughly agree with her interpretation of the results. Like her—and like many others with a significant amount of European ancestry—it has never occurred to me that I could, culturally, be anything but African American, because I was raised that way, I was initiated into that culture, and because my physical features would not allow me to be identified as anything but African American.

Turning to our second admixture test, I told Linda that further analysis of her African heritage suggests that 29 percent of her African ancestors came from Congo Angola, 33 percent came from the region that stretches from Liberia to Senegal—once called Upper Guinea—and 37 percent came from eastern Nigeria. This was exciting news to her, and her mitochondrial DNA testing revealed even more about the broad African heritage she celebrates. Her results included exact matches with a very wide range of African people—from the Mende of Sierra Leone to the Bamileke and Bassa people of Cameroon, from the Luba of what is now the Congo to the Turkana people of Kenya, the Ronga people of Mo-zambique, and people from Bantu-speaking tribes in the Cabinda exclave in modern-day Angola.

In trying to narrow down these results, our historical consultants John Thornton and Linda Heywood concluded that Linda's earliest African fe-male ancestor on her maternal line was probably one of the Luba people, who lived in the central area of what is now the Democratic Republic of Congo. They came to this conclusion because her genetic signature is spread so widely across Africa—which is most likely due to the ancient migration of the Bantu people. This migration would have brought women carrying Linda's mitochondrial DNA down through the center of Africa about a thousand years ago. Centuries later they became part of the Luba kingdom. Then, according to Thornton and Heywood, in the mid- to late eighteenth century, the Lunda Empire waged war against the Luba peo-ple in a fight for control of the region, and the victorious Lunda sold their prisoners—including, perhaps, a direct maternal ancestor of Linda's—to slave traders from the kingdom of Congo called the Zombos, who were ac-tive in the region at that time. The Zombos brought many of their captives to Cabinda, where English slave traders purchased them and took them to Virginia or to South Carolina.

Most of the Luba who went to Virginia arrived there before the 1790s. Most who went to South Carolina arrived between 1790 and 1810. Since we do not know the identity of any of Linda's biological ancestors, Thorn-ton and Heywood could not make a more precise estimate as to when or where her female African ancestor arrived in America. But they were very confident that her original enslaved ancestor was a Luba woman captured during the Lunda-Luba wars of the mid- to late eighteenth century and brought into either Virginia or South Carolina. Slaves coming into these states during this period were often sold to settlers who were opening up new plantations. Thus many of these slaves would later be transported to Alabama, Louisiana, Mississippi, and the like. Linda's ancestors may well have ended up in the Deep South like her adoptive parents' ancestors before moving north in the Great Migration. We'll never know, but it's certainly a strong possibility.

"That's a long journey," said Linda. "A long, tough journey. I never thought I would hear this. It makes me want to know more. I feel that this is the beginning of a wonderful exploration."

As we said good-bye, I asked her to look back on the entire journey she'd taken with me. I was curious as to what the most meaningful stories were for her—and I must confess that I expected her to talk about the DNA results, as those had provided clues to her biological ancestry, which had always been a total mystery to her. But Linda chose to focus on the genealogical work that we'd done and told me something I found very touching.

"The most meaningful things," Linda said, "were really all about my parents. I mean the way that my mother's and my father's ancestors did dovetail in their pursuits and in their quest for knowledge and dissemination of knowledge. To me that was the most fascinating part. I knew that my mother came from a very prominent, very educated family. I knew that my father did not. But the way that those two came together, to me was mind-boggling, just mind-boggling. It sort of sets the tone for my DNA in the publishing business."

Mr. Johnson would have smiled at that.

Kathleen Henderson

January 12, 1959

THE PBS DOCUMENTARIES that led to this book—*African American Lives 1* and *2*—were produced as two separate series, broadcast two years apart. After the first series aired, the response was quite generous. People—and especially African Americans—came up to me on the street, in airports, everywhere, to offer their comments. Mostly they said kind things, but I got one consistent criticism. "Brother," some would say, "you did a good job, we're proud of you. But how come you just pick the big Negroes? How come you didn't pick a person like me?" One of the most important lessons of *African American Lives* is that *all* of our ancestors were "average Negroes," even those of the rich and famous.

I knew what they meant, and I took it to heart. I said to my fellow producers, "Why don't we research a quote/unquote, average African American family?" Everyone loved the idea, so we did a national competition. Over two thousand people responded, writing in to tell us about themselves and explain why they wanted to learn more about their ancestry. The winner, hands down, was a woman named Kathleen Henderson, who was born and raised in Dayton, Ohio, and still lives there, surrounded by her family. She works for the University of Dayton as the director of student engagement, and I am certain that she is great at her job. She's one of the most charming and open people I've met. I'm sure her students just adore her. She told me that she had entered the contest because she loved her family's oral tradition and, like the people who stop me in the street, she came from a family who watched my first series, saying, "Why doesn't he do a family like us?" She appreciated, she said, the fact that I had seen the light. I appreciated her candor in turn—and was pleased by the many richly layered stories we uncovered in her family's past.

Kathleen Henderson was born on January 12, 1959, in Dayton, Ohio. Her parents were Gay Estella Doster, born on February 6, 1935, in Middletown, Ohio, and James Edward Henderson, born on August 13, 1931, also in Middletown. She has two siblings and many aunts, uncles, and cousins.

Kathleen grew up in a changing neighborhood—one that reflected much larger patterns in America at that time. When she was born, the area of Dayton in which she lived was predominantly white, but within a few years that began to change. The white families started moving away and were replaced, almost without exception, by black families. By the time she reached adolescence, the neighborhood had become predominantly black. "It was an interesting experience to have," she reflected. "Not so much watching all the white people pull up and move out, but seeing how everything worked. Because the neighborhood wasn't really segregated by law, but we were still pretty segregated by just what opportunity provided. And there were good things and bad things about this. The good thing was that you had all kinds of black families in the same block, reflecting all classes."

Kathleen and her family were shaped by a complex sociological and economic dynamic with vast implications for the United States. Between 1950 and 1960, census data show that populations in the largest American cities increased negligibly—by just over 3 percent—while suburban populations exploded—going up by well over 60 percent. This is what sociologists have called "white flight." Looking behind the numbers, one learns that almost all the suburban growth was due to the movement of white people from the cities to the suburbs. The cities, even though their overall population numbers stayed relatively flat, became overwhelmingly black. Many believe that this had a devastating effect on the economic life of African Americans, because the removal of middle-class and upper-middle-class whites destroyed the tax base of most cities, wrecking school systems, health care, and other infrastructure, while significantly diminishing business opportunities. Kathleen was a perceptive observer of this phenomenon, and she sees it in very human terms, as a complicated process, almost a mixed blessing, rather than the all-out disaster that many scholars have proclaimed it to be.

"There were people who were striving to do something different, and they moved out," she said. "But there were people who were comfortable in whatever kind of working-class role they had. My great-grandmother, who lived with my grandmother, became kind of the neighborhood grandparent, you know? So you couldn't walk from one block to the other without being reported. So you felt safe and secure. It was a real neighborhood. A mixed-class black neighborhood. At least before integration really took hold."

When the civil-rights movement came, the neighborhood Kathleen knew was thrown into chaos. "It started to be very tense," she recalled. "There was an armory that was about two blocks away from our home. And there was a riot that erupted in Dayton in this armory. This was 1966 or '67. And I can still kind of remember trucks rolling out of that armory. And the neighborhoods were on fire in some places. You knew something was going on."

Kathleen's father, James Henderson, was an active supporter of the civil-rights movement, more sympathetic to the vision of Malcolm X than that of Martin Luther King Jr. Hearing Kathleen describe him, James sounds like Mae Jemison's parents, and he had a profound impact on Kathleen's feelings about her African American heritage, just as Mae's folks did. "My father talked about Africa a lot," Kathleen said. "My father was always saying, you know, 'You came from a great people.' He talked about the Marcus Garvey movement, his 'Back to Africa' movement. I learned about the civilization of Timbuktu, a lot of that. So there was always kind of a connection in our family with Africa and just being black. And that rubbed off."

I wondered why Kathleen's father took such pride in his African ancestors. Though this was not wildly unusual in his generation, it was not by any means the norm—and I'm always eager to learn why some people were on the cutting edge of black culture. Kathleen thinks her father's views had a lot to do with the hue of his skin— a trait he shares with his daughter. "My father was pretty brown," she said. "And so, of course, the kind of colored jokes that you have within the family—he heard a lot of those. And he and I, being the brownest in the household, had a bond. Maybe his talking about Africa, in some ways, was to help me feel comfortable with being as dark as I am and being connected with him."

Kathleen Henderson's mother, Gay Doster, around 1950.

I find this fascinating. I have heard many people tell me why they became cultural nationalists in the 1960s, why they valorized Africa and Malcolm X, but I've never heard anyone explain this intrafamily color dynamic—which, of course, all black people know about. We all discuss who's darker and lighter, sometimes humorously, often with cruel intentions and evil consequences. But we are aware of it. There is no denying that. It is a vital part of our culture. I am not proud of it, but I have participated in it, and I love the way Kathleen frames the discussion so lovingly, in such a moving way, with regard to her father.

There were other reasons, of course, that Kathleen's father—and mother—felt drawn to the civil-rights movement. Like many young black couples in the 1960s, Kathleen's parents knew that the world needed to change. They were both educated and successful, at least as successful as you could be if you were black in 1960s Ohio. Her father, James, was a systems analyst, and her mother, Gay, had done very well in high school. But Kathleen believes that her parents "felt the pains of being colored" from their earliest days in Middletown, attending segregated schools and then living in Dayton, a city that, outside their small neighborhood, was hostile to them.

"My father was a pretty bright man," she said, "and he always felt that there were a lot of opportunities not open to him, even though he could prove himself and he ended up doing a lot of work. And even for my mother—she was going to go to college, but the schools were tracking her very carefully and closely, and she just felt that the message was always, 'You're never gonna go to college. You're gonna do the things that all the other colored girls do.' So things were painful. I even remember there was an amusement park when they were kids. It's now closed. But back then, every year at the end of their year, the kids in the school there in Middletown would go. But it wasn't open for the colored kids to go to. As we got older and things relaxed some, they opened the doors to us. But my father wouldn't have none of it. He wouldn't go. 'You didn't want me before,' he'd say. 'Well, you ain't getting me now.' It was a very, very hard experience for my father."

I'm very familiar with these kinds of experiences—most African Americans of my generation are. We can all remember these humiliations, so blatantly thrown up in our parents' faces, as if they'd happened yesterday. Of course, such humiliations have not entirely stopped, not by any means. America's racism has grown more subtle, perhaps, more diffuse, but it has not disappeared. And I think it is important, as we look around us today, to remember what was so close to the surface just a generation ago. I can feel James Henderson's pain, even today, in his daughter's words.

It is important to note, however, that Kathleen's parents did not lose themselves in their pain. They were determined to transform their world. They became committed civil-rights activists and were also deeply involved in their children's education, knowing from years of accrued experience that schooling was the path to a better life, the only hope to break the shackles of segregation. It is no coincidence that many of the great civil-rights battles were fought over schools and educational issues. These people knew that knowledge was power.

"My parents were very active in our education, growing up," said

Kathleen. "I remember there was a real movement to bring black history into the school. There was a real movement to fix things. They were very involved in that. My father especially. Like, I remember there was a form that you were supposed to get signed and bring back into school. It was just a simple enrollment form, just stating our address, but my father wouldn't sign it. Every year you come back to school, and the teachers will call roll. And, you know, 'Kathy, do you have your paper?' No. 'Well, next time you bring in your paper.' I would go back home, say, 'Daddy, please.' But he wouldn't sign it, because he said he didn't think they were being fair with the money. He said he wouldn't sign it until we had new books in the school. And all those new books were going to the east side of Dayton—to the white kids, with Dayton being segregated. So he wasn't intending to sign nothin'. He was a hardheaded dude. But that was the way my parents were. They always wanted us to have an opportunity. What you did with that opportunity was on you, but you at least had this opportunity."

Turning back a generation on Kathleen's family tree, I was curious to see how her parents were shaped by their families. We were amply rewarded for our efforts. James Henderson's parents—Kathleen's paternal grandparents—were Elwood Henderson and Elizabeth Morton, both born in Kentucky in the early 1900s. Elwood died in Middletown, Ohio, in 1936, so Kathleen never knew him, but she heard many stories about her grandfather when she was growing up, and she believes that Elwood's untimely death had a profound influence on her father.

"My grandfather died when my father was three," she said. "And I think in some ways that probably influenced my father's need or want to make certain that he was there and present with us kids. Because of what he missed early on. I mean, for a young boy, not to have your father there is challenging. And my father made it his goal to meet that challenge, you know? And my dad was a lot of fun. My mother, I think, she sometimes had a difficult time understanding when us siblings would fight. She would be very upset if my sister and brother and I would fight. My father was more carefree. And always very, very family-oriented."

While Kathleen never knew James's father, she had a great deal of contact with his mother, Elizabeth Morton Henderson, who died in 1999

Kathleen remembers her grandmother, Elizabeth Henderson, as a stern and at times intimidating figure in her childhood.

and was a consistent presence in Kathleen's childhood and adult life. "She was a tough lady," Kathleen recalled, smiling. "Thank God that she lived as long as she did, and I was able to grow up and not be afraid of her. When I was a child, she was a little scary. I loved her, but, you know, she'd come to visit us during the summertime and we were excited to go to the Greyhound bus station to pick her up. But we were also excited to take her back."

Kathleen believes that her grandmother Elizabeth was very aware of status and class and that this, in many ways, informed her character, fueling her sense of decorum. "Her mother and brothers, they were the folks who worked in the house," said Kathleen. "They were house servants. And they were just very class-conscious, to be honest. They were always telling stories about what happened. They tended to be a little more secretive about things."

This distinction—between blacks who worked in the house and those who worked in the fields—is as old as the African American experience itself. It not only helped to create a class divide within the black community, it has also contributed to some harmful stereotyping and rather troubled social relations within the race. The simple fact of the matter is that our ancestors who worked in the houses of white people often had access to information and education, which their brethren and sisters in the fields did not. That they also developed a set of social concerns and status concerns that led to tensions in later generations is an undeniable aspect of their experience—and Kathleen perceived these issues in her grandmother Elizabeth's behavior.

We traced Elizabeth Morton back to her parents—Kathleen's great-grandparents—Hummons Allen Morton and Elizabeth Jackson. Hummons was born on October 18, 1883, in Winchester, Kentucky, and Elizabeth was born on March 6, 1883, in nearby Logan County, Kentucky. Both died before Kathleen was born, and she knew little about them. But we were able to trace the family back further, because we found Elizabeth Jackson's death certificate, dated February 4, 1918. It indicates that her parents were Dennis Jackson and Julia Mason. Both were born into slavery around 1845 in Logan County, Kentucky. That means that they spent the first twenty years of their lives as slaves.

"Imagine that," said Kathleen. "To be twenty and a slave, and then suddenly you're free. I bet they were excited—but I'd imagine they were also very afraid, just not knowing what tomorrow is going to bring. I imagine they were pretty frightened."

Searching for records about Dennis and Julia, we uncovered some rather unusual stories. When Dennis died in 1895, Julia applied for a widow's pension, believing that her husband had served in the ranks of the U.S. Colored Troops. But Dennis didn't actually fight in the Civil War. Records tell us that while trying to enlist as a young man, Dennis fell ill and was sent home. So he attempted to enlist but was not accepted into the army. Still, his wife's mistaken recollection—no doubt instilled in her by her husband and perhaps embellished through the years—provided us with a very valuable paper trail to a most unusual story.

In her request for her widow's-pension payment, Julia included a document signed by her friends and family that vouched for her marriage to Dennis. This document states that Dennis and Julia were married "about the year 1864 by Reverend George Downey at the house of William Bryan in Fayette County, Kentucky." This is extraordinarily unusual, because in 1864 Dennis and Julia were slaves and thus legally forbidden to marry. Yet despite the fact that their marriage would not have been recognized by the state or the federal government, they still felt strongly enough about their bond that they held a kind of symbolic wedding in front of their family and friends. Even more unusual is that they were married by an African American minister in the home of a white man named William Bryan, whom we suspect to have been Dennis's slave owner. This means that their master was hosting a wedding of his slaves! I have rarely encountered evidence of this.

We also found another statement filed by Julia Jackson as part of her resolute effort to obtain her husband's nonexistent pension. In this statement one of her friends asserts that Dennis and Julia were married a second time at a courthouse in Lexington, Kentucky, sometime around June of 1874. Second weddings such as this were not uncommon for former slaves and were a legal necessity. They knew that marriages made during the slave era were not valid before the law—no matter what the circumstances. So, as free people, nine years out of slavery, Julia and Dennis reenacted their wedding ceremony and made their relationship legal.

Hearing this, Kathleen began to cry. The desire of these two people, her long-dead ancestors, to stick together and remain a family even in the face of all that slavery had done to them was almost too much for her to bear. There is something so powerful about the will to persevere that our ancestors possessed, the will to build lives for themselves in spite of the worst form of human existence possible, human slavery. We are the beneficiaries of their determination and their will to survive, but so many of us don't know it or don't comprehend its significance. Seeing that story written so plainly in these dusty documents—documents in which so many of our ancestors' lives are trapped, as if in amber—never fails to affect me.

Turning back to Dennis Jackson and his wife, Julia Mason, we tried to identify either of their parents. We could find no evidence that they survived slavery, which rendered this an extremely difficult task. But once again we were very lucky. In 1865 the federal government set up a savings bank for the benefit of newly freed African Americans, called the Freedman's Bank. Among its records we found a file for Isaiah Mason, the brother of Kathleen's great-great-grandmother Julia Mason. The file tells us quite a lot about Isaiah. It says that on April 1, 1873, when Isaiah opened his account, he was twenty-six years old, with a medium-brown complexion, and was working as a "hackler" for a man named Jack Pullman. (A hackler was a worker in the linen industry who used a special kind of tool—a hackle—to comb out the coarse flax.) The file indicates that Isaiah was married with two children. It also lists the names of his eight siblings (including Julia) and his parents, George and Caroline Mason. George and Caroline Mason are, therefore, Kathleen's great-great-great-grandparents.

Digging deeper, we also found Isaiah's enlistment record from the U.S. Colored Troops in the Civil War. Unlike his brother-in-law, Dennis Jackson, Isaiah Mason really did serve in the army. He was mustered in at Camp Nelson in Jessamine County, Kentucky, which was the largest training ground for African American soldiers in the entire Civil War. Many slaves, particularly those from nearby counties in Kentucky, fled to Camp Nelson with their families to find freedom. In fact, one of my own ancestors—J. R. Clifford—served at the very same place. So Kathleen's ancestor and my ancestor may have met one another there. As we shall see, this is not the only ancestral coincidence that Kathleen and I would have.

Isaiah's enlistment records contain one further significant detail: They

Marriages made under slavery were not legal before the law, so Kathleen's ancestors Dennis and Julia Jackson were remarried after the Civil War.

list Isaiah's former slave owner as being a man named William Van Meter. Now, given that he owned Isaiah, it's very likely, of course, that William Van Meter would also have owned the rest of Isaiah's family, including Kathleen's great-great-grandmother Julia. But we wanted proof. So we looked in the census records and found that William Van Meter was living in Fayette County, Kentucky, in 1860. The slave schedule for that county in that year indicates that William Van Meter owned three slaves. One of them fits the profile of Isaiah Mason, but none matches Julia or their parents. However, living next to William Van Meter was his father, Abraham Van Meter, who owned twenty-one slaves. An estate inventory from 1863, made just before Abraham died, contains a list of his slaves. In it we found George, fifty-six years of age, valued at $300; Caroline, thirty-eight years of age, valued at $400; and Julia, eleven years of age, valued at $450. These are Kathleen's ancestors—her great-great-grandmother Julia and Julia's parents, George and Caroline.

"Julia commands a good price," said Kathleen with a sad, ironic laugh.

I explained to Kathleen that Julia was valued so highly at age eleven because of what she was expected to bring her owners as she grew older: new slaves in the form of her children. (Our ancestors were baby machines, in effect: The 388,000 Africans shipped to these shores between 1619 and 1820 directly from the African continent, plus another 60,000 or so shipped via the Caribbean, became 4.5 million by 1860.)

"It's just so disgusting even to have to talk like this," said Kathleen. "I'm amazed. I just wish my father was still alive. The whole family there— it's incredible. And all because a man decided to make an inventory of his property."

I agree. It is disgusting. Though, obviously, I also think that it is terribly important to understand these things. This is our history, after all. And commenting on this, I then showed Kathleen a picture of Abraham Van Meter, the man who owned those two generations of her family.

"Oh, geezy," she said. "There's a part of me that wants to smile, and then there's a part of me that's like—he doesn't look like a very nice man."

Van Meter's twenty-one slaves in 1860 was a fairly large number for that time in Kentucky. He was, it seemed to me at first, a very conventional

white slave owner. But further research revealed that
he was more interesting
than I initially thought. We
found an article published
in 1849 in Van Meter's local
newspaper, the *Lexington
Observer and Reporter*. It
describes "a large and enthusiastic meeting of the
opponents of perpetual slavery in Kentucky and those in
favor of a safe and gradual
plan of emancipation." The
first speaker at this meeting
and, seemingly, its organizer
was Abraham Van Meter.
He owned slaves, but apparently he believed in gradual
emancipation, perhaps starting after he had died.

*Abraham Van Meter, the man who owned
two generations of Kathleen's family.*

"He obviously didn't believe that they should be free in his lifetime,"
Kathleen reflected, laughing. "Not right now, you know? Maybe after I'm
gone. Take care of my needs first. It's all about me."

Kathleen is right, of course. Van Meter's views, whatever they may
have been, did little to help his own slaves, her ancestors. But his views are
illustrative of a moral ambivalence over slavery, nonetheless.

Moreover, Abraham Van Meter provides a remarkable link between
Kathleen's family and my own. I have two ancestors—Joe and Sarah
Bruce, my fourth great-grandparents on my father's mother's side—who
were owned by a man named Abraham Van Meter, who freed them in
1823, long before the Civil War. But my ancestors lived in Hardy County,
Virginia—not Kentucky. Still, I couldn't help but wonder about the connection. So we traced back the family trees of the Abraham Van Meter

who owned Kathleen's ancestors and the Abraham Van Meter who owned mine. And we found that they were cousins! Both started out in Hardy County, Virginia. But while the one who owned my ancestors stayed, Kathleen's Abraham left Virginia for Kentucky in 1838, taking twenty-one slaves with him. This means it is possible that Kathleen's ancestors George and Caroline Mason were born in Hardy County, Virginia, near my ancestors and were then taken to Kentucky by Abraham Van Meter. Kathleen and I both find this an incredible, tantalizing possibility.

Unfortunately, we could not find any records to substantiate the theory. We were also unable to trace Kathleen's paternal line back any further. The paper trail ended with George and Caroline.

Turning to the maternal line of Kathleen's family tree, we found a number of other revealing narratives. Her mother's parents, Kathleen's maternal grandparents, were Charles Reilly Doster and Seda Ruth Pullam. Both were born in Smithville, Georgia—Charles on March 21, 1914, and Seda on February 16, 1917. Kathleen did not know Charles, because he and Seda separated long before she was born. But she knew a great deal about their marriage, because she had just recently found her grandmother's diary. It contains a deeply sad account of a troubled family.

"There are some really poignant moments in the diary," said Kathleen. "She talks about the birth and the death of her first child that she had with Charles Doster. What's really touching is that she calls the baby by name in one entry, and the baby's name was Charlie Mae. And then each day after that she just says 'the baby,' you know? Since the baby has died. She never calls the child by name again. It is really heart-tugging."

After the death of her first child, Seda was sent north to live with her husband's family while Charles attended Fort Valley State College in Georgia. The trip proved disastrous to her marriage. "Charlie's mother never thought anybody was good enough for him," said Kathleen. "And she really kinda carried on. My grandmother was one of those kind of funny people who was very superstitious. Seda swore that Charlie's mother put a hex or something on her, and that's the reason the baby died. And things were going very bad, but then Charlie writes to her and convinces her to come down to Fort Valley for some kind of party. So she goes, and it's there that my mother is conceived. Then my grandmother comes back north and is pregnant. So, supposedly, Charlie's mother, she takes a train to see her son, goes down and brings him some papers to sign, because the family had a little property. And in the stack of papers was a divorce or a dissolution paper. Of course, you know, when your mother gives you something to sign, you just do what she tells you to do. So Charlie signed the papers, and that is how my grandmother learns that this marriage has ended. It was a real kind of heartbreak. There wasn't a whole lot of talk about Charlie when I was growing up. But there were still the pictures that were around, tucked away and hidden."

The story may have elements of family lore, but we were unable to contradict it, and I believe that it may well be true. Regardless, it is an interesting story, and it has a good coda. Seda remarried twice more, eventually settling down very well with a man named Moses Martin, whom Kathleen loved and grew up believing was her maternal grandfather. So in the end Seda found happiness.

Seda's mother was Estella Woodbridge, born in June of 1894 in Lee County, Georgia. Her last name raised an intriguing problem for our researchers. Kathleen has heard many family stories about the origin of the name Woodbridge. "We were told," she said, "that when Papa—and I'm not certain who Papa was—but we all heard at family gatherings that when this man Papa, who was a slave, when emancipation happened and he left his master, he didn't want to carry his master's name anymore. And so when he left from the plantation, he walked—you know, depending on who tells it, the story gets grander—but he walked away, and he decided he was going to rename himself. And the first thing he came across was a wooden bridge. So he was like, 'Hmm, I'll change my name to Woodbridge.'"

Family stories like this are always appealing to me, and I wanted to see if this one had even a kernel of truth to it. Research shows that Kathleen's great-great-great-grandfather on her maternal line was Dudley Woodbridge, born about 1827 in Georgia. He is the first Woodbridge in her family and thus could be the "Papa" in the story. We found a slave schedule from 1860 for a man named Grafton Dudley Woodbridge, who lived in Glynn County, Georgia. There is no definite proof that Grafton

Dudley Woodbridge owned Kathleen's ancestor Dudley Woodbridge, but given the geography and the similarity of name, it seems likely. So I told Kathleen that it appeared to me that Dudley Woodbridge took his favorite parts of his master's name rather than invent a name for himself.

"That makes sense," said Kathleen, with a smile indicating that she never fully believed the family legend. "I think we'll save the other one for late nights around the campfire. It's a good story, you know? It kept me interested for a long time."

At this point our paper trail along Kathleen's maternal line had ended. We could go back no further than Dudley Woodbridge. Turning to her DNA testing, I told her that her admixture test reflected that she was 79 percent sub-Saharan African, 18 percent European, and 3 percent Native American, as are Tom Joyner and Ben Carson, while Quincy Jones and Bliss Broyard have about 5 percent Native American ancestry.

Kathleen was very excited by these results. She had heard family stories of Native American ancestry from her grandmother, like many of the other people I've interviewed. But her family stories turned out to have a bit of truth. This makes her one of the few people in this book (Oprah, Chris Tucker, and Mae Jemison have a significant amount) who actually has even a small amount of measurable Native American ancestry. (As we have seen, only one out of twenty black people has a significant Indian ancestral heritage [12.5 percent], though most of us think otherwise.)

Primarily, however, Kathleen was thrilled to hear about her African results. "I always use the adjective 'African-American,'" she said. "And I'm always really focusing in on that hyphen, because we are African and we are American. And this shows that hyphen. I'm informed and shaped by the American experience. Yet here in these Americas, I'm fully shaped and formed by that 79 percent of the African. So I'm the hyphen."

We did a second admixture test, which indicated that 39 percent of Kathleen's African ancestors came from eastern Nigeria, 31 percent came from Congo Angola, and 30 percent from the region called Upper Guinea, which stretches from Liberia to Senegal. Kathleen's African ancestors were thus almost equally divided among the three main regions that sent slaves to the United States. This, she thought, was welcome news, because she wanted to be connected to as much of Africa as possible.

Our testing of her mitochondrial DNA yielded exact matches with the Mende people of Sierra Leone, the Fula and Balanta people of Guinea-Bissau, and the Mandinka people of Senegal. Based on their knowledge of the slave trade and of Kathleen's family tree, the historians John Thornton and Linda Heywood felt that these results indicated that Kathleen's original enslaved female ancestor came from the Mandinka people. The Mandinka lived near and traded with and fought all the other groups identified in Kathleen's mitochondrial result, but the Mandinka are the group that is best represented among enslaved African Americans brought through South Carolina's ports in the last decades of the eighteenth century and the early nineteenth century. This is significant because many slaves who were brought to Lee County, Georgia, when it was settled in the 1820s— and where Kathleen's oldest known matrilineal ancestor was born—were descendants of slaves who were originally imported into the United States through Charleston and Savannah.

When I told Kathleen that we believed her female ancestor on her direct maternal line most likely was Mandinka from the country now called Senegal, she smiled broadly. "That's amazing," she said. "I don't think Senegal was ever in my mind. I've always wanted to go to Africa. I've always identified with Africa. But I never thought about Senegal. And I think about the students that I've worked with at the University of Dayton who are international students, and, of course, in my head I'm thinking, who did I work with from Senegal? There are a few, and now I can find them and say, 'Guess what? We're related.' I mean, it just opens up the door."

Kathleen seems as happy as anyone involved in this project to learn her roots. "It's very comforting," she said. "It's so very comforting to finally know where. I always wanted to know what tribe I'm from. I think all African Americans do. Because that was stolen from us. And ours being such an oral tradition, you only have the language or those stories that are told. Well, somewhere along the line through slavery, those stories were interrupted. And so there is a real desire to find that connectedness."

At the end I asked Kathleen to think back to her father. He died in

1995. I would like to have met him, and I wanted to know what he would have made of this new knowledge. Would he have said, "We are an African people living in America"? Or would he have said, "We are an American people who happen to be descended in part from Africans"? The difference is crucial.

"I think my father," Kathleen replied, "would join me in saying that it's not an either/or. It is both. We are African and African American."

At this she began to cry, which was one of the most moving moments of this project for me. But after a moment she wiped her eyes and said something that completely surprised me, summing up our work in a way I never could have anticipated—in a way that was important to her sense of what American culture is to her.

"The tears come, thinking about my father and his people," she said. "They just come from thinking about how moved they would have been to know this. It affirms things. I think everybody should do this. Not only African Americans. I think anyone who lives in these United States needs to know this stuff. I mean, when you think about this country being settled and at one point being this wonderful melting pot, well, thank God that we were black, that we didn't quite melt. So we kept some connection back to some country. And it's funny. Because once I started to share this with the people at work, you know, frequently white people would say that they knew their culture and their ancestry, that their culture is hot dogs and apple pie. And I'd say, 'Well, actually, you know, that's not your culture. Apple pie comes out of a slave tradition with cobbler. That's black people. That ain't you. Would your ancestors be happy to know that you have become so melted into this country that you don't know who they are or don't know anything about who they are?' That's my question for them. But for black people, I think the beauty is because we didn't melt, we got to hold on to some of these cultural pieces. And it's hard, but at least we can understand them now. And you know, this information and knowledge, it's priceless. No one can take it away from me. No one will be able to take this experience away from me, no one."

Jackie Joyner-Kersee

March 3, 1962

J ACKIE JOYNER-KERSEE is one of the greatest athletes in the history of track and field. She dominated so many different events for so many years that it's almost impossible to put her accomplishments in perspective. Suffice it to say that she has six Olympic medals, won in four consecutive Olympic Games—an amazing feat that may never be matched again.

I am a huge fan of Jackie's and have followed her career for decades. When she agreed to participate in this project, I was thrilled, because I knew that she had risen to the top against tremendously steep odds, growing up in poverty in the 1960s, struggling every day against the most basic obstacles. I also knew that despite all her success she has remained devoted to her family and her community, and that she works very hard to give back to both. I was eager to see where these values had come from and how they had been shaped. Jackie, for her part, knew little about her family's past and shared my interest in its possible influence on her. Neither of us was disappointed by the results. I was particularly struck by the ways in which Jackie's character seems to be a direct outgrowth of her deepest roots.

Jacqueline Joyner was born on March 3, 1962, in East St. Louis, Illinois. She was named after Jacqueline Kennedy, who was first lady at that time—and her name reflects a confidence that her family had in her from the beginning. "My grandmother Evelyn," said Jackie, laughing, "she named me after the first lady 'cause she thought *I* would be the first lady

Jackie Joyner-Kersee at one of her many charity events.

or something. She always had high hopes and expectations for me."

It is hard to imagine where her grandmother's confidence in her new grandchild's future stemmed from. At the time of Jackie's birth, East St. Louis wasn't likely to be producing any first ladies in the near future. The city, like most of the country, was still locked in the stranglehold of segregation—and the situation was getting worse, not better, as the civil-rights movement accelerated. Indeed, both sets of Jackie's grandparents had moved to East St. Louis from the Deep South in the early years of the twentieth century—part of the Great Migration. Even though the city was the site of huge race riots in 1919, it was still seen as preferable to Mississippi and Alabama. But by the time Jackie was growing up in the 1960s, East St. Louis was changing. It was no longer a northern haven, but rather a place in the throes of an economic decline that would soon make it one of the most dangerous and impoverished environments in the United States, with murder rates and drug-use rates well in excess of those in many larger, better-known cities. This was no place to grow up; it was a metaphor for urban decay and the dissolution of the black family.

Since achieving such great success, Jackie has been deeply involved in helping to rebuild and reinvigorate her hometown, funding an enormous community center and a range of youth programs. But I wanted to know what East St. Louis was like in her childhood—when she was living across the street from a liquor store and a pool hall, in the heart of a violent neighborhood.

"You didn't worry about being hurt," she said with a characteristic shrug, "because your environment is your existence. So for me what was out of the ordinary for someone else was really ordinary. We knew that the tavern, the pool hall, they were okay at times, but then you also saw where there were fights, and then the violence escalated into shooting and then escalated to someone getting killed, you know? So then we'd have our parents or great-grandmother saying, 'Get in the house!' And that's what we did—like every other day. It was like this was just happening. And my mom always wanted me to read the local paper to know about rapes, if someone was missing, that we were not immune to that. To know that if one leaves the house, then everyone leaves all together. To not be overly friendly. My mom taught us all those things. So, I mean, there were drugs, violence, it was a part of life, but I felt safe."

A large part of Jackie's feeling of safety was the powerful presence of her mother, Mary Ruth Gaines, who managed to hold her family together even in these troubled circumstances. Mary Ruth was born on November 14, 1943, in Sunflower, Mississippi. She met and married Jackie's father, Alfred Lee Joyner (no relation to Tom Joyner's family) when they were both still teenagers growing up in East St. Louis. She was sixteen, and he was fifteen. Their children came in rapid succession, so Alfred had to work right out of high school to support the family. It was a very difficult situation, and Jackie recalls her parents' struggles vividly.

"I remember my mom sitting us down and was telling us how tough it was going to be," she said, "And my dad didn't really want her to work, but eventually he lost one job after the other, and he had to move away to Springfield, Ohio. And so my mom said, well, she had to get a job."

With their father gone, Jackie and her siblings spent a great deal of time with their paternal great-grandmother, Ollie Mae Thomas,

Jackie's mother, Mary Ruth Gaines, struggled to hold the family together despite dire circumstances.

while their mother strove to support them. "We would come home, and my great-grandmother would be there," Jackie recalled. "We realized that it was just something my mom had to do. It was very important that she go and try to find a job, and she got one as a nurse's aide. That made a difference. But the hours were just hard. You never knew if she was going to be working early in the morning or late, or if she'd have to do a double shift. It was a very tough time. All of a sudden, the food would run out, and then there were times when there was no heat in the house or there wasn't any hot water."

Jackie says that over the years she has increasingly understood how difficult and chaotic her childhood was. But she does not recall being truly unhappy. To the contrary, she remembers developing an early fixation on athletics; sports were deeply enjoyable for her. And she believes that overall her family life gave her the strength to compete and the inner confidence to succeed. "As a young girl," she said, "I was determined. People would point and say she's a fighter. And I think it was because from my family standpoint I was seeing my mother and father struggle, and never once did my mother ever give up on us or my father, you know? So I had that innately. I just would not give up."

Moreover, Jackie believes that despite the difficulties her parents faced, they were able to provide a loving home that laid the groundwork for her success. As if to illustrate this, even as she tells stories of youthful deprivation, she has a way of laughing about them. The good times, she believes, far outnumbered the bad. "We just made the best of what we had," she said. "We didn't really focus on what we didn't have. Like, when there wasn't food on the table and we just had mayonnaise sandwiches, we made do. And then we'd be waiting for my great-grandmother to get her Social Security check, and after that she'd go to the grocery store to get the cookies, get all kinds of different goodies. We just pulled together."

Jackie's mother's job as a nurse's aide proved critical to the family's stability. It is a mark of her determination and intelligence that her mother was able to get such a job at all. Mary Ruth had never graduated from high school, much less nursing school, but she was smart, had friends to help her, and was determined to give her children a better life. "She always wanted to make sure that myself, my brother, my two sisters, that we graduated from high school, got an education," said Jackie. "So she let us know how hard she had it, how hard it was for her walking the pavement, trying to fill out applications and sometimes not really understanding the applications. It was extremely difficult for her. She was really stressed a lot. And with me being the oldest girl, she would always say to me, 'Don't fall into the same trap.' She didn't ever want us to think that we were a mistake. She loved us and always made that clear. But she was also always saying, 'You can wait for boyfriends, Jackie, and having babies. You get your education. You make something of your life.' That was my mother all the time."

Jackie took her mother's words to heart. She disdained boys, drugs, and alcohol to focus instead on sports and schoolwork. She overcame the racism that had locked her into a segregated, impoverished neighborhood.

"A lot of white schools wouldn't come to our school," she recalled when talking about sporting contests between schools. "They were afraid their bus was going to be rocked or they were going to be jumped on. So a lot of times we had to go to their school. And when we traveled, we all couldn't go into the restaurant. They would take our order and would bring our food back out. And there were certain hotels we couldn't stay in. But it was all a learning experience, just something that as a young person I dealt with."

Jackie and her brother, Al, a few years after their mother's tragic death from cancer.

Graduating in the top 10 percent of her high-school class, Jackie won an athletic scholarship to UCLA, which had some of the most prestigious sports programs in the nation. This gave her access to coaches and trainers who set her on the track to stardom.

Sadly, Mary Ruth did not live to see her daughter's success. She died of cancer in 1981, when Jackie was still in college. Nonetheless, Mary's values endured. Throughout her long years of training, Jackie drew on her mother's strength and sense of purpose, her commitment to making something better out of her life. In our conversations she repeatedly returned to the theme of her mother's example. "I come from a long line of strong-willed, strong-minded women," she said. "I think that was something I definitely got from my mother, and then I'm sure from my grandmother and great-grandmother. But it all started with my mother."

In researching her family tree, I had hoped to prove Jackie right in some measure. Of course, I'm not sure such a thing is really possible. Despite the conventional wisdom, it is very difficult to trace character traits down generations, and even when we think we can, those traits are certainly not genetically transmitted; rather, they are generated through environment, through mimicked behavior, through mother's milk, as it were. Nonetheless, I think we found many strong-willed ancestors in Jackie's tree—more than enough to excite and intrigue her, which every genealogist hopes to do.

Our investigation of Mary Ruth's family began with her parents—Jackie's maternal grandparents—Estella Rainey, who was born in Ruleville, Mississippi, on December 6, 1927, and Sylvester Gaines, born in Vaiden, Mississippi, on March 25, 1925. Tracing Sylvester's family back, we immediately came upon a curious story. His parents were Almeta and Sam Gaines. Census records indicate that both were born in Mississippi—Almeta around 1890 and Sam sometime around 1889. Sam lived until 1964, and his death certificate contains a mystery. On it his parents are listed as Andrew Gaines and Mary Bailey, but the 1910 census records show an Anderson Gaines and a Mary Bailey living *near* each other, but not *with* each other—and certainly not *married* to each other. Instead, in 1910 Anderson Gaines was living with his wife, a woman named Fanny, and Mary Bailey was living in a different household with her seven children, all of whom had her surname: Bailey. One of the children appears to be the man who would later be called Sam Gaines. But in the 1910 census he's called Sam Bailey. Something fishy was clearly going on here.

By examining many records, we finally realized that Anderson Gaines was the father of all of Mary Bailey's children, including Sam Gaines. This means that Jackie's great-great-grandfather Anderson Gaines had two families: one with his legal wife, Fanny, and another with Jackie's great-great-grandmother Mary Bailey. Census records indicate that the situation resolved itself around 1930, by which time Fanny had died and Anderson and Mary were living together. In the coming years, as Anderson and Mary stayed together and had more children together, Sam and many of his siblings ended up taking the Gaines name as well.

"He was a player," said Jackie mischievously, looking at our records. She was clearly curious. She never met either of her mother's parents and had never even heard of Anderson Gaines. When we showed her a photograph of her grandfather Sylvester, she was surprised to see how much he looked like her older brother.

Jackie's lack of familiarity with this branch of her family was partly due to the fact that her mother, Mary Ruth, had had only limited contact with her parents herself. She was raised mainly by her grandmother, Lena Hemingway Rainey, who was born in Mississippi in 1896. Lena was the dominant figure in Mary Ruth's upbringing, and Jackie remembers her vividly from her own childhood. "She was no joker," Jackie said. "Very stern. Very stubborn. She had her house rules, and we couldn't do this and couldn't do that. She would get you when you did wrong, and she'd paddle you. Back then it wasn't called child abuse. That's how they disciplined you. But she could be very warm sometimes, too."

Lena came from a long line of African Americans with roots in the Deep South. What little we know about her parents, James Hemingway and Maggie Robinson, suggests that they were born in Mississippi in the years following the Civil War. Their own parents were slaves born in Alabama and Mississippi. We could find almost no information about them, but in researching Lena we uncovered some revealing stories about her husband's family.

Lena's husband was Andrew Rainey, born in Liberty, Mississippi, around 1891. His father, Jackie's maternal great-great-grandfather, was a man named Drit Rainey, born into slavery in Hinds County, Mississippi, sometime between 1850 and 1855. He seems to have been a remarkable man.

According to the U.S. census in 1870, Drit Rainey was living as a lodger with a mulatto family in Amite County, Mississippi. Ten years later, in 1880, the census indicates that Drit was married to a woman named Ellen Collins. The census also shows that by that time the couple had six children together and were working as tenant farmers in Amite County. This, of course, means that Jackie's great-great-grandparents had to pay enormous amounts of rent to white landowners every year, no matter how their crops fared. And they were vulnerable to unfair treatment by their landlords, many of whom were former Confederates or were the very same planters who had owned them when they were slaves.

Every tenant farmer dreamed of owning a farm. That dream was almost impossible to achieve. But somehow Drit and Ellen succeeded. Census data indicate that by 1900 they owned their own farm in Amite County—free of any mortgage. How did this happen? It was very rare for ex-slaves to become landowners in Mississippi in the 1890s. We went searching through local records and uncovered a fascinating story.

A land deed from late 1890 showed that Drit Rainey purchased 120 acres of land from a white man named G. H. Barney. To pay for it, Drit signed a promissory note with something called the Bank of Gloster to borrow $600 at 10 percent interest. As collateral Drit put up virtually everything he could: all his land, all the crops that he might grow on that land, all future income from tenants or sharecroppers who might live on the land, and all his personal property, including all of his livestock. And then, one year later, Drit signed another deed, whereby his debt was reduced to $485.76—indicating that he was making some progress in spite of the interest. Yet he still had to put up everything he owned as collateral for the lesser amount.

These are extremely disadvantageous terms. Ten percent was exorbitant interest at that time, and the collateral requirements were extraordinarily severe. Moreover, we found unfair notes like this for every subsequent year until Drit had completely paid off his loan. Perhaps unsurprisingly, we also discovered that the president of the Bank of Gloster was none other than G. H. Barney, the white man who'd sold Drit the land in the first place. Furthermore, we learned that Drit could not read or write. His contracts are signed with an *X*, and census data indicate that he was illiterate. He probably had very little idea, if any, of what he was agreeing to or whether it was fair. And if he did, he had no other choice but to sign. His bankers, such as they were, certainly had no incentive to give him an understanding of the terms of his loans.

This transaction is an excellent illustration of how white southerners maintained their power over blacks long after the Civil War—using economic, legal, and political means to hold African Americans in cycles of debt and poverty that were essentially just a new form of slavery. Jackie's ancestor Drit was exploited by the bank and the bank's president—who made money on both ends of the unfair transaction. Moreover, if Drit had failed to pay off his debt, G. H. Barney would have regained his property in foreclosure and most likely repeated the whole deal on another unsuspecting black man.

But here's the incredible thing: Drit Rainey did not fail. He paid off the loan over ten years—most likely by working his farm day and night.

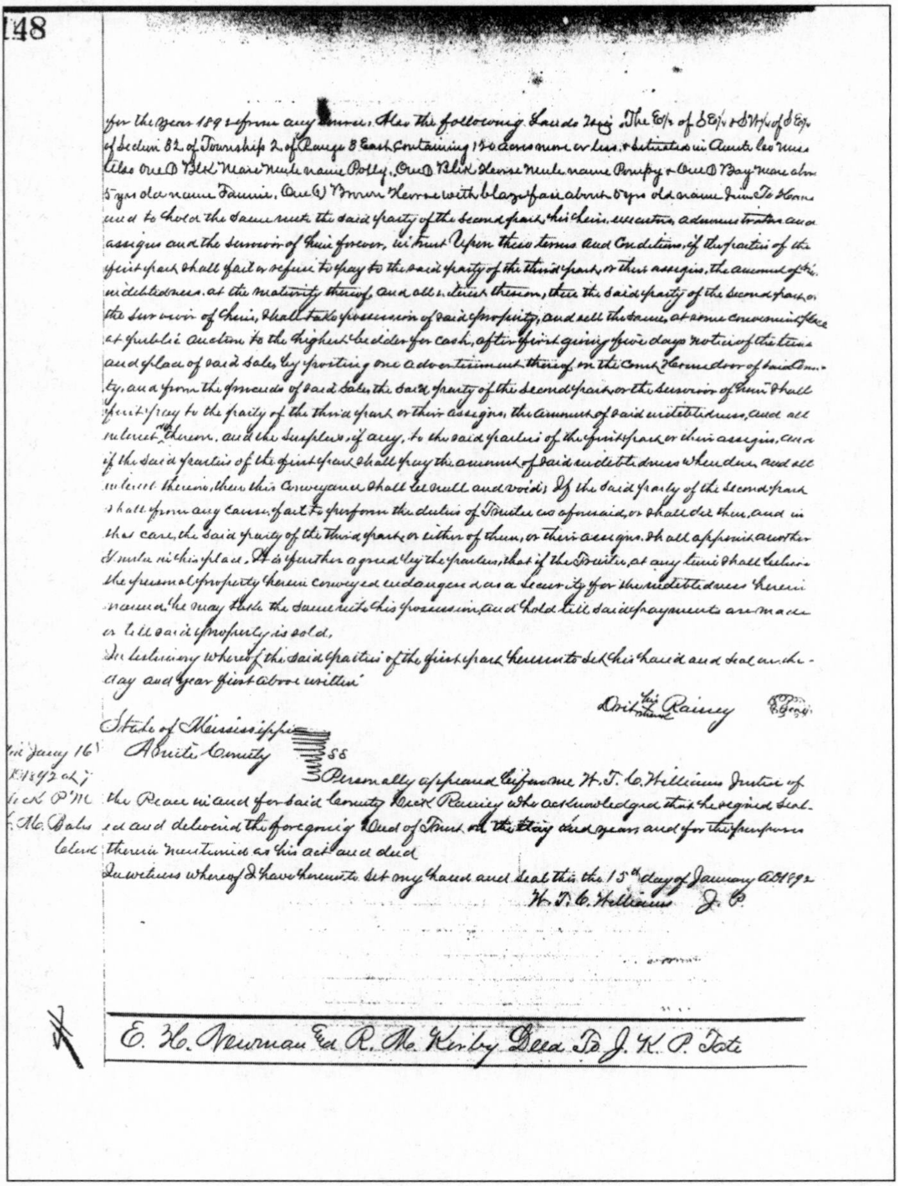

148

for the year 189[illegible] from any source. Also the following Lands to wit: The E½ of SE¼ & SW¼ of SE¼ of Section 32 of Township 2 of Range 8 East containing 120 acres more or less & situated in Amite Co Miss. Also One (1) Blk Mare Mule name Polly, One (1) Blk Horse Mule name Pompy & One (1) Bay mare abt 5 yrs old name Fannie, One (1) Brown Horse with blaze face about 8 yrs old name Jim. To Have and to hold the same unto the said party of the second part his heirs, executors, administrators and assigns and the survivor of them forever, in trust Upon these terms and Conditions, if the parties of the first part shall fail or refuse to pay to the said party of the third part, or their assigns, the amount of the indebtedness at the maturity thereof, and all interest thereon, then the said party of the second part or the survivor of them, shall take possession of said property, and sell the same, at some convenient place at public auction to the highest bidder for cash, after first giving five days notice of the time and place of said sale, by posting one advertisement thereof on the Court House door of said County, and from the proceeds of said sale the said party of the second part or the survivor of them shall first pay to the party of the third part or their assigns, the amount of said indebtedness, and all interest due thereon, and the surplus, if any, to the said parties of the first part or their assigns, and if the said parties of the first part shall pay the amount of said indebtedness when due, and all interest thereon, then this Conveyance shall be null and void; If the said party of the second part shall from any cause fail to perform the duties of Trustee as aforesaid, or shall die then, and in that case, the said party of the third part or either of them, or their assigns shall appoint another Trustee in his place. It is further agreed by the parties, that if the Trustee, at any time shall believe the personal property herein conveyed endangered as a Security for the indebtedness herein named, he may take the same into his possession, and hold till said payments are made or till said property is sold.

In testimony whereof the said parties of the first part hereunto set his hand and seal on the day and year first above written

Drit his X mark Rainey (Seal)

State of Mississippi
Amite County } ss

Filed Jany 16th 1892 at 7 o'ck P.M. [illegible] M. Bates Clerk

Personally appeared before me W. T. C. Williams Justice of the Peace in and for said County Dick Rainey who acknowledged that he signed, sealed and delivered the foregoing Deed of Trust on the day and year and for the purposes therein mentioned as his act and deed

In witness whereof I have hereunto set my hand and seal this the 15th day of January AD 1892

W. T. C. Williams J. P.

E. H. Newman and R. M. Kirby Deed To J. K. P. Tate

Promissory note issued to Jackie's ancestor Drit Rainey, loaning him money to buy his farm. Despite the loan's usurious terms, Drit was able to pay it off and eventually owned his land free and clear.

I would have loved to see G. H. Barney's expression when Drit came in with his payments. I have little doubt that it was a serious shock. And I have great admiration for Drit. Like his family after him, he was stubborn, he was hardheaded, diligent, industrious, and willing to take a risk—a risk that paid off. He beat the system, in his own way and time. Some of his triumph must have been related to luck. If even one year of his crops had failed due to drought or infestation, he'd have lost everything to G. H. Barney and friends. But mostly I think he triumphed by virtue of hard work. And because of that, Drit Rainey managed to carve out a foothold for his family during extremely difficult economic times.

Unfortunately, our research into Jackie's maternal line was not able to reach much further back than Drit Rainey. We know that his father was a man named Carter Rainey, but we do not know where or when he was born. His mother was a woman named Maria or Mollie who was born a slave somewhere in Virginia around 1830. We suspect that both lived their entire lives in slavery, and we cannot trace their families back any further than that.

Turning to Jackie's paternal line, we began to work our way back through the ancestry of her father, Alfred Joyner. He was the son of Jewel Ivory, born on September 19, 1926, in East St. Louis, Illinois, and Evelyn Joyner, born sometime around 1923, probably in Ohio. There is no evidence that they were ever legally married—and indeed Evelyn's entire biography is something of a mystery. She may have been born in Illinois or Ohio, possibly as early as 1921. She lived most of her life in Chicago, and it is unclear how she supported herself. Jackie rarely saw her. However, she has a prominent place in Jackie's memory.

"I don't know what Evelyn did, I really don't," Jackie said. "Within the family we were just like, you know, 'My grandmother is like a gangster.' That was her attitude. She'd come down, and she was just kind of wild. She would teach us all kinds of things—pitching pennies, how to take care of our money. Like, she'd give us a quarter and say, 'How could you turn this quarter into a dollar?' Stuff like that."

Jackie recalls that Evelyn's mother, Ollie Mae, was constantly worried about her daughter. "We spent a lot of time with Ollie Mae," said Jackie.

"We lived in her house, you know, and the conversation we always had was about her Evelyn. She just felt that Evelyn lived a fast life. She wanted her to settle down, and she always feared that something tragic was going to happen to her. I mean, every morning she would talk about it, and you'd just be sitting there and listening, and she'd be drinking her coffee. And then in the evening, at that time she'd drink stag beer. So you'd just sit there listening again. And I was always like, 'Well, why are you so hard on Grandma?' And she goes, 'Well, Jackie, you got to do something with your life, and Evelyn don't know what she want to do.' "

Ollie Mae's fears were well grounded. In 1972, when Evelyn was fifty-one years old, she was murdered by a boyfriend. "It was tragic," said Jackie. "The man she was seeing came in one day and just shot her with a shotgun in her sleep. And my great-grandmother, you know, she always believed something like that was going to happen. She didn't want it, but she could see it happening."

The murder profoundly affected Ollie Mae. "My great-grandmother was very, very strong," said Jackie. "But she was really hurt a lot. You could feel that her soul was hurting. Even though she did everything she possibly could to make us happy, you could just feel that she was sad a lot, really sad. And I don't know if it was because of where she was born and what she had gone through, but at that time, when you'd had a difficult time in your life, that's just not something you talked about. So she kept it all inside and was very tough, but you could feel the hurt."

Ollie Mae Thomas was indeed an exceptionally strong person. She was born in rural Tennessee sometime in the early twentieth century and came from a long line of people who endured great hardship. Her mother was Lee Anna Scott, who was born in Tennessee in the 1870s. Lee Anna's parents were Alex Scott, born a slave in Virginia in 1842, and a woman named Lucy Conner, who was born a slave in Tennessee in 1850. Lucy's father was Gabriel Conner, born into slavery around 1805 in Virginia. He is Jackie's great-great-great-great-grandfather on her father's side, and we uncovered a moving story about him.

Much of what we know about Gabriel comes from a deed that we found, dated October 12, 1827, and signed by a white slaveholder named Uriel Conner, who we believe was Gabriel's original owner. The deed transfers ownership of Gabriel to Uriel's son Francis Lewis Conner and his wife, Mary, so that the couple could move west and start their own farm. Along with Gabriel, Uriel also gave his son a wagon and some livestock. Gabriel, of course, does not have a last name in the document. He was a slave, after all. But he is listed there by his first name. The deed also stipulates that Gabriel the slave technically belongs to Francis's children but that Francis will have possession of him until his children are adults.

This deed interested me for many reasons. Among others, it colors, so to speak, the myth of America's westward expansion. We as a nation cherish the image of the pioneer heading west in the Conestoga wagon—and there are countless images, from the early nineteenth century onward, celebrating these journeys. I cannot think of one that shows a black man riding in the wagon or walking alongside it. Yet, of course, we were there. The story of Jackie's fourth great-grandfather helps prove it. And his story also shows how, as part of this movement to the west, our families were destroyed. Gabriel was ripped away from his parents, his siblings, and his community in Virginia where he had been born and where he grew up. He was then forced to move to a strange new land, to do the backbreaking work of taming the frontier, chopping down trees, and fighting the Native Americans.

Once he got to the frontier, Gabriel's life continued to be emblematic of this cruel aspect of slavery. Francis Lewis Conner took Gabriel to Gibson County, Tennessee. There we found a series of documents showing that Francis was regularly buying and selling land and slaves, including Gabriel, for sums that were so low they did not make sense economically. For instance, in 1842 Francis sold Gabriel, some land, and another slave to one of his relatives for five dollars. Then, in 1849, Francis bought Gabriel and four other slaves back from one of his family members for five dollars. Now, at that time a healthy male slave was worth more than a thousand dollars. What did these transactions mean? They meant that Francis Lewis Conner was dirt poor. He needed cash to make ends meet between cotton growing seasons, and the only valuable asset he had was his slaves. Yet he could not sell them, because his father's will had deeded them to his children—he was simply allowed to use the slaves until his children became adults. So Francis was essentially using Gabriel as collateral on a series of loans he was making with his relatives. The fact that Gabriel and his fellow slaves were being shifted from property to property with no regard for their own families was irrelevant. The white farmers needed cash.

Gabriel's fate was not by any means uncommon. Cotton pioneers like Francis Lewis were taking large risks in a very speculative market. Without slaves Francis probably would never have been able to work his land, much less hold on to it. Yet Gabriel's life—and the lives of thousands like him—was defined first and last in terms of his economic value to his owner.

"It's very sad," said Jackie, shaking her head. "I mean, imagine what it was like for him, not knowing if he was going to have to leave this man and all these relationships that he had built up. Just sitting here listening to this, I'm all in knots, and everything in my stomach is—it's just very unnerving. To have lived through that, you talk about strong will. That is survival and strong will and body and strong mind."

Despite all this buying and selling, despite all the hard labor in the cotton fields, Gabriel survived. In 1865, because of the outcome of the Civil War, when he was sixty years old, he became a free man. He did not, however, move away, like some of the former slaves. The 1870 census shows him living with his family on the property of John Conner, the son of Francis Lewis Conner, the man who brought Gabriel to Tennessee.

"That's strange," said Jackie. "He must have become accustomed to the place and really felt that regardless of how they use you, still they were doing good for him. He felt like he owed them instead of the other way. My mentality is that the only thing I would want to do is to get away. But it's easy for me to say that, 'cause I'm on the outside looking in. But to be in that environment for so many years, I don't know what I would have done. That's just kind of tough."

Jackie is, of course, right. It is very hard for us today to imagine staying in the place where you were owned as a slave. But that is our history, and many, many of our ancestors made that choice, at least initially. With no money, no clothes, no education, how mobile were the newly freed slaves?

The 1870 census contains one other interesting fact about Gabriel and his relationship to the Conner family. It indicates that John Conner's personal wealth was four hundred dollars, while Gabriel, just five years removed from slavery, was worth three hundred dollars. This means that somehow Gabriel was almost as rich as the white man he was living with— which is highly unusual. Most of the former slaves in the 1870 census have a net personal wealth of zero. Gabriel was different. He had almost as much personal property as did the son of his former owner. He must have been an enterprising worker.

We were unable to trace Gabriel's family back any further. But returning to Jackie's paternal family tree, we found several individuals in the ancestry of Ollie Mae's husband, Benjamin Franklin Joyner. Like his wife, Benjamin was born in the early twentieth century in rural Tennessee. His parents—Jackie's great-great-grandparents—were John Henry Joyner, born in December of 1869 in Covington, Tennessee, and Amanda Conner (no relation to Gabriel Conner), born in May of 1875, also in Tennessee. Amanda's parents were Spencer and Angelina Conner; both were born into slavery, Spencer in 1851 and Angelina sometime in 1856. We found their marriage license, which shows that they wed when each was still a teenager, in Tipton County, Tennessee, in January 1870. The license also indicates that Angelina's maiden name was Wortham. This led us to a remarkable discovery.

The 1870 census shows that Spencer and Angelina Conner were at that time living near another couple who shared Angelina's maiden name, Frank and Tabitha Wortham. We were curious to see if Frank and Tabitha (or "Bithey" as she was called in some records) were related to Angelina. They were both born around 1811, so they were in their late fifties in 1870, old enough to be Angelina's parents or perhaps her grandparents. But there were no slaveholders named Wortham in Tipton County, Tennessee, so we could not readily link them to Angelina in any estate records or other records from the slavery era. It seemed as if we had hit a wall. However, as we combed through other records, we puzzled over an apparent error in Amanda Conner's death certificate. It lists her mother's maiden name as Angelina Whitley, not Wortham. And it turns out there was a slaveholder in Tipton County named Daniel Whitley. He died in October 1856, so we checked his estate distribution, and it lists, among Daniel's other property, three slaves: Frank Wortham, age forty-six; Tabitha, also forty-six; and their child Angelina, age three months. So Frank and Tabitha Wortham were in fact Angelina's parents, which means that they were Jackie's great-great-great-great-grandparents. It is exceptionally rare to be able to trace an African American's family tree this deeply into the slave past. Finding a record of Daniel Whitley's estate distribution made this possible.

Looking at the estate division of Daniel Whitley, I was very surprised to see the Worthams identified by first and last name by Whitley in this document. If it is rare to find slaves listed by name, it is extraordinary to find them listed by their first and putative last names, since the law was not at all obliged to recognize these surnames. And many masters used first names merely to distinguish among their property, like naming a sheep or a chicken. Yet here this man Whitley recognized his slaves' last names in his will. I wondered where the name Wortham came from and why Daniel Whitley chose to honor it. The answer to the first question was resolved when our researchers found a bill of sale from 1842 in the property records of Tipton County, Tennessee. It certifies that Daniel Whitley paid eight hundred dollars for "one certain Negro man named Frank, a slave for life, aged thirty-one years." The seller was a man named Thomas Wortham, and that is certainly where Frank Wortham got his surname. As to why Daniel Whitley honored it, and honored the right of slaves to name themselves, no record could tell us.

I found this incident quite telling. We often make the mistake of assuming that because slaves didn't have official surnames in the public records, our ancestors didn't use two names. But they did. Cases like Frank and Tabitha Wortham's show that many slaves did have their own surnames with their own history. Some slaves took the name of a former owner. Some took the name of someone they respected, like George Washington or Thomas Jefferson. And sometimes they just made up a name, like Freeman (though there are plenty of white Freemans, too, a surname inherited from England). We continue to make up names today, often in the most inventive ways.

What's incredible about this discovery is that it shows us how the link between the Wortham and Whitley names was carried forward for decades. Even though Jackie's ancestors probably had no further contact with the Wortham family after they were sold in 1842, they still kept the Wortham name. It shows great continuity within the family, even despite all the obstacles imposed by the slave system. In my own family, we can find no idea of why my great-great-grandmother, Jane Gates, called herself Gates, since we can find no paper trail to an owner named Gates.

Unfortunately, we could not trace Frank or Tabitha Wortham back any further. They, along with Gabriel Conner, are the oldest ancestors we could identify on Jackie's maternal line. Our search for her African American roots thus ended here.

Turning to the DNA, Jackie's admixture test revealed that she is 83 percent sub-Saharan African and 17 percent European. She has no Native American ancestry. I believe that her European heritage, which is average for an African American, probably dates back to her distant ancestors in Virginia and Tennessee, rather than to her more recent ancestors in Mississippi and Illinois. But there is no way to know for certain. And Jackie does not seem to mind either way. She is not in the least bit bothered to think that she has white ancestors.

"There's a mixture in all of us," she said. "And the African American side is the side that I have always embraced and will always embrace, because that is how I see myself. But there are other parts of me, too. So this is really good."

Regarding her African ancestry, a second admixture test revealed that 57 percent comes from Nigeria, 26 percent comes from Congo Angola, and 17 percent from the region that used to be called Upper Guinea. This means Jackie has more Nigerian ancestry than is typical of an African American (the average number is 16 percent) and a smaller number of ancestors from Upper Guinea (the average is 40 percent). Her Congo Angola results are consistent with the average for all African

Americans.

Jackie's mitochondrial DNA testing yielded exact matches with the Kru people of Liberia; the Loko, Temne, and the Mende people of Sierra Leone; the Fulbe and Balanta people of Guinea-Bissau; and the Mandinka people of Senegal, among others. To narrow these results, I asked the historians John Thornton and Linda Heywood which of these groups was most likely to have produced Jackie's first direct matrilineal ancestor from Africa. They told me that only one group among all of these—the Mandinka—lived near and fought all the others, and that this group was also very well represented among slaves brought to South Carolina and Virginia ports in the last decades of the eighteenth century and the early nineteenth century. Thus, according to Thornton and Heywood, the fact that we had been able to trace Jackie's maternal line back to Virginia gave further credence to the idea that her original enslaved ancestor was most likely Mandinka.

Jackie and I then talked about the journey her ancestor must have taken, about the horrors of the Middle Passage. Neither Jackie nor I could imagine what it must have been like, but we both reveled in how strong our ancestors were—how strong their will must have been, as Jackie says. Both of us wondered whether we would have survived the journey. Jackie, ever determined, believes she might well have had the strength to make it. And, looking at her, I cannot help but agree.

"I wish," said Jackie, thinking over the journey her ancestor made, "I really wish I could get people to be able to understand the challenges that other generations had to face. I mean, life didn't just begin today. The benefits that we have today are here because of the work of people who came years and years before. And we need to be able to appreciate that and understand it and not take it for granted. Because I do feel a lot is taken for granted now. And just seeing all this, it's changed me."

As we said good-bye, Jackie told me she couldn't wait for her next family reunion—she had so much to tell her relatives. I asked her what she'd talk about first. Like many of the people in this project, she was intrigued far more by her African American family tree than by the possibilities that lay in the DNA to reveal her more distant African ethnic origins. When I conceived of this series, I had not anticipated this.

"The thing that was really surprising to me," she said, "was just how through slavery they all worked together and in some ways protected one another, you know? I mean, they had that kinship, that bond. Maybe it's because you know that if everybody is working a line and somewhere in that line it breaks down, then we're all going to be penalized for it. But it made them strong."

Jackie is certainly the heir to that strength.

Don Cheadle

November 29, 1964

D ON CHEADLE IS A remarkably adaptable actor, capable of affecting so very many different kinds of characters and performances—from the purely comedic to the tragic. He is, I think, a kind of theatrical chameleon, and watching his films, I always find myself drawn to him, regardless of whether he's the star or just making a cameo. I asked him to participate in this project in part because I had interviewed him once before for another documentary series, and I wanted to try to learn what made him so appealing. I also knew that he had an abiding interest in African American history and in modern Africa, an interest that has guided him in selecting many of his roles. I hoped that by tracing his family roots I'd be able to deepen that interest for him and provide him with some new perspective on his past. In the end I think that happened, but along the way, researching Don's family story taught me a great deal that I did not know about the astonishing intricacies of African American history, and especially about our complex relationship to Native American history.

Don was born on November 29, 1964, in Kansas City, Missouri. His family had deep roots in the area, going back several generations, and Don has very fond memories of his early life there—which he conjures up with an effortless pleasure. "Kansas City was where all my aunts and uncles and grandparents were," he said, grinning. "It was home, and we all lived near each other, spent time at everybody's house. I saw my cousins all the time.

I remember my grandfather hunting and trapping for small game, possums, squirrels, you know? I remember he would throw the skins and whatever in the back of his truck and drive around. And I remember old photo albums from my father's side of the family— my grandmother's photo albums. They had these old, old pictures in them that looked like they were plantations."

Don Cheadle as a toddler with his parents and sister.

I was mesmerized by this flow of images—and by Don's ability to evoke long-lost relatives with a telling detail or gesture. Moreover, I was surprised to learn that within this large family Don was actually lucky enough to grow up knowing his paternal great-grandmother, Clennie Carroll, who was born in Blackwater, Missouri, in 1886. "My great-grandmother lived to be one hundred and seven years old," Don said proudly. "And I spent time with her, so that was a real link to the past. I mean, she was just a stone's throw away from slavery. Just this close— you know? People go, 'Oh, come on, slavery, it's back then.' But it wasn't that far back. I had a personal relationship with somebody who was a generation away from it. And she had real acuity. She was something. Very, very smart, very aware of everything."

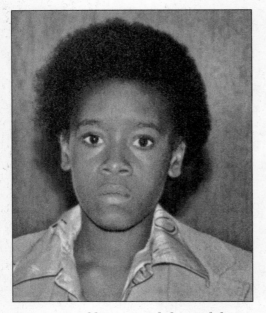

Don, pictured here around eleven, didn't encounter racism until his family left Kansas City for Nebraska.

Talking about his roots in Kansas City, Don seemed genuinely excited. His voice grew a bit sadder, however, when we began to explore the rest of his youth. Unfortunately, Don told me, his family moved away from Kansas City when he was still a child, because his father, Donald Cheadle, a clinical psychologist, was pursuing an academic career. In just a few years, the elder Cheadle moved from the University of Nebraska to the University of Kansas before finally taking a position at the University of Denver. It was hard on his wife and three young children. Don remembers that he first became aware of race when he left Kansas City. "In Kansas City everybody was black," he said. "You know? Everything was black. And that was my whole experience. But when we started moving around, and especially when we went to Nebraska, it got pretty eclectic racially. It was a lot of different people. And I think that was the first time I thought, there's a lot of white people around here. When we were home in Kansas City, I didn't really think about it. I mean, we knew we were black, obviously, but that was the flavor, that was the love. But after that I kind of felt the other side of it."

This feeling, as Don and I both know well, has been shared by almost every African American since they were first brought to this country. There is a moment in virtually all our lives when we become aware of the racial makeup of America, and everything that comes with that. It is a moment we all remember. It is the birth, I think, of a consciousness that binds us one to the other, even as it separates us, painfully, from the larger nation in which we live.

"My mom used to talk with us about racism a lot," said Don, echoing my thoughts. "She would always be concerned, because she raised us to be very open, you know? Not gullible, but just open to life experience. So she would be worried. She'd say, 'You guys are going to get hurt, you are going to be punished.' And race was something that we'd always talk about. She knew that it was very real, and I think that when we moved away, it was very hard for her especially at first, and she really wanted to make sure that we brought black people over to the house and that we had black friends. She wanted us to stay connected to who we were."

Turning to Don's family tree, we found, almost immediately, some very surprising things. Most notably, we learned that Kansas City, and the warm memories it holds for Don even today, is not by any means the only place that is important to his family history. In fact, he has equally important if entangled roots in Oklahoma.

Don's father, Donald Cheadle, was born in Kansas City in August of 1938, but *his* father, Lee Therman Cheadle, was born in 1910 in Oklahoma. Lee moved to Missouri during his youth and married there, but his family was very much a product of his birth state. Growing up, Don spent a great deal of time with his grandfather, yet he knew very little of Lee's story.

"My grandfather was a funny guy," Don recalled. "Sweet but gruff. He worked at the Chevy plant for a lot of his life and sat on the couch and kind of, you know, complained about baseball. He just loved the game and fussing about what people couldn't do. He'd be all like, 'What's wrong with that boy?' You know? He'd just sit there and fuss at the TV. That was my grandfather to me. He never talked about Oklahoma, never once."

This is a real loss to Don's family history. I would love to have heard some stories about Lee's youth, because he grew up in a most unusual historical circumstance, one that genuinely shocked Don and me.

Lee's father, Don's paternal great-grandfather, was William Cheadle, born on September 25, 1882, in what was then known as Indian Territory and what would in 1907 become the state of Oklahoma. The place has such a tragic history. In the 1830s, the United States government forcibly relocated the Five Civilized Tribes (the Cherokee, Chickasaw, Choctaw, Creek, and Seminole) into the region from their homelands in the Deep South (in Mississippi, Alabama, and Florida), as a result of the Indian Removal Act of 1830. The Choctaw were removed in 1831, the Seminole in 1832, the Creek in 1834, the Chickasaw in 1837, and the Cherokee in 1838. This dreadful forced migration, known as the Trail of Tears, cleared lands in Mississippi and Alabama so that white Americans could move in, bringing with them their black slaves and cotton crops, which were perfectly suited for the rich soil. The migration was a fundamental, necessary step in the creation of the Cotton Kingdom, bringing unprecedented wealth to white Americans and immeasurable pain to blacks and Indians alike.

As a historian I knew that very few blacks lived west of the Mississippi in the 1880s, and Don and I were both curious as to how his family ended up living in Indian Territory. The answer lay one generation further back in his father's line, with Don's great-great-grandfather, Henderson Hence Cheadle, born in 1846 in Indian Territory, and his wife, Mary Kemp, born around 1854 in the same area.

Searching for records related to Henderson and Mary, I was astonished when our researchers uncovered an 1898 enrollment card for the Chickasaw freedmen—an official document listing the slaves who had been owned by the Chickasaw nation. The card includes the names of Don's great-great-grandmother Mary and some of her eleven children, including Don's great-grandfather William. And the existence of this card means that Don's ancestors, remarkably, were enslaved by Native Americans, the Chickasaw! That was why they were living in Indian Territory, having been marched from Mississippi with their owners on the Trail of Tears.

"I knew we were owned," said Don, staring at the card. "I mean, you know, we were all owned by somebody. But it's like, ugh, to see it. It raises a lot of questions."

The card also reflects a little known historical fact: Slavery lingered on in the Indian Territory for more than a year after the Civil War. While most African Americans were emancipated in 1865, many of those owned by

	Relationship to Person first Named.	AGE.	SEX.	TRIBAL ENROLLMENT.			SLAVE OF—	REMARKS.
				Year.	County.	No.		
47		43	F				Jimmie Humb.	
28	Son	24	m					
20	Dau	16	F					
20	Son	16	m					
18	Dau	14	F					
17	Son	13	m					
15	Dau	11	F					
13	"	9	"					
12	Son	8	m					
10	"	6	"					
8	"	4	"					
6	Dau	2	F					
3	Son of No. 3	2½	M.					Illegitimate
				No 13 Born Jan. 1900; enrolled Nov 8.1902. Additional proof of birth filed Nov 25.1902				
				No 1 is now wife of Scott Fraley; evidence of marriage filed Nov 25.1902				

Chickasaw Nation. Freedmen Roll.

CARD NO. _____
FIELD NO. 729

COUNTY.

As this document indicates, Don's ancestors were slaves owned by the Chickasaw nation. Their bondage lasted more than a year after the Civil War had ended.

Indians were not freed until at least a year later—including Don's ancestors. This is because when the Civil War ended, the Five Civilized Tribes refused to liberate their slaves, claiming that as self-governing nations they were not a part of the United States and were not subject to its laws.

"That's hard to believe," said Don, stunned. "You'd think that people who had experienced what they had experienced and had lived through what they had lived through would be more—you know—up on human rights. But clearly not. I guess everybody wanted to roll with the slavery thing as long as they could. I had no idea. This is amazing."

I explained to Don that the story grew worse the more one researched it. In fact, his ancestors, as property of the Chickasaw tribe, suffered more than did almost any other African Americans in their situation.

In 1866 the United States government made treaties with the native people in Indian Territory that required them to emancipate their slaves and adopt the freedmen as citizens. The Chickasaws were the only tribe that did not fully comply. Instead they freed their slaves but did not

offer them citizenship in the Chickasaw nation. So, for decades, Chickasaw freedmen like Don's ancestors lived in a state of limbo. They were in
Indian Territory, where many of them had lived since birth, yet they were
neither Chickasaw nor were they American.

"They were in never-never land," said Don, grappling with the reality
of what life must have been like for his ancestors—a people without a
country and without any legal status at all.

"I don't know how I feel about that," he said. "It's crazy, because you
feel like the two biggest blights on the way this country started were slavery and the genocide of the Native Americans, the Trail of Tears and all
those horrible stories of what's happened to the native people here. And
then those are somehow mixed in my past, that our family was owned by
people who had suffered? That's mind-blowing."

Don's ancestors hung in a stateless limbo for over thirty years. All
around them the Creek, Choctaw, Cherokee, and Seminole nations were
offering citizenship to their former slaves. So Don's ancestors probably
hoped and perhaps believed that one day the Chickasaws would embrace
them as well—and indeed the freedmen made many requests for the tribe
to adopt them. But for three decades the answer was no.

The behavior of the Chickasaws seems utterly baffling and cruel
today. But they had their reasons—or justifications—for doing what they
did, and as a historian I find such things curious, even if they are shocking.

We found a letter written by a man named Jonas Wolf, who was the
Chickasaw governor in 1885. He explained the tribe's views succinctly:
"The Chickasaw people cannot see any reason or just cause why they
should be required to do more for their freed slaves than the white people
have done for theirs. It was by the example and teaching of the white man
that we purchased at enormous prices their slaves and used their labor
and were forced by the result of their war to liberate our slaves at a great
loss and sacrifice on our part and we do not hold or consider our nation
responsible for their present situation."

"Wow," said Don, outraged at hearing this. "I love how he just wraps
himself in the cloak of saying, 'Well, you did it.' You know? 'It worked for
you, and now we're supposed to just stop doing it?' It's really typical of

a small politician—it just sounds perfect. But it's amazing that it's coming from that perspective—from somebody who had experienced what he had experienced and who had been a part of that."

Don was surprised by the lack of sympathy in Wolf's words. But at the same time these words are an important reminder of the essence of slavery: It is an economic relationship. In Wolf's view the slaves had been obtained for a significant cost and were playing a significant role in his tribe's economy. They had been freed not for humane reasons but rather because the tribe had been forced to free them by virtue of the outcome of the Civil War. Extending rights to the freedmen would only further the economic loss that the Chickasaws had sustained. There were no human-rights issues at play here at all, just economics, hard and cold.

The story ends in economics, too. In 1893, the United States government set up what was known as the Dawes Commission, to reorganize the Indian Territory by eliminating tribal land titles and instead allocating fixed lots of land to individual Indians. To facilitate this, government agents made official lists, called rolls, of the members of the Five Civilized Tribes and their former slaves. Almost all black people who signed their names to the rolls received forty acres of their own, which sounds generous, but a primary purpose of the whole operation was economic—and deeply cynical. By redistributing land from the tribes to their individual members, the federal government was greatly reducing the power of the tribes and the aggregate amount of land owned by Indians, thus freeing up the Indian Territory for white settlers.

The Dawes Commission proved a disaster for the Native Americans, but it did offer a chance for former slaves like Don's ancestors to claim Chickasaw identity and get some land. With this in mind, Don's great-great-grandparents, Mary Kemp and Henderson Cheadle, traveled to Tishomingo, Oklahoma, the capital of the Chickasaw nation, in order to enroll. And records indicate that they were successful. We found a land deed showing that both of the Hendersons and their child received forty acres each in a town called Wiley, Oklahoma. After suffering for decades as a people with no status at all, in the end Don's ancestors received something that other African Americans only dreamed about: land.

"The vaunted forty acres," said Don, laughing at the irony. "That's huge. That's economic freedom if you can farm it and use it."

The town of Wiley has a very interesting history. It no longer exists, but for a few decades in the late nineteenth century it was a thriving place, with a cotton gin and a sorghum mill and a growing population consisting almost entirely of black families. In those years former slaves from the South were coming to Oklahoma in great numbers, flocking to all black towns like Wiley that had been started by the freedmen of the Native Americans, like Don's ancestors. It was even briefly suggested that Oklahoma be made an all-black state—a haven for all the former slaves. Now, of course that didn't happen. But for a few decades, the state served as a hopeful mecca for freed slaves.

Oklahoma's agricultural depression in the 1920s, followed by the Great Depression of the 1930s, brought all this to an end. Wiley, the all-black town, disappeared in our nation's economic disaster. But there are still reminders of the people who lived there seventy-plus years ago. There is even a Cheadle Road, cut into a vast, largely unpopulated landscape today.

Turning back to his family tree, Don wanted to know where the name Cheadle came from. Henderson Cheadle's Chickasaw enrollment card told us that during slavery he was owned by a man named James Cheadle. So it is likely that Don's surname comes from him. Research revealed that James Cheadle was an influential person in his community. He even served a term as circuit judge of the Chickasaw nation. However, the name Cheadle is not a Native American name. According to many sources, James Cheadle, like many Native American slaveholders, had a significant amount of European ancestry. His mother, Elizabeth, was a Chickasaw Indian, and his father, Thomas F. Cheadle, was a white man whose roots go back to someone named John Cheadle who was born in Middlesex County, Virginia, in 1632. Don's surname therefore most likely finds it origins in the British Isles.

"That name appears in *The Great Gatsby*," said Don. "We had to read it in school, and at one point it talks about all these families that came to Gatsby's big party, and it says the Cheadles were one of the families."

Turning to Don's maternal line, we began to investigate his mother, Bettye North's, family. Her parents were Louisa M. Thompkins and Basil Leon North. Louisa was born in Hartville, Missouri, on September 14, 1903. Basil was born on March 4, 1904, in the same town.

We found some promising information about Basil's father, Don's great-grandfather, Horace North, who was born a slave in Smith County, Tennessee, in 1853. Horace's death certificate indicates that his father was a man named John Ralls. It seemed strange that Horace had not taken his father's last name, so we searched for John Ralls in the United States census records, and in the 1860 census of Smith County we found a white man named John Rawls—the only man with that name in that county in Tennessee. Could this white man have been Don's great-great-grandfather? "Ralls" could certainly be a phonetic transcription of "Rawls."

There is no way to know for certain. But John Rawls's neighbor was a man named Edmund M. North—the same surname Don's great-grandfather took after slavery. This suggested that Horace might have been a slave of Edmund North's, a possibility that grew more likely when our researchers found an 1860 slave schedule showing that Edmund North owned an eight-year-old male slave, which matches the age that Horace would have been at that time. Moreover, the schedule indicates that this eight-year-old slave was a mulatto. So it looks as if John Rawls may have had a child with one of his neighbor's slaves—or perhaps John Rawls may even have sold his own son to his neighbor.

"That's cold, man," said Don. "Really cold."

We were unable to learn very much about John Rawls. Records indicate that he was born in Georgia around 1800 and that he and his wife did not have any biological children. We learned that he had a brother named Horace Rawls, and Don's great-grandfather may be his namesake. But we cannot know for certain, and Horace North's ancestry ends there, with his white father.

Fortunately, we were able to learn a great deal about the ancestors of Horace North's wife, Rachel Kenoly, who was born in Alabama around 1865. Her father was Myers Kenoly, born into slavery in South Carolina in 1835, and her mother was Mary Mathilda Kenoly, born a slave in Alabama

Rachel and Horace North, Don's great-grandparents, with their baby, Basil. Our research indicates that Horace's father may have been a white man named John Rawls.

in 1828.

Our research revealed that, like relatives of Sara Lawrence-Lightfoot, Kathleen Henderson, Chris Rock, and a great-uncle of mine, Myers Kenoly, served in the U.S. Army, enlisting on March 19, 1865, as a private in Company K of the Twenty-fifth Colored Infantry during the last days of the Civil War. His regiment was stationed in western Florida, right next to his home in Alabama. We don't know if he saw combat, but in western Florida skirmishes were still being fought until the bitter end, so it is quite possible that Don's great-great-grandfather had to fight. Regardless, Don was thrilled to learn that he is descended from a Civil War veteran. It's an inspiring story. His great-great-grandfather had spent the first three decades of his life as a slave. He must have been nearly broken when emancipation came. Yet one of the first things he did when he got his freedom was enlist to fight for his country.

To try to find out more about Myers and his wife, Mary, we searched for them in the 1870 census and found that the couple was living in Henry County, Alabama, with their nine children, including Don's great-grandmother Rachel, who was then just six years old. But we could not find any records that would allow us to go back any further in time, and we could not identify a possible slave owner for the Kenolys, so our next step was to talk to as many of Don's family members as possible to see if they had ever heard any clues about this family's experience as slaves in Alabama. As part of this process, we interviewed Melvin Kenoly, a distant cousin of Don's and a keeper of the family history. Melvin told us that this family was owned by a white man in Alabama named Tarwick. He also said that in 1853, Tarwick fathered a child named Hester by Don's great-great-grandmother Mary Mathilda.

We then began searching for evidence to verify or debunk this story. By examining the records of every slave owner named Tarwick around Henry County, Alabama, we discovered an 1860 slave schedule for a man named George Tarwick. If this man owned Don's great-great-grandmother's family, his schedule would have contained slaves whose ages matched Mary, age thirty; Myers, age twenty-five; and their three oldest children, ages ten, four, and two. And indeed the schedule does list slaves of these ages exactly. The slaves have no names, of course, so we cannot know for certain, but I believe that this schedule indicates that Don's ancestors could in fact have been owned by this man Tarwick.

Furthermore, if Don's great-great-grandmother Mary had a child named Hester with this slave owner in 1853, that child would have been seven in 1860. And Tarwick's schedule lists a seven-year-old mulatto girl. So the documentary evidence seems to be very consistent with the oral history that Don's cousin told us.

This realization, of course, was very painful for Don. Looking at the ages of the nine Kenoly children in the 1870 census, it is obvious that this child, Hester, was born in between Myers and Mary's other offspring. This suggests that Myers and Mary were already in the midst of their long-term relationship when the owner impregnated Mary. And this, understandably, was quite upsetting to Don. "What impact did that have on their marriage?" he asked, shaking his head in disbelief. "How devastating must that have been in their relationship to have to endure that? I mean, think about it. And coming from such a great tradition—just a couple generations before that—as Africans, coming from such a huge tradition of family and community. To come to this must have just been awful. The shock of that, the psychic shock. I don't know how you overcome that."

I don't either. It's hard even to imagine how powerless both of Don's great-great-grandparents, Mary and Myers, must have felt being so vulnerable.

"Do you love the child?" asked Don, giving voice to an unanswerable question. "It's a heavy thing. I don't know any guys who could deal with that. I don't know any women who could deal with that. I mean, if you're just not made of more compassionate stuff, how do you live through it? How do you even have the faith and the belief that there is a God and that the goodness does exist and that, you know, 'I just have to hang on to that and try to look forward, although everything in my life is devastation'? I don't know."

I don't know either, but I think slavery necessitated deep religious beliefs and that our people desperately clung to them just to keep on going.

"You have to be an extraordinary person," said Don, "to come from that kind of a background and believe in God, and believe in faith, and think that there is goodness in the world. You'd have to really fight hard to have that. And I think most people aren't extraordinary—black, white, or whatever. Most people just aren't extraordinary. And really, I think you can see a direct line from those days to our own day today—to the tearing apart of black families and a sort of shame from not being able to protect your woman, not having any say over the future of your family. And, you know, always having that hanging over your head?"

Don tells me that he believes many of our woes are generated by a combination of forces that come directly out of our slave past. He believes that after living so long in a society pathologically devoted to and organized around the oppression of black people, in some ways some of our people have internalized these pathological forms of behavior.

"There are so many things that show up nowadays where I feel like you can braid it back directly to slavery," he said emphatically. "There are just all these points where our roots are cut out from under us and it feels like that. You see it in our culture. A lot of people just aimlessly wandering around, and they have no foundation. It manifests itself in a lot of ways. And slavery, it's not that far away, and for us to believe that we somehow have no connection to it and that's not somehow a part of who we are today is foolish and dangerous. And that's why we're, a lot of us are, going down a path that is destructive.

"It makes sense, doesn't it?" he asked. "I mean, why is there this sort of fascination with this death culture? With getting as much as you can, burning up as fast as you can, and then checking out in a blaze of glory? Why is that? Why is that glorified? Why is the height of your manhood getting shot nine times? Why do we aspire to that?"

I have no answers for these questions, though I suspect that Don is right.

At this point our paper trail had run out on both sides of Don's family. The oldest ancestor we could find on Don's maternal line was his great-great-great-great-grandmother Sarah Kenoly, Myers Kenoly's mother. Sarah was born into slavery around 1820 in South Carolina and died in Missouri sometime around 1880. She was married to a man named Anthony Kenoly, who was also a slave in South Carolina, but we know nothing more about him.

Don was grateful that we had been able to go so far back on his family tree, even though the final revelations had proved so upsetting. And he was very eager to learn what our DNA testing had revealed about his African heritage.

He and I were both surprised by the results of the tests. Don's admixture tests revealed that he is 81 percent sub-Saharan African and 19 percent European, with no Native American ancestry, despite his family's long connection to the Chickasaw people.

I explained to him that a 19 percent European result is about average for African Americans. That's the equivalent of having one grandparent who was a European. In Don's case, part of his European DNA could have come from John Rawls, but there were obviously other white ancestors in his family tree as well.

"That's not what I would have thought," said Don, studying the results. "I mean, I didn't think that I would have been so European—as dark-complected as I am. But I guess it makes sense, because at the point in history that we're talking about, they thought of women as chattel and treated them that way. It makes sense to me that it would be that way. But when you have my name on top of it and it's my family that we're talking about, it's not some story in a book—that's a history that nobody in our country really wants to deal with."

I asked him if the result had changed the way he thought of himself and he quickly shook his head. "No," he replied. "It doesn't matter that I'm nineteen percent European and eighty-one percent African. In America I have to deal with the problems that black people in America have to deal with. I have the struggles that black people in America have. So it's interesting to know, but it doesn't change me."

Our analysis of Don's African admixture suggests that around a third of his total African ancestry comes from the region from Senegal down to Liberia, while just over a quarter comes from the Congo Angola region, and the rest comes from the region of western Nigeria and the country of Benin.

Don told me that during one of his many trips to Africa he met a man from Benin who was convinced that he and Don were related—based on their physical resemblance. The man even gave Don a sculpture—a bust—that Don has kept ever since. Our research has confirmed this man's intuition. Forty-three percent of Don's African ancestry comes from the area around Benin. So what the man saw in his face is there in his genes.

"Yeah," said Don, "I mean, he was sure. He was like, 'Oh, I know your people. I know your tribe, I can take you to your people and you would see a bunch of you running around.' And when he gave me this sculpture, he said, 'Now, you can never give that sculpture to anyone, and actually I wasn't supposed to give it to you. That's some serious thing I gave you there, and you have to keep that, and it would be very bad luck on you and your whole line if you give that away or if you sell that.' So, I mean, I'm never going to sell it. But I'm glad it's rightfully mine. I think it gives us a handle on our history in a way that we really don't have. And, it just kind of straightens your backbone in a way, you know? Because this is my lineage, this is the path that I walked, and I can look back and see the footprints that got me here where I'm standing."

I thought this was beautifully put, and I was thrilled to be able to tell Don the results of the rest of our testing, because they were so unusual. Both his mitochondrial and patrilineal DNA indicated matches with individuals in present-day Cameroon: the Bamileke, Masa, and Tikar people on the maternal side and the Ewondo tribe on the paternal side.

This is an exceptional result. It's most unusual for an African American's earliest maternal and paternal ancestry to go back to the same roots in Africa. No one else in the project had a result like this.

"It's amazing," said Don. "I've got to get on the plane and go to Cameroon. I really can't wait to do that. And I can't wait to call my parents and tell them. That's fascinating. I mean, I'm really glad I did this. It's beautiful, that both my parents' lines came from Cameroon. It just feels like a strong bond, even coming through all of that, that could break it apart, that somehow these two people found each other, and it's in their DNA."

I discussed these results with the historians John Thornton and Linda Heywood. They said that it was surprising that both of Don's original enslaved ancestors came from Cameroon, because so few slaves came from that area and that most slaves brought to the Chesapeake Bay region were from Angola. However, they could not rule out the possibility that Don's family did in fact come to the United States from this unusual location.

I explained to Don that his results could be outliers within his DNA profile and that the vast majority of his cousins would probably trace back to a tribe from western Nigeria, Angola, or Benin, not Cameroon. But Don didn't seem to care, and I couldn't blame him. There was something truly romantic about his parents' Cameroon connection.

Before we said good-bye, I asked what he thought would stay with him from our interview. His answer surprised me.

"The history," he said. "It's funny, because I've been in Toronto filming this movie. And in Canada the black people or the dark-skinned people you run into, a lot of them are from the West Indies or they are Jamaican or from somewhere else in the Caribbean. They are not African American.

And so they can run their families all the way back, most of them. And I was talking to one of them, and she said she always forgets that when she talks to black people in the States that there's this big hole where most of them don't know anything past that part of their lives. They don't have any records past their grandparents. And so it's amazing to start plugging these pieces in. It's just fascinating history."

Chris Rock

February 7, 1965

I WANTED TO INVOLVE Chris Rock in this project because I am a huge fan of stand-up comedy, and Chris is one of my favorite stand-up comics today, one of the true heirs, I think, along with Dave Chappelle, to Richard Pryor, who was the funniest stand-up comedian I have ever seen—and one of the most intellectual figures in the history of comedy. (Chris Rock and Dave Chappelle are like the flip sides of Pryor—the light, satiric wit and the tragicomic dark side, the side of Pryor that walked, perilously, along the edge.) When I watch Chris perform, I am always astounded by his powers of social and political observation; by his sensitivity to the way people behave, how they actually think and feel about others and about themselves—white and black, men and women. He's as keen a critic of our times as are any of my peers at Harvard. And I was eager to see how his family's past might have informed his sensitivity as well as his sense of humor. I was not disappointed.

Christopher Julius Rock was born on February 7, 1965. He grew up in Brooklyn, New York, and all his earliest memories are from that city, though his family's roots are mostly in the Deep South. His mother, Rosalie Tingman, was born on February 22, 1945, in Andrews, South Carolina, and his father, Julius Rock, was born on January 6, 1932, in nearby Charleston, South Carolina. Both Rosalie and Julius moved north when they were young, living first in Crown Heights, Brooklyn, before marrying and settling in nearby Bedford-Stuyvesant. Chris is the oldest of their six children, and he remembers his parents as being extremely hardworking people who struggled in the North to support their large family.

"My mom," he said, "she worked with mentally handicapped kids, and sometimes she would take care of other people's kids. So there was always a lot of kids around. My dad drove a truck. First he drove for the Rheingold Brewery for, like, fifteen years. Then he drove for the *Daily News* for, like, twenty years, till he died. And he drove a cab on the side. So my father always kept a job—no matter what."

Growing up at the tail end of the civil-rights movement, Chris remembers spending quite a lot of time at home talking about race and racism with his parents. He vividly recalls his father's devotion to Jackie Robinson and Malcolm X, as well as fights that his parents would have in their house if his mother felt that her husband "was a little too nice" to his white foreman. Though he was only a child, Chris remembers these political discussions between his parents vividly and is readily able to conjure up the complexities of that time, so very different from our own.

"It's weird," he said. "For me, what I remember is, there's before hip-hop and after hip-hop. And before hip-hop, black people were just scared of white people. And literally everything you did was, you know, 'Hey, hey, act right! There are going to be some white people here!' I mean, when I was born, four days later, Malcolm X was shot just over in Harlem, and three years later Martin Luther King goes down. So I was born into a world where my mother just didn't want me to get hurt, you know? And, like, her parents would tell a lot of stories about the old days and segregation. They were in South Carolina—in a little town called Andrews, where they still have a Klan parade every year. There's still a Ku Klux Klan parade through town. It's very kind of accepted, you know? So I grew up hearing a lot of bad-white-man stories."

This landscape of fear is intimately familiar to black people of my generation and older. And I was interested to hear that Chris, though more than a decade younger than I am and raised in a totally different area of the country, shared many of the same experiences and feelings regarding the civil-rights era that I did—albeit from a younger man's perspective.

There was one crucial difference, however. Chris and I attended white schools, though he was bused and I just walked down the hill, like everybody else in my neighborhood, white or black. And whereas my experience in rural West Virginia in the late 1950s was largely positive, his experience in urban Brooklyn in the early 1970s was mostly negative. Indeed, Chris claims that New York City's busing policies "killed his spirit" as a child.

"When I was bused to school," he said, "I encountered a ton of racism. 'Nigger' this, 'nigger' that. Getting beat up. It was just a bad, bad experience. I was bused from Bed-

Chris Rock's parents, Julius and Rose, were both South Carolina natives who settled in Bedford-Stuyvesant.

Stuy to a place called Gerritsen Beach. I was seven years old, in second grade, and I was actually bused to a neighborhood worse than the one I lived in. It was white, but if you looked at those houses and our houses, our houses sold for a lot more than theirs.

"Gerritsen Beach was very working class, very ethnic Irish-Italian, and it was just pretty badly deflating for me. On one hand, I had to go to this school far away from my house. So I got to get up an hour and a half earlier than anybody in my class, and I traveled this long distance and got treated like crap by these kids. And on the other hand, it hurt me in my

own neighborhood, 'cause I didn't know anybody in my own neighborhood, so once I walked off my block, I was a stranger in the ghetto. Which made me prey to crime. If I'd gone to school in my neighborhood, I could have maneuvered around a little more. As it was, I knew people on my block, 'cause they were on my block, but I didn't know anybody else in the neighborhood. So once I got off the block, I got robbed."

According to Chris, busing changed his entire life, altering his feelings about who he was and what he could accomplish. "I realized that I was black when I went to Gerritsen Beach," he said. "It wasn't that I didn't know I was black before I got there. It's just that when I got to school, it was like, 'Oh, this isn't good.' My first day—I'm not going to say the girl's name, 'cause she probably is married with kids now—but literally the first day of school they sit me down next to this little girl, and she goes, 'You're a nigger.' And it hurt, 'cause I knew it was bad. And I knew that no matter what, I wasn't going to overcome my differences—I was always gonna be a nigger to this girl. So it was very painful. Everybody learns they're black in some way. And it's never like, 'Hey, we're giving out money to the first black guy we see!' 'Wow! I am so lucky to be black today! Would have never got this million dollars!' It never works out like that."

I asked Chris if he went home and told his parents about what that little girl had said to him. He didn't—and he's not sure why, even today.

"I can't even answer why," he said. "You know? My father didn't complain. My father went to work, and he came home, and he was obviously tired, and he was obviously beat down, and he was obviously physically exhausted, you know? I had one of those dads who couldn't really throw a baseball with you. Two throws and he was like, 'Ah.' He was obviously falling apart. And my father died at fifty-five. So he was dying when he was thirty-five. But my father didn't complain. So I didn't complain."

Ironically, Chris was bused to the white school in Gerritsen Beach from his Bedford-Stuyvesant home because his parents had volunteered him for it, thinking he would get a better education among whites. The end result, of course, was a disaster. Chris was so unhappy that he dropped out of high school in tenth grade. "It didn't make any sense to keep going," he recalled with a shrug. "I mean, it was dumb to drop out, but from the time I was in grade school to the time I was in high school, I kind of didn't really go to school, anyway. I would just sit in the back and put my head down. I would constantly get D's and F's. It bored me. And it's stupid, because the thing is, if you're going to drop out, just drop out as soon as you can, 'cause dropping out in tenth grade, you might as well have dropped out in the second grade, 'cause you're qualified for the exact same jobs. As a matter of fact, the guy that drops out in the second grade has a better chance of getting a job, 'cause he's got eight years of working experience."

Chris was bused to a white neighborhood for school, an experience he found so miserable that he dropped out of school in tenth grade.

Exploring the story further, I asked Chris if he felt that he'd developed his sense of humor from being such an outsider at school, an underachiever who turned to comedy in the back of the classroom to mask his poor performance in the front of the classroom. I assumed that Chris was concocting jokes sitting in the back, along with the alienated kids—and that his humor would have been widely celebrated, even if his grades were not. His answer surprised me.

"I don't know," said Chris. "I mean, I wasn't that funny back then. Nothing was really funny to me. My grades were horrible, and I was bored. And so, like, I was funny on my block. Sort of. 'Cause I could relax and joke around. But I wasn't funny in school, and I was far from the funniest guy in my neighborhood. Although a lot of the guys that were funnier, you

know, they're dead. Or on drugs. So I guess I was like Jackie Robinson in
the sense that Jackie Robinson was the nineteenth-best player in the Negro
Leagues. So it's like I was about the fifteenth-funniest guy in my neighborhood. But I survived. While my friends, a lot of them are on drugs. I
mean, like even, I was back in my neighborhood a few years ago shooting a
movie. And so I'm, like, eight blocks from my old house. This film crew is
all over the block. And a couple of my friends happened to be driving by,
and they stopped, and we talked, and they probably stayed four minutes.
Why? 'Cause they were going to get high. They were going to the same
spot that they had gone to for years. But I was never the get-high guy. So
I survived, I guess."

Chris says that, growing up, he would tell jokes to his family but that
he didn't have any idea he would one day be a comedian. In fact, as he remembers, he spent more time listening to his relatives' jokes than making
up his own—and he ended up stealing a lot of his material from them.

"I didn't know I was a comedian when I was a kid," he said. "I would
just watch my father be funny, and my grandfather was funny, and all my
uncles on my father's side were hysterical. If I took you to a family reunion
right now, you would never pick me out as the famous guy. 'Cause the
personalities in my family are so big, especially from the men, my God.
Women have good personalities, great personalities, too, but the men can
just talk, and every one of them can hold court."

Turning to our research, Chris and I began to explore these people
who'd had such a strong influence on him. We began with his father's line
and his paternal grandparents, Allen Rock and Mary Vance. Allen was born
on September 22, 1908, in Eutawville, South Carolina, and Mary was born in
the same area on June 9, 1918. The two met and married in South Carolina,
where Chris's father, Julius, was born. Then, during the 1940s, the family
moved north, as many black people did at the time, ending up in Brooklyn.
Chris knew both of his father's parents, Allen and Mary, very well when he
was growing up. "They were great people," he said. "My grandmother was
just a real sweet typical grandmother, you know, bake you a cake, bake you
some pies, fry you up some chicken. My grandfather drove a cab. And I
used to hang out with him. He used to drive me around in his cab a lot of the

time. I never went a week without seeing him, and sometimes I would actually end up in the cab with him driving people around. And he was a preacher, too, at a kind of a storefront church in Brooklyn."

Chris tells me that he writes his jokes the same way his grandfather used to write his sermons. "We both just write bullet points," he said. "My grandfather never really wrote a sermon all down. And I never really write the whole joke, 'cause I want it to come out with the passion of an argument, as opposed to, like, some

Chris's grandparents, Mary Vance and Allen Rock. Chris counts his grandfather as a huge influence on him.

written thing. I mean, things always sound written when they're written. So I used to hang out with him, and he'd write his sermons, and to this day I write my jokes exactly the same way. He was a huge influence on me. And, you know, he cursed all the time. My grandfather the preacher. He would drive: 'Praise the Lord, motherfuck.' Just constant cursing. And he was one of these guys who was quick to jump out of his car when he wanted to fight somebody. We would be driving, and somebody would cut him off, and he had a stick under the seat, and soon as he'd get out, he'd say, 'Christopher, pass me my headache stick.' And I'd pass him his headache stick. A couple of times, we actually ended up in fights. And the headache stick was great, it could do anything, you know? Sometimes, like, the car would break down. He'd be like, 'Pass me my headache stick.' And he'd hit the engine a couple of times, and the car would start."

It is hard to capture accurately on the page just how animated and happy Chris seemed when sharing his recollections about his grandfather. It was a privilege for me just to listen to him. And I could easily see how Chris's comedy had grown out of his affection for a man like this. Unfortunately, our efforts to trace Chris's paternal ancestors past the births of Allen and Mary Rock yielded a series of names but no real stories that could suggest where the strong personalities and strong sense of humor came from. We found records tracing the family back generations to early-nineteenth-century South Carolina, but few anecdotes.

Turning to his mother's side of the family, however, we were much more fortunate in our research. Chris's maternal grandparents were Wesley Tingman and Pearl McClam. Both were born near Andrews, South Carolina—Wesley on October 6, 1915, and Pearl on July 25, 1911. Chris had known both of them growing up and remembered them fondly, but he knew little about their parents and grandparents. "My family never sat around and talked about ancestors," he said, echoing the sentiments of almost everyone involved in this project. "We'd talk about aunts or an uncle or a grandpa, but that's about as far as we got."

Our research revealed that Chris's grandfather Wesley was the son of James Tingman, born in January 1886 in Berkeley County, South Carolina, and a woman named Emma Telefair, who was born in 1890 in the same county. Going back a generation further, we were able to identify James Tingman's parents—Chris's great-great-grandparents—Eliza Moultrie and Julius Caesar Tingman. Both were born into slavery in South Carolina, Julius in 1845 and Eliza sometime around 1850.

Chris was astonished to hear that Julius Tingman served in the U.S. Colored Troops during the Civil War, enrolling on March 7, 1865, just a little over a month after the Confederates evacuated Charleston. At that time South Carolina was filled with Union troops, and the newly freed slaves were enlisting in droves—over two hundred black men were signing up each day. Chris's great-great-grandfather Julius had just become free after twenty-one years living as a slave. Signing up to serve in the U.S. Colored Troops must have been one of the first things he did as a free man. He could have fled to the North or stayed in the South and attempted to make a new life as a farmer, but he risked his life by joining the army and fighting for the freedom of other slaves.

"I can't imagine what making a decision like that would be like," said Chris. "I'm very fortunate. I've never been in any kind of situation like that."

Chris was moved to tears when he saw Julius Tingman's service records. And together, we parsed them closely, looking for details about the man. The records indicated that Julius was a blacksmith, which means he was most likely quite physically strong. They also indicate that he was promoted from private to corporal within four months after he joined the army, which means he must have been a successful soldier.

We discovered that Julius Caesar Tingman, Chris's great-great-grandfather, was elected to the South Carolina state legislature—a revelation that nearly brought Chris to tears.

But the most remarkable aspects of Julius's biography all concern what he did after he left the service in October of 1866. At that point Julius entered a world so far removed from the life of a field hand that one scarcely knows how he could even have imagined it, much less navigated it. South Carolina during the heyday of Reconstruction was a state with an overwhelmingly black majority, enjoying its first days of freedom. More than 60 percent of the population was black, and these new citizens were eager to make the most of their new rights. Chris's great-great-grandfather must have thrived among them, because in 1872, when he was just twenty-four years old, Julius Caesar Tingman was elected to the South Carolina state legislature.

As I explained to Chris, Julius was in the right place at the right time. The South Carolina constitution of 1868 was an exceptionally progressive document. Not only did it give African American men the right to vote, it also removed the property qualifications for holding office. In many other states, no man—white or black—could vote unless he owned property. But Reconstruction South Carolina extended the ballot to all men, regardless of their station in life.

How did Julius get elected to the legislature? We are not certain. He was a former slave with no property to speak of, but census data indicate that he was a literate man and had served honorably in the army. That combination was probably a big part of his candidacy. He was also, most likely, very articulate—like a preacher or a comedian—as he had to convince his fellow citizens to vote for him.

"This makes me feel really proud," said Chris, showing me a side of himself that I had never encountered before. "It's weird. There's a part of me that walks around thinking I'm so lucky. And I am lucky to have grown up where I grew up and end up where I am now. There's a million reasons why I'm lucky. But when you see stuff like this you go, 'Oh, okay, some of it wasn't luck.' Some of it was, sure, but maybe I was actually born to do certain things, you know? I had no idea, but still, if you didn't know Ken Griffey was your dad, you'd probably still play baseball pretty good, right?"

As I told Chris, there was a lot more to Julius Tingman's story. We looked at records of the South Carolina House of Representatives to find out what Julius Caesar Tingman did as a legislator. It turns out that he was an active legislator. He introduced bills attempting to protect the rights of former slaves who had become sharecroppers, as well as bills to protect turpentine workers from unfair price setting and to regulate the conditions for tenant farmers. Not all of these bills passed, but he obviously had a strong sense of social justice—and he clearly worked very hard. He was concerned with the rights of the common man, the workers and the share-croppers—the former slaves—he grew up with.

"It's unbelievable," said Chris, "and it's sad that all this stuff was kind of buried and that I went through a whole childhood and, you know, most of my adulthood not knowing. I mean, how in the world could I not know this?"

Chris has such a noble ancestor in his family. Julius Tingman's picture should have been over the mantelpiece in his descendants' homes. Each successive generation should have been told this man's story. Chris should have known he came from people, as my mother's expression goes. But he didn't. And this, I have found, is remarkably common among African Americans. It is as if we have amnesia, not just about our collective history but also about our individual family history—as if the racism of America in the nineteenth century and the early twentieth century was so pain-ful that we should forget everything that occurred in those years. Indeed, no one I interviewed for this project knew anything about the deep roots of their family trees. A wealth of history and accomplishment has simply been forgotten, which it is incumbent upon our generation of journalists and creative writers and academics to resurrect—so that it will never be lost again.

"It's messed up," said Chris after a moment's reflection. "I was raised in a neighborhood where no one went to college or anything. And I just lucked into a comedy club at age twenty, you know, just on a whim. Up till then I assumed I would pick up things for white people for the rest of my life. Because that's what everyone I knew did. They picked up and cleaned and moved for white people. That was my world, you know? And when I worked in restaurants and whatever, it wasn't like I was working my way through to become a comedian. That was what I thought I'd be doing with my life. But if I'd have known this Julius, it might have taken away the inevitability that I was going to be nothing. And I might not have been a comedian. I might have worked harder in school. I might have been a civil-rights lawyer. Or I don't know what. And it's not just me, you know. Other people in my family would have benefited from knowing that they had this kind of ancestor. You know about a guy like this, it's like that'll make you take school serious."

I understand Chris completely. The memory of this man Julius has been lost to his descendants and to the African American community. There are thousands of Julius Tingmans. And we pay the price, collectively, for that loss. We pay it every day. There are so many people like Julius Caesar Tingman waiting there to be rediscovered, examples of black achievement trapped in the amber of the archives. The records of Chris's ancestor were just sitting in a courthouse in the archives of the city of Charleston, South Carolina, waiting to be rediscovered. Think what else is out there, if we only search.

What's more, Julius's story doesn't end here. After serving in the South Carolina state legislature from 1872 to 1874, he ran for office again in 1876—and his experience in that election is reflective of the tragic betrayal of Reconstruction.

A lot changed in the four years between 1872 and 1876. Disgruntled former Confederates who wanted to regain control of the South were doing so, state by state. The 1876 election had a dreadful result for black people all across the nation. In South Carolina the Republican Party, which in those days was the party of progress—the party of Lincoln— ran a ticket headed by the incumbent governor, Daniel Chamberlain, a friend to African Americans. In opposition the Democrats ran a ticket headed by Wade Hampton, a former Confederate general and war hero— and a leading critic of Reconstruction. The elections were tainted by irregular practices on both sides. There was violence in the streets, with armed clashes between whites who supported Hampton and blacks who supported Chamberlain. In the end Hampton claimed to have won more votes, but Chamberlain refused to concede, and South Carolina actually had two competing state governments for more than six months. And just as there were two competing governors, there were two competing speakers of the house of the state legislature; each with his own posse of legislators. It was utter chaos, and Julius Tingman was in the middle of it, serving in the Republican legislature and supporting Chamberlain.

In 1877 the newly elected president of the United States, Rutherford

B. Hayes, pulled all the federal troops out of the South. Without the support of these troops, Chamberlain had to concede the governorship to Hampton. The ex-Confederate had won. Reconstruction was over in South Carolina—and indeed all over the South. Hampton and his supporters in Charleston acted quickly. Julius Tingman and all his fellow Republican legislators were kicked out of office with the backing of the South Carolina supreme court. Soon thereafter African Americans were effectively disenfranchised by the new legislature. The last black representative left office in 1902, and there would not be another black man elected in South Carolina again until 1970. The "redeemed" former Confederates cleaned Reconstruction's house.

So what happened to Julius Caesar Tingman at this point? He was still a young man when Reconstruction ended, only thirty-two years old. And he clearly had a lot of energy, imagination, and intelligence. But, of course, in 1877, South Carolina was not interested in young black men with these qualities. We found Julius in the 1880 census listed as a tenant farmer, renting ten acres of land from a white man. He owned three cows and grew rice and sweet potatoes. In fifteen years he had gone from being a slave to a soldier to a legislator, and now back to the soil, in another form of servitude, to a life as a hardscrabble farmer.

"What a roller-coaster ride," said Chris, shaking his head. "That is sobering. I mean, he was the man, right? And then these racists come in, kick him out. What's he going to do?"

Chris is right. Julius had very few options. And the ups and downs of his life give us a sense of what it was like to be black in America a century and a third ago. Success, measured by most standards, was quite perilous for a very long time in the lives of the former slaves, especially in the fragile period of massive black vulnerability between the end of Reconstruction in 1876 through the enshrinement of "separate but equal" as the law of the land in 1896. What a hellish twenty years for black people in this country, but especially those in the South. Julius Tingman's rise and fall serves as a metaphor for this fragility of black success, and his turn of fortune had absolutely nothing to do with anything over which he had control.

"I wonder what kind of guy he was," said Chris, realizing all the implications of encountering a family member for the very first time, as if your mother or father had had a child or a sibling long lost but now found. So many stories about our ancestors in the nineteenth century have similarly sad endings. But not, fortunately, the story of Julius Tingman. The answer to Chris's question about what kind of person his ancestor was could be found right there in the historical records. Julius Tingman was a determined guy, an incredibly determined guy. Nothing was going to keep him down. Tenant farming was a most brutal way to earn a living in the Jim Crow South, but Julius found a way to make it work, and to great profit, though Lord knows how. We located a land deed from 1904 that reads, in part, "W. A. Spears of Berkeley County in consideration of $168 sold and released onto the said Julius Caesar Tingman a parcel or lot of land in the parish of St. Stephen's county of Berkeley, 21 acres more or less."

This means that by the age of fifty-six, after working his rented land for twenty-five years, Julius had saved up enough money to buy his own farm. What's more, when the former state legislator died thirteen years later, his will indicates that he owned sixty-five and a half acres and two life-insurance policies. Even though he had no resources when he was kicked out of the legislature in 1876, Julius Tingman still managed over the next thirty years to find a way to provide for his family. He died an extraordinarily successful man, a man wealthy by comparison with his peers.

"I'm very proud of him," said Chris. "I mean, he's a great man. Most people would have given up. And, you know, my family's main attribute has always been hardworking people. I mean, when there is a lazy family member there is, like, an intervention. We treat it like it's drugs. Like, 'Oh, God, what the hell is wrong with you?' So it's nice to know that some of this work ethic actually went back to slavery—that's unbelievable."

I was extremely happy for Chris. The story of Julius Tingman is one of the most inspiring stories that I uncovered in this entire project. Unfortunately, it is also a very singular story within Chris's family. Our additional research into his other maternal ancestors was nearly as fruitless as our work on his paternal side—as almost every line ran into dead ends in that mysteriously dark mausoleum called slavery. We learned, for example, that one of Chris's other maternal great-great-grandfathers was a man named Alex McClam. He was born a slave in South Carolina in about 1837. We found his name on a militia enrollment list from Williamsburg County, South Carolina, taken in 1869, just four years after the Civil War. On the list Alex declares that he was living on the property of a white landowner named Solomon McClam. This, of course, led us to believe that Alex had been the slave of Solomon or his family—because, as we have seen in a surprising number of examples, in the years after the Civil War it was common for freed slaves to remain on the property of their former owner as sharecroppers or tenant farmers. We then began searching McClam's records, and we found a slave schedule from the 1860 census that lists a male slave age twelve—which is roughly how old Alex McClam would have been at that time. So it seems highly likely that Alex was in fact Solomon's slave and that he took his former master's name after gaining his freedom. But though we scoured the rest of Solomon McClam's records, looking for any reference to Alex or his relatives, we could not find any other clues. And, indeed, Alex was the only one of Chris's ancestors for whom we could identify a possible slave owner.

I explained to Chris that, unfortunately, this is pretty normal for African Americans. All African Americans hit a genealogical brick wall somewhere in slavery. Slavery was constructed to deconstruct the Negro, in every way imaginable, except as pure labor, as a measurable commodity.

"Wow," said Chris after a pause. "It's amazing no one's ever been persecuted for treating people like this—taking away their names, taking away everything. And people just treat it like essentially it's a fact. Like disco—or bell-bottoms. It's just something that happened. Slavery. You know? I'm just choked up."

I can sympathize with Chris, of course. There is nothing that upsets me more than the way our ancestors were treated. Nothing is more horrifying, more outrageous, more unjust. And seeing it all written down in these cold, clear documents from a century and a half ago can be terribly sad, even if the thrill of discovering such documents is a rare pleasure scarcely to be described.

I wanted to be able to soothe Chris by telling him more about his family, but I had little to say. The furthest back that we could trace his surname, Rock, was to his great-great-grandfather Josiah Rock, born a slave in 1830 in South Carolina. But we know nothing else about him—or about the source of Chris's surname. There was a famous black abolitionist called John Rock, but we could find no connection between the two families. Nor could we find anyone named Rock who owned slaves who might have been Chris's ancestors. We spoke with researchers who specialize in African American genealogy in the Lowcountry in South Carolina, and they told us that in their experience fewer than 20 percent of the former slaves in this area took their surnames from their previous owners. We don't know why that is. The practice of naming simply varied from county to county and state to state and, indeed, from former slave to former slave. We did find a number of slaveholders of French Huguenot origin named La Roche in this area—and, if anglicized, "La Roche" would be "Rock." But none of these people had slaves we could identify as being Chris's ancestors.

At this point we turned to the DNA portion of our research. Chris's admixture tests reveal that he is 80 percent sub-Saharan African and 20 percent European. He seemed very comfortable with this result.

"You have to assume that any black person has some European ancestry," he said, waving his hand before his face. "And, you know, just the fact that I am not blue-black—I'm a mocha. I knew there's something else in there. I heard stories in my family, stories about Indian ancestry. But I guess they were wrong."

This, as we've seen, is quite common in African American families. Virtually every black person has some white ancestry. Yet so many black people believe they have Native Americans in their family trees.

"It's all about that hair issue," said Chris. "It goes all the way back to the hair issue, and anybody with the so-called good hair, you know, it's easier to say we got a little Indian in us than to say we got raped a few times. It's just a lot easier to say. You make up a myth, sounds much better, a lot smoother."

I asked Chris if it mattered to him how his European ancestors entered his family tree. He shook his head in response.

"The Africans didn't have a choice," he said. "I'm not going to ever say it's by love, you know what I mean? But it doesn't bother me like that. I guess I'm used to it. I mean, you know, you're black so you assume you're whatever, there is some white in you. That was a horrible thing to say but it's true."

Before telling Chris what his DNA had told us about his African ancestry, I wanted to know what his impressions of Africa were. Like many of the people involved in this project, he rarely spoke about Africa with his parents or thought about it much growing up—but as an adult and an international celebrity, he has traveled throughout South Africa extensively.

"I was forty, and I went to South Africa," he said. "I went on safari. I went to Mandela's house and sat with the great man. And then to Robben Island. Unbelievable. Just being on safari was kind of like being underwater and able to breathe without an apparatus. There's that much nature around you. It's like meeting God. But, you know, I also saw some of the worst poverty I've ever seen in my life. Incredible. We can't even imagine it in this country."

I ask him if he felt a deep connection to Africa, and he shook his head.

"No," he said. "A little bit, but not a deep one. You know, I did a joke in my act. It's, like, I sat with Mandela, and, you know, what do you talk about? He's eighty, I'm forty. He's a Rhodes scholar. I dropped out of school. He was in jail for twenty-seven years. I worked at Red Lobster for eight months. So I have so much more in common with Pauly Shore than with Nelson Mandela. That's just the way the world is. But yet we are brothers of the same skin. I am an American person whose ancestors hailed from Africa. And I have African blood flowing through my veins. I know that."

I think Chris's answer here reflects a sentiment that many of the people I interviewed for this project have shared—they are uncertain, at some deep level, as to what their connection to Africa means. I know that I feel the same way—even though I adore Africa and cherish every moment I've spent there. At the most basic level, we are Americans, after all, and it is hard to reconcile the two continents and the tragic history that has passed between them, to reconcile our being descended from

Africans in America with Africans who remained on the African continent. I had hoped, in launching this project, to help make that connection through DNA. I am not certain, however, how well it worked. It is very difficult, I think, to go from test data to an emotional connection. Chris was an especially interesting subject in this regard, because his results were not precise, yet he clearly wished to make the deeper connection that I believe we all crave.

Our African admixture test revealed that just under 25 percent of Chris's African ancestors come from Congo Angola, about a third come from western Nigeria and the country of Benin, and 45 percent come from the region that stretches from Liberia all the way up to Senegal. So Chris is a real reflection of our shared history. In the New World, slaves from different groups were thrown together on plantations where they formed new family bonds and interbred with one another. And his African genetic ancestry reflects that.

Chris's mitochondrial DNA test results are similarly diverse. Many of the people we tested for this project had exact matches with their mitochondrial DNA, tying them to one or two tribes in Africa. Chris does not have that. He has matches all over the African continent, many of them only partial matches. And given the amount of time it has taken for the human genetic code to spread across Africa, it was impossible for the historians John Thornton and Linda Heywood to tell me which group Chris's ancestors on his mother's side come from. They could be from any of a number of tribes in Nigeria, Sierra Leone, Angola, or elsewhere.

I told Chris this meant he had a very ancient genetic signature and that his ancestors had intermingled across Africa perhaps since the time of the first humans. We've never had a result like this. He is the most pan-African person we tested—at least on his mother's line.

Chris seemed somewhat confused by this news. Undoubtedly, he had hoped for more, and I was glad, therefore, to be able to tell him that his Y-DNA yielded something truly concrete: an exact match with the Uldeme people from northern Cameroon.

"Ah, man," said Chris, almost shouting, "that feels complete! You know, that feels great. This was worth getting up early!"

He seemed visibly relieved and truly excited and told me he plans on making a trip to Cameroon as soon as possible. I asked if now he felt that he had that connection we discussed earlier.

"I don't know yet," he replied, shaking my hand and laughing. "You know? It's one of those things we'll see in the coming year and we'll see maybe in my work. I'm curious. I want to see if it rears its head in the work. I remember before I did my last special, for some weird reason I watched *Roots,* like, a week before I did it, and I ended up with all these big, long pieces where I was, you know, playing slaves. So we'll see."

Mostly, he told me as we said good-bye, he was ecstatic to have this news for his children—so that he can, as he said, "start drilling this in their heads." And I understand him. In fact, I think this may be the true purpose of this entire project. I am not certain, not at all, that my peers and I can fully understand the results of these tests. The science is just not fully there yet—but neither are we, emotionally speaking, fully ready to understand our relationship to Africa. We grew up in a maelstrom, amid history that is still unresolved. I hope that restoring the knowledge of our ancestry, on both sides of the Atlantic, can give us new perspectives on the history of our family tree from its roots in Africa to its myriad branches in the New World.

Bliss Broyard

1966

W HEN I BEGAN THIS PROJECT, there was one person whose family history interested me perhaps more than any other: Anatole Broyard, the black writer and longtime literary critic for the *New York Times* who passed as a white man for most of his life. My interest was simple and highly personal: I had researched Anatole in great detail for an essay that I wrote about him more than a decade ago—and his story still haunts me today. And it haunts me because of its typicality. Anatole Broyard, for me, is a metaphor for the African American impulse, as complex as it is, toward what Kwame Anthony Appiah calls "cosmopolitanism." And cosmopolitanism in the black tradition has many forms.

Anatole Broyard was born on July 16, 1920, in New Orleans to Paul Broyard and Edna Miller. He and his parents were black people with light complexions. Anatole was their only son. He had two sisters: One shared his complexion—that is, was not discernibly black—while the other was much darker (the inheritance of melanin is imprecise). In all records and by all accounts, the family was identified as Negro and identified itself as Negro. But when Anatole was still a child, the Broyards moved north to the Bedford-Stuyvesant area of Brooklyn, thus joining the Great Migration that took hundreds of thousands of southern blacks to northern cities and that took the ancestors of so many people in this book to the North as well.

Bliss Broyard with her father, Anatole, the black writer and literary critic who passed as a white man for most of his life.

In the French Quarter, Anatole's father, Paul, had been a legendary dancer, beau, and *galant*. Brooklyn was a less welcoming environment. Though Paul Broyard arrived there a master carpenter, he soon discovered that the carpenters' union was not favorably inclined toward colored applicants. A stranger in a strange city, Paul decided to pass as white in order to join the union and get work. It was strictly a professional decision, which affected his career and nothing else. But his son, Anatole, would make the same decision and expand on it, passing for white in every area of his life—working at the *Times;* living in Southport, Connecticut; and raising two children who believed he was white, in the process alienating himself from his mother and his siblings and countless others from his black past. He died in 1990, having kept his secret from all but a few friends and associates for more than five decades.

I never met Anatole Broyard. I read him regularly in the *New York*

Bliss's grandfather, Paul, who passed as white in order to join the New York carpenter's union.

Times for years—and admired his writing while troubling myself over his secret, which, unlike the vast majority of his readers, I knew. I was told that Anatole was black in 1975, when I was twenty-five years old, by my mentor, Charles T. Davis, the first African American to be tenured in the Yale English department. Charles and his wife, Jean Curtis Davis, were friends with Broyard's sister and brother-in-law, the former ambassador Franklin Williams and his wife, Shirley. Because they knew Shirley so well, they knew all about Anatole's family's past. They were highly amused that the *Times* was unwittingly employing someone who was passing for a white man. I was fascinated and disturbed by this fact. And when Broyard died, I decided to explore it. I interviewed many people who knew him, used a genealogist to track down his family's records in the Louisiana state archives, then published an essay about his life in the *New Yorker*.

In the process of writing my essay, I called Anatole's daughter, Bliss Broyard. We talked a few times on the phone, as I was deciding whether or not to write about her father's story. Finally, after talking to my editors at the *New Yorker,* Tina Brown and Henry Finder, I decided to plunge ahead. I tried to tell Bliss in person, when I thought I would be visiting the campus of the University of Virginia at Charlottesville, where she was a student. But that trip was canceled. So I told her on the phone.

Anatole had a close circle of friends who knew his secret. His wife, Alexandra Nelson, a white woman of Norwegian ancestry, knew it as well. But it was entirely hidden from Bliss and her brother, Todd, almost up until the moment Anatole died. When I told her that I planned to write about her father, Bliss became quite angry with me. I was outing him in a way, and that upset her. But as the years have passed, Bliss's feelings seemed to have softened somewhat. I was delighted this past summer when she left me a copy of her book about her father, *One Drop,* at the house we lease on Martha's Vineyard. When I read her book, I discovered that she was *still* pretty angry at me! Nevertheless, when I began this project, I decided to ask her to participate, precisely because she was so angry and did not, I believe, fully understand how culturally black her father and his father truly had been. I wanted to see how Bliss had been affected, an entire decade after I published my essay, by her father's secret and its revelation, and I wanted to learn what, if anything, DNA testing could add to the story. She was surprised, I believe, but she eagerly agreed.

"When I first met you," Bliss said, "I thought this step of outing him myself would allow me to regain control over my identity. But what I have come to realize is that I am not in control of the way that people see me or my dad. It's always going to be a compromise between how I see myself and how the world sees me. Between how the world sees my dad and how I do."

Bliss took for the title of her book the redolent phrase "one drop"—it refers to one drop of blood, which is the way that blackness was defined legally throughout the United States (if you had one traceable black ancestor—one single drop of black blood—you had the legal standing of a Negro, which, of course, was not a good thing). Her book is fascinating and helped me to understand her father better, yet the essence of his life—his decision to pass as a white man—remains something of a mystery, at least to me. And that mystery, I think, is not his desire to break through the glass ceiling of race but the repudiation of his visibly black sister, Shirley, in the lives of his children.

Bliss and I began our discussion by talking about her memories of

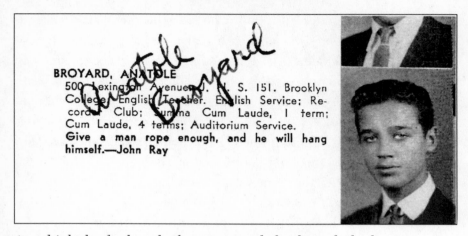

BROYARD, ANATOLE
500 Lexington Avenue. J. H. S. 151. Brooklyn
College English Teacher. English Service; Record Club; Summa Cum Laude, I term;
Cum Laude, 4 terms; Auditorium Service.
Give a man rope enough, and he will hang
himself.—John Ray

Anatole's high-school yearbook entry, a year before he made the decision to begin identifying himself as a white man.

her father, whom she loved and admired profoundly. Flipping through Bliss's photos—past pictures of Anatole walking on the beach in Martha's Vineyard, standing stock-still as an army officer, holding his young daughter—he almost always looks like a white man. It is only in his high-school yearbook photo that he looks, at least to my eyes, unmistakably black. This was, curiously, before he started identifying himself as a white man. According to Bliss, that happened when he filled out an application form for a Social Security card the following year, in 1938. He was seventeen years old. He needed a Social Security number to get a job. In that same year, that same summer, his sister Shirley, who was a couple of years younger, went to the same state office to see if there were any summer jobs. She was told there were no jobs for colored girls.

Looking at Anatole's application, the eye is immediately drawn to question number twelve—the question about color. On Anatole's form there is a check next to "Negro" that has been crossed out, and then there's a check next to "White." The letter *C* has been handwritten as well, which could stand for "Creole" or "colored." There's no way to know. The form is astonishing to behold because of the way that he erased his identity, agonizing over his decision to pass, right there on the form.

"He was confused," Bliss said sadly.

Anatole Broyard's Social Security card application—in which he indicates that he is "white" after first checking the box for "negro."

I asked her how she learned her father's secret. Her mother, Sandy, had told me the story, but I wanted to hear it from Bliss's point of view. She told me that for the first twenty-five years of her life she was, for all intents and purposes, a white person. Though her father was "legally" black, Bliss was raised white in the whitest of white towns—Southport, Connecticut—and she looked white, and believed herself to be white. She did not learn that her father was black until just months before he died of prostate cancer. "My mom said that she and Dad wanted to have a family meeting, which was very out of character for us," she recalled. "And Dad was quite ill at this point. I remember I had to bring a beach chair for him to sit in while we waited for my brother to come. The cancer had metastasized, and the doctors had let us know that there wasn't really anything else they could do.

"I think my mother had been kind of encouraging him to figure out how to finish up his life. And telling my brother and me this secret was one of those things that he needed to do. So we sat down in the living room, and my mom said, 'Anatole, is there anything that you'd like to tell your children?' And he said, 'Oh, I don't want to get into that today.' My brother and I kind of caught eyes and were like, 'Get into what?' And then my mother explained over my father's protesting that there was some secret from my father's childhood that would explain a lot. And she said that the secret was even more painful than this pain of cancer. But he didn't want to talk about it that day. He said that he would tell us eventually—that he needed to think about how to present things, that he wanted to order his vulnerabilities so they didn't get magnified during the discussion. That's a quote. He wanted to 'order his vulnerabilities.' And I remember this because it was so distinctly him."

Ultimately it was her mother, not her father, who revealed the family secret. "What ended up happening," said Bliss, "is my father went back in the hospital after that meeting, with another medical emergency. His bladder burst, and he had to go into emergency surgery, and my mother took it upon herself to tell us then—as my father was about to face the surgery. At that point we had just been watching my father screaming for help as if he were literally drowning, because he was in such terrible pain. So my mom simply said, 'I think I better tell you what the secret is.' And she said, 'Your father is part black.' That was her language. Then she sort of talked a little more, and she said that he was mixed and that his parents were Creoles from New Orleans, where there had been a lot of race mixing at one point, and that when he was growing up, his parents had had to pass in order to get work, and it had confused him about what the family was supposed to be. And she told us that his two sisters, Lorraine and Shirley, had stayed in the black community and they both lived as black, and that's why we never saw them."

Bliss's mother also said that when Anatole was growing up, he was a victim of frequent abuse due to his color—and Bliss believes that this in many ways shaped his decisions in later life. "My mother," said Bliss, "told us that when he was a child, my father used to come home with his jacket torn from getting into fights, that the black kids would pick on him because he looked white and the white kids would pick on him because he looked black, and his parents would just ignore it. They wouldn't ask what happened. And he didn't want his own kids to go through the same thing he did."

Bliss says that she had no inkling that her father had been conceal-ing his race, but she also recalls feeling no shock upon learning this se-cret. Her father was dying—and *would* die in just a few days—and her thoughts were focused on his health. The fact that he was part black was immaterial. "We laughed," said Bliss. "I thought the secret was going to be some horrible thing like a murder or incest or something. And it was just, like, he's part black. You know? This is the terrible secret from his childhood that's caused so much pain? We didn't get it. In fact, it seemed kind of cool, like, I remember saying to my mother, 'Oh, that means that we're part black, too!' Because I had always bought into this idea of the American melting pot, and here I was an example of it."

While Bliss does not seem the least bit concerned about the content of her father's secret—and the realization that she is part black—she re-mains deeply concerned over why he felt the need to keep the secret from her, his daughter. Indeed, in talking with her it is palpably clear that she still struggles with this—and still wonders why her father concealed so much from one of the people in the world who was closest to him. In the end she believes that he did so for a variety of complex reasons, all deeply intertwined with our nation's tortured past. "I think," she said, "that a big part of it was just that he didn't want us to have to struggle with our ra-cial identity the way that he had. He just thought that he'd saved us from having that struggle. I think that, you know, he didn't want us to be black, that for him, growing up in Bed-Stuy in the forties, being black wasn't a good thing. And he always was sort of encouraging us to meet the kind of people who could help us later. I think that's what we were supposed to do in Connecticut. He was always telling us that we should learn how to play squash, because, you know, those are the kinds of people who can give you jobs. For him there was a kind of social cachet."

There are, of course, overwhelming advantages to being white in America. When Anatole surveyed the racial landscape and decided that his children would have an easier time of it if they were white, he knew what he was doing. And about this he was, without a doubt, correct. Being white, in general, in America, has had enormous historical and economic advantages. The cost, however, could be enormous as well. Anatole's life and virtually all his personal relationships were contorted by his decision. Bliss has great sympathy for him but also clearly recognizes the consequences of his decision—the internal chaos that it may have spawned.

"I think he wanted to spare us from a lot of pain that he had as a child," said Bliss. "But I don't know that he wanted to be white, either. He just wanted to be a kind of outsider to both these racial labels and expectations and prejudices that went with them, 'cause, you know, he was kind of a cool cat. He didn't want to be some white guy. He held black people up on a pedestal and was always making these comments about black athletes being better than white athletes, always the stereotypes, or black musicians being better than white musicians. At the same time, though, he also had some prejudicial feelings about blacks himself, and I think that my dad looked down on black people. I mean, I heard him saying prejudiced things when I was growing up sometimes. There was this time he was trying to sell our house in Cambridge. It was a very nice house, but down the block there was some low-income housing. And these buyers were coming back to look at the house for the third time, and even though he was sick, he walked up and down the street, picked up all the trash so it would look nicer. And then he came back fuming. I said, 'What's wrong?' He said, 'There are some black kids playing down the street. And these people are never going to want to buy this house if they see that.' And I was shocked. I remember saying, 'Dad, you sound like a goddamn racist.' And then he got up and left the table."

In this regard Anatole was acting like many black people, meaning that we make comments of this sort all the time. Nonetheless, the comment is startling—and as Bliss and I explored the implications of her father's decision to keep his race secret, similarly ironic contradictions arose. When I think about Bliss's father, I am reminded of how hard it is to be black and successful. His story is among the saddest I know, not because of its abstract implications but because of the costs to his mother and sisters. Anatole gained a world; they lost a son and brother. And how does one measure the comparative costs of that trade-off?

Bliss believes that her father liked to pretend that he had put his family in the past, but in reality she thinks he lived with the guilt or struggle of his decision on a daily basis.

"He was a family man," said Bliss, shaking her head. "He loved our family, and I think that he loved his family, and I think he had terrible guilt about it. I remember in 1979, when I was twelve, it was Mother's Day, and my father had decided to get my mom these really fancy earrings from Tiffany's, a kind of much nicer present than he usually did. He told me all about it, and I picked them out in the catalog with him, and then when he came down to give her the present, she was making dinner, even though it was Mother's Day, and she didn't sort of turn around and sit down quickly enough to accept the present. He abruptly lost his temper and threw the Tiffany box across the room. And I couldn't believe it. It was just so irrational. Then, later that night, I just went to bed, and my parents were kind of fighting, and then my mom woke me up in the middle of a deep sleep. She was looking for the bologna. She wanted to know where I had put the bologna when I had helped her unpack the groceries earlier that day. Because every night my dad had a bologna and cheese sandwich. Every night—with a single beer. So I told her, you know, 'It's in the meat drawer, I think.' And she went running back downstairs. I followed her, because I couldn't figure out what was going on."

When Bliss arrived in her family's kitchen, she was confronted by a scene of utter chaos. "My mother was kneeling in front of the refrigerator," she said, "and there were all these broken mayonnaise jars and things all over the floor. Because my dad had ransacked the refrigerator. I couldn't believe it. I said, 'What has got into him? It's Mother's Day. He got you this nice gift.' And my mother said, 'Well, his mother died, and I think he's feeling guilty.' This was the first I had heard that she was dead—and she had died nine months earlier."

Bliss can remember meeting her grandmother Edna Broyard only once in her life. "I had just turned seven," she recalled, "and my grand-mother came out for the day to Connecticut where we were living and sat in a lawn chair in the backyard for a while, and then we went to the local country club and all had dinner, and then she went back home with my Aunt Lorraine. Then later, when I was going through my father's letters—he kept every letter he had ever received—I found a letter from my grandmother, who was living in a nursing home, dated a few weeks prior to this visit saying, 'Dear Anatole, I am not that young anymore. I am just going to be seventy-six. I want to meet my grandchildren for once in my life.' So she had requested this visit. And then she had her one visit."

Bliss says that her requests to see her grandmother again were always met with excuses. To me this story encapsulates what would be the unimaginably painful consequences of Anatole Broyard's decision to pass.

Turning to her family tree, Bliss told me that before she began writing her book, she had no knowledge of her family history as it related to her father's line beyond the fact that they came from New Orleans. Her research on her book revealed much more. Bliss was able to trace her family back to the middle of the eighteenth century, to her great-great-great-great-great-great-grandfather, a white Frenchman named Étienne Broyard who was born in 1729 and arrived in New Orleans in 1753, when it was part of New France. I wondered how her father would have felt about that. No doubt he would have been pleased; it certainly wouldn't have threatened his sense of the black identity that he had fled. It would have confirmed what was written right on his face: that he had a long, mixed racial heritage. Indeed, it probably would have impressed him, just as Bliss's research skills impressed me.

Bliss and I then began to explore the part of her heritage that had so tormented her father: her African ancestry—which, as it turns out, is filled with remarkably fascinating and quite unusual stories. It can be traced back to the marriage of her great-great-grandparents, Henry Antoine Broyard, a white man born on July 18, 1829, and Marie Pauline Bonnet, a free woman of color. They married in 1855. Marie's family came from the French colony of Saint-Domingue, now Haiti, as refugees of Toussaint-Louverture's revolution, the only successful slave revolt in the Western Hemisphere. The Bonnets were expelled from Haiti along with thousands of other free people of color, because the new government feared they might still be loyal to France. And like many of their fellow refugees, they came to New Orleans because of the French culture there and its relatively large mulatto, elite population.

The fact that Henry and Marie formed a mixed-race couple is not surprising. Marie Pauline's parents were educated. Her father was a carpenter, and in fact he may even have worked with her future husband, who was also a carpenter. They all lived in the New Orleans neighborhood known as Treme, which has been called the oldest black neighborhood in America, though in fact it was quite mixed, even back in the 1850s—as was all of New Orleans, much more so than anywhere else in the South at that time. So to some extent Henry and Marie were mimicking the behaviors and mores of their city when they joined together. There were other factors as well. Records show that Henry's father had had children with a black woman—and so Henry had half siblings living as free people of color. Moreover, there is evidence that Henry himself had a child with another free woman of color before he married Marie. So Henry and Marie were surrounded by interracial couples.

Nonetheless, these two people did something very unusual: They got married. It was illegal for blacks and whites to get married in 1855 Louisiana. Even though Marie was free, she was visibly and officially black, and in the years leading up to the Civil War anti-black feelings in the South were rising and free people of color were being viewed with ever-mounting suspicion as possible instigators of slave revolts. Yet Marie and Henry were able to marry. How was this possible? Bliss's novel theory is that it was facilitated by the same means that Anatole Broyard would use a century later—only in reverse: She believes that Henry Broyard passed as black! His race, on his marriage license, is listed as "Negro." He even volunteered for the army in the Civil War as a colored man, serving in the famous Louisiana Native Guard, one of the first all-black regiments in the war.

Tellingly, after black-and-white marriages were legalized again in 1870, Henry Broyard indicated that he was white on the census, and his family indicated the same on his death certificate. If Bliss is indeed right about her ancestor's origins, it would seem that following the Civil War he stopped passing, although his wife and all their children continued to list themselves as mulattoes.

Bliss is struck by the irony of this. "I thought, how could it be that my great-great-grandfather passed from white to black?" Passing, it would seem, has a long history in her family.

I have consulted with many scholars about Bliss's ancestor, and I am convinced that Henry Broyard could possibly have decided to pass for black, although for obvious reasons this was extraordinarily rare. On the other hand, he could have been a mulatto himself. Race is such a tenuous thing, especially in New Orleans.

"I come from a very illustrious line," said Bliss, laughing. "I like to think of it as a little bit of a love story. It was important for me to find that moment of mixing, and I thought it was a rape in a slave cabin. I mean, that was the sort of image you always have, right? But I think this was a love relationship. It's quite unusual."

Henry and Marie Pauline's oldest son was Nat Broyard. He is Bliss's paternal great-grandfather, and according to her research, he was a carpenter who built some of the biggest buildings in New Orleans in the 1890s. He was also, according to Bliss, very active in Republican politics at that time and may have been friends with Homer Plessy and the group of Creoles in Louisiana who pressed one of the most important civil-rights lawsuits in American history—an early and unsuccessful challenge to segregation that ended up in the infamous 1896 Supreme Court decision *Plessy v. Ferguson.* The failure of Plessy's case cemented the "separate but equal" doctrine and helped institutionalize Jim Crow racism in this country for another six decades. If Nat Broyard knew and helped Homer Plessy, he has my deepest admiration. Plessy and his friends stood up for racial justice in the worst of times.

In his life of passing, Anatole Broyard was a virtuoso of ambiguity and equivocation. People who learned about his secret generally heard rumors about "distant" black ancestry—perhaps a great-grandfather. Anatole wanted things vague. He rarely spoke directly to anyone about his racial background.

"My father," recalled Bliss, "never said anything about it to me, but he said it to, I guess, my mother and some other friends who had asked. He'd say, 'Oh, you know, my great-grandfather found his wife under a coconut tree.' That was his way of saying that she was from the islands. Or he would say that there were some 'Caribbean influences' in his past. But he'd never come out and say 'black.' "

The truth, of course, was very different. Nat Broyard, Anatole's paternal grandfather, was half black, and he married a half-black woman named Rosa Cousin. Her father was a white man named Anatole Cousin (the source of Anatole Broyard's name), and her mother was Marie Evalina Xavier, whose family was also part of this Haitian refugee community in early-nineteenth-century New Orleans.

Nat and Rosa Broyard's son was Paul Broyard, Anatole's father. Paul followed in his father's footsteps, working as a carpenter and builder in New Orleans. His wife was Edna Miller. She was from a colored Creole family in New Orleans, and in her photographs she looks like an elegant African American woman of her day. There is simply no doubt, based on Bliss's book and my own research, that Anatole Broyard was at best confused if he did in fact believe that he had only one black ancestor. He had many black ancestors, just as he had white ancestors, and in the United States when he was born—and in the United States today—he would be defined as an African American. And so would Bliss.

Our DNA testing further confirmed this. Bliss's admixture test revealed that she is 17.2 percent sub-Saharan African, 78 percent European, and 4.7 percent East Asian. Her African results indicate that 37 percent of her African ancestry came from Upper Guinea and 63 percent comes from Congo Angola, which is where more than a quarter of all the slaves brought to America came from.

"I'm an octoroon," she said. "My daughter is a steeth—she's a sixteenth black. My dad was a quadroon. A quarter black."

I asked Bliss if she saw race as a matter of choice. "I'm in a very unusual situation," she said. "I can decide how much I want this to be a part of who I am. In a lot of people, their race is so apparent that they don't have any control over how they are seen. I think race is the sum of experience and a state of mind. When I went to New Orleans and did my genealogy and learned about my family history, that made me feel like a different person. When I look in the mirror, I see a different person now.

But without having grown up as black and without looking black, it's hard for me to feel that I am black, you know? I don't feel that I have earned the right to call myself black, since I wasn't raised that way and I don't look black. But, you know, at the same time, my father was black. I'm black. There's just a lot of explaining to do."

I told Bliss that based on her DNA she most certainly has a significant amount of African ancestry. And she was fascinated to hear that her results indicate that her first enslaved maternal ancestor on her father's side (we tested her father's sister) was most likely shipped from what is now Angola to the New World sometime between 1750 and 1808. The slaves shipped from Angola were generally handled by Portuguese slave traders—which triggered an interesting memory in Bliss.

"Edna Miller," she said, "my father's mother. When they moved to New York in 1930, the census taker came around, and she said that her family was Portuguese. And Portuguese keeps cropping up in her family line, and I always suspected that somebody in her family had been a slave in the United States, and maybe they came over with a Portuguese slave trader or something."

Before we said good-bye, I told Bliss once again how powerfully her father's story had affected me. I still remember when I learned that Anatole was black. I was stunned. And I remember thinking, "He's a reviewer for the *New York Times,* but he's passing." And I had very mixed emotions about that. I was proud of him, but I wanted him to have fought the battle as a black man and not as a black man passing as a white man. I wanted him to have made it as a daily reviewer at the *New York Times* with everyone knowing his race. And I have often wondered whether he ever felt this, too—could he have achieved so much if he had identified himself as a black man? And would it have made him happier?

Bliss does not know any better than I do. "He believed in that kind of modernist notion of self-invention," she said. "He thought that he could create himself and be who he wanted to be and that the only authority on his identity was himself. And he was ahead of his time in that way."

The irony, of course, is that he should have been able to define himself. I deeply believe that. But Anatole was trapped in a system of racist class values—deeply American racist class values. And he couldn't re-create his conscience. He couldn't obliterate this sense of rejecting actual people with whom he had grown up. But what kind of person could? And that was naïve on his part.

"It's also naïve," Bliss said, nodding her head, "that he believed that people who looked like himself, who didn't look visibly black, could make race not matter. I think that he wildly underestimated the level of racism and prejudice that people experience every day. It was very easy for him to say, 'Forget your race.' But some people don't want to forget their race."

This is very true. And it is also true that there is probably no way in the world her father could have achieved what he did had he identified him-self as black rather than white. "He never could have gotten that job at the *Times*," Bliss said. "If he had been openly black at that time? There was no other black critic on staff of a daily major paper in the United States. And one of the reasons he couldn't have gotten the job is that if he had been openly black, he would have been expected to write only about, to know only about black subjects."

Nonetheless, I believe that Anatole Broyard made a terrible mistake. And I've had people pass in my own family. My cousin Pat Carpenter was black, divorced his first wife, and married a white woman, and he didn't want anybody in the family to contact him. My father's Uncle Roscoe married a white woman and passed. When my great-grandmother died, my grandpa, my father's father, wouldn't tell his own brother that their mother had died, because he was so angry at him for having passed. I was raised with these stories. I know firsthand that the black experience has al-ways been multicolored. But Anatole's decision will always, on some level, be a puzzle to me—especially the fact that he couldn't talk to his children about it.

In parting, I told Bliss that I wish I could have met her father just to console him, just to encourage him to talk to the people who loved him. Hearing this, Bliss smiled knowingly. "If I could say something to him now, it would be something simple," she told me. "I'd just say, 'I can un-derstand why you were trying to protect yourself and protect your family, but you don't have to anymore. Times have changed, and being black can be a wonderful thing. There are so many great aspects of the culture and your own family history that should not be buried, and we'd like to know. I'd like to know.' "

I am very sorry she never got the chance to say this. I think it would have unburdened him in some way to hear it.

Chris Tucker

August 31, 1971

T HE COMEDIAN CHRIS TUCKER is the youngest person I
involved in this project. He is roughly the same age as my own
daughters, and I asked him to participate in part because I wanted
to see how family history influenced someone of their generation. It was
a lucky choice, as Chris proved an ideal subject. He was just beginning to
learn about his past, but at the same time I was struck by the many ways
this A-list movie star remains deeply involved with his close-knit family.
By his own admission, they laid the foundation for all his success. And in
researching their stories, I found myself appreciating anew the traditional
ways in which our people have raised their children, even in my generation.

Chris was born on August 31, 1971, in Decatur, Georgia, a suburb just
east of Atlanta. His father, Norris Tucker, was born March 26, 1946, in
Atlanta. His mother, Mary Louise Bryant, was born November 21, 1943,
in nearby Lithonia, Georgia. Chris was the youngest of their six children,
and although Norris and Mary separated when he was a teenager, his father did not move far away and maintained close contact with the family.
Looking back, Chris remembers his childhood warmly, saying that he developed his comedic skills sparring with his siblings.

"My strongest memories," said Chris, "are just of my family and hanging around each other in Decatur. It was always a lot of fun. We enter-
tained ourselves just being together. We didn't try to be funny, it was just
natural. Like, I shared a bedroom with my brother, you know? Called

Chris Tucker around seven years old.

him my prison mate. And we never got along. But we had fun. A lot of good times. And I think comedy comes out of real stuff. Something funny happens all the time in a family if you watch what's going on. And with a big family, you got so many people interacting, something's always going on."

When Chris was growing up, Decatur was a community made up almost entirely of African Americans. "It was mostly black schools," he recalled, "and church was black. Of course, when we'd go outside, we'd see white people, but in our community it was black." This would change over the course of Chris's upbringing, as the neighborhood would become a relatively affluent mixture of many races, but the changes did not affect Chris's family. Indeed, Decatur provided a very stable environment for Chris. When he was five years old, his family moved into the house where he would live until he was eighteen and finally moved away to pursue his career. He spent almost his entire youth in that house, sharing it happily with brothers and sisters, weathering the good and bad times in his parents' marriage.

His father provided a very strong role model, working long hours to keep his family in this secure setting. "My father always had jobs," recalled Chris. "Always two or three jobs. He worked for Atlanta Dairy. Then he started his own business, a cleaning company. And that's the only real job I've ever had in my life—working for my daddy. We cleaned everything—toilets, we used to clean Burger Kings, McDonald's, office buildings. My daddy had a lot of buildings, a lot of people working for him, and me and my brothers were part of that workforce."

Laughing, Chris told me that having his father for a boss was not by any means easy. "You don't want to work for your family," he said. "Because if you don't do a good job, you get a whipping. I used to get a lot of whippings from my daddy." Nonetheless, Chris grew up thinking that he would one day follow in his father's footsteps, owning and operating his own business—and he did everything he could to learn from his father. But he was a poor student, and along the way he also realized that he had a unique gift for comedy.

"I was the class clown," he said, with a wide grin. "I used to joke around just to take attention off my bad grades. I was like, 'I got to make the teacher laugh so she'll pass me.' And I got kept back so many times they finally said, 'Look, just go. You got nothing to learn.' Because all I was doing was jokes."

Chris started hosting talent shows in high school, succeeding onstage in a way he had never imagined possible. "It felt so good," he recalled. "Right then and there, I said 'This is what I'm going to do the rest of my life.' And, my career, it just sort of happened. I mean, I wanted to go to college, but I didn't think that was a good idea 'cause I barely got out of high school. So I just stuck with comedy. It was like I didn't have no choice. I was acting up in class, so I said, 'Might as well keep doing this.' I just found my calling early, you know? And I always knew I had a strong family. Even when I moved out to California, if it didn't work out, I'd come back home and tell jokes in the living room. So it didn't matter."

Unlike most of the other people involved in this project, Chris seems to have been truly insulated from the effects of racism. By his own admission, it's almost as if racism did not affect him or limit his life choices at all—which is not the popular conception of growing up black in the South. But Chris insists that it was his experience.

"I believed that I could do anything," he said. "I didn't think about race. I told my mother when I was in high school, 'After I graduate, I'm going to go to California. I want to be a comedian.' And I was kind of nervous telling people, because being from Georgia, saying you're going to be a comedian in the entertainment business, it's like that's not possible. But my mother never said I couldn't do it. She didn't laugh in my face. She just said all right. She didn't know what I was going to do, 'cause I wasn't exactly doing anything in school. So she was just happy I was going to do *something*. So it was cool."

As we began to explore his family tree, I was repeatedly struck by his values and his fundamental sense of security, by the warmth and pleasure he took from learning about his ancestors—and by the delight he seemed to derive from telling stories about the ones he actually knew or had heard about. "The oldest ancestor I can remember is my great-great-grandmother Mimaw," he said, elated upon first glimpsing the charts I had made. "She lived to one hundred and four. I remember Mimaw. I was, like, five or six when she was alive. I remember she used to grow her own food in the backyard. They said she was so old she grew a new set of teeth."

Mimaw, as her family called her, was Chris's great-great-grandmother on his mother's side. She was born Flora Harris in Henry County, Georgia, sometime around 1870, so she did indeed live more than a hundred years. "She was beautiful," said Chris. "She had long, wavy beautiful hair. And they said she had some Indian in her."

Chris also remembers "Little Ma"—Mimaw's daughter—his mother's grandmother, Mary Harris, born in July of 1897 in Henry County, Georgia. He happily recalls visiting her rural home. "We used to go get water out of the well," he said. "And then we had to use the bathroom late at night, and we'd be all scared because we had to go to the outhouse, and we'd be hearing pigs and goats and all that, chickens, stepping on chickens and stuff." It sounds exotic, but his great-grandmother lived in what is known as the Flat Rock community of Lithonia, Georgia, just a few dozen miles east of where Chris grew up. So did many of his other relatives and ancestors. In fact, the first thing that I noticed in researching Chris's family is that it has been in Georgia continuously since slavery. This is highly unusual. Could it account for his great sense of security, his values and confidence? Perhaps. Aside from my own family, his family is the only one I researched that refused to join the mass migration from the South to the North.

The more I thought about this fact, the more significant I found it. Whereas most of the families I traced fled the South as part of the Great Migration sometime in the first half of the twentieth century, Chris's ancestors chose to stay. They chose to deal with the situation they found themselves in—an environment that they knew and were comfortable with—rather than risk everything in the uncertain, unfamiliar cities of the North. Chris appreciates this decision. He loves Georgia and is proud of his southern roots. But he nonetheless acknowledges that his ancestors must have made some great sacrifices to stay in the region throughout the Jim Crow era. He vividly recalls listening to his parents and grandparents talk about segregation and the violence that surrounded them.

"I remember hearing, 'Don't go through Stone Mountain!' " he said, recalling advice he'd received often as a child. "They'd say that all the time, because the Ku Klux Klan was still alive and going on around Stone Mountain, still wearing them masks and all that stuff. So they said don't go through Stone Mountain. And then also in Atlanta, back when I was growing up, there was still a lot of racial tension, a lot of fear. Even now you can't go to some parts of Georgia, you know."

I wanted to learn more about why Chris's family chose to stay in the South—and about how this decision may have affected him. Turning back to his mother's side, we looked at Mary Louise Bryant's family, tracing her through her mother, Flora Robinson, born in the Flat Rock community on August 4, 1925, and then back to Little Ma and Mimaw. Consulting the 1870 census, we were even able to identify Mimaw's mother, Amanda Harper, born a slave sometime around 1850 in Henry County, Georgia. Unfortunately, though, after Amanda we could go back no further along this line. So we returned to Chris's mother and began researching the line of her father, the Reverend Theodore Arthur Bryant Jr., born in the Flat Rock community on November 24, 1922, and still alive today.

The Reverend Bryant has vivid memories of life in the Jim Crow South. "In that time," he told us, "back in the twenties and thirties, you had to be careful and know what to say, when to say it, and who to say

Chris's grandfather, Theodore Arthur Bryant Jr., at right, in an undated photo. Bryant, born in 1922, has vivid memories of growing up during the height of segregation.

it to—or know what not to say, mostly. You had to walk a tightrope to survive."

Moreover, the Reverend Bryant was able to help us learn about his own father, Theodore Arthur Bryant Sr., who helped cement a relationship between Chris's family and the small rural community of Flat Rock, Georgia. Chris knew his great-grandfather. He called him "Papa" and visited him often as a child. "Papa had all this property," said Chris, "and all these animals and stuff. We saw him a lot. He had this big old fat pig, and it was always laying in the mud when we went over there. We used to go back there and mess with him all the time. He had a lot of animals, we always had fun with him. He was just a nice man, just a great man—a lot of wisdom."

Theodore Arthur Bryant Sr. was born December 13, 1896, in Rockdale, Georgia, which is part of DeKalb County and located very near the Flat Rock community where so many of his family members would live for generations. Theodore was a farmer and, for his time, a reasonably wealthy one. This, as Chris knows, is remarkable. When Bryant was growing up, economic opportunities for African Americans in the South were as scarce as hen's teeth. In the late nineteenth century and for much of the twentieth century, most blacks who did not migrate north could not afford to own land and were condemned to the sharecropping system. Most worked for low wages or had to rent land at exorbitant rates that made just breaking even difficult. Booker T. Washington famously called the region the "Black Belt" in those years, because the soil was very dark and very rich—but so was the skin of the people who were working it. The land itself, however, was overwhelmingly owned by whites, many of them former slaveholders or the descendants of former slaveholders. Their black workers were bound to them by the sharecropper relationship, which they could not break. And many times the white man they worked for had been the person who'd owned them under slavery. It was a crushingly unfair system, but somehow Chris's ancestors managed to be free of it.

To learn how they accomplished this, we set out looking for records relating to Theodore Bryant Sr., and we found a land deed from 1925 indicating that Bryant had purchased forty-five acres of farmland in Flat Rock for six hundred dollars. This is a major accomplishment. In 1925, six hundred dollars was a lot of money, and very few black people in the United States had anything close to that much land.

Chris's grandfather, the Reverend Bryant, took us to the original piece of land that his father purchased some eighty years ago, showing us the old home where he himself was born and raised. "My dad accumulated all of this himself," the reverend said proudly. "He was the type of person who wanted to do things his way, and owning his own land, he *could* do it his way. He didn't have to answer to anybody. And we plowed all of the land. And we grew cotton as far as you could see."

The Reverend Bryant rightly sees this house as the heroic monument that it surely is: For this was the very first property that any member of his family ever owned. This is the farm that sustained and supported his people for forty years. And digging deeper into the historical record, we learned that Theodore's actions were even more significant than they first seemed. Land deeds revealed that between 1925 and 1945, Bryant Sr. sold off pieces of his property at least thirty different times. Sometimes the lots were as small as two acres. I was fascinated by this, never having seen anything like it before. Why did he sell little bits of property here and there? What story did these land deeds tell? The answer came from the Reverend Bryant, shocking both Chris and me.

"Dad sold the land to relatives and some other people," said the reverend. "To keep them here. Some was going north because of better jobs, in some cases to get away from segregation. Dad was determined to try to keep enough people in the community to keep the church going. If he hadn't, then the community would have gone down. There was another church in an adjoining community that didn't survive. It just ceased to exist. And Dad, he was a church person, and he realized that if the people didn't have anywhere to live in the community, they were gonna move out and then the church and everything would, you know, go down. My mother complained a couple of times about him selling the land. Some of us, too, we complained about him selling it, because we thought that he ought to keep it and let us inherit it. I guess that's what we thought. But I am proud of him now. I think about it quite often. How my dad sacrificed."

"That's amazing," said Chris, solemnly looking at one of these deeds of sale. Frankly, I thought the same thing. What he tried to do was deeply touching. And the story matches the historical record. When Bryant was selling land in tiny parcels to his neighbors, black people all around him were moving to the North, fleeing the South. But Bryant thought that the South was their ancestral home—all black people were from the South, by and large—and he did not want to see them move. He wanted to hold his Flat Rock community together. So he divided up his farm, and by so doing he kept his community intact.

"I know I wouldn't do that today," said Chris, laughing. "I'd be like, 'I'll see you later—land for me.'"

He and I were both impressed with his great-grandfather's actions. I myself have never heard of a story like this. And we were curious as to why Bryant was so concerned about the community and its church. So we investigated further and found another fascinating story. Theodore's father, Chris's great-great-grandfather, was Spencer Bryant, who was born

Spencer Bryant, at center, was Chris's great-great-grandfather. He moved to Flat Rock in the 1880s and helped found the Flat Rock United Methodist Church.

a slave around 1862 in Newton County, Georgia. We found him in the 1870 census, which indicates that at that time Spencer was living in the household of his mother, Jemima Bryant, who is listed as being a thirty-five-year-old farmer. Later census records tell us that in the 1880s the Bryant family moved from Newton County to the Flat Rock community in DeKalb County.

So Spencer Bryant is most likely the man who set down Chris's family roots in Flat Rock, having been brought there by his mother. Spencer also seems to have had a very early involvement with the Flat Rock United Methodist Church—the church that so concerned his son Theodore. We found a photograph from around 1890 of the church's trustees and deacons, with Spencer Bryant at its center. He is listed as being the principal deacon of the church.

Chris was raised very religiously. His grandfather, the Reverend Bryant, is a retired deacon from this Flat Rock United Methodist Church

The Flat Rock Church, seen here in 1916, plays a multigenerational role in Chris's family history, also figuring large in the lives of his grandfather and great-grandfather.

and remains active in its congregation. Chris's mother took him to church every Sunday and instilled in him a sense of spirituality that still seems to undergird him. And he and I both know how important religion is for our people today. But neither of us can fully understand how much more important it was to keep the community together in the late nineteenth and early twentieth centuries. At that time the church was the main institution for African American culture and society. It would continue to be so right up through the civil-rights movement and beyond. This gives tremendous added meaning to the sacrifices that Theodore Bryant made to preserve this small church in rural Georgia. His ancestor's sacrifice seemed truly humbling to Chris.

"We go way back in church," said Chris quietly. "I didn't know that we go *all* the way back—but our family was always in church. Church is very important to us, very important. I know all my blessings come from God. And spirituality—my mother, she raised me in church, and that really molded me and helped me deal with every part of life. And this is just—it's so important."

Looking at this photograph, which is well more than a hundred years old, you can see the family resemblance between Chris and his ancestor, as if they were brothers. "Whom does he look like?" I had asked Chris. "Me!" he exclaimed. Unfortunately, we were not able to learn anything more about Spencer Bryant. The 1870 census lists his mother, Jemima, but no father. And we could find no other documents to trace either Spencer or Jemima back into slavery.

We did, however, find more about Spencer's wife, Mary Ann Shoemaker. She was born a slave in 1864 in Morgan County, Georgia, and census records indicate that her parents were Rebecca and Richard Shoemaker. Searching for a possible slave owner with their name, we found a white farmer named Charles Shoemaker who owned fourteen hundred acres of land and thirty-three slaves in 1860. So we began looking through Charles Shoemaker's records to see if he had any slaves named Mary Ann or Rebecca or Richard. It was a long shot. More often than not, the slaves listed in property records aren't listed by their first names. But we found something very interesting in this case. Charles Shoemaker died in 1864, a year before the end of the Civil War. And because he didn't leave a will, his estate was administered by his son, who had to divide up all of his father's property—including his slaves. The records of the division of this property indicate that the Shoemaker slaves were divided into groups of equal value and parceled out to Shoemaker's heirs. And they clearly identify two slaves named Mary Ann and Rebecca. These were, I am confident, Chris's great-great-grandmother and her mother. The total value of the lot in which they were included was seven thousand five hundred dollars. Ironically, these ancestors of Chris's who were slaves survive in the historical record only because their master died. (And this is something that Chris shares with seven of the other people in this project: Morgan Freeman, Benjamin Carson, Mae Jemison, T. D. Jakes, Kathleen Henderson, Linda Johnson Rice, and Jackie Joyner-Kersee all learned about the existence of enslaved ancestors only through the estate papers and wills left by the white folks who owned them.)

Charles Shoemaker's records also contained the name of the man who I believe is Mary Ann's father, Richard Shoemaker. And they contained one other interesting fact. We knew from the 1870 census that Richard and Rebecca were both born slaves around 1830 in Virginia. And Charles Shoemaker's records indicate that he moved to Georgia from Virginia for economic reasons in the mid–nineteenth century. This is further confirmation, I believe, that Shoemaker was the owner of Chris's ancestors.

Unfortunately, we were unable to find any records in Virginia that identify either Richard's or Rebecca's parents, so our trail goes cold with them.

Still, Chris was thrilled that we were able to take his family back even this far. "I didn't know this was going to be like this," he said gleefully. "I thought you'd tell me where I'm from, and then I'd be excited about that. But this knowledge—it's just instilling something in me that has been missing, you know? A sense of history, of my family. It gives me another look at life, a better outlook. I mean, seeing my great-great-grandfather who was a slave—it makes me appreciate right now where I'm at in life and take advantage of life."

We had now reached as far back in Chris's ancestry as genealogical research could take us. The paper trail on every line had ended in slavery, and it was time to turn to our DNA testing. Before doing so, however, I wanted to know what Chris thought of Africa. I knew that as a young man he'd had a fairly typical exposure to it—which is to say no exposure at all. "Africa to me when I was growing up was a far, faraway place, and I never thought I would ever go," he had told me when we first met. But I also knew that since his career had catapulted him to fame, he had toured Africa several times, visiting many of its countries, giving money and time to African causes. I knew that he felt very emotionally connected to it. And I wanted to know—given this—why he wanted to learn where exactly he was from in Africa. What difference would it make to him? "It's wisdom," he replied without hesitating. "Knowing where you're from is wisdom. I will just be proud—like knowing what my grandfathers did. Because even though we were slaves, even though it was a sad situation, to me it is exciting because I know now. I've got a wealth of knowledge that can't ever be taken away from me."

This, I thought, was an excellent way of putting it. And I was excited to realize that even someone who had seen so much of Africa was still eager to personalize it. I was doubly excited when Chris's DNA tests revealed some very interesting things. His admixture test showed that he was 83 percent sub-Saharan African, 10 percent Native American, and 7 percent European. Like Oprah Winfrey's and Mae Jemison's, his Native American ancestry is quite high—and strongly suggests that the stories about Chris's maternal grandmother's having "Indian blood" are true. Even more interesting, at least to my mind, was the fact that we were able to trace Chris's genetic signatures back to Africa on both his mother's and his father's lines. This is not possible for a lot of black Americans because of the high degree of European admixture on many of our fathers' family lines. But with Chris we got very lucky.

His mitochondrial DNA testing gave us a wide range of results. We learned that he shared ancestry with the Bamileke people in western Cameroon, but it is unlikely that his original female ancestor was a member of this tribe. Only about 2 percent of the total number of Africans brought to this country as slaves came from what is now western Cameroon—and they weren't exported as slaves until quite late in the history of the slave trade, by which time the vast majority of slaves were being sent into the Deep South, not into Georgia where Chris's family ended up.

We also learned that Chris shares mitochondrial DNA with the Bassa people of Nigeria, the Ewondo of Cameroon, the Biaka and Mbenzele of the Central African Republic, the Chwabo of Mozambique, and others. John Thornton and Linda Heywood were convinced that this wide array of results—combined with our knowledge that the Tucker family is based in Georgia—indicates that Chris's original female African ancestor was most likely a genetic product of the great Bantu migration and that regardless of which tribe she belonged to, she was probably taken into slavery in the area around modern-day Angola in Central Africa. Even though none of Chris's exact matches were with tribes from Angola, Thornton and Heywood felt that the fact that so many enslaved people from the area were shipped to Virginia and South Carolina (and then on to Georgia) makes the area the most likely source of Chris's ancestor. These results, Thornton and Heywood told me, were very consistent with the history of both the slave trade and the Bantu migration. Though they did not allow us to pinpoint the ethnic group of Chris's original enslaved ancestors, they do indicate that he shares ancestry with a very wide range of modern-day Africans on his mother's side.

Fortunately, reconstructing the journey of Chris's first African ancestor on his father's side was much easier. Indeed, of all the people involved in this project, Chris's patrilineal line provided the greatest overlap between history and genetics. His Y-DNA testing revealed that he shares genetic material with the Mbundu people in northern Angola. As Thornton and Heywood explained to me, this match made perfect sense historically, as many of the enslaved people from this area ended up in the same region of the United States as Chris's family.

This was exciting news to me. The Mbundu are a very interesting people. They were fiercely independent and are of great consequence to historians. In fact, they were led by a famous queen, Queen Nzinga, born sometime in the early seventeenth century. She organized a revolt against the Portuguese, who were trying to colonize Angola. Beginning in 1619 and almost continuously until 1657, Nzinga effectively held the Portuguese at bay, often personally leading her troops into battle and ultimately winning international renown for her military and diplomatic skills. She is, I believe, one of the most impressive rulers of her age, somebody about whom we should all know more.

Chris was fascinated to hear about Nzinga. He was also interested to learn, given the role of religion in his family, that the Mbundu people converted to Christianity very early, relative to other African tribes. Furthermore, according to our researchers, Chris's Y-chromosome test was unusual in that it was a very strong match with the Mbundu people in present-day Angola. I asked Chris if he would want to return to Africa in search of his genetic cousins.

Chris seemed thrilled when I asked him to accompany me back to Angola. He cleared his schedule, and we flew out within a matter of weeks.

It was one of the most interesting trips of my life. Located on the Atlantic coast of south-central Africa, Angola is one of the continent's truly fascinating countries. Conquered by the Portuguese in the late seventeenth century, after the demise of Queen Nzinga, Angola remained a colony until 1975. Then it was torn apart by twenty-seven years of civil war. Today the country is finally at peace; it's rebuilding, and it's eager to reconnect with the rest of world.

Chris is not the only African American to have roots here. The Trans-Atlantic Slave Trade Database suggests that one out of every four slaves who reached the United States came from the Congo Angola region. To begin to understand what they endured, we drove one hour south of Angola's capital, Luanda, to visit the country's National Slavery Museum, situated on the edge of the ocean that so many of our ancestors were forced to cross.

The museum's director, Aniceto do Amaral Gourgel, gave us a very moving tour, showing us shackles and other horrifying tools of the trade, describing in detail how many Africans died long before even being thrown onto the dreadful ships that would take them to the New World—dying in forced marches, of disease, or committing suicide rather than facing the ordeal.

One of the most chilling aspects of this museum to Chris was the fact that it was once a chapel, a reminder that slavery was once seen as being good for an African's soul. Gourgel showed us the door that the slaves entered—and the spot nearby where a priest would greet them. He then explained how they would kneel in front of a crucifix and be baptized before being led down to the ships in chains. The irony was appalling, and Chris and I stepped outside sickened.

Surveying the magnificent Atlantic, Chris wondered how a place that was so peaceful and calm today could have been a focus of the bloodiest industry and trade of its age, if not in all of human history. The magnitude and cruelty of the African slave trade never fails to shock me. I don't think that I could have survived the journey from the interior to here—the two- or three-month walking journey before you even got on this torture chamber they called a slave ship. Neither does Chris. We both agreed that our ancestors who showed up in the New World were some strong people.

To go further back in time, to the time Chris's Mbundu ancestor was first enslaved, we then traveled to Angola's National Historical Archive, where they keep shipping records concerning the slave trade. The records are very straightforward and extremely telling. Because slavery was a commercial venture, the Europeans wrote down everything that they cared about. I have studied similar records and found page after page of ship ledgers, detailing how many slaves were captured and sold, how much they cost, and everything else pertaining to their transport. It is shocking how impersonal it all is, but it makes you realize that we truly were chattel once. Slaves were not people in the eyes of the Europeans who bought and sold them. They were just property. And there was a lot of property moving through this place.

"Somewhere in there is my great-great-great-great-great-great-great-granddaddy," said Chris, quietly looking at the mountain of records. He's probably right.

I was especially interested in these archives, because the Portuguese sometimes recorded the names of the Africans who were taken into slavery and shipped to Brazil. This is highly unusual. In fact, I had never seen it before. Typically records from the slave trade do not list the individual slaves' names; instead, they will just say "nineteen slaves from the Gold Coast"—cold and simple. But here, in Angola, the Portuguese sometimes listed the actual names of the people they sold into slavery. This offered us a slim chance of finding something that might relate to Chris's family. I didn't expect anything, but I thought it was worth a try. And it was, to my mind, a very valuable learning experience, though we were unable to find anything related to Chris. We did learn, however, from the archive's director, Dr. Rosa Cruz e Silva, that African names on the records indicate the individuals who had not been baptized yet. So, on a ledger, names like Joaquin referred to baptized slaves, while names like Quiambo were African.

Dr. Silva also told us, based on what we knew of Chris's heritage, that she believed that his ancestors may have been taken into slavery during a war waged in the early 1700s between Portuguese forces who colonized the country and the African kingdom of Matamba. The kingdom of Matamba, according to Dr. Silva, resisted the Portuguese occupation for a long time but eventually lost and saw a large number of its population enslaved and shipped to America.

To visit the place where those events took place, Chris and I flew east to where the kingdom of Matamba once lay. For Chris's ancestor, walking in chains, the agonizing journey to the coast would have taken over a month. In the air, retracing his steps took us less than an hour. Then Chris and I drove another hour—deep into the bush—to visit one of the oldest villages in the area. We were met warmly by the village elder, a man named Vincente João Manuel. I asked him if his people knew anything about their ancestors who were sold into slavery. He shrugged and said sadly, "They were sent away. They couldn't come back. They were separated from their families."

I then explained to him that the man I'd brought with me, Chris Tucker, was perhaps one of the lost members of his people, that hundreds of years ago his descendant was taken to the New World. João Manuel beamed. "I'm happy to see a member of my family!" he said, exuberant. Chris looked every bit as happy as children from the village mobbed him.

We will never know for sure if this is where Chris's ancestor came from. But under the village's sacred tree, he felt a kind of homecoming he had never experienced before. "I just fell in love," he said. "There's wisdom in knowing where you're from, and I know now. This is the greatest thing that's ever happened to me."

Sitting with Chris, watching how warmly the Angolans welcomed him back, I have to confess that I was a little envious. Whereas Chris can trace his ancestry to Africa on both his mother's side and his father's side, my paternal and maternal lines go straight to Europe! (On other lines, however, such as my father's mother's father's side, I can trace my African ancestry.) It's a strange feeling—I call it "Roots" envy.

Of course, our ability to travel back into the past is still in its infancy.

As DNA databases grow and as genealogical research techniques develop, we'll be able to find, ever more exactly, the identity of our ancestors and the roots of our family trees. As we do this, we'll not only begin to heal the wounds of the Middle Passage, but we'll be able to stake our claim, ever more deeply, within the American tradition. In the meantime I was delighted to have made this journey with Chris, and I felt I understood better than ever how the shared values of our people are based so deeply in the soil of the South, and how they have been passed from one generation to the next, in spite of the hardships of segregation and discrimination.

How to Trace

Your Own Roots

If you have gotten this far into my book, you have probably figured out
something that it took me an awfully long time to learn: Genealogy is
hard work. It is intensely rewarding, and I would encourage everyone—black and white—to try it. But there is no quick and easy way to
build your family tree.

Of course, that doesn't mean you have to quit your job to do it. You
can spend as much or as little time on your genealogy as you want to—
you'll start learning things right away, so there is a reward to even the
tiniest bit of effort. And the more time you put into the work, the more
you'll get out of it. As my professional genealogy guru Jane Ailes says, the
deeper you go into researching each person on your tree, the more you'll
get to feel as if you know those people, the more interested you'll be in the
process, and the less your tree will seem like just a list of names.

Furthermore, while there is also no one right way to do your tree, in
my experience there is a step-by-step methodology you can follow that will
help streamline the work. My researchers and I employed this methodology, with some slight variations, for every subject in this book. I've tried to
set it down here, in brief, so that you can do this yourself.

First, you should begin by gathering basic information regarding who
your ancestors were, when they were born and died, and where they lived.
This will allow you to start mapping out the branches of your family tree.
Over time you'll learn details about these people's lives that will ultimately
make your work more interesting and fulfilling, but at the outset focus on

information and gather as much as possible. Write down everything you know about yourself and your family, then start interviewing your relatives. Meet with the oldest ones first, as they have the least time left and can give you the most information on past generations. Ask them everything—their birthdays, anniversaries, where they lived and worked, who their siblings were, their parents, their colleagues and friends. (You never know what you may glean from a call to your long-dead grandmother's old best friend.)

Bring a tape recorder and record the interviews, but also take good notes—write down everything that comes into your head, because you'll often think things during an interview that won't be captured on the tape, and you might want to ask questions about those things later. And plan to do at least one follow-up interview with everybody you talk to. (This is very important, as your grandfather's memory may change from the first interview to the second.) Also, when you conduct your interviews, ask your relatives if they have documents to support their memories—birth certificates, marriage licenses, diaries, newspaper clippings—anything, really. Take whatever they'll give you, and make copies.

As you're conducting your interviews, you should be sorting out the data you're collecting. I'd suggest organizing it all into charts that trace bloodlines and group people into family units. You can post index cards on a wall if you like, one with each family member's name on it, as well as their relevant dates and locations. Then you can make connections between individuals by using pieces of string or tape. I find that having a visual image of the family tree is a great organizational help—you understand the data better if you can see it in this familiar form.

At the same time, you need to start checking everything you've learned against the public record. Remember: Don't just take what your relatives say as gospel truth, no matter how sweet and trustworthy they may seem. Go find some records to back it up. I'd suggest you start with census records. If you know the name of one of your ancestors, you can search for him or her in the census, which will allow you to place that individual in a particular state, town, and county. From there you can begin to flesh out people's lives and relations by tapping into all possible record sources in that area. You can search marriage records, death records, cemetery records, Social Security applications, military records, immigration records, trial records, tax filings, voting records, land deeds, slave-trade records, wills and other estate records, newspaper obituaries, school records, funeral-home records and church records, as well as local genealogies, county histories, and private journals and letters.

Just writing all that makes *me* dizzy. But don't let it overwhelm you. Go slowly, generation by generation. Don't try to leap all the way back to the 1800s, or else you'll likely as not reach a dead end (or worse, waste your time researching somebody who isn't even related to you). If you go slowly, though, you'll build a solid tree and you'll find that the records are much easier to work with.

Where should you look for these records? Professional genealogists often start by using the website www.ancestry.com. They log on, search by name to get an overview of what records are available on a given individual, and then they go to the libraries, archives, and historical societies to see the original records. For a lot of research—including census research—my professional friends tell me that ancestry.com is hands-down the best place because of the power and convenience of its indexes and search tools. It offers sound matches for names and wildcard searches (and once you realize that the spelling of an individual or a family name can change dramatically over time, you'll understand that these kinds of searches are very important). As one genealogist told me, if you can't find someone at ancestry, either they somehow managed to skip every census or they never existed in the first place.

However, ancestry.com is by no means one-stop shopping for genealogists. It's full of errors and omissions, and you still have to go check what you learn there against the original records. It's just a good place to start, that's all. It is also not free. The site charges a subscription fee, and it isn't cheap. So if you are on a budget, I'd suggest that you start your document search instead with the Mormon Church. You don't have to go to Salt Lake City, though. The church has what are called Family History

Centers worldwide. You can go to any of these centers and order the microfilms you need on interlibrary loan, then keep them as long as you have a use for them. (They also have an excellent website, www.familysearch. org.) You should be warned, however, that the Family History Centers are not nearly as easy to use as ancestry.com. They may contain more records, but the records are organized state by state, county by county, private collection by private collection. There is no central indexing. It is the largest source of genealogical data in the world—there's nothing comparable— and it's constantly expanding, but you need to know what you want to find before you start looking around, or else you will waste an incredible amount of time. So before you go to one of these centers, figure out all the variant spellings of your ancestors' names and where they lived. Then, when you get to the center, you'll find the computerized catalog, which you generally search by place name. So you'll type in "Montgomery," and it will give you a whole list of places that have the word "Montgomery" in their jurisdiction—and then it will give you a list of all the types of records—court documents, land deeds, census data, and so on—from that jurisdiction. Then you can request microfilm of each record, put it on a reader, and scan through it for your ancestor's name. There is no indexing by name (although some records may themselves contain indexes).

Of course, just like ancestry.com, the Family History Centers are by no means exhaustive. You will also find important documents in the Freedmen's Bureau records (part of the National Archives and available online at www.archives.gov or www.freedmensbureau.com), as well as at many historical societies, public and university libraries, and newspaper archives around the country and online. The specific demands of your own search will guide you.

There are a number of excellent reference books that can also help. According to one of my genealogist gurus, Jane Ailes, the best sources for learning the techniques of professional genealogists are the following:

Henry Campbell Black. *Black's Law Dictionary.* 1st edition 1891 and 2nd edition 1910. (CD-ROM edition of the two editions of the dictionary, Archive CD Books USA, ISBN 1-933828-08-0.)

Joan F. Curran, Madilyn C. Crane, and John H. Wray. *Numbering Your Geneal-ogy: Basic Systems, Complex Families, and International Kin*. Arlington, VA: National Genealogical Society, 2000.

William Dollarhide. *The Census Book: A Genealogist's Guide to Federal Census Facts, Schedules and Indexes*. North Salt Lake, UT: Heritage Quest, 2000.

Colleen Fitzpatrick and Andrew Yeiser. *DNA & Genealogy*. Fountain Valley, CA: Rice Book Press, 2005.

Val. D. Greenwood. *The Researcher's Guide to American Genealogy*. Baltimore, MD: Genealogical Publishing, 3rd edition, 2000.

E. Wade Hone. *Land & Property Research in the United States*. Salt Lake City, UT: Ancestry, 1997.

Elizabeth S. Mills. *Evidence! Citation & Analysis for the Family Historian*. Balti-more, MD: Genealogical Publishing, 1997.

Elizabeth S. Mills, ed. *Professional Genealogy: A Manual for Researchers, Writ-ers, Editors, Lecturers, and Librarians*. Baltimore, MD: Genealogical Pub-lishing, 2001.

James C. Neagles. *U.S. Military Records: A Guide to Federal and State Sources, Colonial America to the Present*. Orem, UT: Ancestry Publishing, an imprint of MyFamily.com, 1994.

Christine Rose. *Genealogical Proof Standard: Building a Solid Case*. San Jose, CA: CR Publications, 2005.

Loretto D. Szucs and Sandra H. Luebking, editors. *The Source: A Guidebook to American Genealogy*. Provo, UT: Ancestry Publishing, an imprint of MyFam-ily.com, 3rd edition, 2006.

William Thorndale and William Dollarhide. *Map Guide to the U.S. Federal Cen-suses, 1790–1920*. Baltimore, MD: Genealogical Publishing, 1987.

You can also find articles in the journal of the National Genealogi-cal Society—the *National Genealogical Society Quarterly*, which covers a myriad of topics related to genealogical research, including African Amer-ican research. These articles are juried and go through an editorial pro-cess, so they are of good quality. The journal is usually available at any library that has a section on genealogy.

African Americans, of course, face unique problems in researching their family trees. The fact that the vast majority of our ancestors were slaves until 1865 means that no census prior to 1870 is going to contain their names. So black Americans who are trying to trace their families back past 1870 must try to find the name of their last enslaved ancestor's owner prior to emancipation. These can be found in the slave schedules that were part of the census in 1850 and 1840 and in the estate records of the Old South. But that search will often prove fruitless, and even under the best circumstances you will have great difficulty tracing your family into the slave period. There are many excellent books and articles on this subject. As a start I'd recommend the following few:

Curtis G. Brasfield. "Tracing Slave Ancestors: Batchelor, Bradley, Branch, and Wright of Desha County, Arkansas," *National Genealogical Society Quarterly*, vol. 92, no. 1 (March 2004), pp. 6–30.

James F. Brooks. *Confounding the Color Line: The Indian-Black Experience in North America*. Lincoln and London: University of Nebraska Press, 2002.

Tony Burroughs. *Black Roots*. New York: Fireside Books, 2001.

Virginia E. DeMarce. "Verry Slitly Mixt": Tri-Racial Isolate Families of the Upper South—A Genealogical Study," *National Genealogical Society Quarterly*, vol. 80, no. 1 (March 1992), pp. 5–35.

———. "Looking at Legends—Lumbee and Melungeon: Applied Genealogy and the Origins of Tri-racial Isolate Settlements," *National Genealogical Society Quarterly*, vol. 81, no. 1 (March 1993), pp. 24–45.

———. "Review Essay: *The Melungeons*," *National Genealogical Society Quarterly*, vol. 84, no. 2 (June 1996), pp. 135–49.

Herbert G. Gutman. *The Black Family in Slavery & Freedom, 1750–1925*. New York: Pantheon Books, 1976.

Jefferson-Hemings: A Special Issue of the National Genealogical Society Quarterly. *National Genealogical Society Quarterly*, vol. 89, no. 3 (September 2001).

Elizabeth Shown Mills. "Ethnicity and the Southern Genealogist: Myths and Misconceptions, Resources and Opportunities," chapter 5, in Robert M. Taylor Jr. and Ralph J. Crandall, ed. *Generations and Change: Genealogical Perspectives in Social History*. Macon, Georgia: Mercer University Press, 1986, pp. 89–108.

Gary B. Mills. "Tracing Free People of Color in the Antebellum South: Methods, Sources, and Perspectives," *National Genealogical Society Quarterly*, vol. 78, no. 4 (December 1990), pp. 262–78.

————. "Can Researchers 'Prove' the 'Unprovable'? A Selective Bibliography of Efforts to Genealogically Document Children of Master-Slave Relationships," *National Genealogical Society Quarterly,* vol. 89, no. 3 (September 2001), pp. 234–37.

Christopher A. Nordmann. "Jumping Over the Broomstick: Resources for Documenting Slave 'Marriages,' " *National Genealogical Society Quarterly,* vol. 91, no. 3, pp. 196–216.

David E. Paterson. "Georgia's Slave Population in Legal Records: Where and How to Look, an Introduction to Courthouse Resources," digital image (www.rootsweb.com/~gapike/slave.htm).

Edward T. Price. "A Geographic Analysis of White-Negro-Indian Racial Mixtures in Eastern United States," *Annals of the Association of American Geographers,* vol. 43, no. 2, pp. 138–55.

Dee Parmer Woodtor. *Finding a Place Called Home.* New York: Random House, 1999.

Additionally, I would recommend consulting the following websites:

Information Regarding the Table of Slaves, Age 100 and Up. Tom Blake, compiler.
http://freepages.genealogy.rootsweb.ancestry.com/~ajac/slave100up.htm

Large Slaveholders of 1860 and African-American Surname Matches from 1870. Tom Blake, compiler.
http://freepages.genealogy.rootsweb.ancestry.com/~ajac/

Mississippi Department of Archives and History.
http://www.mdah.ms.gov/new/

North American Slave Narratives. University of North Carolina Library, Documenting the American South.
http://docsouth.unc.edu/neh/

Records of the Bureau of Refugees, Freedmen, and Abandoned Lands. Record Group 105.
www.archives.gov/research/guide-fed-records/groups/105.html

Researching Southern Claims Commission Records. St. Louis County Library.
http://www.slcl.org/content/researching-southern-claims-commission-records-resources

Slave Narratives from the Federal Writers' Project, 1936–1938. Library of Congress, American Memory.
http://memory.loc.gov/ammem/snhtml/snhome.html

In the end, African Americans who've taken their family tree back as far as traditional genealogical research will allow have to decide if they want to undergo DNA testing to try to take it back even further. Understanding how this is done begins with a little biology. As you may remember from school, the only elements of our entire genome that we inherit unchanged from our parents are our mitochondrial DNA (or mtDNA) and—if we are male—our patrilineal DNA (or Y-DNA). Because these strands of DNA are not "recombined" as they pass from parent to child, a man's Y-DNA is the same as his father's, which is the same as *his* father's, and so on, back up the direct paternal line of his family tree, much like a family name. The same goes for mtDNA on the direct maternal side of all our family trees.

If you are black, imagine your two family lines extending back through the generations: They will more than likely lead to African ancestors who survived the horrors of the Middle Passage and then back still further, to their ancestors who lived and died in Africa before the slave trade ravaged their communities and stole their descendants.

Thinking about those African ancestors, you should know that not all of their descendants would have been enslaved. Many would have remained in Africa and passed on their Y-DNA and mtDNA to their children and grandchildren and so on, right up to the present day. These people are, effectively, very distant cousins of ours. They have not been cut off from their ancestral origins as we were, and they have the potential to tell us the tribe and region of Africa from where our shared ancestors originated. To access this vital information, all we have to do is *find* them.

This is where breakthroughs in DNA analysis come in. Today it's possible for any of us to take either a patrilineal DNA or a mitochondrial DNA test, which more often than not involves swabbing the inside of our cheek and sending those cells to a laboratory for analysis. Having extracted sections of our DNA from these cells, geneticists can then compare our genetic signature with samples taken from people living in Africa today. If they find a match, they've located one of our very distant cousins and, by extension, a long-lost fragment of our family history.

These tests are not yet very specific. The process is still in its infancy, the data is not by any means complete. They will not yield the names of any of the individuals on our distant family trees, just the general geographic areas in which our ancestors lived. Yet tens of thousands of African Americans are now paying to receive kits through the mail that promise to tell them whence their more remote ancestors hailed. Learning these results can be enormously satisfying; I know it has been for me.

There are quite a large number of companies that will do this. FamilyTreeDNA has joined the Inkwell Foundation to form a new company, AfricanDNA.com, which is the first company to offer one-stop shopping so that you can have your family tree traced (prices start at $399) and your DNA analyzed (their twenty-five marker tests for Y-DNA and their high-resolution mtDNA test are both $189). AfricanAncestry.com offers their single-marker tests for $349, and RootsforReal.com charges $300.

If you can afford it, I recommend that you do the tests twice, with two different companies, so that you can better evaluate the results. The tests are simple—usually just a swab of your cheek is all they want—and the whole thing can be done through the mail. They are not cheap, though, and the results can be inconclusive or very complicated to assess. In the end you will learn the names of one or more ethnic groups that share genetic markers with you. It will then be up to you to learn as much as you care to about those groups—which will almost invariably involve studying the history of Africa and of the transatlantic slave trade.

There are innumerable excellent books on this subject. I'd recommend the following as a start:

John W. Blassingame. *The Slave Community.* New York: Oxford University Press, 1972.

Sylviane A. Diouf, ed. *Fighting the Slave Trade: West African Strategies.* Athens: Ohio University Press, 2003.

David Eltis. *The Rise of African Slavery in the Americas.* New York: Cambridge University Press, 1999.

Michael Angelo Gomez. *Exchanging Our Country Marks: The Transformation of African Identities in the Colonial and Antebellum South.* Chapel Hill: University of North Carolina Press, 1998.

Walter Hawthorne. *Planting Rice and Harvesting Slaves: Transformations Along the Guinea-Bissau Coast, 1400–1900.* Portsmouth, NH: Heinemann, 2003.

Linda Heywood, ed. *Central Africans and Cultural Transformations in the American Diaspora.* New York: Cambridge University Press, 2000.

———— and John Thornton. *Central Africans, Atlantic Creoles, and the Foundation of the Americas, 1585–1660.* New York: Cambridge University Press, 2007.

Adam Jones. *From Slaves to Palm Kernels: A History of the Galinhas Country (West Africa) 1730–1890.* Wiesbaden, Germany: F. Steiner, 1983.

James A. McMillan. *The Final Victims: Foreign Slave Trade to North America, 1783–1810.* Columbia: University of South Carolina Press, 2004.

Joseph Miller. *Way of Death: Merchant Capitalism and the Atlantic Slave Trade, 1730–1830.* Madison: University of Wisconsin Press, 1988.

Walter Rodney. *History of the Upper Guinea Coast, 1545–1800.* Oxford: Clarendon Press, 1970. (Reprint, New York: Monthly Review Press, 1980.)

Robert B. Shaw. *A Legal History of Slavery in the United States.* Potsdam, NY: Northern Press, 1991.

John Thornton. *Africa and Africans in the Making of the Atlantic World, 1400–1800.* New York: Cambridge University Press, 1998.

————. *Warfare in Atlantic Africa, 1500–1800.* London: Routledge, 1998.

I don't know if this brief overview has made you any more confident about researching your own family tree. I hope it has, though, because in my experience there are few things more rewarding than knowing where you came from.

Acknowledgments

T his project would not have been possible without the absolutely top-notch genealogists and DNA scientists who guided its research and grounded its claims. I will be forever in their debt. Of special note are the genealogists Jane Ailes, Johni Cerny, Megan Smolenyak, and Jan Hillegas, who spent years combing over state and federal records, digging around in libraries and attics and churches all over the country, and even visiting a few old graveyards. Their efforts yielded invaluable results. I would also like to especially thank the brilliant researcher and editor Sabin Streeter, who searched through hundreds of hours of interviews and a mountain of scientific data to help identify the narrative threads of the stories found in this book, the historians Ira Berlin, Evelyn Brooks Higginbotham, Hollis Robbins, and Susan O'Donovan, and the scientists Dr. Fatimah Jackson at the University of Maryland, Dr. Peter Forster at the University of Cambridge, Dr. Rick Kittles at the University of Chicago, and Dr. Mark Shriver at Pennsylvania State University. These people did our DNA testing and, no less significantly, explained the results to me in simple English. Thanks as well to Julian Pavia for shepherding the manuscript through the editing process, to Rick Horgan for all of his support, and to my agents Tina Bennett, Lynn Nesbit, and Bennett Ashley at Janklow & Nesbit, who believed in this project from the beginning. Sabin Streeter and Donald Yacovone carefully read through the manuscript for consistency and accuracy, and Joanne Kendall, as always, kept my life on track.

I would like to thank my partners on the two PBS documentary series—*African American Lives 1* and *2*—that were at the heart of this project: Peter Kunhardt, Dyllan McGee, Graham Judd, Leslie Asako Gladsjo, Jesse Sweet, Amilca Palmer, Julia Marchesi, Sandra McDaniel, Leslie Farrell, Jack Youngelson, Jill Cowan, Mary Farley, and Michael Maron.

My thanks to Ingrid Saunders Jones and Chuck Fruit at Coca-Cola for their enthusiastic and consistent support as the founding sponsor of the *African American Lives* series and *Finding Oprah's Roots;* Anne Sempowski Ward and Najoh Tita-Reid for their support of the first *African American Lives* series at Procter & Gamble; and Rod Gillum, Betsy Lazar, Dino Bernacchi, and Maria Rohrer for their support of *African American Lives 2* at General Motors.

And, finally, I would like to thank everyone at WNET/Channel 13 who made the *African American Lives* series a reality, including Steven Rattner, Bill Baker, Tammy Robinson, Neal Shapiro, William Grant, Stephen Segaller, Stephanie Carter, Donna Williams, Ron Thorpe, Joseph Pullen, Julie Schapiro, Barbara Bantivoglio, and Bruce McArthur.

Index

Adams, Charles, 260
Adams, John Quincy, 19, 239
Admixture tests, 37, 54, 77, 99, 125, 147, 176, 197, 224, 238, 305, 322, 341, 357, 358, 376, 378, 393
Aflao, 37–38
African American Lives 1 and *2* (PBS documentary series), 13, 41, 242, 308, 426
African slave trade, 6, 9, 15–22, 38, 98, 101, 151, 198, 238, 283, 284, 411
AfricanAncestry.com, 423
AfricanDNA.com, 423
Ailes, Jane, 415, 418, 425
Akan people, 257
Alabama Baptist Convention of 1893, 299
Alabama Baptist Normal and Theological School, 299
Alachua County, Florida, 232, 237
Amistad (slave ship), 19, 239, 240
Amite County, Mississippi, 332
Ancestry
    of Angelou, 31–39, 160, 253
    of Broyard, 390–394
    of Carson, 187–199, 407
    of Cheadle, 69, 100, 192, 348–359
    of Freeman, 52, 67–78, 167, 170, 252, 254, 407
    of Goldberg, 159–160, 234–240
    of Gomes, 104, 110, 113, 118–129
    of Henderson, 313–314, 354, 407
    of Jakes, 69, 270–286, 407
    of Jemison, 242, 250–258, 322, 407
    of Jones, 49–57, 75, 253
    of Joyner, 69, 92, 159–178, 191, 254
    of Joyner-Kersee, 330–342, 407
    of Lawrence-Lightfoot, 104, 124, 135–152, 354
    of Rice, 69, 292–307, 407
    of Rock, 354, 366–379
    of Tucker, 322, 400–414
    of Turner, 85, 91–102
    of Winfrey, 92, 211–224, 255, 409
Ancestry.com, 417, 418
Anderson, Albert, 68
Anderson, Evie, 65, 68, 71
Anderson, Lucinda Cain ("Cindy"), 68–71, 252
Anderson, Marian, 132
Andrews, South Carolina, 362, 368
Angelou, Maya, 23–40, 49, 211
    ancestry of, 31–39, 160, 253
    birth of, 24
    childhood of, 24–29
    DNA testing and, 37, 38
    I Know Why the Caged Bird Sings by, 23, 34
    mother, relationship with, 25–27
    segregation and, 28–29
    sexual abuse of, 24–25
Angola, 8, 9, 19, 56, 101, 176, 223, 257, 305, 306, 359, 394, 409–416
Appiah, Kwame Anthony, 380
Archives.gov, 418
Arkansas City, Arkansas, 289, 290, 293
Armstrong, Louis, 47
Ash, Green, 191–194
Ash, Indiana, 190, 192
Ash, James, 190–192
Ash, Millie, 190
Ash, Thomas, 190–192

Ashkenazi Jews, 127
Attala County, Mississippi, 72, 212

Back to Africa movement, 310
Bailey, Anselm, 121, 123
Bailey, Antoinette, 118
Bailey, Ben, 121, 122
Bailey, Ben, Sr., 123–125
Bailey, Isaac, 118–122, 143
Bailey, Lucy, 124, 125
Bailey, Mary, 331
Bailey, Marya, 118–120
Bailey, Rose, 121, 122
Bailey, Samuel, 121
Baiote people, 239
Balanta people, 38, 150, 151, 175, 323, 342
Baldwin, James, 80, 132
Balm in Gilead (Lawrence-Lightfoot), 130
Baltimore Afro-American, 154
Bamenda Grassfields, Cameroon, 55
Bamileke people, 101, 198, 222, 223, 305, 359, 409
Bantu people, 55, 56, 101, 198, 222, 223, 257, 306, 409–410
Barney, G. H., 333, 335
Basie, Count, 47
Bassa people, 198, 305, 409
Baxter, Addison, 34
Baxter, Ira, 34
Baxter, Jane, 34
Baxter, Thomas, 33–34, 36, 160
Behrendt, Stephen D., 17
Beloved (movie), 213–214
Bemba people, 56
Benin, 19, 358, 359, 378
Biaka people, 409
Bight of Biafra, 19, 78
Black Power era, 222
Blackstock, South Carolina, 162
Blight, David, 16
Blount, Lucius, 248–249, 255
Blum, John Morton, 236
Bonnet, Marie Pauline, 390–392
Boston, Massachusetts, 115–116, 181–182
Bovina, Mississippi, 51
Boykens, Sam, 279
Bradford, Fannie, 253
Brava, Cape Verde, 105, 126
Brazil, 21, 412
Bremerton, Washington, 46
Brice, Nelson, 164
Briggs, Frances, 167
Brokers, 187–188

Brooklyn, New York, 361, 363
Brooks, Walter Henderson, 301
Brotherhood of Sleeping Car Porters, The, 230
Brown, Abraham, 144
Brown, Dixon, Jr., 144–145
Brown, Dixon, Sr., 145–146
Brown, Eliza, 144
Brown, H. Rap, 246
Brown, James, 144
Brown, Lucy, 144
Brown, Susannah, 145, 146
Brown, Tina, 382
Brown, William Wells, 70
Brown v. Board of Education (1954), 134, 158, 226
Broyard, Alexandra Nelson, 383
Broyard, Anatole, 380–395
Broyard, Bliss, 380–396
    ancestry of, 390–394
    childhood of, 389
    DNA testing and, 322, 393, 394
    father of, 381–396
    One Drop by, 383
Broyard, Edna Miller, 380, 389–390, 393, 394
Broyard, Étienne, 390
Broyard, Henry Antoine, 390–392
Broyard, Lorraine, 386, 389
Broyard, Nat, 392, 393
Broyard, Paul, 380–382, 393
Broyard, Sandy, 385–387
Broyard, Shirley, 383, 384, 386
Broyard, Todd, 383
Bruce, Joe, 319
Bruce, Sarah, 319
Bryan, William, 315, 316
Bryant, Jemima, 405, 407
Bryant, Spencer, 404–407
Bryant, Theodore Arthur, Jr., 401–405
Bryant, Theodore Arthur, Sr., 402–406
Buckingham County, Virginia, 298
Budget, Hattie, 163–164
Bullock, Alex, Jr., 82–83
Bullock, Anna Mae (*see* Turner, Tina)
Bullock, Floyd Richard (father of Tina Turner), 81, 101
Bullock, Floyd Richard (half-brother of Tina Turner), 101
Bullock, Gil, 81
Bullock, Tom, 98–99
Bullocks, Charles, 210
Burgess, Elizabeth Betsy, 50

Burgess, Osborne, 50
Burgess, Susannah, 45–46, 50
Bushwick County, Virginia, 98
Butler, Benjamin F., 141

Cabinda enclave, 198, 306
Cain, Patrick Hub, 68, 69
Cain, Sylvia, 69, 71
Cameroon, 19, 55, 56, 101102, 128, 176, 198,
    222, 223, 257, 258, 283, 305, 359, 378,
    379, 409
Camp Nelson, Jessamine County, Kentucky,
    317
Cape Verde, 105–109, 125–127
Caribbean slave trade, 6, 17
Carlisle, Illinois, 34–35
Carmichael, Stokely, 246
Carpenter, Pat, 395
Carr, Alfred, 71–76, 170
Carr, Celia (Celie) Johnson, 71–77, 170
Carr, Elizabeth, 71, 72
Carr, James, 74
Carroll, Clennie, 345
Carroll County, Mississippi, 214
Carson, Benjamin Solomon, 179–198
    ancestry of, 187–199, 407
    birth of, 180
    childhood of, 181–182
    DNA testing and, 197–198, 322
    education of, 183–185
    mother, relationship with, 182–186
    racism and, 185–186
    as surgeon, 179, 185–186
Carson, Curtis, 183
Carson, Robert, 180
Carson, Sonya Copeland, 180–187, 189–190
Carver, George Washington, 46, 136, 154,
    156
Central African Republic, 102, 409
Cerny, Johni, 178
Chamberlain, Daniel, 372
Chapelle, Dave, 361
Charles, Ray, 47–48
Charles City County, Virginia, 140, 142–145,
    147
Charleston, Mississippi, 59, 65, 66
Cheadle, Bettye North, 353
Cheadle, Don, 344–360
    ancestry of, 69, 100, 192, 348–359
    birth of, 344
    childhood of, 344–346
    DNA testing and, 357–359
    racism and, 346–347

Cheadle, Donald, 346–347
Cheadle, Elizabeth, 352
Cheadle, Henderson Hence, 348, 351
Cheadle, James, 352
Cheadle, John, 352
Cheadle, Lee Thurman, 347
Cheadle, Mary Kemp, 348, 351
Cheadle, Thomas F., 352
Cheadle, William, 347–348
Cherokee Indians, 100, 250, 348
Chicago, Illinois, 42–43, 242, 245–246
Chicago Defender, 246
Chickasaw Indians, 100, 348–352, 357
Chicot County, Arkansas, 292, 294, 295
Chinese laborers, 255–256
Choctaw County, Mississippi, 216
Choctaw Indians, 100, 216, 348
Chokwe people, 56
Chwabo people, 409
Cinque, 19, 239
Civil-rights movement, 13, 25, 131–133,
    155–156, 160, 215–216, 228, 230, 246,
    264, 265, 301, 310–312, 326, 362, 406
Civil War, 8, 12, 16, 33, 34, 53, 67, 69, 72,
    93–95, 97, 98, 118, 120, 122, 140–142,
    144, 163, 165, 171, 173, 187, 194, 213,
    221, 232, 237, 250–255, 273, 279, 280,
    295, 298, 299, 304, 315, 317, 319, 332,
    338, 348, 349, 351, 354, 368, 375,
    391, 407
Clifford, J. R., 317
Cole, Nat King, 204
Collier, Caroline, 171
Collins, Ellen, 332
Columbia County, Arkansas, 28, 29
Congo Angola, 37, 77, 305, 322, 341, 358,
    378, 393, 411
Conner, Amanda, 339
Conner, Angelina Wortham, 339–340
Conner, Francis Lewis, 337–338
Conner, Gabriel, 336–339, 341
Conner, John, 338, 339
Conner, Lucy, 336
Conner, Mary, 337
Conner, Spencer, 339
Conner, Uriel, 337
Coosa County, Alabama, 302
Copeland, Alexander, 193
Copeland, John H., 190, 192–194
Copeland, John Martin, 187, 189–190
Copeland, Spencer, 194
Copeland, Tom, 189
Copeland, William, Jr., 192, 193

Copeland, William, Sr., 192–194
Cornell Medical School, 247
Cottman, Sarah J., 140, 144
Cottman, Tom, 144
Cotton gin, invention of, 192
Cotton Kingdom, 69, 98, 172, 296, 348
Cousin, Anatole, 393
Cousin, Rosa, 393
Covington, Tennessee, 339
Crawley, Leota, 294
Creek Indians, 100, 348
Crosby, John, 164
Cumberland, Maryland, 2–3
Cumberland Evening Times, 13
Cunningham, Chaney, 254–255
Cunningham, Joseph T., 254–255
Cunningham, Letitia, 254
Cunningham, William J., 254
Currie, Betty, 93, 97
Currie, Jesse, 93–96
Currie, Josephus Cecil ("Papa Joe"), 83–84,
    93
Currie, Logan, Jr., 93–97
Currie, Logan, Sr., 93, 97
Currie, Zelma Priscilla, 81, 93
Cutlip, Alonzo, 65–66

Davis, Charles T., 382
Davis, Jean Curtis, 382
Dawes Commission, 351
Dayton, Ohio, 308–310, 312, 313
Decatur, Alabama, 242, 247, 249
Decatur, Georgia, 397, 398
Decatur County, Georgia, 230
Declaration of Independence, 18, 191
Democratic Republic of Congo, 19, 101, 198,
    257, 305, 306
Detroit, Michigan, 180–183, 262
Dickerson, Charlie, 253, 254
Dickerson, Henry, 254
Dickerson, Susie Anna, 250, 253
Dickinson, Wiley, 254
Dickson, Cordelia, 51–53, 55
Dickson, Henry, 53
DNA testing, 10, 20–21, 42, 422–423
    Angelou and, 37, 38
    Broyard and, 322, 393, 394
    Carson and, 197–198, 322
    Cheadle and, 357–359
    Freeman and, 77–78
    Goldberg and, 238
    Gomes and, 125–128
    Henderson and, 322–323
    Jakes and, 283
    Jemison and, 255–258, 409

Jones and, 54–55
Joyner and, 175–176
Joyner-Kersee and, 341–342
Lawrence-Lightfoot and, 147, 150
Rice and, 288, 304–307
Rock and, 376–378
Tucker and, 409–410
Turner and, 99, 101–102
Winfrey and, 221–224, 409
Doster, Charles Reilly, 320
Doster, Charlie Mae, 320
Doster, Gay Estella, 309, 311
Douglass, Frederick, 6, 20, 111, 231
Downey, George, 315
Du Bois, W. E. B., 6
Dumas, Clara, 171–173, 178
Dumas, Frances Lincoln, 158
Dumas, Isaac, 167, 171
Dumas, Isaac Lafayette, 165–166
Dumas, Mary, 171, 173–174
Dumas, Obediah, 171–173
Dumas, Ralph, 171–173
Dumas, Tony, 171–176, 178
Dunaway, W. M., 96

East St. Louis, Illinois, 325–327
Ebony magazine, 287, 288, 292
Edo people, 198
Edward I, King of England, 53
Elam Baptist Church, Charles City County,
    Virginia, 144–145
Ellington, Duke, 47
Ellison, Ralph, 132
Eltis, David, 17–19, 175
Emancipation Proclamation, 16
Equatorial Guinea, 55
Esthers, Katherine, 210
Eutawville, South Carolina, 366
Ewondo people, 359, 409

Faceville, Georgia, 230–231
Family History Centers, 417–418
Familysearch.org, 418
FamilyTreeDNA, 423
Fang people, 55
Fayette County, Kentucky, 315, 318
Federal Writers' Project, 68, 252, 303
Fifth Virginia Regiment, 124
Finder, Henry, 382
Five Civilized Tribes, 100, 348–351
Flagg, Benjamin B., 92
Flagg, George, 92
Flagg, Georgianna, 83–85, 87, 91
Flagg Grove Elementary School, 92
Flat Rock, Georgia, 402–405

Flat Rock United Methodist Church, Georgia, 405
Florentino, Manolo, 17
Fogo, Cape Verde, 126
Fon people, 19
Ford, W. W., 295
Free blacks, 97, 119–122, 140, 142–147
Freedman, Rachel, 231
Freedman's Bank, 316
Freedmens bureau.com, 418
Freedmen's Bureau, 94, 418
Freeman, Hubert, 65, 68, 78
Freeman, Jesse, 65–66
Freeman, Morgan, 58–79
   ancestry of, 52, 67–78, 167, 170, 252, 254, 407
   birth of, 58
   childhood of, 58–59, 67
   DNA testing and, 77–78
   education of, 59–60
   father, relationship with, 65–68
   in military, 60
   mother, relationship with, 62–67
   origins of surname of, 67–68
   stage and screen career of, 58, 61–62
Freeman, Morgan Porterfield, 65–67
Freeman, Willie, 65–66
Fula people, 19, 38, 323
Fulani people, 128, 257, 284
Fulbe people, 39, 77, 257–258, 342
Futa Jallon, 38–39

Gaines, Almeta, 331
Gaines, Andrew, 331
Gaines, Fanny, 331
Gaines, Mary Ruth, 327–332
Gaines, Sam, 331
Gaines, Sylvester, 331
Gambia, 19, 39, 78, 150
Garvey, Marcus, 310
Gates, Edward Lawrence, Jr. "Pop," 1–3, 13
Gates, Jane, 4, 5, 341
Ghana, 19, 37, 38, 257
GI homes, 180–181
Gibson County, Tennessee, 337
Gill, Mary, 164
Glen, Kesiah, 294–295
Goldberg, Whoopi, 225–241
   ancestry of, 159–160, 234–240
   childhood of, 225–229
   DNA testing and, 238
   education of, 227
   parents of, 225–226, 229
   racism and, 226–227
Gomes, Christiano, 126–127

Gomes, Manuel Lobo, 107, 109, 125
Gomes, Orissa Josephine White, 104–111
Gomes, Peter J., 104–129, 143, 146, 281
   ancestry of, 104, 110, 113, 118–129
   birth of, 104
   childhood of, 109–113
   DNA testing and, 125–128
   education of, 111
   parents of, 105–111, 117, 123–125
   racism and, 112
   religion and, 112–114, 116–117
Gomes, Peter Lobo, 105
Gourgel, Aniceto do Amaral, 411
Great Migration, 42, 115, 135, 166, 201, 227, 262, 306, 326, 380, 401
Green, Ada, 247
Green, John, 247
Green, Major, 248
Greene County, Georgia, 193
Greenlee, Samuel, 71, 77
Griffin, Franklin, 162
Griffin, Julia, 162
Griffin, Meeks, 162–164
Griffin, Tom, 162–164
Guinea-Bissau, Republic of, 37, 38, 150, 175, 238, 323, 342
Gullah people, 222, 223
Gumwood Plantation, Bovina, Mississippi, 51, 53

Haley, Alex, 9, 41, 42
Hall, Edward, 168–171, 176
Hall, Isaac, 169
Hall, Jane, 168–171, 176–178
Hall, Janet Wilson, 167–169
Hall, John, 169–170
Hall, Robert, 168
Hampshire County, West Virginia, 16–17
Hampton, Lionel, 48
Hampton, Wade, 372
Haplotypes, 10
Hardy County, Virginia, 319–320
Harper, Amanda, 401
Harris, Emma, 225–226, 231
Harris, Flora ("Mimaw"), 400, 401
Harris, James, 231, 233
Harris, Latitia Burnett, 135–136, 140
Harris, Malakiah, 231
Harris, Martha, 143
Harris, Mary ("Little Ma"), 400, 401
Harris, Mitchell, 140–144
Harris, Morris, 143–144
Harris, Sandy Mitchell, 140–144, 147
Harris County, Georgia, 187–188, 193, 198
Harvard University, 127

Hattiesburg, Mississippi, 262
Hausa people, 102, 128, 257, 258, 283, 284
Hayes, Rutherford B., 372–373
Haywood County, Tennessee, 80–83, 92–93,
    97–98, 102
Heinegg, Paul, 73
Hemings, Sally, 168
Hemingway, James, 332
Henderson, Anna, 27–29, 38
Henderson, Elizabeth Morton, 313–315
Henderson, Elwood, 313
Henderson, James Edward, 309–313
Henderson, Kathleen, 308–324
    ancestry of, 313–314, 354, 407
    birth of, 309
    childhood of, 309
    DNA testing and, 322–323
    education of, 312–313
    parents of, 310–313
Henry County, Alabama, 354–355
Henry County, Georgia, 400, 401
Heywood, Linda, 19, 38–39, 55, 56, 77, 78,
    101, 128, 151, 176, 177, 198, 223, 224,
    238, 257–258, 283–284, 306, 323, 342,
    359, 378, 409–410
Higginbotham, Evelyn Brooks, 301
Hinds County, Mississippi, 212, 332

I Know Why the Caged Bird Sings (Ange-
    lou), 23, 34
Igbo people, 19, 78, 283–284
Indian Removal Act of 1830, 348
Indian Territory, 347–351
Inkwell Foundation, 423
Inman, Alberta, 247–249
Inman, Jones, 248–249
Inman, Molly Ray, 258
Itta Bena, Mississippi, 62
Ivory, Jewel, 335

Jackson, Dennis, 315–317
Jackson, Elizabeth, 315
Jackson, Julia Mason, 315–318
Jake, Lemon, 278–279
Jake, Thomas D., 274–278
Jakes, Ernest, 262–268, 271, 274, 275
Jakes, Jamar, 269
Jakes, Jermaine, 269
Jakes, Nancy Boykens, 279
Jakes, Odith Thelma Patton, 262–263,
    271–272
Jakes, Serita Ann Jamison, 269
Jakes, T. D., 260–286, 407
    ancestry of, 69, 270–286, 407
    birth of, 262, 263

childhood of, 262–268
    DNA testing and, 283
    parents of, 262–267, 270
    as preacher, 260, 268–270
    racism and, 262, 264
    Woman, Thou Art Loosed by, 270
Jalonke people, 39
Jefferson, Thomas, 121, 168, 197, 340
Jefferson, Zenia, 279
Jemison, Ada, 242, 247–249, 253–254
Jemison, Adam, 250–253
Jemison, Annie, 250, 251
Jemison, Charles, 242
Jemison, Charlie, 242–245, 249, 255
Jemison, Dorothy Mae Green, 242–249, 256,
    310
Jemison, Edward Primus, 250
Jemison, Lewis, 250
Jemison, Mae, 242–259
    ancestry of, 242, 250–258, 322, 407
    as astronaut, 242, 247
    birth of, 242
    childhood of, 242–247
    DNA testing and, 255–258, 409
    education of, 244–248
    parents of, 242–245, 256, 310
    racism and, 245–246, 247
Jemison, Perry Sid, 252
Jemison, Robert, Sr., 250
Jemison, Shadrack, 250
Jemison, Shadrack Mims, 251
Jenkins, William, 294
Jessamine County, Kentucky, 317
Jet magazine, 287, 292
Jews, in Portugal, 127
Jim Crow era, 13, 28, 29, 53, 65, 81, 82, 155,
    202, 210, 214, 262, 271, 285, 392, 401
Johnson, Abner, 297
Johnson, Alex, 231
Johnson, Andrew, 72, 73
Johnson, Bailey, Jr., 24
Johnson, Bailey, Sr., 24
Johnson, Caryn Elaine (*see* Goldberg,
    Whoopi)
Johnson, Clyde, 225, 226, 230
Johnson, Emaline Lankford, 32
Johnson, Eunice Walker, 287–289, 298, 300
Johnson, James, 294
Johnson, John, 231
Johnson, John Harold, 289–294
Johnson, Leroy, 292, 294
Johnson, Marguerite (*see* Angelou, Maya)
Johnson, Matilda, 295
Johnson, Nelson, 294–295, 297
Johnson, Robert, Sr., 160

Johnson, Robert James, Jr., 225, 229–230
Johnson, Robert Sr., 229–230
Johnson, Simon, 32
Johnson, Steven, 295
Johnson, Vivian Baxter, 24–26
Johnson, William, 32
Johnson Publishing Company, 287
Jones, Caesar James, 49–50, 54–55
Jones, LeRoi, 246
Jones, Quincy, 41–57, 149, 305
    ancestry of, 49–57, 75, 253
    birth of, 42
    childhood of, 42–48
    DNA testing and, 54–55, 322
    mother, relationship with, 43–48
    music career of, 47–49
    segregation and, 46
Jones, Quincy Delight, Sr., 42–44, 46–48
Jones, Sarah Wells, 42–45
Jones Boys, 42
Joyner, Al, 330
Joyner, Alfred Lee, 327, 335
Joyner, Benjamin Franklin, 339
Joyner, Benjamin John Henry, 339
Joyner, Evelyn, 325–326, 335–336
Joyner, Hercules L., 158
Joyner, Oscar Albert, 159–162, 165
Joyner, Ruth Griffin, 162, 165
Joyner, Tom, 64, 153–178
    ancestry of, 69, 92, 159–178, 191, 254
    birth of, 153
    childhood of, 155–158
    DNA testing and, 175–176, 322
    parents of, 154–158
    radio and, 153, 156–157
Joyner-Kersee, Jackie, 325–343
    ancestry of, 330–342, 407
    as athlete, 325, 328–330
    birth of, 325
    childhood of, 327–329
    DNA testing and, 341–342
    education of, 329
    parents of, 327–331

Kansas City, Missouri, 344, 346
Kanuri people, 150, 151
Karamoko Alpha, 38
Kennedy, Jacqueline, 325
Kenoly, Anthony, 357
Kenoly, Mary Mathilda, 353–356
Kenoly, Melvin, 355
Kenoly, Myers, 353–357
Kenoly, Rachel, 353
Kenoly, Sarah, 357
Kenya, 101, 150, 198, 247, 257, 306

Keys, Janet, 166–169
Kikuyu people, 257
Kimbro, Lucy, 97–99
Kimbrough, Lucy, 97
Kimbrough, William, 97
King, Coretta Scott, 271
King, Martin Luther, Jr., 13, 133, 156, 228, 246, 301, 310, 362
Koronko people, 19
Kosciusko, Mississippi, 201, 202, 209
Koto people, 257, 258
Kpelle people, 222–224
Kru people, 238, 239, 342
Ku Klux Klan, 235, 362, 401

L3d, 150
Lanier, James Balance, 51–54
Lanier, Mary Bell, 51–52
Lankford, Stephen, 33
Lawrence, Charles, 131, 134
Lawrence, Charles Radford, Jr., 135, 138
Lawrence, Charles Radford, Sr., 135, 138
Lawrence, Margaret Cornelia Morgan, 135, 146
Lawrence-Lightfoot, Sara, 130–152, 305
    ancestry of, 104, 124, 135–152, 354
    Balm in Gilead by, 130
    birth of, 131
    childhood of, 131–133
    DNA testing and, 147, 150
    parents of, 131–140, 150, 152
Lee, Earlist, 201, 208, 212
Lee, Ed, 37
Lee, Elizabeth, 212
Lee, Grace, 212
Lee, Harold, 212–213
Lee, Hattie Mae Presley, 201–203, 205, 208–210
Lee, John, 212
Lee, Mary, 35–39
Lee, S. E., 212–213
Lee County, Georgia, 321, 323
Lewis, John, 163–164
Lexington Observer and Reporter, 319
Liberator magazine, 246
Liberia, 19, 38, 39, 77, 177, 222–224, 238, 239, 305, 322, 342, 358, 378
Liberty, Mississippi, 332
Library of Congress, 252
Limba people, 176
Lithonia, Georgia, 397, 400
Logan County, Kentucky, 315
Loko people, 176, 342
Long, Huey, 39
Louis, Joe, 42

Louisiana Native Guard, 391
Lozi people, 56
Luba people, 305, 306
Lucedale, Mississippi, 275
Lunda Empire, 56, 101, 257, 306
Lyerson (Larson), Malinda, 294

Macklin, Nathaniel, 97–98
Madison County, Tennessee, 83, 93, 96
Mafa people, 257
Makeba, Miriam, 245
Makua people, 197–198
Malcolm X, 110, 310, 311, 362
Mali, 77
Mallet, Luther, 216, 217
Mandela, Nelson, 377
Mandingo people, 19
Mandinka people, 38, 39, 150, 151, 257, 258,
     323, 342
Manuel, Vincente Joao, 413
Marion, Alabama, 271, 273
Marshall, Paule, 284
Martin, Moses, 321
Mary Holmes Missionary School, Clay Coun-
     ty, Mississippi, 63, 64
Masa people, 359
Mason, Caroline, 317, 318, 320
Mason, George, 317, 318, 320
Mason, Isaiah, 316–318
Matamba, kingdom of, 413
Mbenzele people, 102, 409
Mbundu people, 410–412
McAlpine, Augustus, 302–304
McAlpine, Emily, 302, 303
McAlpine, Ethel, 298
McAlpine, Park, 302
McAlpine, Robert, 302
McAlpine, Tom, 304
McAlpine, William, 298–304
McClam, Alex, 375
McClam, Pearl, 368
McClam, Solomon, 375
McCool, Mississippi, 216
McKenzie, John, 253
Meharry Medical College, Nashville, Ten-
     nessee, 160–161
Memphis, Tennessee, 58
Mende people, 19, 20, 38, 39, 176, 198, 238,
     239, 257, 258, 305, 323, 342
Middle Passage (see African slave trade)
Miller, Ms., 203–204
Milwaukee, Wisconsin, 201–204, 306
Minerva ("Mother Kitty"), 52–53
Mongolia, 6

Montgomery, West Virginia, 269
Montgomery Advertiser, 156
Montgomery Bus Boycott, 155, 291
Montgomery County School Board, 218
Montrose, Mississippi, 277
Moonves, Alan, 217
Morgan, Sandy Alonzo, 146
Morgan County, Georgia, 407
Morris, Emmaline, 238
Morton, Hummons Allen, 315
Moton, Robert Russa, 155
Moultrie, Eliza, 368
Mozambique, 19, 55, 197, 306, 409
Muhammad Speaks, 246

NAACP (National Association for the
     Advancement of Colored People),
     13, 210
Nashville, Tennessee, 201, 204
Nation of Islam, 246
National Archives, 140, 418
National Baptist Convention, 301, 302
National Genealogical Society, 419
National Historical Archive, Angola, 412
National Slavery Museum, Angola, 411
Native Americans, 20, 21, 54, 69, 77, 84–85,
     99–101, 147–148, 192, 224, 250, 255,
     256, 322, 344, 348–352, 376, 409
New, Miss, 205
New Orleans, Louisiana, 390–392
New York Amsterdam News, 155
New York Times, 380, 394
Newmarket Heights, Battle of, 141
Newton County, Georgia, 405
Niger, 77, 78, 101
Niger River, 77
Nigeria, 19, 21, 37, 78, 150, 198, 257,
     282–285, 305, 322, 341, 358, 359,
     378, 409
Noland, Judge Pearce, 51–53
North, Basil Leon, 353, 354
North, Edmund M., 353
North, Horace, 353, 354
North, Rachel Kenoly, 353, 354
Nutbush, Tennessee, 81
Nzinga, Queen, 410, 411

O'Malley, Greg, 17
One Drop (Broyard), 383

Palatka, Florida, 231
Papel people, 238–239
Parks, Rosa, 155–156
Patton, Ann Chatman, 273

Patton, Leander, 273–274
Patton, Richard David, 273–274
Patton, Susie Mae Williams, 272–274
Peace Corps, 247
Pentecostalism, 268, 269
Perry County, Alabama, 273
Pilgrims, 110
Pittsburgh Courier, 154
Plant City, Florida, 161, 165
Plessy, Homer, 392
Plessy v. Ferguson (1896), 301, 392
Plymouth, Massachusetts, 104–110, 112–113
Poplar Creek, Mississippi, 214, 220
Portuguese Inquisition, 127
Potter's House, Dallas, Texas, 270
Powell, Colin, 58, 66
Presbyterian Church, 64, 166–167
Presley, Nelson Alexander, 210
Pretlow, Ann Bailey, 120
Pretlow, D. L., 122
Pretlow, Joshua, 120
Pretlow, Thomas, 120
Pryor, Richard, 361
Pullam, Seda Ruth, 320
Pullman, Jack, 317
Pullman porters, 154, 159–160, 230
Pygmies, 102

Quakers, 122–123
Quilts, 30–31

Racism, 13, 42, 65, 86, 112, 136, 155, 160,
      165, 179, 183, 185, 202, 204, 214–215,
      226–227, 262, 264, 289–291, 300, 312,
      346–347, 363, 371, 392, 395, 399
Rainey, Andrew, 332
Rainey, Carter, 335
Rainey, Drit, 332–335
Rainey, Estella, 331
Rainey, Lena Hemingway, 331–332
Ralls, John, 353
Randolph, A. Philip, 230
Rawls, Horace, 353
Rawls, John, 353, 354, 357
Ray, Mollie, 249
Reconstruction, 12, 92, 219, 232–234,
      369–370, 372–373
Redman, Jane, 73
Redman, John, 73, 124
Redman family, 5
Revere, Lenora Greenlee, 63, 71
Revere, Mayme Edna, 62–67
Revolutionary War, 123, 124, 145, 146
Rice, Linda Johnson, 287–307

adoption of, 288, 289
ancestry of, 69, 292–307, 407
birth of, 289
DNA testing and, 288, 304–307
parents of, 287–293, 307
Richardson, David, 17
Richie, Lionel, 154
Richmond, Virginia, 141
Rinaldi, Matthew, 216
Robeson, Paul, 132
Robinson, Flora, 401
Robinson, Jackie, 362, 366
Robinson, Maggie, 332
Rock, Allen, 366–368
Rock, Chris, 148, 361–379
      ancestry of, 354, 366–379
      birth of, 361
      childhood of, 362–366
      as comedian, 361, 366
      DNA testing and, 376–378
      education of, 362–365
      parents of, 361–362
      racism and, 363
Rock, John, 376
Rock, Josiah, 376
Rock, Julius, 361–363, 366
Rock, Mary Vance, 366, 367
Rock, Rosalie Tingman, 361
Rockdale, Georgia, 402
Ronga people, 306
Roots (Haley), 41, 125, 379
RootsforReal.com, 423
Rosenwald, Julius, 210
Ruleville, Mississippi, 331
Russell, Miss Sarah, 260, 272, 276
Rustin, Bayard, 132

St. Louis, Missouri, 24, 25, 87, 88
Savin, John, 35–37
Savin, Marguerite, 34–35
Scott, Alex, 336
Scott, Lee Anna, 336
Second U.S. Colored Cavalry, 140
Segregation, 28–29, 42, 46, 60, 86, 211, 264,
      291, 309, 312, 313, 326
Selma Seminary, 298
Selma University, 298, 299
Seminole Indians, 100, 348
Senegal, 19, 37, 38, 77, 78, 128, 150, 223,
      257, 305, 322, 342, 358, 378
Senegambia, 39
Sephardic Jews, 127
Sharecropping system, 86, 95, 209, 214, 253,
      295, 403

Sherman, Estella, 230–231
Sherman, William Tecumseh, 232
Shoemaker, Charles, 407–408
Shoemaker, Mary Ann, 407
Shoemaker, Rebecca, 407–408
Shoemaker, Richard, 407–408
Shriver, Mark, 20
Sierra Leone, 37–39, 176, 177, 198, 238, 239,
    257, 323, 342
Silva, Rosa Cruz e, 412
Sky View Acres, New York, 131–132
Slave auctions, 17
Slave marriages, 33, 97, 172, 315–317, 391
Slave narratives, 68–70, 119, 252–253, 303
Slave revolts, 239, 284, 390, 391
Slave schedules, 93, 97, 168, 187, 212, 213,
    218, 273, 318, 355, 375, 420
Slavery, 5–7, 12, 15–21 (*see also* Ancestry)
Smiley, Lorena, 277
Smiley, Willie, Jr., 278
Smiley, Willie, Sr., 278
Smith, Emily, 188, 198
Smith, Green, 188
Smith, Lucy, 187–189
Smith, Mary Elizabeth, 146
Smith County, Tennessee, 353
Smithville, Georgia, 320
Songhai people, 77
Soundex code, 254
South Carolina constitution of 1868, 370
South Charleston, West Virginia, 262, 263
Southampton County, Virginia, 118, 120, 122
Southern Homestead Act of 1866, 233
Southport, Connecticut, 385
Stamps, Arkansas, 28–29
Stanback, Nettie Lavinia, 166–168
Stanback, Zacharia, 167
Stanford University, 247, 248
Stanley, Coleman, 187–188
Stanley, John D., 188–189
Stanley, Ruby, 187–190
Staple Singers, 216
Staples, Ella, 216
Stevenson, John "Monk", 163
Stockton, California, 25
Stockton Black Women for Humanity, 25
Stowe, Harriet Beecher, 7
Stuart, Sally, 144
Stuart, William, 144
Sukuma people, 55
Sunnyside Plantation, Chicot County, Arkan-
    sas, 295, 296
Sunnyside Plantation, Talladega, Alabama,
    251
Supreme Court of the United States, 301,
    392

Surry County, Virginia, 118, 119, 121
Susu people, 19, 39

Talbot County, Georgia, 193, 194
Talladega, Alabama, 249–254, 303, 304
Talladega College, 299
Tanzania, 55
Tarwick, George, 355
Tarwick, Hester, 355
Taylor, Emanuel, 29
Telefair, Emma, 368
Temne people, 176, 342
Temple of Faith Pentecostal Church, Mont-
    gomery, West Virginia, 269
Tenant farming, 96, 295, 332, 373, 374
Tennessee State University, 207
Terrell, Mary Church, 6
Thomas, Ollie Mae, 327–329, 335–336, 339
Thompkins, Louisa M., 353
Thornton, John, 19, 38–39, 55, 56, 77, 78,
    101, 128, 151, 176, 177, 197–198, 223,
    224, 239, 257–258, 283–284, 306, 323,
    342, 359, 378, 409–410
Thredkil, Reginald, 175
Tikar people, 55, 128, 359
Timbuktu, 77, 310
Tingman, James, 368
Tingman, Julius Caesar, 368–374
Tingman, Wesley, 368
Tipton County, Tennessee, 339–340
Tom Joyner Morning Show, The, 153
Tonga people, 55
Toussaint-Louverture, 390
Trail of Tears, 69, 100, 192, 224, 348, 350
Trans-Atlantic Slave Trade Database, 17, 39,
    55, 78, 175, 177, 411
Truth, Sojourner, 6
Tuareg people, 77, 101
Tucker, Chris, 397–414
    ancestry of, 322, 400–414
    birth of, 397
    childhood of, 397–399
    as comedian, 399
    DNA testing and, 409–410
    education of, 399
    racism and, 399
    religion and, 406
Tucker, Daniel, 236, 237
Tucker, Dinah, 236–238
Tucker, Mary Louise Bryant, 397, 401
Tucker, Norris, 397
Turkana people, 101, 198, 306
Turner, Ike, 80, 88–91, 94–95, 101
Turner, Tina, 80–103

ancestry of, 85, 91–102
birth of, 80
childhood of, 81–85
in cotton fields, 85–86
DNA testing and, 99, 101–102
education of, 86, 88, 92
grandparents and, 82–85, 87, 91
Ike, relationship with, 88–91, 94–95, 101
mother, relationship with, 81–89
music career of, 80, 87, 88, 90, 91
Tuskegee, Alabama, 153–158
Tuskegee Airmen program, 154, 155
Tuskegee Institute, 137, 154, 167, 271
Twenty-fifth Colored Infantry, 354

Uldeme people, 378
Uncle Tom's Cabin (Stowe), 7
Underground Railroad, 119
Union Baptist Church, Boston, 115–116
Union Carbide, 263, 269
U.S. census
    of 1790, 144
    of 1810, 144
    of 1840, 420
    of 1850, 16–17, 93, 143, 420
    of 1860, 16–17, 72, 93, 143, 273, 353, 375
    of 1870, 8, 35, 71, 170, 171, 189, 190, 191,
        193, 195, 211, 212, 218, 254, 297, 332,
        338, 339, 401, 405, 407
    of 1880, 72, 75, 96–98, 218, 237, 373
    of 1900, 230–232
    of 1910, 33, 189, 231, 278, 331
    of 1920, 63, 65
    of 1930, 63, 66, 166, 249
U.S. Colored Troops, 315, 317, 368
University of Michigan Medical School, 185
Upper Guinea, 19, 39, 77, 305, 322–323,
    341, 393
Utica Normal and Industrial Institute, Mis-
    sissippi, 135–139

Vaiden, Mississippi, 331
Van Buren, Angelica, 295
Van Buren, Martin, 295
Van Meter, Abraham, 318–320
Van Meter, William, 318
Vicksburg, siege of, 53
Vikings, 176

Wafford, Mary "Kentucky," 29–31
Wafford, Miles, 31
Wafford, Washington, 31
Wafford, William, 31
Walker, Nathaniel, 298
Walker, Wyatt T., 260

Washington, Booker T., 6, 46, 111, 137, 138,
    154, 155, 167, 184, 271, 403
Washington, Clander, 231, 232, 235
Washington, Elsa Tucker, 231–237
Washington, George, 54, 121, 340
Washington, William, 231–237
Watson, John R., 219
Wayne County, North Carolina, 254
Waynesboro, Mississippi, 279
Webb, John Henry, 273–274
Wells, Love Adam, 50
West Virginia State College, 268
Westward expansion, 337
What's Love Got to Do with It? (movie),
    89–90
Wheatley, Phyllis, 6
White, Candace Annabelle Williams, 115
White, Henry, 118
White, Jacob Merritt Pedford, 114–115, 118
White flight, 309
Whitelaw, Roxanna, 82
Whitley, Daniel, 340
Wilberforce University, 209
Wilcox County, Alabama, 166, 171, 173–175
Wiley, Oklahoma, 351–352
Williams, Adam Daniel, 301
Williams, Alexander "Sandy," 125
Williams, Franklin, 382
Williams, Gertrude Jenkins, 292–294
Williams, James, 292
Williams, Leola Gregory, 59, 62
Williams, Quilley, 231
Williams, Shirley, 382
Williams, Tennessee, 54
Williams, Tye, 273
Williamsburg County, South Carolina, 375
Winfrey, Absalom F., 218
Winfrey, Beatrice Woods, 214–216, 224
Winfrey, Constantine, 11, 13, 216–221, 224
Winfrey, Elmore, 214–217, 224
Winfrey, Oprah, 11, 200–224
    ancestry of, 92, 211–224, 255, 409
    broadcasting career of, 207–208
    childhood of, 201–205, 208
    DNA testing and, 221–224, 409
    father, relationship with, 206–207
    mother, relationship with, 202–203
    pregnancy of, 206–207
    sexual abuse of, 204–206
Winfrey, Sanford, 216
Winfrey, Vernita Lee, 201
Winfrey, Vernon, 201, 206, 209, 215, 216
Winfrey, Violet, 216–218
Winfrey, Zelma, 207
Winters, Amanda, 209–212, 224

Winters, Henrietta, 209, 211–212, 223
Winters, Jesse, 209
Winters, Matilda, 209
Winters, Pearce, 209, 211
Wolf, Jonas, 350
Woman, Thou Art Loosed (Jakes), 270
Woodbridge, Dudley, 321–322
Woodbridge, Estella, 321
Woodbridge, Grafton Dudley, 321–322
Works Progress Administration (WPA), 68,
    252
World War II, 46, 66, 154
Wortham, Frank, 339–341
Wortham, Tabitha ("Bithey"), 339–341
Wortham, Thomas, 340
Worthington, Elijah, 295–298

Wright, Milton, 69, 71

Xavier, Marie Evalina, 393

Yale University, 179, 185, 186, 199
Yoruba people, 19, 198, 282

Zambia, 56, 222, 223
Zombo people, 56, 101, 306
Zulu people, 222–224